Conference of the North American Chapter of the Association for Computational Linguistics (NAACL 2024)

Languages of Latin America

AA001571

Demonstrations Session

Mexico City, Mexico
16-21 June 2024

ISBN: 978-1-7138-9896-2

Printed from e-media with permission by:

Curran Associates, Inc.
57 Morehouse Lane
Red Hook, NY 12571

Some format issues inherent in the e-media version may also appear in this print version.

Copyright© (2024) by the Association for Computational Linguistics
All rights reserved.

Printed with permission by Curran Associates, Inc. (2024)

For permission requests, please contact the Association for Computational Linguistics at the address below.

Association for Computational Linguistics
209 N. Eighth Street
Stroudsburg, Pennsylvania 18360

Phone: 1-570-476-8006
Fax: 1-570-476-0860

acl@aclweb.org

Additional copies of this publication are available from:

Curran Associates, Inc.
57 Morehouse Lane
Red Hook, NY 12571 USA
Phone: 845-758-0400
Fax: 845-758-2633
Email: curran@proceedings.com
Web: www.proceedings.com

NAACL 2024

The 2024 Conference of the North American Chapter of the Association for Computational Linguistics

Proceedings of the Demonstrations Session

June 16-21, 2024

©2024 Association for Computational Linguistics

Introduction

Welcome to the proceedings of the System Demonstration Track at NAACL 2024, taking place from June 16 to June 21.

The System Demonstration Track at NAACL 2024 serves as a platform for presenting papers that describe system demonstrations, ranging from early prototypes to mature, production-ready systems. Publicly available open-source or open-access systems are of special interest.

This year, we received 48 submissions, and 21 were selected for inclusion in the program, resulting in an acceptance rate of 43

We would like to thank the members of the program committee for their timely assistance in reviewing the submissions and to the authors who submitted their work to the demonstration track.

Best,
Kai-Wei Chang, En-Shiun Annie Lee, and Nazneen Rajani,
NAACL 2024 Demonstration Track Chairs

Program Committee

Program Chairs

Kai-Wei Chang, University of California, Los Angeles
En-Shiun Annie Lee, OntarioTech University, Oshawa, and University of Toronto, Toronto
Nazneen Rajani

Reviewers

Ahmed Abdelali, Hamad Bin Khalifa University
Rodrigo Agerri, University of the Basque Country
Zeynep Akkalyoncu, StackAdapt
Miguel A. Alonso, Universidade da Coruña
Rafael Anchiêta, Federal Institute of Piauí
Lisa Bauer, Amazon
Shubhang Bhatnagar, University of Illinois, Urbana-Champaign
Aljoscha Burchardt, German Research Center for AI
Daniel F Campos, Snowflake
Daniel Cer, Google
Wei-Rui Chen, University of British Columbia
Guanyi Chen, Central China Normal University
Jhih-Jie Chen, National Tsinghua University
Chung-Chi Chen, AIST, National Institute of Advanced Industrial Science and Technology
Christos Christodoulopoulos, Amazon
Marina Danilevsky, International Business Machines
Michael Desmond, IBM
Shizhe Diao, Hong Kong University of Science and Technology
James Fan
Chi Han, University of Illinois Urbana-Champaign
Ales Horak, Masaryk University
Claudiu Daniel Hromei, University of Roma Tor Vergata
Ziniu Hu, Caltech
Xiaodan Hu, University of Illinois, Urbana-Champaign
Kuan-Hao Huang, University of Illinois Urbana-Champaign
Ali Hürriyetoğlu, Wageningen University & Research
Vivek Iyer, University of Edinburgh, University of Edinburgh
Sneha Jha, Imperial College London
Pratik Joshi, Google DeepMind
Khalid Al Khatib, University of Groningen
Philipp Koehn, Johns Hopkins University
Mamoru Komachi, Hitotsubashi University
Tuan Lai, University of Illinois Urbana Champaign
Mark Last, Ben-Gurion University of the Negev
Xintong Li, Apple
Yanran Li
Bill Yuchen Lin, AI2
Ye Liu, Universität Ulm
Pan Lu, University of California, Los Angeles
Wolfgang Maier, Mercedes Benz Research & Development

Tao Meng, University of California, Los Angeles
Margot Mieskes, University of Applied Sciences Darmstadt
Aldrian Obaja Muis
Pierre Nugues, Lund University
Tsuyoshi Okita, Kyushu Institute of Technology
Eda Okur, Intel Labs
Tanmay Parekh, University of California, Los Angeles
Xutan Peng, Huawei Technologies Ltd.
Prokopis Prokopidis, Institute for Language and Speech Processing, Athena Research Center
Saurav Sahay, Intel
Jaydeep Sen, IBM
Sheng Shen, University of California Berkeley
Chenkai Sun, University of Illinois at Urbana-Champaign
Yufei Tian, University of California, Los Angeles
Natalia Vanetik, SCE
Andrea Varga, Theta Lake Ltd
Nikhil Verma, LG Toronto AI Lab
Xuan Wang, Virginia Polytechnic Institute and State University
Qingyun Wang, University of Illinois, Urbana Champaign
Jingjing Wang, soochow university
Yiwei Wang, University of California, Los Angeles
Xianchao Wu, NVIDIA
Di Wu, University of California, Los Angeles
Zhen Xu, PCG Tencent
Ashok Yadav, Indian Institute of Information Technology Allahabad
Seid Muhie Yimam, University Hamburg
Pengfei Yu, University of Illinois at Urbana-Champaign
Dian Yu, Google
Qi Zeng, Facebook
Wenjie Zi, Borealis AI
Imed Zitouni, Google

Table of Contents

TOPICAL: TOPIC Pages AutomagicaLly

John Giorgi[1,2,3*] **Amanpreet Singh**[4] **Doug Downey**[4,5]
Sergey Feldman[4] **Lucy Lu Wang**[4,6]

[1]University of Toronto [2]Terrence Donnelly Centre [3]Vector Institute for AI
[4]Allen Institute for AI [5]Northwestern University [6]University of Washington

`john.giorgi@utoronto.ca, lucylw@uw.edu, {sergey, dougd}@allenai.org`

Abstract

Topic pages aggregate useful information about an entity or concept into a single succinct and accessible article. Automated creation of topic pages would enable their rapid curation as information resources, providing an alternative to traditional web search. While most prior work has focused on generating topic pages about biographical entities, in this work, we develop a completely automated process to generate high-quality topic pages for scientific entities, with a focus on biomedical concepts. We release TOPICAL, a web app and associated open-source code, comprising a model pipeline combining retrieval, clustering, and prompting, that makes it easy for anyone to generate topic pages for a wide variety of biomedical entities on demand. In a human evaluation of 150 diverse topic pages generated using TOPICAL, we find that the vast majority were considered relevant, accurate, and coherent, with correct supporting citations. We make all code publicly available and host a free-to-use web app at: `https://s2-topical.apps.allenai.org`.

1 Introduction

The automatic generation of topic pages is a longstanding goal of the NLP community (Balasubramanian and Cucerzan, 2009, 2010a,b; Pochampally et al., 2021). In contrast to web search results—displayed as ranked lists of hyperlinks with short text snippets across many pages—topic pages aggregate useful information about various aspects of an entity or concept in a single, concise location. *Scientific* topic pages (Wodak et al., 2012; Azarbonyad et al., 2023) apply this thinking to scientific concepts by aggregating information from the primary literature to produce succinct and accessible summaries useful to both experts and non-experts alike (Figure 1). Among other things, high-quality scientific topic pages hold the promise of:

[*] Work performed during internship at AI2

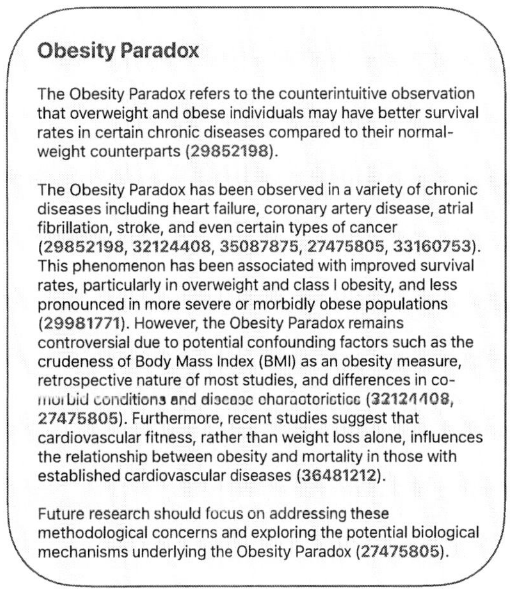

Figure 1: Example of a scientific topic page generated by our system. Citations are provided as hyperlinks to PubMed articles and denoted by their PMID. The topic page is divided into the definition statement, main content, and future directions and open research questions.

1. **Helping manage the torrent of scientific literature**. A staggering amount of scientific information is published daily. In biomedicine alone, nearly 4,000 papers (>2 per minute) are deposited in PubMed or bioRxiv each day, leading to a general state of "information overload" (Landhuis, 2016; Hope et al., 2023). Automatically generated topic pages allow researchers to quickly familiarize themselves with an area and its most active research directions, while citations to source articles provide an entry-point into the literature for in-depth exploration.[1]

2. **Improving the accessibility of scientific texts**. Encyclopedic resources like Wikipedia contain

[1]Topic pages generated by our system provide citations to highly relevant primary literature. See §3.2 for details.

Proceedings of the 2024 Conference of the North American Chapter of the Association for Computational Linguistics: Human Language Technologies (Volume 3: System Demonstrations), pages 1–11
June 16-21, 2024 ©2024 Association for Computational Linguistics

descriptions for a small fraction of scientific concepts (King et al., 2020). Therefore, non-expert readers may turn to the primary literature for information (August et al., 2022), e.g., a patient or caregiver wishing to learn about a new drug or rare disease. However, most scientific text assumes extensive background knowledge that a non-expert reader is unlikely to possess (Portenoy et al., 2021; Murthy et al., 2022). Automatically generated topic pages hold the promise of improving the accessibility of scientific texts, both by providing an *alternative* to the primary literature and by serving as a *resource* to help fill in the gaps in a reader's background knowledge.

In this work, we develop a fully automated process leveraging large language models (LLMs) to generate high-quality scientific topic pages, with a focus on biomedical topics (§3). Our solution is available as an easy-to-use and publicly available web app (§4), and associated source code.[2] We validate the quality of TOPICAL via extensive human evaluation on 150 diverse biomedical terms from the MeSH[3] hierarchy (§5) and find that the vast majority of topic pages are rated as relevant, accurate, and coherent, with correct citations to primary sources (§6).

2 Related Work

Topic page generation Topic page generation is usually framed as a topic-focused, open-domain multi-document summarization (MDS) task (Giorgi et al., 2023). Most prior work is concerned with generating Wikipedia-like pages for general-domain entities and concepts (often biographical in nature). Early work clustered the web search query logs for an entity of interest to determine its various aspects, used each aspect cluster to retrieve and rank relevant sentences, and then re-organized the retrieved sentences for coherence to produce a bullet-list style topic page (Balasubramanian and Cucerzan, 2009, 2010a,b).

More recent work—also focused on biographical entities—first templates the topic page by copying common section headings from Wikipedia pages for related topics and trains a supervised model to select the text content for each section. An unsupervised component then creates topic-specific sections, and several post-processing steps are applied to reduce redundancy and improve coherence (Pochampally et al., 2021). In contrast, our work focuses on topics of scientific interest, does not try to match a Wikipedia-like structure, and generates topic pages in a *abstractive* fashion.

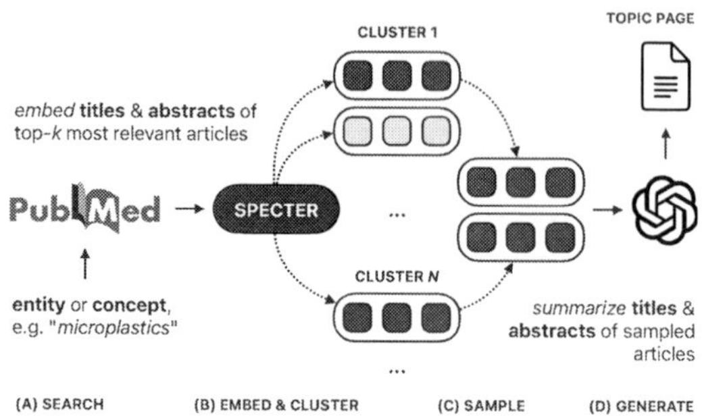

Figure 2: Overview of TOPICAL. Given a biomedical entity, we query PubMed for relevant literature (**A**). The titles and abstracts of the results are embedded with SPECTER (Singh et al., 2023) and clustered based on semantic similarity (**B**). We sample titles and abstracts from the clusters (**C**) and feed them to GPT-4 (OpenAI, 2023), alongside publication metadata and natural language instructions, to generate the topic page (**D**).

Scientific topic pages Azarbonyad et al. (2023) investigate generating scientific topic pages at scale; however, they do not synthesize a summary but focus rather on extracting a definition statement verbatim, alongside "mention snippets" and related concepts. In contrast, we attempt to synthesize more comprehensive topic pages, including a definition statement and content about the entity's main and future research directions. King et al. (2022) introduce a Scientific Concept Description task with similar motivation to our work, but focus on earlier, smaller generative models for describing computer science concepts, and find the systems to hallucinate relatively frequently. WikiCrow, based on PaperQA (L'ala et al., 2023), provides scientific topic pages generated by an LLM-based system for human protein-coding genes. In contrast to our approach, their publicly available demo is limited to 15,616 pre-generated topic pages and does not allow a user to generate topic pages for a new entity of interest on demand.[4]

3 Approach

Our approach follows a retrieval-augmented generation (RAG) setup (Guu et al., 2020; Lewis et al., 2020; Petroni et al., 2021; Izacard et al., 2022). A

[2] https://github.com/allenai/TOPICAL

[3] Medical Subject Headings (MeSH) is a hierarchical vocabulary used to index articles and books in the life sciences.

[4] https://www.futurehouse.org/wikicrow

Microplastics

CLUSTER 1 (Size: 24)

Interactions between microplastics and unit processes of ***wastewater treatment plants****: a critical review.*

Effects of ***Wastewater Treatment*** *Processes on the Removal Efficiency of Microplastics Based on Meta-analysis*

Removal of microplastics from ***wastewater****: available techniques and way forward.*

CLUSTER 2 (Size: 23)

Microplastics in ***aquatic environments****: Occurrence, accumulation, and biological effects.*

Microplastics in ***aquatic environments****: Toxicity to trigger ecological consequences.*

Microplastics in ***aquatic environment****: Challenges and perspectives.*

Obesity Paradox

CLUSTER 1 (Size: 31)

Obesity and the Obesity Paradox in ***Heart Failure****.*

Impact of obesity and the obesity paradox on prevalence and prognosis in ***heart failure****.*

Obesity paradox and ***heart failure****.*

CLUSTER 4 (Size: 26)

Obesity paradox and ***stroke****: a narrative review.*

Obesity paradox and ***stroke*** *outcomes according to stroke subtype: a propensity score-matched analysis.*

*Obesity-****stroke*** *paradox and initial neurological severity.*

CLUSTER 5 (Size: 23)

The true obesity paradox: obese and malnourished?

Obesity paradox?

Obesity Paradox - Truth or Misconception?

Monkeypox

CLUSTER 2 (Size: 30)

Monkeypox: ***epidemiology****, pathogenesis,* ***treatment*** *and* ***prevention****.*

Monkeypox: A ***clinical update*** *for paediatricians.*

The changing ***epidemiology*** *of monkeypox and* ***preventive measures****: an update.*

CLUSTER 5 (Size: 14)

MonkeyNet: A robust ***deep convolutional neural network*** *for monkeypox disease detection and classification*

Utilizing ***convolutional neural networks*** *to classify monkeypox skin lesions.*

Hyper-parameter tuned ***deep learning approach*** *for effective human monkeypox disease detection.*

CLUSTER 9 (Size: 8)

Monkeypox: Considerations as a ***New Pandemic*** *Looms.*

Monkeypox: A ***potential global threat****?*

Monkeypox and human transmission: Are we on the verge of ***another pandemic****?*

Figure 3: Example clusters. Three titles from a selection of clusters for each concept are shown. **Emphasis** ours.

large body of literature (up to 10k papers) is retrieved for a given entity (§3.1) and fed to a LLM alongside publication metadata and instructions (§3.3). Because the amount of retrieved literature is often many times larger than the LLM's maximum context size, we design a clustering step to loosely group the literature into areas of study and sample from these clusters for input (§3.2). During prompting, the model is instructed to provide in-line citations for all claims by outputting one or more PubMed IDs (PMIDs). See Figure 2 for an overview.

3.1 Querying PubMed

The generation of each topic page begins with a user-provided biomedical entity or concept. This entity is expected to be covered by papers indexed in PubMed,[5] a free search engine that indexes over 36 million papers on life science and biomedical topics. TOPICAL, our system, leverages the Entrez ESearch API (Kans, 2023) to query PubMed and supports the full syntax of the PubMed Advanced Search Builder; however, simply inputting the entity or concept verbatim is often sufficient, e.g. "*microplastic*," as the ESearch API will apply 'automatic term mapping' (ATM)[6] to this query to include, among other things, matching MeSH descriptors and pluralization (e.g. "*microplastics*"). We then download the titles and abstracts of the top 10,000 most relevant papers returned by ESearch.

[5] `https://pubmed.ncbi.nlm.nih.gov/`

[6] `https://pubmed.ncbi.nlm.nih.gov/help/#automatic-term-mapping`

3.2 Clustering and sampling the literature

The amount of retrieved literature is usually many times the maximum context size of the LLM. Therefore, we first cluster titles & abstracts by semantic similarity to identify major areas of study, then sample from these clusters to produce a diverse set of inputs. The steps are described below:

Embedding Titles and abstracts are jointly embedded using the SPECTER2 PRX model (Singh et al., 2023), a text encoder specifically designed for producing highly-quality representations of scientific text from a paper's title and abstract. We formatted each input as: "`{title}` [SEP] `{abstract}`".

Clustering We apply a clustering algorithm which identifies 'communities': clusters of embeddings of a minimum size with a pairwise cosine similarity greater than or equal to some threshold.[7] We set the similarity threshold to `0.96` and the minimum cluster size to 5. In degenerate cases where fewer than 2 clusters are identified, we iteratively reduce the similarity threshold by `0.02`, stopping when at least 2 clusters are identified or the threshold falls below `0.90`—in which case we skip the clustering step. See Figure 3 for examples of clusters produced by this process.

Sampling We sample as many titles and abstracts as will fit in the prompt to the LLM. If the number of papers returned in the search step is 100 or

[7] `https://www.sbert.net/examples/applications/clustering/README.html#fast-clustering`

Algorithm 1 Sampling Procedure for Papers

Require: Collection of clustered titles + abstracts, $\mathcal{C}$
Require: Maximum number of input tokens, $T_{\max}$
$\mathcal{C} \leftarrow \text{sorted}(\mathcal{C})$ ▷ By descending cluster size
Initialize $\mathcal{S} \leftarrow \emptyset$ ▷ Sampled papers
$t \leftarrow 0$ ▷ Current token count
for each C_i in $\mathcal{C}$ **do**
  $c \leftarrow$ centroid of C_i
  if $t + |c| \leq T_{\max}$ **then**
    Append c to $\mathcal{S}$
    $t \leftarrow t + |c|$ ▷ $|c|$ is the number of tokens in c
  end if
end for
while $t < T_{\max}$ and there exist unsampled papers in $\mathcal{C}$ **do**
  Sample a paper p from $\mathcal{C}$ with a probability $\propto \sqrt{|C_i|}$
  if $t + |p| \leq T_{\max}$ **then**
    Append p to $\mathcal{S}$
    $t \leftarrow t + |p|$ ▷ $|p|$ is the number of tokens in p
  end if
end while
Ensure: Return $\mathcal{S}$ as a list of lists (outer: unique clusters, inner: papers from the cluster)

less, or no clusters were identified in the clustering step, we randomly sample papers for inclusion. Otherwise, we do the following: first, sort clusters by decreasing size. Then, select each *centroid* for inclusion, starting with the largest cluster and continuing until the centroids of all clusters have been selected or the model's maximum input size has been reached. If all centroids have been selected and the model's maximum input tokens are not exhausted, we sample from the remaining clusters with a probability proportional to the square root of the cluster size (see Algorithm 1 for details).[8] This sampling strategy is motivated by the idea that we should aim to capture as many and as diverse areas of study for a concept as possible (hence the selection of centroids) while favouring more commonly studied subtopics (hence the weighted sampling).

3.3 Generating the topic page

We chose GPT-4[9] as the LLM due to its state-of-the-art performance across many text generation tasks (OpenAI, 2023). We designed a prompt including natural language instructions, publication metadata, and the sampled titles and abstracts. The prompt is broken into system and user roles (truncated example in Figure 4). In the system role, we provide instructions about the task and what constitutes a good topic page. The user role provides instruction about what the model will receive as input, followed by a description of how to cite its

TOPICAL Prompt

System Role

You are a biomedical domain expert. Your job is to produce a high-quality, scientifically-orientated topic page for a given biomedical entity or concept grounded in the provided literature. [...]

A good scientific topic page is: [...]

Assume the target audience of this topic page will have basic scientific literacy (i.e. undergraduate-level biology). [...]

User Role

INSTRUCTIONS

I will provide you with a biomedical entity or concept, titles and abstracts that mention this entity. [...]

HOW TO CITE YOUR CLAIMS

Every scientific claim in the topic page should be followed by an in-line citation to PubMed using the provided PMIDs. [...]

ENTITY OR CONCEPT

Canonicalized entity name: `Microplastics`
Publications per year: `2006: 1, 2007: 1, [...] 2023: 2288`
Total number of publications: 8217
Supporting literature:

Cluster 1
PMID: 37079238 **PubDate:** May 2023 **Title:** [...] **Abstract:** [...]
PMID: 35301580 **PubDate:** Mar. 2023 **Title:** [...] **Abstract:** [...]
[...]

Cluster N
PMID: 30036839 **PubDate:** Nov 2018 **Title:** [...] **Abstract:** [...]
[...]

TOPIC PAGE

Now, generate the scientific topic page section by section following the instructions below.

First, provide a short textbook or Wikipedia-like description of the entity that is easy to understand for a non-expert audience (1 sentence max).

Next, produce the main content of the topic page (6 sentences max). Summarize the main reasons for this entities notability and interest to science. [...]

Finish by commenting on any open questions or future research directions mentioned in the supporting literature [...] (1 sentence max).

Figure 4: Truncated example prompt. The prompt is divided into system and user roles. In the user role, we provide instructions about the input, how to cite a claim, details about the entity or concept like publication metadata, the sampled literature, and guidance about the expected sections and lengths for the topic page. Emphasis is provided for visualization purposes only.

sources. We then provide information about the entity or concept, including the publications per year, total number of publications, and sampled titles and abstracts. These include a PMID and publication date and are sorted by decreasing cluster size. Finally, we provide instructions about the expected format of the topic page.

The model is instructed to produce three sections: a **definition statement** (1-2 sentences), **main content** (5-8 sentences) and a concluding remark about **future research directions and open questions** (1 sentence). We model the components of our target

[8] `https://en.wikipedia.org/wiki/Square_root_biased_sampling`

[9] Specifically, the 06/13/2023 snapshot, "`gpt-4-0613`"

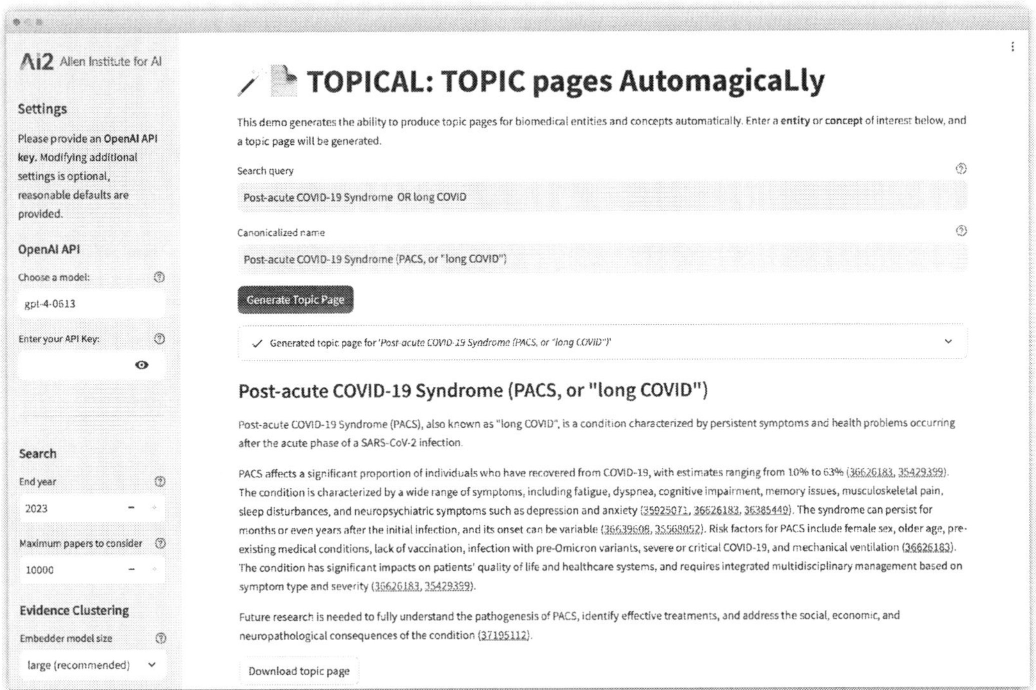

Figure 5: TOPICAL web app. Given a search query for a biomedical entity or concept of interest and a canonicalized name, it automatically generates a topic page for the concept. An expandable section provides additional information, like a histogram of publication dates for the query and the number of clusters identified.

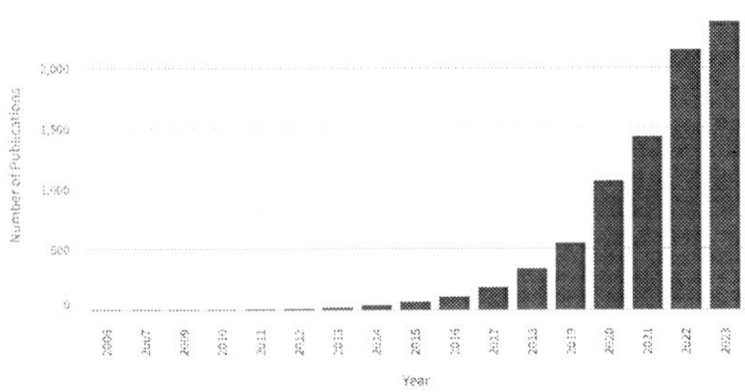

Figure 6: Example publications per year histogram displayed to users for the entity: "*Microplastics*".

topic pages based on the structure of existing scientific topic pages and the information researchers are likely to seek from a topical review. Curated topic pages typically begin with definitions,[10] so we also begin by generating a definition statement. Per the PRISMA guidelines for systematic reviews (Page et al., 2020), a primary goal of reviews is to provide "syntheses of the state of knowledge in a field, from which future research priorities can be identified"; from this goal, we derive the main content, which summarizes the main directions of research, and future research directions.

[10]e.g., `https://www.sciencedirect.com/topics`

We set `temperature` to 0.0, `max_tokens` to 512, (the maximum tokens to generate for the topic page), and kept all other hyperparmeters of the OpenAI API at default values.[11] The model's maximum context size is 8,192 tokens, which is approximately enough for the prompt instructions and 16 abstracts. To fit more abstracts into the prompt, we take only the first three and last two sentences of each, joining them with a "`[TRUNCATE]`" token. These sentences tend to be rich in the type of content expected in a topic page, e.g., definition-like content, conclusions, major findings, and future directions.

4 TOPICAL Web App

TOPICAL is available as a web app (see Figure 5 for an overview). The web app can be run locally as a standalone python package but is also publicly available at `https://s2-topical.apps.allenai.org`. A user first inputs a PubMed search query, which supports the full syntax of the PubMed Advanced Search Builder (see Appendix A for details). However, in most cases, sim-

[11]`https://platform.openai.com/docs/api-reference/completions`

ply inputting the entity or concept name directly and allowing ESearch to expand the query via automatic term mapping (ATM) works well, especially with respect to recall. A user can optionally provide alternative names for the entity, referred to as 'canonicalized names,' which are provided to the LLM as additional context. Once a user clicks the button to generate a topic page, the search, embedding, clustering, and generation steps are executed. An expandable section in the app displays progress, as well as additional information about the search, e.g., any query expansions made via ATM and a histogram of publications per year (see Figure 6). The generated topic pages can be downloaded as JSON files. A video demonstration of the system is available here: `https://youtu.be/hgnG7BnIeAY`.

5 Human evaluation

We conduct human evaluation to determine the quality of the automatically generated topic pages. The evaluation consists of two tasks, described below. All annotations were performed by three full-time, paid annotation specialists with undergraduate training spanning the biosciences, materials science, environmental science, and data science.

5.1 Annotation Task 1: Topic Page

In task 1, the goal was to evaluate the overall quality of the topic page along three facets, **relevance**, **accuracy**, and **coherence**, defined as:

- **Relevance**: whether the topic page covers only important aspects of the entity or concept; unimportant or excess information is penalized
- **Accuracy**: whether the topic page is free of obvious factual errors or contradictory information
- **Coherence**: whether sentences and sections fit together and sound natural, with little to no redundancy within or across sections

We adapt these facets and their definitions from the summarization evaluation facets used in Fabbri et al. (2021); we assess Accuracy instead of Consistency due to the infeasibility of comparing a generated topic page against all input documents. Relevance and accuracy were assessed per topic page *section* (definition statement, main content and future directions), while coherence was assessed globally. The annotation interface (see Appendix B) displayed each section of the topic page, and the annotators were provided instructions about how to evaluate topic pages along each facet. The annotation interface also provided a link to the PubMed query issued when building the topic page. Annotators were instructed to follow the link and skim a handful of abstracts to familiarize themselves with the entity or concept before evaluation.

For each facet, annotators selected from one of three options: 'not' {relevant, accurate, coherent}, 'somewhat' {relevant, accurate, coherent} or simply: {relevant, accurate, coherent}. We included a fourth option for relevance and accuracy: 'missing/invalid', in case the LLM failed to generate a particular topic page section.

5.2 Annotation Task 2: Citations

In task 2, the goal was to evaluate the relevance and sufficiency of model-provided citations. One citation from each topic page was sampled at random. Annotators were shown the citation in context and the cited article's title and abstract. They were instructed to annotate the citation as:

- **Correct**: citation is topically *relevant* (i.e., the cited article is about the target entity or concept) and provides sufficient evidence for the corresponding claim(s) in the topic page.
- **Incorrect (topically relevant)**: citation is topically relevant but does not provide sufficient evidence for the corresponding claim(s).
- **Incorrect (topically irrelevant)**: citation is topically *irrelevant*.
- **Incorrect (invalid)**: citation is not valid, e.g. the PMID does not exist or was truncated.

5.3 Choosing topics for evaluation

In order to choose a broad selection of topics for evaluation, we collected all terms added to the MeSH vocabulary in the last 10 years (01/01/2013–16/10/2023, inclusive). We only include terms with a maximum tree depth[12] of at least 7 as we found terms with a tree depth less than this tended to be overly broad and non-specific, e.g. "*Metadata*", "*Rural Nursing*", "*Infant Health*", and "*Missed Diagnosis*". The end result is 981 biomedical terms or concepts spanning a wide range of semantic types, including diseases (e.g. "*Charles Bonnet Syndrome*"), drugs (e.g. "*Modafinil*"), proteins (e.g. "*beta-Arrestin 1*), organisms (e.g "*Fallopia multiflora*"), cell types (e.g. "*Memory T Cells*") and broader concepts like "*Glycemic Load*". We subsampled from this set to produce the final list of entities for evaluation: 15 per annotator for the an-

[12]MeSH terms are organized in a polyhierarchical ontology, where more specific terms exist deeper in the tree.

Table 1: Results of human evaluation for annotation task 1. Total ratings for each facet and label are shown, along with agreement percentage. Two annotators rated 100 pages each (with 50% overlap). Each facet for each section was rated on an ordinal scale: "not", "somewhat", or "(yes)" relevant/accurate/coherent.

	Definition		Main content		Future directions		
Rating	relevant	accurate	relevant	accurate	relevant	accurate	coherent
missing/invalid	0	0	0	0	0	0	–
not	0	0	1	0	3	0	0
somewhat	4	1	7	0	15	0	15
yes	196	199	192	200	182	200	185
Percent agreement	94	98	94	100	88	100	82

Table 2: Results of human evaluation for annotation task 2. Total ratings per label are shown, along with agreement percentage. Each annotator rated 100 citations, with 50% overlap between annotators.

Rating	Number of Ratings
Incorrect (invalid)	0
Incorrect (topically irrelevant)	2
Incorrect (topically relevant)	32
Correct	166
Percent agreement	88

notation pilots (with 100% overlap) and 100 per annotator for the final evaluation (50% overlap).

6 Results

We find that the majority of topic pages are rated by our annotators as relevant, accurate, and coherent (Table 1), with high inter-annotator agreement ($\geq$ 82%).[13] We note that in no case did the model fail to output a topic page with the expected three-section structure. All sections received nearly perfect ratings for accuracy. The future direction section received the lowest rating for relevancy (18/200 ratings of 'not' or 'somewhat' relevant). Examining these instances reveals that the LLM often states vague or even obvious future directions, such as: "*[...] Future research is needed to further clarify the most effective use of this drug combination in the treatment of respiratory diseases*" or "*Future research directions include further investigation into the exact mechanisms of resveratrol's action in diseases such as cancer and diabetes [...].*" We believe this reflects the inherent difficulty of identifying future research directions and open questions about a given topic. Coherence was the next lowest-rated aspect, with 15/200 ratings of 'somewhat' coherent. The most common reason for this according to the annotators, by far, was extensive use of highly-specific jargon, making the topic page difficult to read as a non-expert.

Similarly, most model-provided citations were rated as correct (Table 2) with high inter-annotator agreement ($\geq$ 88%); in no case were the citations invalid, e.g., a hallucinated PMID. Most incorrect citations were marked as 'Incorrect (topically relevant)' (32/200), denoting cases where the citation was *on-topic*, but the cited article did not provide sufficient evidence for the corresponding claim(s).

7 Conclusion

In this paper, we present TOPICAL, a new approach for the automatic generation of high-quality scientific topic pages that leverages large language models (LLMs) and retrieval-augmented generation (RAG). We conducted an extensive human evaluation of 150 diverse topics from the biomedical literature and our annotators rated the vast majority of generated topic pages as relevant, accurate, and coherent; and model-provided citations as correct. Promising future directions include allowing users to provide custom instructions with respect to structure, focus and length of the automatically generated topic pages, and the investigation of open-source LLMs in place of the closed-source LLM we experimented with (GPT-4). We release a publicly available web app so that others can experiment with generating topic pages for entities or concepts of interest on demand.

Limitations

Context window Due to the limited context window of GPT-4 (8192 tokens), our system only ingests a small fraction of literature for most entities

[13] We report inter-annotator agreement as the percent agreement: (fraction of cases where annotators agree) / (total number of annotations).

or concepts. We tried to partially alleviate this through our clustering and sampling procedure, which is designed to encourage diversity in the selected literature while maintaining the representation of common research threads. A promising future direction is to explore the use of language models with significantly larger context windows, such as the recently announced GPT-4-turbo (128,000 tokens).

Unclear provenance Our evaluation is not able to determine to what degree the information in the resulting topic pages is derived from the learned weights of the language model itself, versus the retrieved literature. This is partially alleviated by requiring the language model to provide citations for all scientific claims, allowing a user to verify the information.

Unit of retrieval We do not explore retrieving information other than titles or abstracts. It is possible that retrieving information on another level of granularity, e.g. sentences or "chunks", could improve the quality of the topic pages. It is also possible that extending retrieval to the full-content of a scientific paper could further improve quality. Determining the most performant granularity for the retrieval step is an exciting future direction.

Acknowledgements

This research was enabled in part by support provided by the Digital Research Alliance of Canada (alliancecan.ca) and Compute Ontario (www.computeontario.ca). We thank Jenna Sparks, Erin Bransom, and Bailey Kuehl for helping to conduct human evaluations. We thank the AI2 Reviz team for assistance with hosting the web application. We thank all internal and external reviewers for their thoughtful feedback, which improved earlier drafts of this manuscript.

Author Contributions

John Giorgi conducted data processing, engineered prompts, ran experiments, and implemented the evaluation. John also contributed to project scoping and ideation and wrote the paper with feedback from others. Sergey, Doug, and Lucy were project mentors, contributing equally to project scoping and experimental design and providing core ideas and direction throughout the course of the project and paper writing. Aman made technical contributions around scaling and hosting of the demo.

References

Tal August, Lucy Lu Wang, Jonathan Bragg, Marti A. Hearst, Andrew Head, and Kyle Lo. 2022. Paper plain: Making medical research papers approachable to healthcare consumers with natural language processing. *ACM Transactions on Computer-Human Interaction*, 30:1 – 38.

Hosein Azarbonyad, Zubair Afzal, and George Tsatsaronis. 2023. Generating topic pages for scientific concepts using scientific publications. In *Advances in Information Retrieval: 45th European Conference on Information Retrieval, ECIR 2023, Dublin, Ireland, April 2–6, 2023, Proceedings, Part II*, page 341–349, Berlin, Heidelberg. Springer-Verlag.

Niranjan Balasubramanian and Silviu Cucerzan. 2009. Automatic generation of topic pages using query-based aspect models. In *Proceedings of the 18th ACM Conference on Information and Knowledge Management*, CIKM '09, page 2049–2052, New York, NY, USA. Association for Computing Machinery.

Niranjan Balasubramanian and Silviu Cucerzan. 2010a. Beyond ranked lists in web search: Aggregating web content into topic pages. *Int. J. Semantic Comput.*, 4:509–534.

Niranjan Balasubramanian and Silviu Cucerzan. 2010b. Topic pages: An alternative to the ten blue links. In *2010 IEEE Fourth International Conference on Semantic Computing*, pages 353–360.

Alexander R. Fabbri, Wojciech Kryściński, Bryan McCann, Caiming Xiong, Richard Socher, and Dragomir Radev. 2021. SummEval: Re-evaluating summarization evaluation. *Transactions of the Association for Computational Linguistics*, 9:391–409.

John Giorgi, Luca Soldaini, Bo Wang, Gary Bader, Kyle Lo, Lucy Wang, and Arman Cohan. 2023. Open domain multi-document summarization: A comprehensive study of model brittleness under retrieval. In *Findings of the Association for Computational Linguistics: EMNLP 2023*, pages 8177–8199, Singapore. Association for Computational Linguistics.

Kelvin Guu, Kenton Lee, Zora Tung, Panupong Pasupat, and Ming-Wei Chang. 2020. Realm: Retrieval-augmented language model pre-training. *ArXiv*, abs/2002.08909.

Tom Hope, Doug Downey, Daniel S Weld, Oren Etzioni, and Eric Horvitz. 2023. A computational inflection for scientific discovery. *Communications of the ACM*, 66(8):62–73.

Gautier Izacard, Patrick Lewis, Maria Lomeli, Lucas Hosseini, Fabio Petroni, Timo Schick, Jane A. Yu, Armand Joulin, Sebastian Riedel, and Edouard Grave. 2022. Few-shot learning with retrieval augmented language models. *ArXiv*, abs/2208.03299.

Jonathan Kans. 2023. Entrez direct: e-utilities on the unix command line. In *Entrez programming utilities help [Internet]*. National Center for Biotechnology Information (US).

Daniel King, Doug Downey, and Daniel S. Weld. 2020. High-precision extraction of emerging concepts from scientific literature. *Proceedings of the 43rd International ACM SIGIR Conference on Research and Development in Information Retrieval*.

Daniel King, Zejiang Shen, Nishant Subramani, Daniel S. Weld, Iz Beltagy, and Doug Downey. 2022. Don't say what you don't know: Improving the consistency of abstractive summarization by constraining beam search. In *Proceedings of the 2nd Workshop on Natural Language Generation, Evaluation, and Metrics (GEM)*, pages 555–571, Abu Dhabi, United Arab Emirates (Hybrid). Association for Computational Linguistics.

Jakub L'ala, Odhran O'Donoghue, Aleksandar Shtedritski, Sam Cox, Samuel G. Rodriques, and Andrew D. White. 2023. Paperqa: Retrieval-augmented generative agent for scientific research. *ArXiv*, abs/2312.07559.

Esther Landhuis. 2016. Scientific literature: Information overload. *Nature*, 535:457 – 458.

Patrick Lewis, Ethan Perez, Aleksandara Piktus, Fabio Petroni, Vladimir Karpukhin, Naman Goyal, Heinrich Kuttler, Mike Lewis, Wen tau Yih, Tim Rocktäschel, Sebastian Riedel, and Douwe Kiela. 2020. Retrieval-augmented generation for knowledge-intensive nlp tasks. *ArXiv*, abs/2005.11401.

Sonia Murthy, Kyle Lo, Daniel King, Chandra Bhagavatula, Bailey Kuehl, Sophie Johnson, Jonathan Borchardt, Daniel Weld, Tom Hope, and Doug Downey. 2022. ACCoRD: A multi-document approach to generating diverse descriptions of scientific concepts. In *Proceedings of the 2022 Conference on Empirical Methods in Natural Language Processing: System Demonstrations*, pages 200–213, Abu Dhabi, UAE. Association for Computational Linguistics.

OpenAI. 2023. Gpt-4 technical report. *ArXiv*, abs/2303.08774.

Matthew J. Page, Joanne E. McKenzie, Patrick M. M. Bossuyt, Isabelle Boutron, Tammy C. Hoffmann, Cynthia D. Mulrow, Larissa Shamseer, Jennifer Marie Tetzlaff, Elie A. Akl, Sue E. Brennan, Roger Chou, Julie May Glanville, Jeremy M. Grimshaw, Asbjørn Hrõbjartsson, Manoj Mathew Lalu, Tianjing Li, Elizabeth W. Loder, Evan Mayo-Wilson, Steve McDonald, Luke A. McGuinness, Lesley A Stewart, James Thomas, Andrea C. Tricco, Vivian A Welch, Penny F. Whiting, and David Moher. 2020. The prisma 2020 statement: an updated guideline for reporting systematic reviews. *Systematic Reviews*, 10.

Fabio Petroni, Aleksandra Piktus, Angela Fan, Patrick Lewis, Majid Yazdani, Nicola De Cao, James Thorne, Yacine Jernite, Vladimir Karpukhin, Jean Maillard, Vassilis Plachouras, Tim Rocktäschel, and Sebastian Riedel. 2021. KILT: a benchmark for knowledge intensive language tasks. In *Proceedings of the 2021 Conference of the North American Chapter of the Association for Computational Linguistics: Human Language Technologies*, pages 2523–2544, Online. Association for Computational Linguistics.

Yashaswi Pochampally, Kamalakar Karlapalem, and Navya Yarrabelly. 2021. Semi-supervised automatic generation of wikipedia articles for named entities. *Proceedings of the International AAAI Conference on Web and Social Media*, 10(2):72–79.

Jason Portenoy, Marissa Radensky, Jevin D. West, Eric Horvitz, Daniel S. Weld, and Tom Hope. 2021. Bursting scientific filter bubbles: Boosting innovation via novel author discovery. *Proceedings of the 2022 CHI Conference on Human Factors in Computing Systems*.

Amanpreet Singh, Mike D'Arcy, Arman Cohan, Doug Downey, and Sergey Feldman. 2023. SciRepEval: A multi-format benchmark for scientific document representations. In *Proceedings of the 2023 Conference on Empirical Methods in Natural Language Processing*, pages 5548–5566, Singapore. Association for Computational Linguistics.

Shoshana J. Wodak, Daniel Mietchen, Andrew M. Collings, Robert B. Russell, and Philip E. Bourne. 2012. Topic pages: Plos computational biology meets wikipedia. *PLoS Computational Biology*, 8.

A PubMed Advanced Search Builder

TOPICAL supports the full syntax of the PubMed Advanced Search Builder. For example, to search for mentions of an entity in the title only:

```
Post-acute COVID-19 Syndrome[Title]
```

or for papers with the corresponding MeSH term:

```
Post-acute COVID-19 Syndrome[MeSH Terms]
```

Search terms can be further combined with `AND`, `OR` and `NOT` operators:

```
Post-acute COVID-19 Syndrome[Title] AND
Post-acute COVID-19 Syndrome[MeSH Terms]
```

However, in most cases, we found that simply inputting the entity or concept name directly and allowing ESearch to expand the query via automatic term mapping (ATM) works best, especially with respect to recall.

B Annotation Interface

In Figure 7, we provide a screenshot of the annotation interface built in Google Sheets used for the human evaluation. Annotators were provided the contents of the topic page segmented into the three sections (definition statement, main content, and open research questions and future directions)

C Annotation pilots

Before the full evaluation, we ran 2 pilots with 3 annotators. The annotators evaluated the same 10 topic pages in the first pilot. We used their feedback to improve the annotation guidelines and identify the main sources of inter-annotator disagreement. Most notably, task 2 originally had annotators identify all unique claims in each section of the topic page and then annotate each following the guidelines. This turned out to be overly time-intensive, and determining the specific number of claims had a very low-inter-annotator agreement. Task 2 was therefore simplified by randomly sampling one citation in the topic page and having the annotators assess its relevance and sufficiency. We then ran a second pilot on a new set of 5 topic pages to finalize the annotation guidelines and identify any remaining sources of significant annotator disagreement.

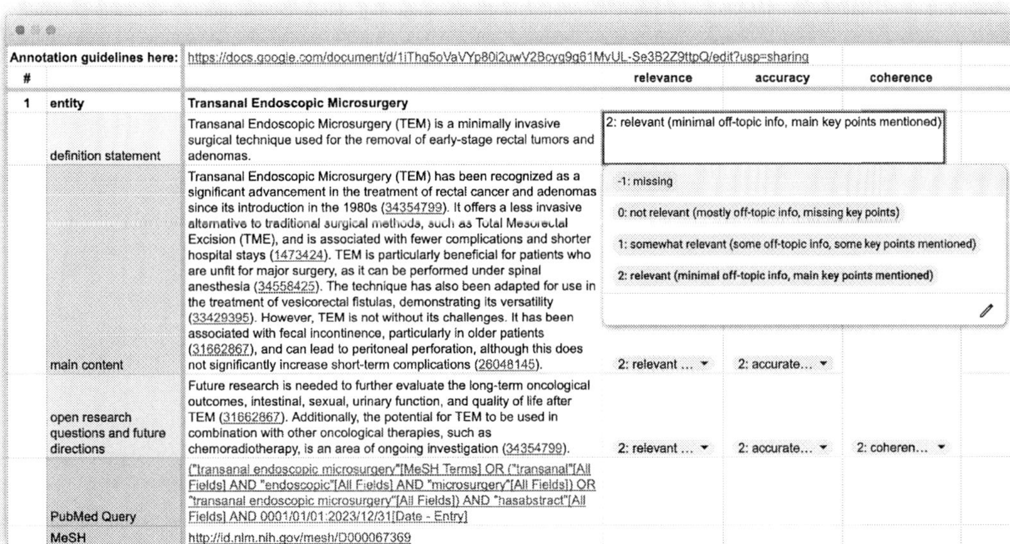

Figure 7: Annotation interface for annotation task 1.

Low-code LLM: Graphical User Interface over Large Language Models

Yuzhe Cai*, Shaoguang Mao*, Wenshan Wu, Zehua Wang, Yaobo Liang, Tao Ge
Chenfei Wu, Wang You, Ting Song, Yan Xia, Nan Duan and **Furu Wei**
Microsoft Research Asia
v-yuzhecai, shaoguang.mao, wenswu, zehwang, yalia, tage, chewu, v-wangyou, tsong, yanxia, nanduan, fuwei@microsoft.com

Abstract

Utilizing Large Language Models (LLMs) for complex tasks is challenging, often involving a time-consuming and uncontrollable prompt engineering process. This paper introduces a novel human-LLM interaction framework, **Low-code LLM**. It incorporates six types of simple low-code visual programming interactions to achieve more controllable and stable responses. Through visual interaction with a graphical user interface, users can incorporate their ideas into the process without writing trivial prompts. The proposed Low-code LLM framework consists of a Planning LLM that designs a structured planning workflow for complex tasks, which can be correspondingly edited and confirmed by users through low-code visual programming operations, and an Executing LLM that generates responses following the user-confirmed workflow. We highlight three advantages of the low-code LLM: user-friendly interaction, controllable generation, and wide applicability. We demonstrate its benefits using four typical applications. By introducing this framework, we aim to bridge the gap between humans and LLMs, enabling more effective and efficient utilization of LLMs for complex tasks. The code, prompts, and experimental details are available at LowcodeLLM. A system demonstration video can be found at LowcodeLLM.

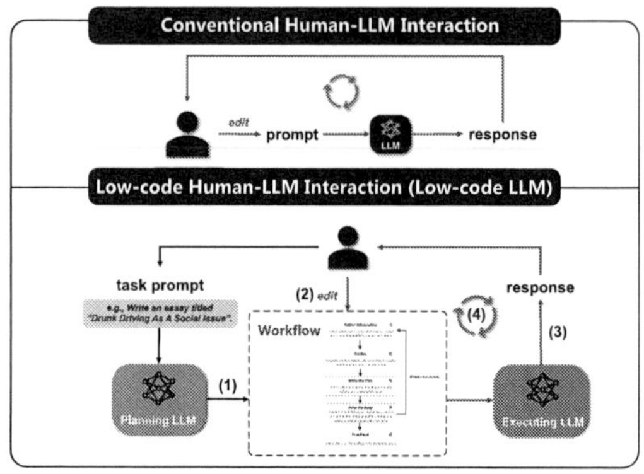

Figure 1: Overview of the Low-code human-LLM interaction (Low-code LLM) and its comparison with the conventional interaction. The red arrow indicates the main human-model interaction loop.

1 Introduction

Large language models (LLMs), such as ChatGPT(OpenAI, 2022) and GPT-4(OpenAI, 2023), have garnered significant interest from both academia and industry, as they demonstrate impressive capability across a range of tasks(Bubeck et al., 2023), and are increasingly utilized in a variety of other fields as well(Nori et al., 2023; Choi et al., 2023; Baidoo-Anu and Owusu Ansah, 2023). However, it is not yet perfect in handling complex tasks. For example, when generating a long paper, the presented arguments, supporting evidence, and overall structure may not always meet expectations in diverse user scenarios. Or, when serving as a task completion virtual assistant, ChatGPT may not always interact with users in the intended manner and may even display inappropriate behavior in various business environments.

Effective utilization of LLMs like ChatGPT requires careful prompt engineering(Zhou et al., 2022; Wang et al., 2023b). However, prompt engineering can be particularly challenging when instructing LLMs to perform complex tasks, as reflected in more uncontrollable responses and more time-consuming prompt refining(Tan et al., 2023). There exists a gap between providing prompts and receiving responses, and the process of generating responses is not accessible to humans.

To reduce this gap, this paper proposes a new human-LLM interaction pattern **Low-code LLM**, which refers to the concept of low-code visual programming(Hirzel, 2022), like Visual Ba-

* The first two authors contributed equally. This work was performed during the first author's internship at Microsoft Research Asia

Proceedings of the 2024 Conference of the North American Chapter of the Association for Computational Linguistics: Human Language Technologies (Volume 3: System Demonstrations), pages 12–25
June 16-21, 2024 ©2024 Association for Computational Linguistics

sic(Microsoft, 1991) or Scratch(Resnick et al., 2009). Users can confirm the complex execution processes through six predefined simple operations on an automatically generated workflow, such as adding or deleting, graphical dragging, and text editing.

As shown in Figure 1, human-LLM interaction can be completed through the following steps: (1) A Planning LLM generates a highly structured workflow for complex tasks. (2) Users edit the workflow using predefined low-code operations, which are all supported by clicking, dragging, or text editing. (3) An Executing LLM generates responses based on the reviewed workflow. (4) Users continue to refine the workflow until satisfactory results are obtained.

Compared with the conventional human-LLM interaction pattern, Low-code LLM has the following advantages:

1. User-friendly Interaction. The visible workflow provides users with a clear understanding of how LLMs execute tasks, and enable users to easily edit it through a graphical user interface.

2. Controllable Generation. Complex tasks are decomposed into structured workflows and presented to users. Users control the LLMs' execution through low-code operations to achieve more controllable responses.

3. Wide applicability. The proposed framework can be applied to various complex tasks across various domains, especially in situations where human's intelligence or preference are critical.

2 Low-code LLM

2.1 Overview

Figure 1 demonstrates the overview framework of the Low-code LLM. Different from conventional prompt engineering, in Low-code LLM, users first input a task prompt, which could be a very brief description of the task they want to achieve. Then (1) a **Planning LLM** will design a **workflow** for completing the task. The workflow is a kind of structured plan, including execution procedure and jump logic. (2) The user will edit the workflow using six pre-defined **low-code visual programming operations**. (3) Once the user confirms workflow, it is interpreted into natural language and inputted to the **Executing LLM**, which will generate a response with the user's guide. (4) The user can iteratively refine the workflow until satisfactory results are achieved.

```
STEP 1: [Step Name] [Step Description] [[[If ...][Jump to STEP...]][...]]
STEP 2: [Step Name] [Step Description] [[[If ...][Jump to STEP...]][...]]
...
```

Table 1: Format of Structured Planning Workflow. For each item, it consists of two parts: execution procedure (i.e. step name and description), and jump logic (null for sequential execution).

2.2 Planning LLM and Structured Planning Workflow

A structured planning workflow is designed by the Planning LLM based on user input task prompt. Generally, the workflow consists of multiple steps and jump logic between steps. To facilitate the transformation from a workflow in natural language to an intuitive graphical flowchart, Planning LLM is instructed to produce structured workflows, as shown in Table 1, with every step consisting of two parts: (1) Step: including step name and step description that users can directly revise; (2) Jump logic. Additionally, users can extend every step of the workflow into a sub-workflow with more details according to their preferences, and keep extending until reaching their desired level of detail.

We implement the Planning LLM with ChatGPT[1] and educate it to draft a plan with *education prompts*, which consists of (1) **Role of Planning LLM**: a powerful problem-solving assistant that provides a standard operating procedure (i.e., workflow) for the user's task; (2) **Generation of overall workflow**: Planning LLM is instructed to analyze the task and provide standard operating procedure as guidance, but is not required actually to solve the task; (3) **Generation of sub-workflow**: If a user intends to extend a step, the Planning LLM is provided with the dialogue history of the previous generation of the overall workflow to ensure logical consistency and prevent duplication of content between the sub-workflow the other steps of the overall workflow. (4) **Basic rules**: Planning LLM must follow the instructions and be strict to the output format defined in Table 1.

With the *education prompts*, Appendix A.2 exhibits an example of a workflow for the task "Write an essay titled 'Drunk Driving As A Social Issue'" generated by the Planning LLM.

[1]GPT-3.5-turbo on Azure. Model version: 2023-06-13

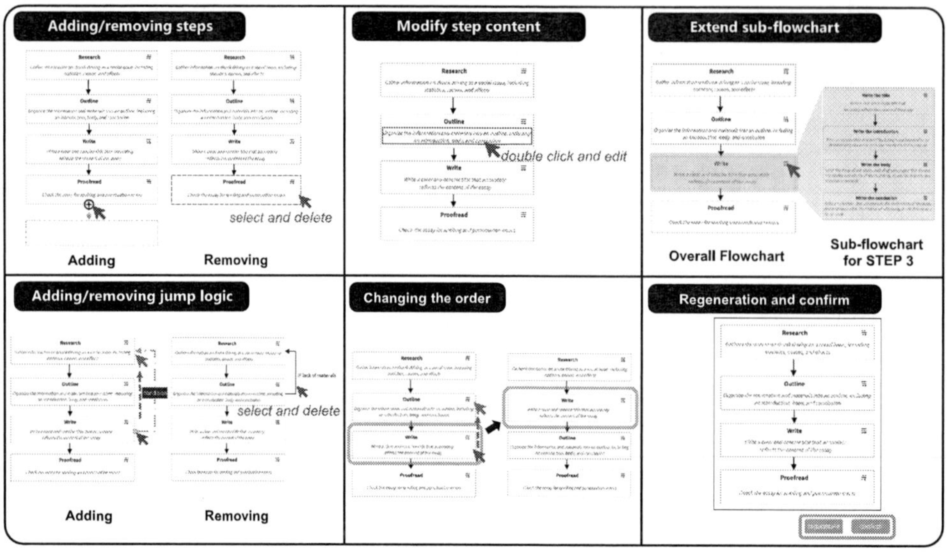

Figure 2: Six kinds of pre-defined low-code operations: (1) adding/removing steps; (2) modifying step name or descriptions; (3) adding/removing a jump logic; (4) changing the processing order; (5) extending a part of the flowchart; (6) regeneration and confirmation.

2.3 Low-code Interaction with Planning Workflow

To more intuitively present users with the workflow, a flowchart is utilized to visualize the workflow and presented it to users. The structured workflow (e.g., workflow in Appendix A.2) can be conveniently converted to a flowchart. Then, low-code visual programming operations enable users to easily implement sequential execution, conditional execution, and recursive execution.

As shown in Figure 2, there are six pre-defined low-code interactions on graphical flowchart. We define six types of low-code interactions for users to edit the workflow, including:

- Extending a step in the flowchart by clicking the button;
- Adding or removing steps by clicking buttons;
- Modifying step names or descriptions by clicking and text editing;
- Adding/removing a jump logic by clicking;
- Changing the processing order by dragging;
- Regeneration by clicking buttons.

These operations can be efficiently completed in a graphical user interface to achieve a very user-friendly interaction. Besides, a prototype has also been designed, featuring a clear interactive interface that enhances the usability of the Low-code LLM.

2.4 Executing LLM

The modified flowchart is converted back to a natural language based workflow (referred to as modified workflow) so that it can be understood by LLMs. Executing LLM is designed to generate responses by following the user-confirmed workflow and engaging in interactions with users via a conversational interface. Thanks to the user's explicit confirmation of the task execution logic in the workflow, the results generated by LLMs will be more controllable and satisfactory.

We implement the Executing LLM with ChatGPT and educate it to generate responses by providing it with *education prompts*, which instruct the ChatGPT to generate responses by strictly following the provided workflow.

2.5 Application Scenarios

We believe that, no matter how powerful large language models will be in the future, some tasks inevitably require users' participation. For example, users need to communicate their ideas and preferences, their understanding of the task, and their desired output format to the large language models. The traditional approach is to iterate through cumbersome prompt engineering, but the interaction method of Low-code LLM will greatly liberate users from such tedious prompt engineering. Workflow is an effective intermediate language that both humans and large language models can understand. This simple low-code operation in graphical user interface allows users to easily complete their logical ideas, while the structured planning process allows large language models to execute tasks more strictly according to the logic.

3 Experiments

3.1 Experimental Setup

We demonstrate the power and potential of Low-code LLM in assisting users with four categories of tasks:

(1) **Long Content Generation**, including long texts (such as blogs, business plans, and papers), and posters, wherein users interact with the flowchart generated by the Planning LLM to specify the structure, idea, and focus of the generation.

(2) **Large Project Development**, including complex object relations and system design. Users can educate LLMs about their architect design through low-code interactions.

(3) **Task-completion Virtual Assistant**, where developers can predefine the interaction logic between the virtual assistant and customers by editing the flowchart, and the Executing LLM will strictly follow the logic specified by the developer to minimize potential risks.

(4) **Knowledge-embedded System**, where domain experts can embed their experience or knowledge into a conducting workflow. Then, the counseling assistant will follow a pre-defined pattern and act as a coach to scaffold users to complete their tasks.

In particular, the Low-code LLM experiments are carried out using the OpenAI service (gpt-3.5-turbo). In each experiment, we detail the user-defined requirements, the user-provided input prompt, the flowchart created by the Planning LLM, user edits on the flowchart, and the final generation results.

In the qualitative analysis, we examined four pilot cases in the above categories to demonstrate the benefits of Low-code LLM in achieving controllable and satisfactory results.

3.2 Qualitative Analysis

Pilot Case 1: Essay Writing As shown in Figure 3, by enabling users to make specific edits to the flowchart, users can easily communicate with the system on their ideas and writing structures. As a result, the generated results are very controllable and highly aligned with users' writing plans. Low-code interaction is a win-win collaboration of the user's intelligence and LLM's powerful text generation ability.

Pilot Case 2: Object-oriented Programming Even though large language models demonstrate significant capabilities in code generation, it can be challenging for users to precisely instruct their requirements to an LLM in building complex systems. However, as shown in Figure 4 in Appendix A.1 , Low-code LLM enables professional programming architects to easily input their system design through low-code interaction. The results verify that the generated codes strictly follow the expert's design. With the Low-code LLM interaction, constructing a complex system becomes much more convenient for users.

Pilot Case 3: Virtual Hotel Service Figure 5 in Appendix A.1 shows the advantages of Low-code LLM over traditional prompt engineering for implementing a task-completion virtual assistant. By using Low-code LLM, users, probably hotel managers, can take advantage of a structured planning flowchart and interactively define the necessary execution logic for the virtual assistant. This ensures that the virtual assistant operates according to the managers' exact intentions, reducing potential errors and misbehavior. The intuitive, visual nature of the flowchart allows for easy editing and modification, and the result shows the behaviors are tightly aligned with the specified requirements.

Pilot Case 4: Resume Helper Figure 6 in Appendix A.1 shows another scenario where Low-code LLM is helpful. In some professional, knowledge-driven scenarios, experts can integrate execution logic and knowledge into the workflow through low-code interactions. By embedding expert knowledge, users can be scaffolded to complete their tasks. In this case, a human resource expert inputs resume creation experiences into Resume Helper, and when users use it to complete their resumes, the Executing LLM strictly follows the expert-defined workflow to communicate with users. Some similar scenarios may include psychological counseling, medical diagnosis, mock interviews, and others.

Low-code

Prompt: Write an essay titled "Advertising: Information or Manipulation".

The user-specified preferences:

- Support that advertising is primarily a form of manipulation
- Expound the argument in the introduction paragraph
- Use three paragraphs to dialectically analyze

Flowchart generated by Planning LLM and then revised by user: (The red text is the part edited by the user)

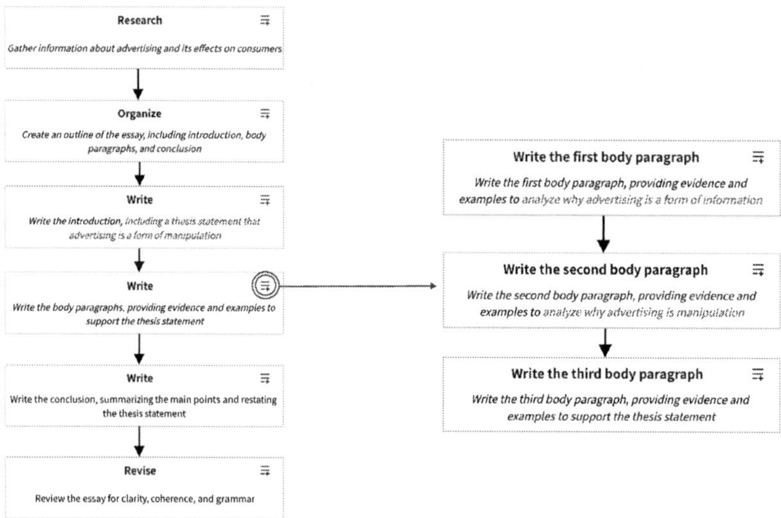

Low-code LLM:

Certainly, here is the essay I have written on the topic "Advertising:

Information or Manipulation": Advertising: Information or Manipulation

Advertising is a ubiquitous presence in modern society, with advertisements appearing on television, billboards, and social media platforms. While some argue that advertising provides valuable information to consumers, others contend that it is a form of manipulation that exploits people's desires and insecurities. In this essay, I will explore both sides of the debate and argue that advertising is primarily a form of manipulation.

On the one hand, proponents of advertising argue that it provides valuable information to consumers. For example, advertisements for new products can inform people about the latest technological advancements or health benefits. Additionally, advertisements can help consumers make informed decisions by providing information about the features and benefits of different products. In this sense, advertising can be seen as a useful tool for consumers to make informed choices.

On the other hand, critics of advertising argue that it is primarily a form of manipulation. Advertisements often appeal to people's emotions and desires, rather than providing objective information. For example, advertisements for beauty products often use images of flawless models to create an unrealistic standard of beauty that can make people feel inadequate. Similarly, advertisements for fast food restaurants often use images of delicious food to create cravings that can lead to unhealthy eating habits. In this sense, advertising can be seen as a form of manipulation that exploits people's desires and insecurities.

While there are certainly benefits to advertising, I believe that it is primarily a form of manipulation. Advertisements often use psychological tactics to influence people's behavior, such as creating a sense of urgency or scarcity. Additionally, advertisements often rely on stereotypes and cultural norms to appeal to people's emotions. For example, advertisements for cleaning products often feature women as the primary users, reinforcing gender stereotypes and limiting women's roles to domestic tasks. In this sense, advertising can be seen as a powerful tool for shaping people's beliefs and behaviors.

In conclusion, while some argue that advertising provides valuable information to consumers, I believe that it is primarily a form of manipulation that exploits people's desires and insecurities. By using psychological tactics and appealing to people's emotions, advertising can shape people's beliefs and behaviors in powerful ways. As consumers, it is important to be aware of these tactics and to critically evaluate the messages that we receive from advertisements.

Figure 3: Essay Generation through Low-Code LLM: Users interact with the LLM by editing a flowchart, resulting in responses that are more closely aligned with their requirements. The red section in the flowchart illustrates how users modify the workflow. The generated output is highly tailored to the user's specific needs (see the highlighted parts). To obtain similar controllable results, conventional prompt engineering requires complex prompt and heavy prompt modification works.

4 Related Work

Large Language Models Large language models (LLMs) have emerged as a prominent area of research in recent years. Recent LLMs, such as GPT-4 and ChatGPT, have made impressive strides in generating more coherent and contextually relevant responses. They have been applied in various industries and fields, including content creation, code development(Chen et al., 2021), customer support(George and George, 2023), and more. However, while LLMs have demonstrated promising potential, they still face limitations(Bowman, 2023; Borji, 2023; Bang et al., 2023). In particular, controlling the behavior and output of LLMs for complex tasks remains a challenge, which has led to the development of new techniques, such as prompt engineering, and methods to improve results(Wu et al., 2023; Ge et al., 2022; Wu et al., 2022; Shen et al., 2023; Wang et al., 2023b).

Prompt Engineering Prompt engineering has emerged as an essential technique for interacting with LLMs to achieve desired outcomes. The success of large language models relies heavily on their ability to produce answers to various queries(Zuccon and Koopman, 2023). However, providing effective prompts that convey the exact intent of humans is a non-trivial task, especially when it comes to complex tasks and requirements.

The challenge in prompt engineering lies in crafting prompts that can manipulate the LLM into generating specific outcomes. Researchers have explored various techniques to simplify prompt engineering, ranging from giving explicit instructions to providing context for LLMs to understand the desired output better(White et al., 2023).

Some recent advancements in prompt engineering include techniques such as few-shot learning(Wang et al., 2023a; Brown et al., 2020; Min et al., 2022), reinforcement-learning(Deng et al., 2022; Cao et al., 2023). However, these techniques often demand substantial expertise and time, making it difficult for end-users to leverage the full potential of these LLMs.

The Low-code LLM framework proposed in our paper provides an innovative solution by involving the users in the process of designing workflows, which ultimately controls the LLM's response generation.

Task Automation with LLMs Recently, various research studies have focused on leveraging large language models for task automation(Auto-GPT, 2023; Liang et al., 2023; Kim et al., 2023). Task automation with LLMs usually involves the model analyzing a given input, breaking it down into subtasks, and generating desired outputs accordingly.

However, the black-box nature of the interaction and the difficulty in controlling their output have remained significant challenges in deploying LLMs for complex tasks(Tan et al., 2023). Users often face difficulties when attempting to direct LLMs to adhere to specific requirements or constraints.

By offering a user-friendly and efficient way of specifying preferences and constraints, Low-code LLM contributes to research on task automation with LLMs, while further bridging the gap between users and LLMs for achieving more structured and fine-grained control.

5 Limitations

While the Low-code LLM framework promises a more controllable and user-friendly interaction with LLMs, there are some limitations.

One such limitation is the increase in the **cognitive load** for users, who now need to understand and modify the generated workflows.

Furthermore, accurate and effective **structured planning** within the Planning LLM may be challenging, and bad structured planning poses a heavy user editing burden. But we believe with the evolution of LLMs and research on task automation, the planning ability will be getting satisfactory.

Lastly, the current design assumes that users have sufficient **domain knowledge and skills** to modify the generated workflows effectively.

6 Conclusion

We proposed a novel human-LLM interaction framework, which aims to improve the control and efficiency of utilizing large language models for complex tasks. Low-code LLM allows users to better understand and modify the logic and workflow underlying the LLMs' execution of instructions. Compared with traditional prompt engineering, the proposed Low-code LLM framework advances the state-of-the-art in human-LLM interactions by bridging the gap of communication and collaboration between humans and LLMs. We believe the Low-code LLM framework presents a promising solution to many of the challenges faced by LLM users today and has the potential to greatly impact a wide range of industries and applications.

References

Auto-GPT. 2023. Auto-gpt.

David Baidoo-Anu and Leticia Owusu Ansah. 2023. Education in the era of generative artificial intelligence (ai): Understanding the potential benefits of chatgpt in promoting teaching and learning. *Available at SSRN 4337484*.

Yejin Bang, Samuel Cahyawijaya, Nayeon Lee, Wenliang Dai, Dan Su, Bryan Wilie, Holy Lovenia, Ziwei Ji, Tiezheng Yu, Willy Chung, et al. 2023. A multitask, multilingual, multimodal evaluation of chatgpt on reasoning, hallucination, and interactivity. *arXiv preprint arXiv:2302.04023*.

Ali Borji. 2023. A categorical archive of chatgpt failures. *arXiv preprint arXiv:2302.03494*.

Samuel R Bowman. 2023. Eight things to know about large language models. *arXiv preprint arXiv:2304.00612*.

Tom B. Brown, Benjamin Mann, Nick Ryder, Melanie Subbiah, Jared Kaplan, Prafulla Dhariwal, Arvind Neelakantan, Pranav Shyam, Girish Sastry, Amanda Askell, Sandhini Agarwal, Ariel Herbert-Voss, Gretchen Krueger, Tom Henighan, Rewon Child, Aditya Ramesh, Daniel M. Ziegler, Jeffrey Wu, Clemens Winter, Christopher Hesse, Mark Chen, Eric Sigler, Mateusz Litwin, Scott Gray, Benjamin Chess, Jack Clark, Christopher Berner, Sam McCandlish, Alec Radford, Ilya Sutskever, and Dario Amodei. 2020. Language models are few-shot learners.

Sébastien Bubeck, Varun Chandrasekaran, Ronen Eldan, Johannes Gehrke, Eric Horvitz, Ece Kamar, Peter Lee, Yin Tat Lee, Yuanzhi Li, Scott Lundberg, et al. 2023. Sparks of artificial general intelligence: Early experiments with gpt-4. *arXiv preprint arXiv:2303.12712*.

Tingfeng Cao, Chengyu Wang, Bingyan Liu, Ziheng Wu, Jinhui Zhu, and Jun Huang. 2023. BeautifulPrompt: Towards automatic prompt engineering for text-to-image synthesis. In *Proceedings of the 2023 Conference on Empirical Methods in Natural Language Processing: Industry Track*, pages 1–11, Singapore. Association for Computational Linguistics.

Mark Chen, Jerry Tworek, Heewoo Jun, Qiming Yuan, Henrique Ponde de Oliveira Pinto, Jared Kaplan, Harri Edwards, Yuri Burda, Nicholas Joseph, Greg Brockman, et al. 2021. Evaluating large language models trained on code. *arXiv preprint arXiv:2107.03374*.

Jonathan H Choi, Kristin E Hickman, Amy Monahan, and Daniel Schwarcz. 2023. Chatgpt goes to law school. *Available at SSRN*.

Mingkai Deng, Jianyu Wang, Cheng-Ping Hsieh, Yihan Wang, Han Guo, Tianmin Shu, Meng Song, Eric P. Xing, and Zhiting Hu. 2022. Rlprompt: Optimizing discrete text prompts with reinforcement learning.

Tao Ge, Jing Hu, Li Dong, Shaoguang Mao, Yan Xia, Xun Wang, Si-Qing Chen, and Furu Wei. 2022. Extensible prompts for language models. *arXiv preprint arXiv:2212.00616*.

A Shaji George and AS Hovan George. 2023. A review of chatgpt ai's impact on several business sectors. *Partners Universal International Innovation Journal*, 1(1):9–23.

Martin Hirzel. 2022. Low-code programming models. *arXiv preprint arXiv:2205.02282*.

Geunwoo Kim, Pierre Baldi, and Stephen McAleer. 2023. Language models can solve computer tasks. *arXiv preprint arXiv:2303.17491*.

Yaobo Liang, Chenfei Wu, Ting Song, Wenshan Wu, Yan Xia, Yu Liu, Yang Ou, Shuai Lu, Lei Ji, Shaoguang Mao, et al. 2023. Taskmatrix. ai: Completing tasks by connecting foundation models with millions of apis. *arXiv preprint arXiv:2303.16434*.

Microsoft. 1991. Visual basic.

Sewon Min, Xinxi Lyu, Ari Holtzman, Mikel Artetxe, Mike Lewis, Hannaneh Hajishirzi, and Luke Zettlemoyer. 2022. Rethinking the role of demonstrations: What makes in-context learning work?

Harsha Nori, Nicholas King, Scott Mayer McKinney, Dean Carignan, and Eric Horvitz. 2023. Capabilities of gpt-4 on medical challenge problems. *arXiv preprint arXiv:2303.13375*.

OpenAI. 2022. Chatgpt.

OpenAI. 2023. Gpt-4 technical report.

Mitchel Resnick, John Maloney, Andrés Monroy-Hernández, Natalie Rusk, Evelyn Eastmond, Karen Brennan, Amon Millner, Eric Rosenbaum, Jay Silver, Brian Silverman, et al. 2009. Scratch: programming for all. *Communications of the ACM*, 52(11):60–67.

Yongliang Shen, Kaitao Song, Xu Tan, Dongsheng Li, Weiming Lu, and Yueting Zhuang. 2023. Hugginggpt: Solving ai tasks with chatgpt and its friends in huggingface. *arXiv preprint arXiv:2303.17580*.

Yiming Tan, Dehai Min, Yu Li, Wenbo Li, Nan Hu, Yongrui Chen, and Guilin Qi. 2023. Evaluation of chatgpt as a question answering system for answering complex questions. *arXiv preprint arXiv:2303.07992*.

Lean Wang, Lei Li, Damai Dai, Deli Chen, Hao Zhou, Fandong Meng, Jie Zhou, and Xu Sun. 2023a. Label words are anchors: An information flow perspective for understanding in-context learning. In *Proceedings of the 2023 Conference on Empirical Methods in Natural Language Processing*, pages 9840–9855, Singapore. Association for Computational Linguistics.

Zhenhailong Wang, Shaoguang Mao, Wenshan Wu, Tao Ge, Furu Wei, and Heng Ji. 2023b. Unleashing the emergent cognitive synergy in large language models: A task-solving agent through multi-persona self-collaboration. *arXiv preprint arXiv:2307.05300*.

Jules White, Quchen Fu, Sam Hays, Michael Sandborn, Carlos Olea, Henry Gilbert, Ashraf Elnashar, Jesse Spencer-Smith, and Douglas C Schmidt. 2023. A prompt pattern catalog to enhance prompt engineering with chatgpt. *arXiv preprint arXiv:2302.11382*.

Chenfei Wu, Shengming Yin, Weizhen Qi, Xiaodong Wang, Zecheng Tang, and Nan Duan. 2023. Visual chatgpt: Talking, drawing and editing with visual foundation models. *arXiv preprint arXiv:2303.04671*.

Tongshuang Wu, Ellen Jiang, Aaron Donsbach, Jeff Gray, Alejandra Molina, Michael Terry, and Carrie J Cai. 2022. Promptchainer: Chaining large language model prompts through visual programming. In *CHI Conference on Human Factors in Computing Systems Extended Abstracts*, pages 1–10.

Yongchao Zhou, Andrei Ioan Muresanu, Ziwen Han, Keiran Paster, Silviu Pitis, Harris Chan, and Jimmy Ba. 2022. Large language models are human-level prompt engineers. *arXiv preprint arXiv:2211.01910*.

Guido Zuccon and Bevan Koopman. 2023. Dr chatgpt, tell me what i want to hear: How prompt knowledge impacts health answer correctness. *arXiv preprint arXiv:2302.13793*.

A Appendix

A.1 Pliot Cases

Figure 4, Figure 5 and Figure 6 demonstrate the details of pilot case 2, 3 and 4 in Section 3.2.

A.2 Workflow Example

Table 2 is an example of workflow generated by Planing LLM.

A.3 Discussion on System Robustness

Although the proposed Low-code LLM framework offers a user-friendly and easy-to-control environment for managing complex tasks with large language models, LLMs sometimes generate unexpected results, which may affect the robustness of the Low-Code LLM framework. We have observed the following potential problems in the system: (1) The generated workflows from Planing LLM may be either too sketchy or overly detailed. Users may need to regenerate the workflow or specify some key points. (2) Planning LLM might generate workflow that does not adhere to format requirements, potentially impacting subsequent processes. However, with the enhancement of LLMs such as GPT-4, their instruction following ability is continuously improving, thus mitigating this issue. Furthermore, rule-based post-processing methods can also address such problems. (3) In rare cases, despite being aware of all existing hierarchical levels of the workflow, LLMs may still generate sub-workflow that contains redundant content and logical inconsistencies compared to the original workflow, even when instructed to avoid such errors in the prompt. We believe this limitation is inherent to the model's capabilities. In such instances, users have the option to regenerate the workflow to obtain a satisfactory result.

Overall, the potential uncertainty in the outputs of large language models (LLMs) may affect the robustness of the system. However, in our experiments, such cases are very rare. These situations can be simply resolved by clicking the 'Regenerate' button. We believe that as the capabilities of foundation models improve, low-code LLMs will offer more robust, user-friendly, and efficient services.

Low-code

Prompt:
Write a two-person battle game with python where both game characters have two attributes: health and combat power. Player 1 has only two skills about attacking and plays 2 has only two skills about healing.

The user-specified preferences :
Defining parent class and implementing each game character by inheriting can improve the scalability and flexibility of the code.

Flowchart generated by Planning LLM and then revised by user: (The red text is the part edited by the user)

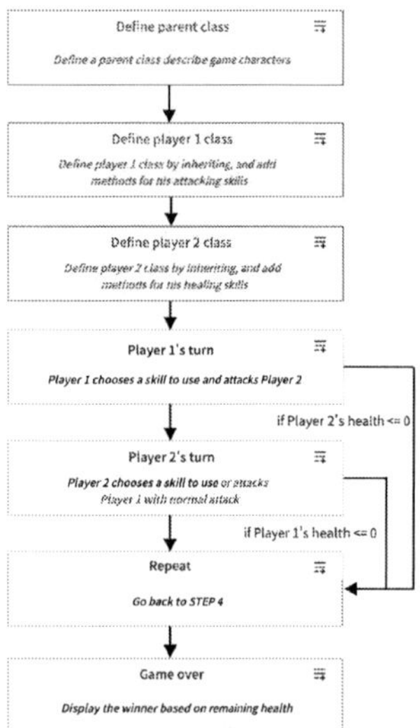

Utilizing ChatGPT directly:

```
```python
import random

class Player:
    def __init__(self, name, health, combat_power):
        self.name = name
        self.health = health
        self.combat_power = combat_power

    def attack(self, other_player):
        damage = random.randint(1, self.combat_power)
        print(f" {self.name} attacks
                {other_player.name} for
                {damage} damage!")
        other_player.health -= damage

    def heal(self):
        heal_amount = random.randint(1, 10)
        print(f"{self.name} heals for {heal_amount} health!")
        self.health += heal_amount

# Create the two players
player1 = Player("Player 1", 100, 20)
player2 = Player("Player 2", 100, 10)

# Game loop
Omitted due to limited space
```
```

Low-code LLM:

Sure, here is the code for the two person battle game:

```
```
class GameCharacter:
    def __init__(self, health, combat_power):
        self.health = health
        self.combat_power = combat_power

class Player1(GameCharacter):
    def __init__(self, health, combat_power):
        super().__init__(health, combat_power)

    def skill1(self, player2):
        player2.health -= self.combat_power * 2

    def skill2(self, player2):
        player2.health -= self.combat_power * 3

class Player2(GameCharacter):
    def __init__(self, health, combat_power):
        super().__init__(health, combat_power)

    def skill1(self):
        self.health += 20

    def skill2(self):
        self.health += 50

def main():
    player1 = Player1(100, 20)
    player2 = Player2(100, 10)

    while player1.health > 0 and player2.health > 0:
        print("Player 1's turn.")
        choice = input("Choose a skill to use (1 or 2): ")
        if choice == "1":
            player1.skill1(player2)
        elif choice == "2":
            player1.skill2(player2)

        if player2.health <= 0:
            break

        print("Player 2's turn.")
        choice = input("Choose a skill to use (1 or 2) or attack normally (3): ")
        if choice == "1":
            player2.skill1()
        elif choice == "2":
            player2.skill2()
        else:
            damage = random.randint(5, 15)
            player1.health -= damage
            print("Player 2 attacked normally and dealt", damage, "damage to Player 1.")

        if player1.health <= 0:
            break

    if player1.health > 0:
        print("Player 1 wins!")
    else:
        print("Player 2 wins!")

if __name__ == "__main__":
    main()
```
```

Figure 4: This case demonstrates how to empower LLMs coding using object-oriented programming patterns via the proposed approach. Architecture design is a professional skill for deveoping large scale project. With Low-code LLM, architects can easily educate the model about well-designed architecture, allowing Executing LLM to generate code based on flowcharts. The results from ChatGPT performed poorly in object design. After incorporating a human-edited workflow, the model was able to generate correct codes.

Low-code

Prompt: You are a hotel customer service, and someone calls to reserve a room.

The user-specified necessary requirements:

- Necessary processes: warm greeting, check on the availability of rooms, and confirmation of reservations
- Necessary information: name, check-in and check-out date, room options, contact information, payment method

Flowchart generated by Planning LLM and then revised by user : (The red text is the part edited by the user)

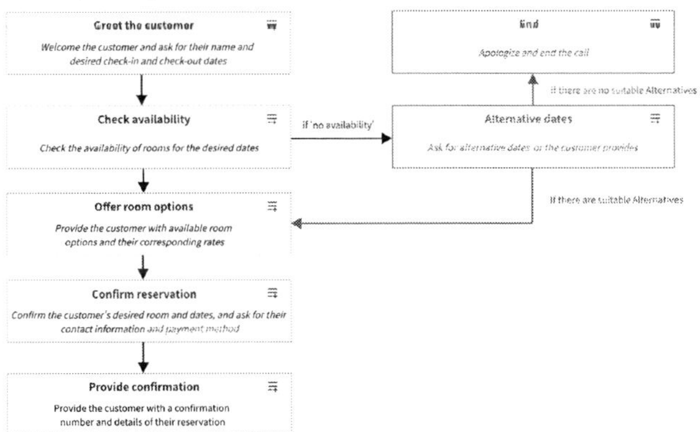

Low-code LLM:

Customer: Hi.

Service: Hello! Thank you for calling. How may I assist you today?

Customer: I want to reserve a room.

Service: Of course! May I have your name and the dates you would like to check in and check out?

Customer: Sure, my name is David Lee, and I will check in next Monday, and check out next Friday.

Service: Thank you, David Lee. Let me check our availability for those dates.

Customer: OK.

Service: I apologize, but we do not have any available rooms for those dates. Would you like me to check for any other dates?

Customer: What if I check out one day earlier?

Service: Let me check for you. Yes, we do have availability if you check out on Thursday instead of Friday. Would you like me to proceed with the reservation?

Customer: Sure.

Service: Great! We have a few room options available for those dates. We have a standard room available for $150 per night, a deluxe room for $200 per night, and a suite for $300 per night. Which one would you like to reserve?

Customer: Standard room is OK.

Service: Great choice! Can I have your contact information and payment method to confirm the reservation?

Customer: My phone number is 123456, and I will pay in cash.

Service: Thank you, David Lee. Your reservation for a standard room from next Monday to Thursday has been confirmed. Your confirmation number is 123456. We look forward to seeing you soon!

Customer: OK, many thanks.

Service: You're welcome! If you have any further questions or concerns, please don't hesitate to contact us. Have a great day!

Figure 5: A virtual hotel service using Low-code LLM allows users, such as hotel managers, to clearly define the execution logic through interaction with the structured planning flowchart, ensuring that the conduction logic strictly follows the user's intent. The red part in the flowchart shows how the user edits the workflow. As a result, the generated system is highly aligned with the user's specified requirements (refer to the highlighted part). Without the low-code LLM interaction, it becomes difficult to control how virtual hotel service communicates with customers.

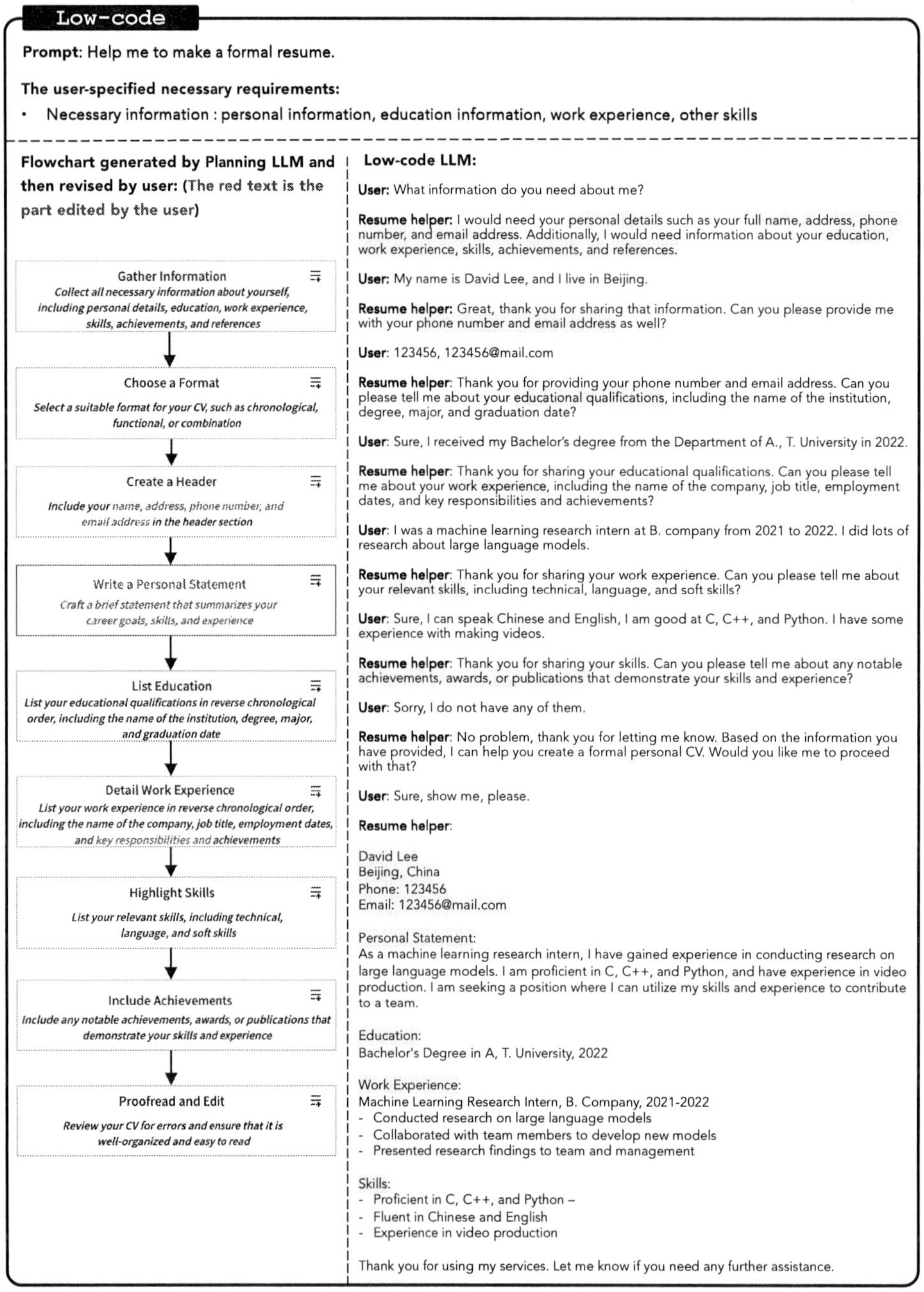

Figure 6: Resume Helper via Low-code LLM. In this case, domain experts, maybe human resource experts, can embed their resume-creating knowledge into a workflow. With the embedding of expert knowledge, Executing LLM can scaffold users to complete their resumes. Similar examples may also include psychological counseling, medical diagnosis, interview mock, etc.

Table 2: A workflow generated by Planing LLM when the user inputs "Write an essay titled 'Drunk Driving As A Social Issue'". STEP 3 is appointed by the user to provide a more detailed sub-workflow.

STEP	Step Name	Step Description	Jump Logic
STEP 1	Research	Gather information on drunk driving as a social issue, including statistics, causes, and effects	
STEP 2	Outline	Organize the information and materials into an outline, including an introduction, body, and conclusion	If lack of materials, jump to STEP 1
STEP 3	Write	Write the essay, including an introduction that defines drunk driving as a social issue, a body that discusses the causes and effects of drunk driving, and a conclusion that emphasizes the importance of addressing this issue	
STEP 3.1	Write the introduction	Write an introduction that provides background information on drunk driving as a social issue and clearly states the purpose of the essay	
STEP 3.2	Write the body	Write the body of the essay, including paragraphs that discuss the causes and effects of drunk driving, as well as any relevant statistics or research	
STEP 3.3	Write the conclusion	Write a conclusion that summarizes the main points of the essay and emphasizes the importance of addressing drunk driving as a social issue	
STEP 4	Proofread	Check the essay for spelling and punctuation errors	

A.4 Prompts

Planning LLM

PLANNING_LLM_PREFIX = Planning LLM is designed to provide a standard operating procedure so that an abstract and difficult task will be broken down into several steps, and the task will be easily solved by following these steps.

Planning LLM is a powerful problem-solving assistant, so it only needs to analyze the task and provide standard operating procedure as guidance, but does not need actually to solve the problem.

Sometimes there exists some unknown or undetermined situation, thus judgmental logic is needed: some "conditions" are listed, and the next step that should be carried out if a "condition" is satisfied is also listed. The judgmental logics are not necessary, so the jump actions are provided only when needed. Planning LLM MUST only provide standard operating procedure in the following format without any other words:

STEP 1: [step name][step descriptions][[[if 'condition1'][Jump to STEP]], [[[if 'condition1'][Jump to STEP]], [[if 'condition2'][Jump to STEP]], ...]
STEP 2: [step name][step descriptions][[[if 'condition1'][Jump to STEP]], [[[if 'condition1'][Jump to STEP]], [[if 'condition2'][Jump to STEP]], ...] ...

For example:

STEP 1: [Brainstorming][Choose a topic or prompt, and generate ideas and organize them into an outline][]
STEP 2: [Research][Gather information, take notes and organize them into the outline][[[lack of ideas][Jump to STEP 1]]] ...

EXTEND_PREFIX = Some steps of the SOP provided by Planning LLM are too rough, so Planning LLM can also provide a detailed sub-SOP for the given step.

Remember, Planning LLM take the overall SOP into consideration, and the sub-SOP MUST be consistent with the rest of the steps, and there MUST be no duplication in content between the extension and the original SOP. Besides, the extension MUST be logically consistent with the given step.

For example: If the overall SOP is:

STEP 1: [Brainstorming][Choose a topic or prompt, and generate ideas and organize them into an outline][]
STEP 2: [Research][Gather information from credible sources, and take notes and organize them into the outline][[[if lack of ideas][Jump to STEP 1]]]
STEP 3: [Write][write the text][]

If the STEP 3: "write the text" is too rough and needs to be extended, then the response could be:

STEP 3.1: [Write the title][write the title of the essay][]
STEP 3.2: [Write the body][write the body of the essay][[[if lack of materials][Jump to STEP 2]]]
STEP 3.3: [Write the conclusion][write the conclusion of the essay][]

Remember:
1. Extension is focused on the step descriptions, but not on the judgmental logic;
2. Planning LLM ONLY needs to response the extension.

PLANNING_LLM_SUFFIX = Remember: Planning LLM is very strict to the format and NEVER reply any word other than the standard operating procedure. The reply MUST start with "STEP".

Executing LLM

EXECUTING_LLM_PREFIX = Executing LLM is designed to provide outstanding responses.

Executing LLM will be given a overall task as the background of the conversation between the Executing LLM and human.

When providing response, Executing LLM MUST STICTLY follow the provided standard operating procedure (SOP). the SOP is formatted as:

STEP 1: [step name][step descriptions][[[if 'condition1'][Jump to STEP]], [[if 'condition2'][Jump to STEP]], ...]
STEP 2: [step name][step descriptions][[[if 'condition1'][Jump to STEP]], [[if 'condition2'][Jump to STEP]], ...]

Here "[[[if 'condition1'][Jump to STEP n]], [[if 'condition2'][Jump to STEP m]], ...]" is judgmental logic. It means when you're performing this step, and if 'condition1' is satisfied, you will perform STEP n next. If 'condition2' is satisfied, you will perform STEP m next.

Remember:

Executing LLM is facing a real human, who does not know what SOP is. So, Do not show him/her the SOP steps you are following, or the process and middle results of performing the SOP. It will make him/her confused. Just response the answer.

EXECUTING_LLM_SUFFIX = Remember:

Executing LLM is facing a real human, who does not know what SOP is.

So, Do not show him/her the SOP steps you are following, or the process and middle results of performing the SOP. It will make him/her confused. Just response the answer.

EdTec-QBuilder: A Semantic Retrieval Tool for Assembling Vocational Training Exams in German Language

Alonso Palomino[1,3], Andreas Fischer[2], Jakub Kuzilek[1], Jarek Nitsch[4], Niels Pinkwart[1], Benjamin Paaßen[1,3]

[1]Educational Technology Lab, DFKI, alonso.palomino@dfki.de
[2]Forschungsinstitut Betriebliche Bildung (f-bb), andreas.fischer@f-bb.de
[3]Universität Bielefeld, benjamin.paasen@uni-bielefeld.de
[4]bfz gGmbH

Abstract

Selecting and assembling test items from a validated item database into comprehensive exam forms is an under-researched but significant challenge in education. Search and retrieval methods provide a robust framework to assist educators when filtering and assembling relevant test items. In this work, we present EdTec-QBuilder[1], a semantic search tool developed to assist vocational educators in assembling exam forms. To implement EdTec-QBuilder's core search functionality, we evaluated eight retrieval strategies and twenty-five popular pre-trained sentence similarity models. Our evaluation revealed that employing cross-encoders to re-rank an initial list of relevant items is best for assisting vocational trainers in assembling examination forms. Beyond topic-based exam assembly, EdTec-QBuilder aims to provide a crowdsourcing infrastructure enabling manual exam assembly data collection, which is critical for future research and development in assisted and automatic exam assembly models.

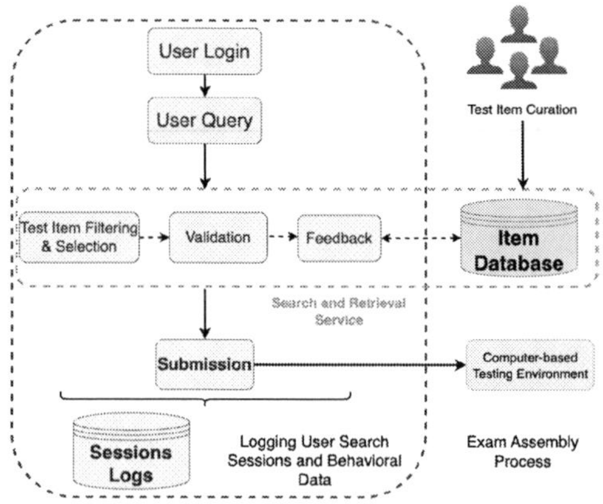

Figure 1: The operational flowchart scenario of EdTec-QBuilder.

1 Introduction

Examination forms consisting of validated, high-quality test items are a crucial tool for estimating the current competence of students in education. While much research has covered the task of *generating* such items, relatively little research has focused on *assembling* new exams from a database of existing, validated test items (Kurdi et al., 2020). Exam assembly is a challenging task on its own as exams need to cover all skills in a given topic comprehensively, at multiple levels of difficulty, and such that the resulting exam is psychometrically valid (Armendariz et al., 2012; Lane et al., 2015; Fischer and Neubert, 2015).

To support educational experts in formative exam assembly, we present EdTec-QBuilder[1], a service and tool to search a database of (validated and high-quality) test items and assemble them for an exam. Beyond its practical utility for exam assembly, our tool is also intended to be a crowdsourcing platform to collect data on exam assembly processes and thus provide data for future research on assisted and automated exam assembly.

Figure 1 summarizes the operational flow of our tool. After logging in, users query, filter, and annotate relevant items from a validated item database. While selecting, confirming, and submitting exam forms, users assess the quality of their search experience. Finally, search sessions are stored for analysis and exam assembly model development.

To implement EdTec-QBuilder's semantic search functionality, we evaluated the performance of eight search and retrieval strategies in combination with the top twenty-five trending pre-trained sentence similarity models (representing over 176 different combinations, overall; refer to Section 4). We selected the best-performing strategy and pre-trained model from our evaluation to include it as a core search and retrieval module. Our work makes the following key contributions:

[1]The EdTec-QBuilder system demo version is publicly accessible at: https://www.dfki.de/kiperweb/about.html

Proceedings of the 2024 Conference of the North American Chapter of the Association for Computational Linguistics: Human Language Technologies (Volume 3: System Demonstrations), pages 26–35
June 16-21, 2024 ©2024 Association for Computational Linguistics

- A new perspective to tackle the topic-based exam assembly task, framed as an information retrieval problem.
- A new data resource to study exam assembly[2].
- A system demonstration of the deployed service and tool used by vocational educators[1].
- An extensive evaluation and performance analysis of popular pre-trained sentence similarity models for the exam assembly task.

The evaluation and selection of the best-performing core semantic search functionality can be found in Section 4. The implementation and features of EdTec-QBuilder are described in Section 5. Finally, we discuss future directions and opportunities for improvement in Section 6.

2 Related Work

Research on assisted and automated exam assembly can be traced back to the EVALING system (Fairon, 1999), a platform that employed rule-based and finite state transducers to compile and update language proficiency exams from a question bank. Piton-Gonçalves and Aluísio (2012) presented a multidimensional adaptive test architecture and system that selects test items based on a student's profile and previous performance. Qin et al. (2019) utilized named entity recognition to build a knowledge graph of skills, which a recommendation method harnessed to suggest personalized interview questions. Sangodiah et al. (2016) used text classification methods to estimate exam difficulty from question bank's items via Bloom's taxonomy categories. Han (2018) introduced selection methods for complying with test item criteria for automated item selection, fostering adaptive learning and individualized learning. Ruan et al. (2019) developed a dialog agent to teach factual knowledge of science and safety. When contrasting system usage with a flashcard system, students increased their response accuracy significantly when using the agent. Cole et al. (2020) leveraged classic natural language processing methods with a cluster-based test item generation approach aligned to a dashboard that enables test designers to select generated questions from the available clusters. Datta et al. (2021) tackled the task of automatically generating an interview question plan from the applicant's resume, harnessing knowledge graphs and integer programming methods. Upadhyay et al. (2023) employed large language models to develop a suite for automated item generation and exam assembly. However, the suite delegates the assembly process to human experts to ensure the test items' quality.

Most of the prior research focuses exclusively on test item generation, utilizing either classical NLP methods such as text classification and topic modeling (Brown et al., 2005; Mitkov et al., 2006; Rus et al., 2011; Heilman and Smith, 2010; Chali and Hasan, 2015), or deep neural networks and transformer-based architectures (Du et al., 2017; Chan and Fan, 2019; Tuan et al., 2020; Qu et al., 2021; Yoshimi et al., 2023). However, in real scenarios, where contextual knowledge, quality control, and topic alignment with curricular standards are necessary for effective student skill development, it is not sufficient to generate items; we also need to assemble them to exams that are psychometrically suited to test the competencies they ought to assess. Therefore, in contrast to prior work, our contribution focuses on assisted exam assembly rather than item generation. Further, we conceptualize exam assembly as an information retrieval problem.

3 Methods

EdTec-Qbuilder aims to assist in tackling the topic-based exam assembly task. We formalize the task as an information retrieval problem. Given a query $q \in Q$ – e.g. a text describing the topic of a exam – and a database of possible items $B = \{x_1, \ldots, x_N\}$, we wish to compute similarity scores $s_1 = S(q, x_1), \ldots, s_N = S(q, x_N)$ for some similarity function $S : Q \times B \to \mathbb{R}$. Based on these scores, we rank all possible items from most similar to least similar and let an educational expert assemble an exam from the ranked list. In other words, we support educational experts in exam assembly by assisting them in searching a large item database according to their query (refer to Figure 1). Therefore, the similarity function S needs to correspond to educational experts' notion of relevance. In other words, S must assign higher similarity values to the items experts want to include in their exam. This is precisely the criterion we evaluate in Section 4.

3.1 Item Database

The item database B for our investigation has been provided by the bfz group, one of the largest voca-

[2]The public data fold available under CC BY license at: `https://www.dfki.de/kiperweb/about.html#dataset`

tional training providers in Germany. The database consists of 2,812 test items across 34 in-demand vocational training topics. For the purpose of a freely available version of our tool (the original 2,812 items are proprietary) and to increase the amount of training data, we augmented the item database with another 2,812 items generated via ChatGPT3.5[23]. All generated items were manually inspected, and duplicates/low-quality items were removed. The remaining items form the basis for our tool's openly available demo version.

Table 1a displays the most prominent topics in the item database, with their three most used terms. Specifically, the topics "Professional Counseling/Learning Skills/Self-assessment", "Business Knowledge", "Communication/Negotiation and Etiquette in the Workplace", "Information Technology Competence" and "Presentation and Visualization Techniques" cover 2,329 items, meaning 41.41% of all items. The average length of the questions is 17.76 words. Overall, the most used terms throughout the collection correspond to "company", "product" and "important". To estimate the difficulty of 2,812 test items of the bfz data datafold, we fitted a 1parameter item response theory model to the answers of prior respondents. Table 1b shows the distribution of the resulting difficulty values, grouped into three levels: easy, medium, and hard. We observed that 78.91% of test items have a medium difficulty, 20.98% were easy to answer, and only 0.10% were hard. Table 1c outlines the question type distribution in the item database. We observed that 64.83% are multiple and single choice test item types, whereas other formats are less frequent.

4 Experiments and Analysis

Our experiments aim to evaluate the capability of various (semantic) search strategies to retrieve matching test items for typical queries in our item database[4]. Due to the lack of historical search data and insufficient human annotation capacity that would allow us to obtain ground-truth data, we opted to use an automated relevance labeling approach. Using the following approach, we built a new synthetic TREC-style (Voorhees et al., 2005; Teufel, 2007; Voorhees et al., 2022) data set of queries and corresponding relevancy items.

[3] `https://chat.openai.com/`

[4] The experiments were conducted on a macOS with an ARM64 processor, 32 GB of memory, and 12 physical cores.

Testbed We randomly generated synthetic queries by selecting 15 syntactically different synonyms from the 34 available topic dimensions of the item database (refer to Table 1a). By aggregating the top 100 agreeing search results of 25 trending multilingual and German sentence similarity models (refer to Appendix A.1), with the trec-tools library (Palotti et al., 2019), we constructed a synthetic test dataset for evaluating our experiments. To attach relevance judgments to the elements of the test dataset, we calculated the average similarity score with the available pre-trained models for each query and item pair. Pairs with an average similarity score between 0.60 and 0.75 were labeled as moderately relevant; pairs above 0.75 were labeled as highly relevant. We acknowledge that this labeling strategy could introduce a bias as the assumed ground truth is influenced by the same language models later used as part of the search strategies. However, the labeling was obtained by averaging the similarity scores of all language models, thus reducing the bias toward any single model and enhancing the robustness of the obtained labeling.

Evaluation We employed the ranx library (Bassani, 2022) to calculate standard information retrieval metrics as an evaluation method to identify and select the best-performing strategy to include as a search module in our tool. In addition to Precision, Recall, F1, and mean average precision (MAP), we used normalized discounted cumulative gain (nDCG) and mean reciprocal rank (MRR). The former expresses the relevance of documents ranked at the top, whereas the latter expresses relevant documents' (reciprocal) rank. Both metrics are better if higher.

Search and retrieval strategies We tested eight different search and retrieval strategies:

1. BM25: As a baseline method, we fitted a standard BM25 model (Řehůřek and Sojka, 2010). BM25 is a probabilistic model that, given a query, calculates term and inverse document frequencies to retrieve relevant items.
2. LM+ANN: We employed 25 trending multilingual and German sentence similarity pre-trained language models (LM) (see Appendix A.1) to approximate the top nearest neighbors (ANN) with the NMSLIB library (Boytsov and Naidan, 2013).
3. TF-IDF Weighted Average: To improve the se-

(a)

Top 5 Topics	Avg. Terms per Item	Unique Terms	Top 3 Terms	Dist.
Professional Counseling, Learning Skills Self-assessment	11.96	2495	learn (140) work (93) professional (91)	671
Business Knowledge	18.25	2495	company (328) product (210) business plan (199)	586
Workplace Communication, Negotiation & Etiquette	18.75	2490	customer (184) product (182) communication (177)	514
Information Technology Competence	17.01	2064	internet (58) digital (47) program (43)	322
Presentation & Visualization Techniques	17.45	1014	presentation (241) audience (184) represent (86)	236
Total 34	17.76	15023	company (1017) product (639) important (492)	5624

(b)

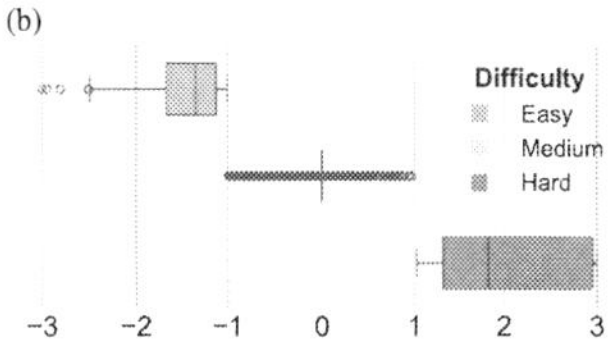

(c)

	Attribute	Dist.
	Multiple Choice	1902
	Single Choice	1745
	Scale	732
	Single Choice Matrix	753
	Page type	146
	Multiple Choice Matrix	144
	Word Problem	58
	Fill in The Blank	46
	Other	125
Source	bfz	2812
	ChatGPT3.5	2812

Table 1: Summary of (a) topical, (b) test item dificulty, and (c) structural contents of the bfz-EdTec dataset, where topic categories and top terms are translated in English language

mantic representation of the existing pre-trained language models, we averaged the embedding vectors by weighting the term frequency and the inverse document frequency scores (TF-IDF) of the represented terms.

4. Query-term expansion: We expanded search queries and documents with synonym terms as listed in OdeNet (Siegel and Bond, 2021), the German language version of Wordnet.
5. Vertical search: To reduce the search space to only relevant topics, we truncated the search to the top ten most semantically similar topics in terms of cosine similarity, where topics were defined by the item data base (refer to Table 1, first column).
6. MILP: After computing the top 100 most similar items to the query according to cosine similarity of sentence embeddings, we applied the method of (Mitchell et al., 2011) to re-rank the items to optimize the nDCG score via mixed integer linear programming (MILP) with a CBC Solver.
7. LambdaMART: We employed a LambdaMART (Burges, 2010; Chen and Guestrin, 2016) regressor for re-ranking the top 100 most similar items to the query. We evaluated our model with a ten-cross-validation schema. The average nDCG score of the model in cross-validation was 0.35.
8. Cross-encoder: We re-ranked the top 100 most similar items to the query with a multilingual MS Marco cross-encoder (Reimers and Gurevych, 2019)[5]. To re-rank, cross-encoders concatenate query and items, passing them to a transformer model. With a self-attention mechanism, the transformer learns the importance of weights across the concatenated inputs, scoring its relevance. Finally, the model re-orders an initial list of candidates by its relevance scores.

Note that each strategy may have several representatives. Overall, we evaluated 176 different combinations of search strategies and pre-trained sentence similarity models.

4.1 Results and Analysis

Table 2 reports each strategy's top three best-performing representatives (regarding nDCG) for the 100 highest-ranked items. We observed that the most effective strategy for our task is re-ranking an initial candidate list of relevant items with a cross-encoder (0.516 nDCG and 0.713 MRR), followed by a vertical search approach (0.468 nDCG and 0.245 MRR). The least effective strategies were BM25 and query expansion. Overall, we observed that using a pre-trained sentence similarity German language model[6] in conjunction with a multilingual cross-encoder[5] outperformed all the proposed strategies with their corresponding pre-trained sentence similarity model.

We conduct a correlation analysis via Kendall's τ between the best-performing search runs (refer to A.2) to analyze the differences across the best-performing strategies' search results. The LambdaMART re-ranker and the TF-IDF weighted average model had the most similar search results ($\tau = 0.59$). However, considering the nDCG

[5] amberoad/bert-multilingual-passage-reranking-msmarco

[6] deutsche-telekom/gbert-large-paraphrase-cosine

Strategy	Pre-trained Language Model	nDCG@100	MRR@100	Prec@100	Recall@100	F1@100	MAP@100
Baseline	bm25	0.07	0.12	0.05	0.09	0.06	0.01
LM+ANN	deutsche-telekom_gbert-large-paraphrase-cosine	0.43	0.20	0.31	0.53	0.37	0.25
	deutsche-telekom_gbert-large-paraphrase-euclidean	0.43	0.20	0.31	0.53	0.37	0.24
	sentence-transformers_paraphrase-multilingual-mpnet-base-v2	0.42	0.24	0.30	0.51	0.36	0.24
TF-IDF Weighted Average	deutsche-telekom_gbert-large-paraphrase-cosine	0.32	0.14	0.24	0.40	0.29	0.15
	PM-AI_sts_paraphrase_xlm-roberta-base_de-en	0.31	0.18	0.23	0.39	0.28	0.15
	nblokker_debatenet-2-cat	0.30	0.14	0.22	0.36	0.26	0.13
Query-Term Expansion	deutsche-telekom_gbert-large-paraphrase-euclidean	0.26	0.08	0.21	0.33	0.24	0.13
	deutsche-telekom_gbert-large-paraphrase-cosine	0.25	0.10	0.20	0.32	0.23	0.13
	PM-AI_sts_paraphrase_xlm-roberta-base_de-en	0.24	0.10	0.18	0.30	0.22	0.13
Vertical Search	deutsche-telekom_gbert-large-paraphrase-euclidean	0.46	0.24	0.34	0.58	0.41	0.26
	deutsche-telekom_gbert-large-paraphrase-cosine	0.45	0.23	0.33	0.57	0.40	0.25
	sentence-transformers_paraphrase-multilingual-mpnet-base-v2	0.44	0.24	0.32	0.55	0.39	0.25
MILP Re-ranker	deutsche-telekom_gbert-large-paraphrase-euclidean	0.39	0.26	0.31	0.53	0.37	0.15
	deutsche-telekom_gbert-large-paraphrase-cosine	0.38	0.18	0.31	0.53	0.37	0.14
	sentence-transformers_paraphrase-multilingual-mpnet-base-v2	0.38	0.18	0.30	0.51	0.36	0.14
LambdaMART Re-ranker	deutsche-telekom_gbert-large-paraphrase-euclidean	0.42	0.32	0.31	0.53	0.37	0.17
	deutsche-telekom_gbert-large-paraphrase-cosine	0.41	0.27	0.31	0.53	0.37	0.16
	sentence-transformers_paraphrase-multilingual-mpnet-base-v2	0.40	0.28	0.30	0.51	0.36	0.16
Cross-encoder Re-ranker	deutsche-telekom_gbert-large-paraphrase-cosine	0.51	0.70	0.31	0.53	0.37	0.28
	deutsche-telekom_gbert-large-paraphrase-euclidean	0.51	0.71	0.31	0.53	0.37	0.28
	0_Transformer	0.49	0.70	0.27	0.49	0.34	0.27

Table 2: Performance metrics for the eight search strategies (rows), combined with the respective best-performing language models, evaluated at a cut-off of 100.

scores, the ranking quality produced by the LambdaMART re-ranker model was 10% better compared to the TF-IDF weighted average. With a correlation of -0.89, the models that showed the slightest similarity in terms of the produced rankings were the MILP re-ranker and the BM25 model.

5 Tool Overview

This section presents EdTec-QBuilder, a semantic search service and web tool to support exam assembly. Figure 2 provides an overview of the tool. While the frontend is a website implemented in HTML and JavaScript, the backend is implemented in Python and Flask. Below, we summarize each of the main components.

User workflow Figure 2a illustrates EdTec-QBuilder's user workflow. First, after notifying users that we will only collect click data from the user interface and annotations for future research and development, users land on the search result page (SERP) interface after successfully authenticating themselves. Second, once in the SERP view, the web application provides a search bar where users can browse and search across the test items in the item database. Third, after triggering a search, the tool returns the top 100 items relevant to their query, grouped on pages with ten results each. We employed a cross-encoder as a re-ranking strategy because it showed the best performance (see Section 4). Fourth, as illustrated in Figure 2b, to assemble exams, users click on the test items they wish to include in their exam. When users click on an item in the ranked list, the item changes to green, indicating its inclusion in the exam. Any selected item can be de-selected by clicking again. Users can flag items if they consider them outdated or inconsistent by pressing a red flag button. Finally, after annotating, users submit the selected test items to another endpoint, e.g., to publish the exam or deliver it to a computer-based testing environment (CBTE). Note that our interface also crowdsources ground-truth annotation data by internally logging and sending the selected items to the tool's backend (refer to Appendix 4 for more details about the user interface).

API endpoints We implemented 13 interoperable functionalities coupled with the search and data collection processes. Figure 2c summarizes the endpoint's inter-module coordination. We provide a JSON Web Token-based service[7] to authenticate and serve client requests from the SERP. After user authentication, the endpoint validates the users' credentials in the user's database. When a user submits a query, the query is embedded as a vector via the deutsche-telekom_gbert-large-paraphrase-cosine model and the 100 closest items according to cosine similarity are retrieved via NMSLIB. To optimize the output of the initial search, the tool

[7] https://jwt.io/

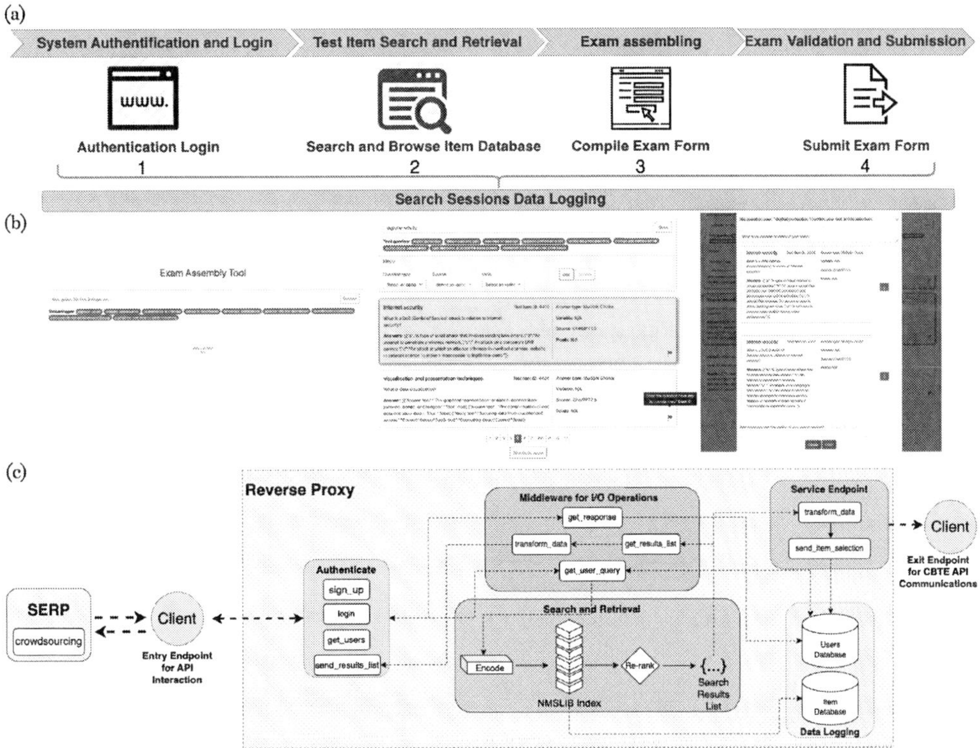

Figure 2: Summary of user workflow (a), API/endpoints architecture (b), SERP user interface (c).

re-ranks the top 100 results with a cross-encoder. Then, it returns a response in JSON format with the resulting test items and their corresponding attributes. The client receives the system's output, and the SERP maps the JSON into a suitable format for the visualization of results. The client then allows users to select relevant items; in the background, the SERP logs the selected items and sends this data to the web tool in a JSON format.

6 Conclusions

More than item generation is required to build high-quality exams in education; items must also be assembled into comprehensive examination forms (Lane et al., 2015; Kurdi et al., 2020). We framed assisted topic-based exam assembly as an information retrieval problem, evaluating 176 search and retrieval strategies and language model combinations on a 5,624-item database from the vocational education domain. The most promising strategy is to embed queries via language models, identify the closest 100 items regarding cosine similarity, and re-rank these 100 results via a cross-encoder, yielding 0.516 nDCG and 0.713 MRR. In other words, about half of the top-ranked results were relevant, and the highest-ranked relevant result was, on average, on rank 1 or 2. Using the cross-encoder re-ranking strategy, we developed EdTec-QBuilder[1], a semantic search service and tool to support exam assembly, which is currently in use at bfz, one of the leading vocational training providers in Bavaria. As competencies are known to be heterogenous constructs, test developers are well advised to combine items on multiple topics and items of varying difficulty (Fischer and Neubert, 2015). Future work should investigate leveraging crowdsourced search sessions and developing models for estimating test item difficulty without entirely depending on respondent data beforehand. Lastly, exploring and incorporating large language models could significantly aid the assembly process.

Limitations and Ethics Statement

While EdTec-QBuilder already supports assisted topic-based exam assembly significantly, some limitations remain. To overcome the cold start problem and rapidly transfer a tool to our industry partner to assist them in exam assembly, we based our evaluation on a synthetic and automated labeling scheme instead of using human judgments as ground truth. However, our tool establishes a research infrastructure for crowdsourcing ground truth expert data that can be used to improve or train future assisted or automatic test assembly models.

Exam assembly is an ethically charged subject matter because exam results can severely impact students' future learning and prospects. Therefore, our system does *not* automate exam assembly but, instead, serves as a tool for vocational educators who still have to make the final test item selection and take responsibility for the assembled examination form. Our system does not reason about the item quality but focuses on scoring the similarity between queries and test items. Finally, we may encounter a popularity bias for items that educators prefer in the early use of the system, and these preferences are "locked in" by using teacher preferences as training data. Our current training data is synthetically generated and thereby circumvents this particular bias, but future work should investigate this issue more closely.

References

Anaje Armendariz, Tomás A Pérez, and Javier López-Cuadrado. 2012. Compiling a test: how to solve calibration issues. *Procedia-Social and Behavioral Sciences*, 46:2253–2257.

Elias Bassani. 2022. ranx: A blazing-fast python library for ranking evaluation and comparison. In *ECIR (2)*, volume 13186 of *Lecture Notes in Computer Science*, pages 259–264. Springer.

Leonid Boytsov and Bilegsaikhan Naidan. 2013. Engineering efficient and effective non-metric space library. In *Similarity Search and Applications - 6th International Conference, SISAP 2013, A Coruña, Spain, October 2-4, 2013, Proceedings*, volume 8199 of *Lecture Notes in Computer Science*, pages 280–293. Springer.

Jonathan Brown, Gwen Frishkoff, and Maxine Eskenazi. 2005. Automatic question generation for vocabulary assessment. In *Proceedings of Human Language Technology Conference and Conference on Empirical Methods in Natural Language Processing*, pages 819–826, Vancouver, British Columbia, Canada. Association for Computational Linguistics.

Christopher JC Burges. 2010. From ranknet to lambdarank to lambdamart: An overview. *Learning*, 11(23-581):81.

Yllias Chali and Sadid A. Hasan. 2015. Towards topic-to-question generation. *Computational Linguistics*, 41(1):1–20.

Ying-Hong Chan and Yao-Chung Fan. 2019. A recurrent BERT-based model for question generation. In *Proceedings of the 2nd Workshop on Machine Reading for Question Answering*, pages 154–162, Hong Kong, China. Association for Computational Linguistics.

Tianqi Chen and Carlos Guestrin. 2016. Xgboost: A scalable tree boosting system. In *Proceedings of the 22nd acm sigkdd international conference on knowledge discovery and data mining*, pages 785–794.

Brian S Cole, Elia Lima-Walton, Kim Brunnert, Winona Burt Vesey, and Kaushik Raha. 2020. Taming the firehose: Unsupervised machine learning for syntactic partitioning of large volumes of automatically generated items to assist automated test assembly. *Journal of Applied Testing Technology*, pages 1–11.

Soham Datta, Prabir Mallick, Sangameshwar Patil, Indrajit Bhattacharya, and Girish Palshikar. 2021. Generating an optimal interview question plan using a knowledge graph and integer linear programming. In *Proceedings of the 2021 Conference of the North American Chapter of the Association for Computational Linguistics: Human Language Technologies*, pages 1996–2005, Online. Association for Computational Linguistics.

Xinya Du, Junru Shao, and Claire Cardie. 2017. Learning to ask: Neural question generation for reading comprehension. In *Proceedings of the 55th Annual Meeting of the Association for Computational Linguistics (Volume 1: Long Papers)*, pages 1342–1352, Vancouver, Canada. Association for Computational Linguistics.

Cédrick Fairon. 1999. A web-based system for automatic language skill assessment: Evaling. In *Computer Mediated Language Assessment and Evaluation in Natural Language Processing*.

Andreas Fischer and Jonas Neubert. 2015. The multiple faces of complex problems: A model of problem solving competency and its implications for training and assessment. *Journal of Dynamic Decision Making*, 1(6):1–14.

Kyung Chris Tyek Han. 2018. Components of the item selection algorithm in computerized adaptive testing. *Journal of Educational Evaluation for Health Professions*, 15.

Michael Heilman and Noah A. Smith. 2010. Good question! statistical ranking for question generation. In *Human Language Technologies: The 2010 Annual Conference of the North American Chapter of the Association for Computational Linguistics*, pages 609–617, Los Angeles, California. Association for Computational Linguistics.

Ghader Kurdi, Jared Leo, Bijan Parsia, Uli Sattler, and Salam Al-Emari. 2020. A systematic review of automatic question generation for educational purposes. *International Journal of Artificial Intelligence in Education*, 30:121–204.

Suzanne Lane, Mark R Raymond, and Thomas M Haladyna. 2015. *Handbook of test development*. Routledge.

Stuart Mitchell, Michael OSullivan, and Iain Dunning. 2011. Pulp: a linear programming toolkit for python.

The University of Auckland, Auckland, New Zealand, 65.

Ruslan Mitkov, Ha Le An, and Nikiforos Karamanis. 2006. A computer-aided environment for generating multiple-choice test items. *Natural language engineering*, 12(2):177–194.

Joao Palotti, Harrisen Scells, and Guido Zuccon. 2019. Trectools: an open-source python library for information retrieval practitioners involved in trec-like campaigns. In *Proceedings of the 42nd International ACM SIGIR Conference on Research and Development in Information Retrieval*, pages 1325–1328.

Jean Piton-Gonçalves and Sandra Maria Aluísio. 2012. An architecture for multidimensional computer adaptive test with educational purposes. In *Proceedings of the 18th Brazilian Symposium on Multimedia and the Web*, WebMedia '12, page 17–24, New York, NY, USA. Association for Computing Machinery.

Chuan Qin, Hengshu Zhu, Chen Zhu, Tong Xu, Fuzhen Zhuang, Chao Ma, Jingshuai Zhang, and Hui Xiong. 2019. Duerquiz: A personalized question recommender system for intelligent job interview. In *Proceedings of the 25th ACM SIGKDD International Conference on Knowledge Discovery & Data Mining*, KDD '19, page 2165–2173, New York, NY, USA. Association for Computing Machinery.

Fanyi Qu, Xin Jia, and Yunfang Wu. 2021. Asking questions like educational experts: Automatically generating question-answer pairs on real-world examination data. In *Proceedings of the 2021 Conference on Empirical Methods in Natural Language Processing*, pages 2583–2593, Online and Punta Cana, Dominican Republic. Association for Computational Linguistics.

Radim Řehůřek and Petr Sojka. 2010. Software Framework for Topic Modelling with Large Corpora. In *Proceedings of the LREC 2010 Workshop on New Challenges for NLP Frameworks*, pages 45–50, Valletta, Malta. ELRA. http://is.muni.cz/publication/884893/en.

Nils Reimers and Iryna Gurevych. 2019. Sentence-bert: Sentence embeddings using siamese bert-networks. In *Proceedings of the 2019 Conference on Empirical Methods in Natural Language Processing*. Association for Computational Linguistics.

Sherry Ruan, Liwei Jiang, Justin Xu, Bryce Joe-Kun Tham, Zhengneng Qiu, Yeshuang Zhu, Elizabeth L Murnane, Emma Brunskill, and James A Landay. 2019. Quizbot: A dialogue-based adaptive learning system for factual knowledge. In *Proceedings of the 2019 CHI Conference on Human Factors in Computing Systems*, pages 1–13.

Vasile Rus, Paul Piwek, Svetlana Stoyanchev, Brendan Wyse, Mihai Lintean, and Cristian Moldovan. 2011. Question generation shared task and evaluation challenge: Status report. In *Proceedings of the 13th European Workshop on Natural Language Generation*, ENLG '11, page 318–320, USA. Association for Computational Linguistics.

Anbuselvan Sangodiah, Rohiza Ahmad, and Wan Fatimah Wan Ahmad. 2016. Integration of machine learning approach in item bank test system. In *2016 3rd International Conference on Computer and Information Sciences (ICCOINS)*, pages 164–168.

Melanie Siegel and Francis Bond. 2021. OdeNet: Compiling a German wordnet from other resources. In *Proceedings of the 11th Global Wordnet Conference (GWC 2021)*, pages 192–198.

Simone Teufel. 2007. An overview of evaluation methods in trec ad hoc information retrieval and trec question answering. *Evaluation of text and speech systems*, pages 163–186.

Luu Anh Tuan, Darsh Shah, and Regina Barzilay. 2020. Capturing greater context for question generation. *Proceedings of the AAAI Conference on Artificial Intelligence*, 34(05):9065–9072.

Shriyash Upadhyay, Chris Callison-burch, and Etan Ginsberg. 2023. Learn with martian: A tool for creating assignments that can write and re-write themselves. In *Proceedings of the 17th Conference of the European Chapter of the Association for Computational Linguistics: System Demonstrations*, pages 267–276, Dubrovnik, Croatia. Association for Computational Linguistics.

Ellen M Voorhees, Donna K Harman, et al. 2005. *TREC: Experiment and evaluation in information retrieval*, volume 63. MIT press Cambridge.

Ellen M Voorhees, Ian Soboroff, and Jimmy Lin. 2022. Can old trec collections reliably evaluate modern neural retrieval models?

Nana Yoshimi, Tomoyuki Kajiwara, Satoru Uchida, Yuki Arase, and Takashi Ninomiya. 2023. Distractor generation for fill-in-the-blank exercises by question type. In *Proceedings of the 61st Annual Meeting of the Association for Computational Linguistics (Volume 4: Student Research Workshop)*, pages 276–281, Toronto, Canada. Association for Computational Linguistics.

A Appendix

A.1 Pre-trained sentence similarity models Details

Table 3 displays the complete list of pre-trained semantic sentence similarity models used in the experiments.

The language models in this list were the top-trending pre-trained sentence similarity language models as of December 1, 2023, according to huggingface[8]. These models were evaluated in combination with the eight search strategies in Section 4.

[8] https://huggingface.co/models?pipeline_tag=sentence-similarity&language=de&sort=trending

#	Pre-trained Language Model
1	sentence-transformers/paraphrase-multilingual-mpnet-base-v2
2	aari1995/German_Semantic_STS_V2
3	sentence-transformers/LaBSE
4	PM-AI/bi-encoder_msmarco_bert-base_german
5	efederici/e5-base-multilingual-4096
6	intfloat/multilingual-e5-base
7	clips/mfaq
8	PM-AI/sts_paraphrase_xlm-roberta-base_de-en
9	deutsche-telekom/gbert-large-paraphrase-euclidean
10	LLukas22/all-MiniLM-L12-v2-embedding-all
11	LLukas22/paraphrase-multilingual-mpnet-base-v2-embedding-all
12	sentence-transformers/distiluse-base-multilingual-cased-v1
13	sentence-transformers/distiluse-base-multilingual-cased-v2
14	deutsche-telekom/gbert-large-paraphrase-cosine
15	shibing624/text2vec-base-multilingual
16	Sahajtomar/German-semantic
17	setu4993/LaBSE
18	symanto/sn-xlm-roberta-base-snli-mnli-anli-xnli
19	and-effect/musterdatenkatalog_clf
20	nblokker/debatenet-2-cat
21	setu4993/LEALLA-large
22	dell-research-harvard/lt-wikidata-comp-de
23	ef-zulla/e5-multi-sml-torch
24	barisaydin/text2vec-base-multilingual
25	meta-llama/Llama-2-7b-chat-hf

Table 3: The full list of tested pre-trained language models.

A.2 Kendall Tau Correlation Analysis

To understand how much the different search strategies (in combination with the respective best-performing language odel) agree in their search results, we calculated Kendall's τ coefficients (refer to Section 4.1). Figure 3 summarizes the correlation coefficients when comparing the best search run outputs.

A.3 Search Results Page

An essential component of our search service and tool is the search results page (SERP), which allows and simplifies browsing and assembling test items from the item database. The SERP will also enable us to gather expert crowdsourced data from manual exam assembly processes, which was nonexistent at the time of development (refer to Section 5).

User Interface Client: The user interface client of the SERP primarily consists of 12 major elements. Figure 4 summarizes these major components. After the search module retrieves relevant test items from the database, the response is sent to the user interface client in JSON format. Then, users can select and determine for each query what items are relevant (Figure 4a, the item filtering mode). Once relevant items are identified, the users validate their selections by leaving or removing them (Figure 4b, the validation mode). The user interface requests the intent of the exam and explicit feedback about the quality of the search. The feedback is collected by grading the search experience from one to five stars. Finally, when users finish validating their selection, a submit button sends the selected items to another endpoint, e.g. a computer-based testing environment. All the interactions and annotations are securely stored in the database. When users accept the general data protection regulation policy, we inform them that we only collect relevant judgments and annotations that we will use later for future improvements and development of exam assembly models.

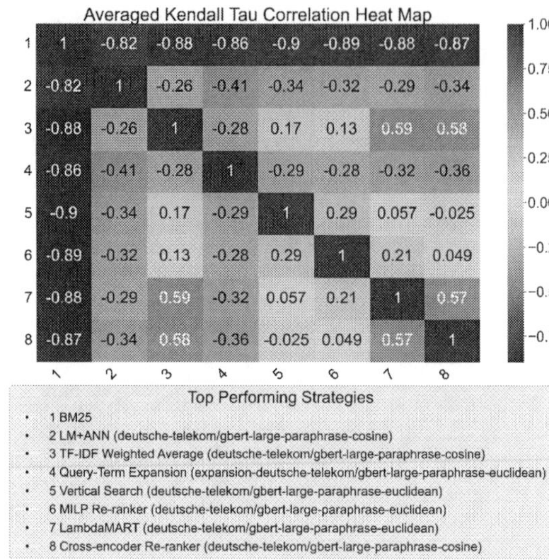

Figure 3: The averaged Kendall τ rank correlation coefficient across all the best-performing search runs for each search strategy.

Crowdsourcing Functionality: In addition to serving as a user interface, the SERP interface stores selected and not-selected items for each query and sends them back to an internal API endpoint. We will later use the stored interactions to develop assisted and automatic exam assembly models further. Figure 5 summarizes an example of a compressed version of an interaction captured and stored in the search service database. The system stores the search queries, the IDs of the elements marked as relevant, all elements not selected but displayed in the user interface, the selected filters, the value of the feedback, and the intention of the query (for more details, refer to 5).

A.4 Backend

As mentioned in section 5, the backend of the search service is fully implemented as a Flask web

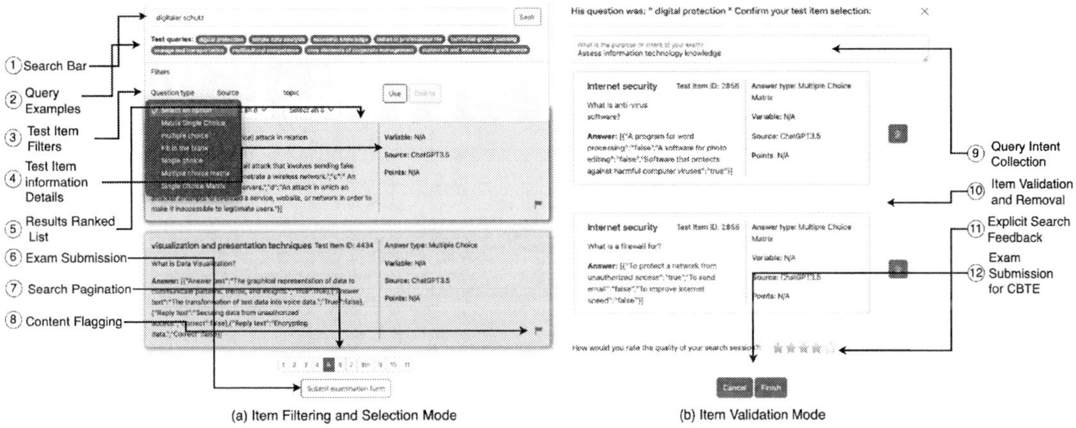

Figure 4: EdTec-QBuilder's search results page fuctionality details (contents automatically translated to English language).


```
{
    "search_log": {
        "query": "digitaler schutz",
        "relevant_ids": ["2856", "2858"],
        "irrelevant_ids": ["4753", "5035",
                            ...,"4086"],
        "filters": ["filters"],
        "seconds": "88",
        "timestamp": "1/14/2024 5:22:28 AM",
        "intent": "the query intent",
        "feedback": {"value": "4"},
        "user_id": "83ee3871840871c2a3a7"
    },
    "browsed_ids": ["2815", "2832",
                          ..., "2879"]
}
```


Figure 5: A compressed representation of the captured interactions, as stored in the backend database of the search service.

application. All the API endpoints are implemented in the Flask framework. All the search sessions are securely stored in an SQLite[9] database. The backend is mounted on an Amazon EC2 instance with four processor cores, 15GB of total memory, and a storage drive of 16 GB.

[9]https://www.sqlite.org/

DiaLight: Lightweight Multilingual Development and Evaluation of Task-Oriented Dialogue Systems with Large Language Models

Songbo Hu[1] **Xiaobin Wang**[2] **Zhangdie Yuan**[3] **Anna Korhonen**[1] **Ivan Vulić**[1]
[1]Language Technology Lab, University of Cambridge, UK
[2]Independent Researcher
[3]Department of Computer Science and Technology, University of Cambridge, UK
[1,3]{sh2091,zy317,alk23,iv250}@cam.ac.uk
[2]wxb9585@gmail.com

Abstract

We present DiaLight, a toolkit for developing and evaluating multilingual Task-Oriented Dialogue (ToD) systems which facilitates systematic evaluations and comparisons between ToD systems using fine-tuning of Pretrained Language Models (PLMs) and those utilising the zero-shot and in-context learning capabilities of Large Language Models (LLMs). In addition to automatic evaluation, this toolkit features (i) a secure, user-friendly web interface for fine-grained human evaluation at both local utterance level and global dialogue level, and (ii) a microservice-based backend, improving efficiency and scalability. Our evaluations reveal that while PLM fine-tuning leads to higher accuracy and coherence, LLM-based systems excel in producing diverse and likeable responses. However, we also identify significant challenges of LLMs in adherence to task-specific instructions and generating outputs in multiple languages, highlighting areas for future research. We hope this open-sourced toolkit will serve as a valuable resource for researchers aiming to develop and properly evaluate multilingual ToD systems and will lower, currently still high, entry barriers in this field.

1 Introduction

Task-oriented dialogue (ToD) systems are designed to model interactions between human users and system agents, focusing on accomplishing specific, predefined tasks such as assisting with hotel or restaurant bookings, or providing domain-specific FAQ information (Gupta et al., 2006; Tür et al., 2010; Young, 2010). These systems serve not only as access points to cutting-edge AI applications but also as drivers of technological expansion.

The prevailing approach in ToD system development has predominantly involved fine-tuning Pretrained Language Models (PLMs), like T5 (Raffel et al., 2020) and BART (Lewis et al., 2020), on task-specific dialogue datasets (Budzianowski et al., 2018a; Byrne et al., 2019). However, recent research trends indicate a paradigm shift from fine-tuning to an increased reliance on Large Language Models' (LLMs) inherent capacity for in-context learning and generalisation for natural language understanding and generation. In our work, we categorise systems as fine-tuned-based using PLMs (hereafter FT-based) or in-context-learning-based using LLMs (ICL-based), noting that LLMs can be fine-tuned and smaller PLMs can use ICL.[1]

Several pilot works (Hudeček and Dusek, 2023; Heck et al., 2023; Zhang et al., 2023; Chung et al., 2023) have explored the integration of LLMs into ToD systems. These studies indicate that FT-based approaches outperform ICL-based approaches, as evidenced by superior automatic evaluation scores. This applies even with smaller PLMs and when the number of training examples is limited. On the other hand, instruction-based training of LLMs demonstrates its potential in aligning model outputs more closely with human preferences (Ouyang et al., 2022; Wang et al., 2022). In ToD, ICL-based systems (Chung et al., 2023) have been shown to generate responses that exceed previous models in critical human evaluation dimensions such as informativeness, helpfulness, and perceived humanness. Despite these early results, a systematic, comparative human evaluation of these two approaches in ToD systems remains a gap in current research.[2]

[1]**Disclaimer:** Here, we (coarsely) differentiate between PLMs and LLMs in terms of their dependency on fine-tuning with task-specific datasets for achieving optimal performance. LLMs, such as LLaMA (Touvron et al., 2023) and GPT-4 (OpenAI, 2023), are characterised by their extensive training on a broad spectrum of data. This approach enables LLMs to adapt to diverse tasks with minimal reliance on task-specific data. Empirical evidence suggests that LLMs demonstrate remarkable capabilities, nearing or 'surpassing' human-level performance on NLP benchmarks such as SuperGLUE (Wang et al., 2019) and BIG-Bench (Srivastava et al., 2023).

[2]The study by Chung et al. (2023) lacks full details on their human evaluation protocol, leading to potential ambiguities in interpretation. Moreover, current research infrastructure falls short in facilitating extensive human evaluation of end-to-end

Proceedings of the 2024 Conference of the North American Chapter of the Association for Computational Linguistics: Human Language Technologies (Volume 3: System Demonstrations), pages 36–52
June 16-21, 2024 ©2024 Association for Computational Linguistics

Toolkit	Human Evaluation	Multilinguality	LLM+E2E	Comparative Experiment
PyDial (Ultes et al., 2017)	✓	✗	✗	✗
ConvLab2 (Zhu et al., 2020)	✓	✗	✗	✗
ConvLab3 (Zhu et al., 2022)	✓	✓	✗	✗
to-llm-bot (Hudeček and Dusek, 2023)	✗	✗	✓	✗
other E2E baselines	✗(∗)	✗(∗)	✗	✗
DIALIGHT (this work)	✓	✓	✓	✓

Table 1: A comparative overview of ToD system toolkits supporting E2E modelling. This summary excludes system components focused solely on dialogue state tracking (DST) and response generation (RG). Key features include **Human Evaluation**, indicating support for online (crowdsourcing) human evaluation, **Multilinguality** capabilities for development and evaluation across various languages and in monolingual, multilingual, and cross-lingual setups, **LLM+E2E** for in-context learning with LLMs in E2E modelling, and **Comparative Experiment**, denoting a unified framework for evaluating both FT-based and ICL-based systems. Detailed comparisons are presented in § 2. (∗) We acknowledge that while some ToD systems support human evaluation and multilingualism, it is recognised that a significant majority lack these crucial features.

Furthermore, the development of ToD systems has historically been confined to a limited number of high-resourced languages (Razumovskaia et al., 2022). The recent release of the Multi3WOZ dataset (Hu et al., 2023a) expands the linguistic scope, introducing the same-level data support for Arabic, English, French, and Turkish ToD. Nevertheless, there are still noticeable disparities in system performance across different languages even with the fully comparable training data (Hu et al., 2023b), raising questions about system utility and user satisfaction with ToD in non-English contexts. To facilitate future research in minimising these performance disparities, a toolkit that supports developing and evaluating multilingual dialogue systems is critically needed.

Aiming to address these gaps, this paper introduces DIALIGHT, a novel toolkit for developing and evaluating multilingual end-to-end (E2E) ToD systems. DIALIGHT is specifically designed for comprehensive comparative analyses between FT-based and ICL-based systems (see §3). It supports an array of ToD datasets from the MultiWOZ family (Budzianowski et al., 2018b; Ding et al., 2022; Hu et al., 2023a, *inter alia*), and enables seamless evaluations in monolingual, multilingual, and cross-lingual setups (§4). Given often the moderate correlation between automatic evaluation metrics and human judgements (Yeh et al., 2021; Mehri et al., 2022), our toolkit places a special emphasis on human evaluation, facilitating both utterance-level and full dialogue-level assessments (§5). The toolkit is available online at: `github.com/cambridgeltl/e2e_tod_toolkit`.

ToD systems, especially for comparative analyses between FT-based and ICL-based systems.

2 Related Work

DIALIGHT represents a novel addition to the landscape of ToD system toolkits, complementing existing frameworks such as PyDial (Ultes et al., 2017), ConvLab-3 (Zhu et al., 2022), and their antecedents (Zhu et al., 2020; Lee et al., 2019), as shown in Table 1. DIALIGHT is unique in offering support for ICL-based implementations in E2E ToD systems, a feature not yet available in existing toolkits. Moreover, DIALIGHT diverges in its core design philosophy. Instead of incorporating extensive and intricate systems and components, it is meticulously crafted to reduce entry barrier and learning curve for researchers engaging in multilingual ToD research. Our objective is to provide a streamlined codebase that facilitates rapid development of multilingual ToD systems.

Another range of publicly available implementations exists for both traditional FT-based and ICL-based E2E ToD systems, typically accompanying research publications as supplementary code. For traditional FT-based approaches, works include those by Wen et al. (2017); Bordes et al. (2017); Lei et al. (2018); Eric and Manning (2017); Eric et al. (2017); Lin et al. (2020); Peng et al. (2021); He et al. (2022) . The ICL-based category is exemplified by the work of Hudeček and Dusek (2023).[3] However, these systems lack a unified setup for comparative experimentation. Our toolkit fills this gap, enabling fair and comprehensive comparisons between the aforementioned two types of systems. Additionally, many of these systems, primarily designed to enhance benchmark results, exhibit key limitations, such as: 1. absence of implementation for lexicalisation in utterances, 2. lack of a dialogue

[3]To date (December 2023), the implementations by Zhang et al. (2023); Chung et al. (2023) have not been released.

system agent for real user interaction, 3. existence of English-centric heuristics in evaluation,[4] 4. inadequate support for human evaluation. DIALIGHT specifically addresses these limitations.

While existing tools for human evaluation, such as DialCrowd (Lee et al., 2018; Huynh et al., 2022), offer simple approaches for conducting human evaluation experiments in ToD systems, they are not without limitations. DialCrowd is not open-sourced, available solely via its designated website, which imposes significant constraints. These include limited customisation flexibility, increased maintenance complexity,[5] and challenges in aligning with data protection regulations such as GDPR, thus affecting its broader applicability in research. In contrast, our human evaluation tool is open-sourced, enabling 'one-click' deployment on local or cloud servers.

3 System Architecture

This section delineates the architecture and implementation of the proposed E2E dialogue system within DIALIGHT. As illustrated in Figure 2 in the Appendix, despite the term 'end-to-end', state-of-the-art E2E ToD systems typically employ a pipelined approach in the background, incorporating three key components: **1)** a dialogue state tracking (DST) model, **2)** a database interface, and **3)** a response generation (RG) model. In the following, we describe the system pipeline and provide an in-depth examination of each constituent component.

3.1 System Pipeline

Our E2E ToD system operates by processing a dialogue history, represented as the concatenation of a list of preceding dialogue utterances $[\mathbf{u}_1, \mathbf{u}_2, \cdots, \mathbf{u}_{t-1}]$ with the latest user utterance $\mathbf{u}_t$. Specifically, the DST model, denoted as $\mathrm{DST}(\cdot)$, takes this concatenated input dialogue utterances to predict the current dialogue state, formulated as $\mathbf{s}_t = \mathrm{DST}([\mathbf{u}_1, \mathbf{u}_2, \cdots, \mathbf{u}_t])$. Within the context of MultiWOZ datasets, a dialogue state is defined as a set of tuples $\mathbf{s} = \{(d_1, s_1, v_1), \cdots, (d_k, s_k, v_k)\}$, where each tuple consists of domain d, slot s, and slot value v. Then, this state is sent to a database $\mathrm{DB}(\cdot)$, from which a set of entities satisfying the requirements specified by the state $\mathbf{s}_t$ are retrieved. Namely, $\{\mathcal{E}_1, \cdots \mathcal{E}_l\} = \mathrm{DB}(\mathbf{s}_t)$, where $\mathcal{E}$ is a data entry in the database. The RG model, denoted as $\mathrm{RG}(\cdot)$, is then tasked to consume the sequence of dialogue utterances with the retrieved set of entities as input and generate a dialogue response $\mathbf{u}_{t+1}$. The process can be formally expressed as $\mathbf{u}_{t+1} = \mathrm{RG}([\mathbf{u}_1, \cdots, \mathbf{u}_t], \{\mathcal{E}_1, \cdots, \mathcal{E}_l\})$, where $\mathbf{u}_{t+1}$ represents the generated dialogue response to user input $\mathbf{u}_t$, taken as the next system turn.

In the proposed toolkit, DST models and RG models can be implemented using both FT-based and ICL-based methods. In what follows, we detail the implementation for each system component, applying both methods.

3.2 Dialogue State Tracking Models

Fine-Tuning with PLMs. The dialogue state $\mathbf{s}_t$ is transformed into a flattened string representation. For example, consider a dialogue state $\{(d_1, s_1, v_1), \cdots, (d_k, s_k, v_k)\}$: it gets transformed into the string $d_1\#s_1{=}v_1;s_2{=}v_2|\cdots|d_k\#s_k{=}v_k$. In this representation, slots and their corresponding values within the same domain are merged. For example, the dialogue state '{(taxi, departure, saint johns college), (taxi, destination, pizza hut fenditton)}' is linearised as 'taxi # departure = saint johns college ; destination = pizza hut fenditton'. At each dialogue turn t, a PLM is trained to take the input of the concatenated dialogue history $[\mathbf{u}_1, \mathbf{u}_2, \cdots, \mathbf{u}_t]$, and generates the linearised dialogue state.

In-Context Learning with LLMs. We use LLMs for direct generation of dialogue states in JSON format, guided by task-specific prompts and training examples for in-context learning. The instruction prompt consists of six parts: 1. *Task instruction* for generating the dialogue state. 2. *Output format instruction* to produce results in JSON format. 3. *Ontology instruction* detailing available domains and slots. 4. *Categorical slot instruction*, guiding LLMs to choose from predefined options for categorical slots. 5. *Time slot instruction* for generating times in 24-hour format (`hh:mm`). 6. *Number slot instruction*, directing LLMs to produce non-negative integer values for numeric slots, such as the quantity of individuals in a booking. After these instructions, we incorporate a list of training examples, randomly chosen from the training dataset, to provide a baseline for future research. The final

[4]For instance, the official evaluation script for MultiWOZ (Nekvinda and Dušek, 2021) employs a string matching algorithm that normalises English slot values to their canonical forms. This approach, however, introduces a bias in evaluation, leading to potentially unfair comparisons when extending the framework to other languages.

[5]E.g., DialCrowd is currently offline (December 2023).

step involves appending the concatenated dialogue history $[\mathbf{u}_1, \mathbf{u}_2, \cdots, \mathbf{u}_t]$ to the prompt, enabling the LLMs to generate the corresponding state $\mathbf{s}_t$.

Implementation and Setup. In DIALIGHT, the FT-based DST models can be instantiated with any of the PLMs available in the Huggingface repository (Wolf et al., 2020). Additionally, we provide comprehensive support for various models in ICL-based systems, including: 1. Models from the Huggingface repository, 2. Models accessible through the OpenAI API,[6] 3. LLaMA.cpp models, tailored for on-device LLM inferences.[7] For evaluation of FT-based DST in this paper, we utilise the $\mathrm{mT5}_{\mathrm{small}}$ and $\mathrm{mT5}_{\mathrm{large}}$ (Xue et al., 2021). For ICL-based DST experiments, we employ the GPT-3.5, LLaMA2 (Touvron et al., 2023), and OpenChat-3.5 (Wang et al., 2023) models.[8]

3.3 Database Interface

We adapt the implementation of our database interface from the official MultiWOZ evaluation scripts (Nekvinda and Dušek, 2021) with minor modifications. Each data entity across different domains within the database can be represented as a set of slot-value pairs. In response to each user utterance $\mathbf{u}_t$, our system executes a database query using the predicted dialogue state $\mathbf{s}_t$, to independently retrieve relevant data entries from each respective domain. For each domain, a database entry is retrieved if it meets the following criteria: 1. exact matching of categorical slot values with those prescribed in the dialogue state, 2. achieving a Levenshtein distance for non-categorical slot values that is below a predefined threshold when compared with the dialogue state.[9]

3.4 Response Generation Models

Fine-Tuning with PLMs. In the context of the MultiWOZ datasets, our approach follows the conventional two-step process: initially generating a delexicalised response and subsequently lexicalising this response with slot values from dialogue states and retrieved entities.[10] It is worth noting that the majority of prevalent automatic evaluation metrics predominantly focus on delexicalised responses. However, incorporating lexicalisation is a more realistic scenario, which is also a necessity for proper human evaluation.

The generation of a delexicalised response is modelled as a transduction problem, converting dialogue history into a natural response. To integrate database outcomes, we initially create a summary (e.g., *'attraction has one result found; hotel has no result found'*). Subsequently, a PLM is trained to process the input, which is a combination of dialogue history and the database summary, to produce the delexicalised system response. The lexicalisation process is carried out through a systematic replacement of placeholders with the relevant values from the current dialogue state $\mathbf{s}_t$ and from the retrieved entities.

In-Context Learning with LLMs. The ICL-based method also follows the conventional two-step process. However, instead of fine-tuning, this approach involves prompting LLMs with a task-specific instruction that encompasses four parts: 1. *Task instruction*, which directs the generation of the dialogue response. 2. *Ontology instruction*, providing details on the available domains and slots. 3. *Delexicalisation instruction*, informing the LLM about all available placeholders and guiding it to substitute slot values with these placeholders. 4. *Language instruction*, specifying the target language for the generated response. A set of training examples, randomly selected from the dataset, is appended to these instructions. The LLM is then tasked to generate the corresponding dialogue response based on this augmented prompt, the database summary, and the concatenated dialogue history $[\mathbf{u}_1, \mathbf{u}_2, \cdots, \mathbf{u}_t]$.

Implementation and Setup. Similarly as before with DST models, we employ the $\mathrm{mT5}_{\mathrm{small}}$ and $\mathrm{mT5}_{\mathrm{large}}$ models for FT-based response generation. For ICL-based experiments, we employ the GPT-3.5, LLaMA2, and OpenChat-3.5 models.

4 Automatic Evaluation

As part of DIALIGHT, we have implemented a range of automatic evaluation metrics: 1. For DST evaluation, metrics include Joint Goal Accuracy (JGA), Slot F1, Slot Recall, and Slot Precision. 2. For response generation evaluation, we utilize the BLEU score (Papineni et al., 2002), ROUGE-L (Lin, 2004), and METEOR (Banerjee

[6] openai.com/blog/openai-api

[7] LLaMA.cpp is open-sourced and accessible at github.com/ggerganov/llama.cpp.

[8] All the other experimental details are in Appendix C.

[9] We use 90% as the ratio with the fuzzywuzzy package for matching.

[10] In the case of delexicalised dialogues, all the slot values in the context and responses are replaced a predefined placeholder (e.g. *[value_name] is an [value_price] [value_food] restaurant on the [value_area] . do you need to know more ?*).

Language	Dialogue State Tracking				Response Generation			End-to-end Modelling		
	JGA	Slot F1	Slot Precision	Slot Recall	BLEU	ROUGE	METEOR	Inform Rate	Success Rate	BLEU
FT-mT5$_{small}$										
ENG	56.4	83.4	83.7	83.1	16.3	24.5	27.2	70.7	46.0	16.3
ARA	43.8	77.5	78.7	76.3	15.0	28.8	26.4	70.2	42.6	15.0
FRA	47.0	79.6	79.5	79.8	14.3	25.5	26.3	71.5	41.5	14.1
TUR	48.9	80.7	78.8	82.6	21.0	33.7	33.3	77.7	48.0	21.4
AVG.	49.0	80.3	80.2	80.5	16.6	28.1	28.3	72.4	44.4	16.7
ICL-GPT-3.5 (∗)										
ENG	13.5	37.6	26.3	65.8	1.8	12.2	11.4	33.0	16.0	1.8
ARA	7.6	31.9	22.6	60.2	0.1	2.2	1.5	36.0	18.0	0.1
FRA	12.5	39.4	29.0	61.2	0.9	8.7	7.2	40.0	24.0	0.8
TUR	7.7	34.5	24.7	57.4	0.8	6.1	5.0	32.0	13.0	0.8
AVG.	10.3	35.9	25.7	61.2	1.2	7.3	6.3	35.3	17.8	0.9

Table 2: Performance across fully supervised variants of DST models, RG models, and E2E systems on the MULTI3WOZ dataset. This table reports the performance metrics for each language, evaluated across different models. 'AVG.' represents the mean average of the evaluation scores aggregated across all four languages. We note that for these metrics the ground truth score is set at 100, with the exception of the Inform Rate and Success Rate, which are measured as 89.3 ± 0.2 and 68.6 ± 0.2 across the four languages, respectively. ($*$) For practical considerations, the evaluation of ChatGPT-3.5-based models and systems is limited to a randomly selected sample of 100 dialogues from the full test set, due to the significant time and resource requirements of full-scale evaluation.

and Lavie, 2005). 3. For evaluating the overall systems, we report Inform Rate, Success Rate, and BLEU. Additionally, we provide an interface to facilitate easy extension for future additional metrics.

Table 2 presents the performance of implemented systems across various languages and backbone models, evaluated using the aforementioned automatic metrics.[11] The main results indicate a performance advantage of FT-based systems over their ICL-based counterparts. Specifically, the ICL-GPT-3.5-based TOD system demonstrates inferior performance when compared to the FT-based systems.[12] Subsequently, we present a detailed analysis aimed at identifying the root causes of this performance discrepancy. Initially, we observe that a substantial portion, 42.7%, of the system predictions generated by the English ICL-based DST model do not adhere to the prescribed dialogue state format specified by the instruction and ontology. Furthermore, with the given instructions, the ICL-GPT-3.5 system generates delexicalised English system responses that recall only 3.6% of the placeholders found in the ground-truth utterances. Concerning other languages, even when explicitly instructed to generate responses in the target language, the GPT-3.5 model produces utterances thare are only 18.4% in Arabic, 78.0% in French, and 70.5% in Turkish.[13] We hypothesise that this is attributed to the fact that our prompt is provided in English, and future work should experiment with additional and more sophisticated prompt designs (Shaham et al., 2024).

5 Human Evaluation

In DIALIGHT, we offer an open-sourced human evaluation tool specifically designed for TOD systems. This tool is comprehensive, providing all essential functionalities to conducting human evaluation experiments in a production setting. In the following, we detail the features supported by our web interface, provide an overview of the high-level design of our backend servers, and present a case study of human evaluation experiments.

5.1 Web Interface

The web interface of the tool offers a range of features, including user registration, account login, consent acquisition for data collection, and the execution of human evaluation tasks. In this section, we highlight two critical features that distinguish our tool from existing work.

Fine-Grained User Feedback. As shown in Figure 7 in the Appendix, our web interface is designed to support the collection of user feedback and scores at both the (local) utterance and (global) dialogue levels. Furthermore, all evaluation questions can be fully customised with minimal programming effort.[14]

Secure Authentication and Access Management. A high priority has been placed on data security

[11]We show the performance of the FT-mT5$_{large}$, ICL-LLaMA2, and ICL-OpenChat-3.5 systems in Table 6 in the Appendix. Additionally, Table 7 in the Appendix presents the evaluation results of FT-based systems on the same selected subset of 100 dialogues for consistency in comparison.

[12]It is worth noting that our system's simplicity, as opposed to the more complex system proposed by Hudeček and Dusek (2023), leads to its lower absolute performance. Our system is primarily designed to serve as a baseline for future research.

[13]Language detection was performed using the tool developed by Nakatani (2010).

[14]The tool supports all components provided by the AntDesign toolkit: `ant.design/components/overview`.

and the incorporation of authentication measures. An authentication system employing JSON Web Tokens (JWT) and a basic role management framework has been implemented. This arrangement ensures that access to specific task groups is limited to authorised users, and only task administrators are permitted to access submitted data in the database. Moreover, the web interface is integrated with an nginx reverse proxy, enhancing data and communication security through SSL encryption.

5.2 Back-End Servers

Our human evaluation tool is architected using a microservice design, a choice that significantly enhances its scalability and adaptability. Another standout feature of the tool is the 'one-click' deployment option, making it more accessible for users. This tool sets itself apart from its predecessors by being easy-to-use and tailored for the prevailing trend of LLMs.

Microservice with Scalability. In a microservice architecture, each service operates independently, managing a specific task or functionality. Our tool adopts this modular framework, partitioning each task model into its own independent service on a dedicated server, as depicted in Figure 3 in the Appendix. The design of these stateless services offers several benefits: firstly, it enables a single model to be concurrently shared by multiple systems, each with different configurations; secondly, it allows for the deployment of multiple instances of the same model within the same system.

On-click Deployment. The tool is designed with an 'out-of-the-box' capability, facilitated by full containerisation using docker and docker-compose (see docs.docker.com/) This approach ensures a simple and efficient deployment process. The versatility of these containers supports deployment in various environments, ranging from local machines to cloud-based platforms. The entire build process is governed by a central configuration file, which users can modify according to their specific requirements, thus enhancing the tool's adaptability.

5.3 A Pilot Analysis of FT-based versus ICL-based Systems in English

Relying on DIALIGHT, we conduct a human evaluation experiment comparing the performance of the English system with FT-mT5$_{\text{small}}$ and the system utilising the ICL-GPT-3.5 model. In this study, each of the 10 participants has completed 2 dialogues for each system, resulting in a total of 40 data entries. The FT-based system attains an overall score of 3.8 ± 0.9, while the ICL-based system achieves 1.6 ± 0.9. Furthermore, Figure 1 demonstrates the number of dialogues for each system based on a set of dialogue-level evaluation dimensions (Mehri and Eskenazi, 2020). The results indicate that the FT-based system outperforms the ICL-based system in terms of maintaining conversation coherence, providing consistent information, understanding the user, and delivering informative responses. Conversely, the ICL-based system generates more diverse responses and exhibits a more favourable personality.

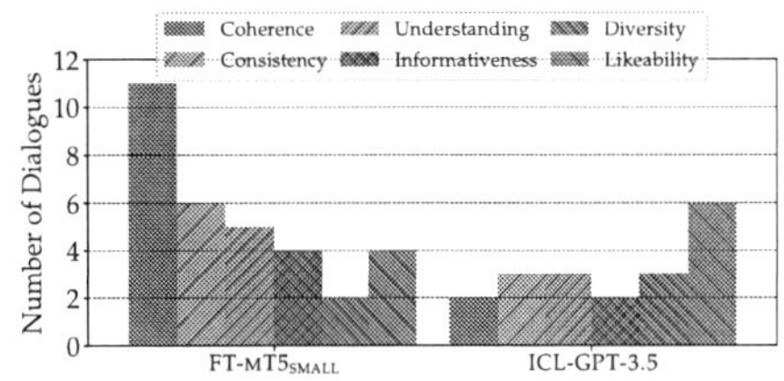

Figure 1: Number of dialogues (from the total of 20) assessed by human evaluators according to the desirable properties that align with the dialogue-level evaluation dimensions outlined in Mehri and Eskenazi (2020).

6 Conclusion and Outlook

We introduced DIALIGHT, a comprehensive toolkit for advancing multilingual TOD systems supported by language models of different families, offering the essential infrastructure for system development and evaluation. DIALIGHT supports the development of and includes baseline systems for fine-tuning and in-context learning paradigms, enabling comparative experiments within a unified setup for automatic and human evaluation. We have publicly released all our source code to facilitate future research and invite the research community to adapt and contribute to this toolkit.

Utilising this toolkit, we executed a performance analysis across several languages and models for the two modeling paradigms. The results indicate that despite their potential, LLMs, even the most powerful ones, are far from 'solving' the TOD task, especially in a multilingual context. Instead, our results open up new avenues for future research and exploration. In Appendix B, we provide some examples of future work aimed at addressing the bottlenecks identified in the baseline systems.

Ethics Statement

The experimental study obtained the full Ethics Approval from the University of Cambridge in advance of its implementation and execution. Informed consent was obtained from every individual participant involved in the study, all of whom participated voluntarily. Our models leverage two data sources: the MULTI3WOZ dataset and the pretraining data of each PLM employed in this study. Hu et al. (2023a) highlights that the creation and publication of MULTI3WOZ comply with the GDPR. Particularly, this dataset consists solely of hypothetical dialogues in which the domains and content have been restricted and predefined, minimising the risk of personal data being present. On the other hand, it is important to acknowledge that although these PLMs and LLMs are publicly available, there exists a potential risk of privacy violations (Carlini et al., 2021; Brown et al., 2022).

Acknowledgements

Songbo Hu is supported by the Cambridge International Scholarship. Anna Korhonen acknowledges the support of the UK EPSRC grant EP/T02450X/1 and the UKRI Frontier grant EP/Y031350/1. Ivan Vulić acknowledges the support of a personal Royal Society University Research Fellowship *'Inclusive and Sustainable Language Technology for a Truly Multilingual World'* (no 221137; 2022–). We are grateful to our diligent participants for their efforts and contributions in our human evaluation experiment.

References

Satanjeev Banerjee and Alon Lavie. 2005. METEOR: An automatic metric for MT evaluation with improved correlation with human judgments. In *Proceedings of the ACL Workshop on Intrinsic and Extrinsic Evaluation Measures for Machine Translation and/or Summarization*, pages 65–72, Ann Arbor, Michigan. Association for Computational Linguistics.

Antoine Bordes, Y-Lan Boureau, and Jason Weston. 2017. Learning end-to-end goal-oriented dialog. In *International Conference on Learning Representations*.

Hannah Brown, Katherine Lee, Fatemehsadat Mireshghallah, Reza Shokri, and Florian Tramèr. 2022. What does it mean for a language model to preserve privacy? In *Proceedings of the 2022 ACM Conference on Fairness, Accountability, and Transparency*, FAccT '22, page 2280–2292, New York, NY, USA. Association for Computing Machinery.

Paweł Budzianowski, Tsung-Hsien Wen, Bo-Hsiang Tseng, Iñigo Casanueva, Stefan Ultes, Osman Ramadan, and Milica Gašić. 2018a. MultiWOZ - a large-scale multi-domain Wizard-of-Oz dataset for task-oriented dialogue modelling. In *Proceedings of the 2018 Conference on Empirical Methods in Natural Language Processing*, pages 5016–5026, Brussels, Belgium. Association for Computational Linguistics.

Paweł Budzianowski, Tsung-Hsien Wen, Bo-Hsiang Tseng, Iñigo Casanueva, Stefan Ultes, Osman Ramadan, and Milica Gašić. 2018b. MultiWOZ - a large-scale multi-domain Wizard-of-Oz dataset for task-oriented dialogue modelling. In *Proceedings of the 2018 Conference on Empirical Methods in Natural Language Processing*, pages 5016–5026, Brussels, Belgium. Association for Computational Linguistics.

Bill Byrne, Karthik Krishnamoorthi, Chinnadhurai Sankar, Arvind Neelakantan, Ben Goodrich, Daniel Duckworth, Semih Yavuz, Amit Dubey, Kyu-Young Kim, and Andy Cedilnik. 2019. Taskmaster-1: Toward a realistic and diverse dialog dataset. In *Proceedings of the 2019 Conference on Empirical Methods in Natural Language Processing and the 9th International Joint Conference on Natural Language Processing (EMNLP-IJCNLP)*, pages 4516–4525, Hong Kong, China. Association for Computational Linguistics.

Nicholas Carlini, Florian Tramer, Eric Wallace, Matthew Jagielski, Ariel Herbert-Voss, Katherine Lee, Adam Roberts, Tom B Brown, Dawn Song, Ulfar Erlingsson, et al. 2021. Extracting training data from large language models. In *USENIX Security Symposium*, volume 6.

Willy Chung, Samuel Cahyawijaya, Bryan Wilie, Holy Lovenia, and Pascale Fung. 2023. Instructtods: Large language models for end-to-end task-oriented dialogue systems. *arXiv preprint arXiv:2310.08885*.

Bosheng Ding, Junjie Hu, Lidong Bing, Mahani Aljunied, Shafiq Joty, Luo Si, and Chunyan Miao. 2022. GlobalWoZ: Globalizing MultiWoZ to develop multilingual task-oriented dialogue systems. In *Proceedings of the 60th Annual Meeting of the Association for Computational Linguistics (Volume 1: Long Papers)*, pages 1639–1657, Dublin, Ireland. Association for Computational Linguistics.

Mihail Eric, Lakshmi Krishnan, Francois Charette, and Christopher D. Manning. 2017. Key-value retrieval networks for task-oriented dialogue. In *Proceedings of the 18th Annual SIGdial Meeting on Discourse and Dialogue*, pages 37–49, Saarbrücken, Germany. Association for Computational Linguistics.

Mihail Eric and Christopher Manning. 2017. A copy-augmented sequence-to-sequence architecture gives good performance on task-oriented dialogue. In *Proceedings of the 15th Conference of the European Chapter of the Association for Computational Linguistics: Volume 2, Short Papers*, pages 468–473, Valencia, Spain. Association for Computational Linguistics.

Narendra K. Gupta, Gökhan Tür, Dilek Hakkani-Tür, Srinivas Bangalore, Giuseppe Riccardi, and Mazin Gilbert. 2006. The at&t spoken language understanding system. *IEEE Transactions on Speech and Audio Processing*, 14(1):213–222.

Wanwei He, Yinpei Dai, Yinhe Zheng, Yuchuan Wu, Zheng Cao, Dermot Liu, Peng Jiang, Min Yang, Fei Huang, Luo Si, et al. 2022. Galaxy: A generative pre-trained model for task-oriented dialog with semi-supervised learning and explicit policy injection. *Proceedings of the AAAI Conference on Artificial Intelligence*.

Michael Heck, Nurul Lubis, Benjamin Ruppik, Renato Vukovic, Shutong Feng, Christian Geishauser, Hsien-chin Lin, Carel van Niekerk, and Milica Gasic. 2023. ChatGPT for zero-shot dialogue state tracking: A solution or an opportunity? In *Proceedings of the 61st Annual Meeting of the Association for Computational Linguistics (Volume 2: Short Papers)*, pages 936–950, Toronto, Canada. Association for Computational Linguistics.

Songbo Hu, Han Zhou, Mete Hergul, Milan Gritta, Guchun Zhang, Ignacio Iacobacci, Ivan Vulić, and Anna Korhonen. 2023a. Multi 3 WOZ: A multilingual, multi-domain, multi-parallel dataset for training and evaluating culturally adapted task-oriented dialog systems. *Transactions of the Association for Computational Linguistics*, 11:1396–1415.

Songbo Hu, Han Zhou, Moy Yuan, Milan Gritta, Guchun Zhang, Ignacio Iacobacci, Anna Korhonen, and Ivan Vulić. 2023b. A systematic study of performance disparities in multilingual task-oriented dialogue systems. In *Proceedings of the 2023 Conference on Empirical Methods in Natural Language Processing*, pages 6825–6851, Singapore. Association for Computational Linguistics.

Vojtěch Hudeček and Ondrej Dusek. 2023. Are large language models all you need for task-oriented dialogue? In *Proceedings of the 24th Meeting of the Special Interest Group on Discourse and Dialogue*, pages 216–228, Prague, Czechia. Association for Computational Linguistics.

Jessica Huynh, Ting-Rui Chiang, Jeffrey Bigham, and Maxine Eskenazi. 2022. DialCrowd 2.0: A quality-focused dialog system crowdsourcing toolkit. In *Proceedings of the Thirteenth Language Resources and Evaluation Conference*, pages 1256–1263, Marseille, France. European Language Resources Association.

Kyusong Lee, Tiancheng Zhao, Alan W. Black, and Maxine Eskenazi. 2018. DialCrowd: A toolkit for easy dialog system assessment. In *Proceedings of the 19th Annual SIGdial Meeting on Discourse and Dialogue*, pages 245–248, Melbourne, Australia. Association for Computational Linguistics.

Sungjin Lee, Qi Zhu, Ryuichi Takanobu, Zheng Zhang, Yaoqin Zhang, Xiang Li, Jinchao Li, Baolin Peng, Xiujun Li, Minlie Huang, and Jianfeng Gao. 2019. ConvLab: Multi-domain end-to-end dialog system platform. In *Proceedings of the 57th Annual Meeting of the Association for Computational Linguistics: System Demonstrations*, pages 64–69, Florence, Italy. Association for Computational Linguistics.

Wenqiang Lei, Xisen Jin, Min-Yen Kan, Zhaochun Ren, Xiangnan He, and Dawei Yin. 2018. Sequicity: Simplifying task-oriented dialogue systems with single sequence-to-sequence architectures. In *Proceedings of the 56th Annual Meeting of the Association for Computational Linguistics (Volume 1: Long Papers)*, pages 1437–1447, Melbourne, Australia. Association for Computational Linguistics.

Mike Lewis, Yinhan Liu, Naman Goyal, Marjan Ghazvininejad, Abdelrahman Mohamed, Omer Levy, Veselin Stoyanov, and Luke Zettlemoyer. 2020. BART: Denoising sequence-to-sequence pre-training for natural language generation, translation, and comprehension. In *Proceedings of the 58th Annual Meeting of the Association for Computational Linguistics*, pages 7871–7880, Online. Association for Computational Linguistics.

Haonan Li, Fajri Koto, Minghao Wu, Alham Fikri Aji, and Timothy Baldwin. 2023. Bactrian-X: A multilingual replicable instruction-following model with low-rank adaptation. *CoRR*, abs/2305.15011.

Chin-Yew Lin. 2004. ROUGE: A package for automatic evaluation of summaries. In *Text Summarization Branches Out*, pages 74–81, Barcelona, Spain. Association for Computational Linguistics.

Zhaojiang Lin, Andrea Madotto, Genta Indra Winata, and Pascale Fung. 2020. MinTL: Minimalist transfer learning for task-oriented dialogue systems. In *Proceedings of the 2020 Conference on Empirical Methods in Natural Language Processing (EMNLP)*, pages 3391–3405, Online. Association for Computational Linguistics.

Shikib Mehri, Jinho Choi, Luis Fernando D'Haro, Jan Deriu, Maxine Eskenazi, Milica Gasic, Kallirroi Georgila, Dilek Hakkani-Tur, Zekang Li, Verena Rieser, Samira Shaikh, David Traum, Yi-Ting Yeh, Zhou Yu, Yizhe Zhang, and Chen Zhang. 2022. Report from the nsf future directions workshop on automatic evaluation of dialog: Research directions and challenges.

Shikib Mehri and Maxine Eskenazi. 2020. Unsupervised evaluation of interactive dialog with DialoGPT. In *Proceedings of the 21th Annual Meeting of the Special Interest Group on Discourse and Dialogue*, pages 225–235, 1st virtual meeting. Association for Computational Linguistics.

Shuyo Nakatani. 2010. Language detection library for java.

Tomáš Nekvinda and Ondřej Dušek. 2021. Shades of BLEU, flavours of success: The case of MultiWOZ. In *Proceedings of the 1st Workshop on Natural Language Generation, Evaluation, and Metrics (GEM 2021)*, pages 34–46, Online. Association for Computational Linguistics.

OpenAI. 2023. Gpt-4 technical report. *ArXiv*, abs/2303.08774.

Long Ouyang, Jeffrey Wu, Xu Jiang, Diogo Almeida, Carroll Wainwright, Pamela Mishkin, Chong Zhang, Sandhini Agarwal, Katarina Slama, Alex Ray, et al. 2022. Training language models to follow instructions with human feedback. *Advances in Neural Information Processing Systems*, 35:27730–27744.

Kishore Papineni, Salim Roukos, Todd Ward, and Wei-Jing Zhu. 2002. Bleu: a method for automatic evaluation of machine translation. In *Proceedings of the 40th Annual Meeting of the Association for Computational Linguistics*, pages 311–318, Philadelphia, Pennsylvania, USA. Association for Computational Linguistics.

Baolin Peng, Chunyuan Li, Jinchao Li, Shahin Shayandeh, Lars Liden, and Jianfeng Gao. 2021. Soloist: Building task bots at scale with transfer learning and machine teaching. *Transactions of the Association for Computational Linguistics*, 9:807–824.

Colin Raffel, Noam Shazeer, Adam Roberts, Katherine Lee, Sharan Narang, Michael Matena, Yanqi Zhou, Wei Li, and Peter J. Liu. 2020. Exploring the limits of transfer learning with a unified text-to-text transformer. *J. Mach. Learn. Res.*, 21(1).

Evgeniia Razumovskaia, Goran Glavaš, Olga Majewska, Edoardo Maria Ponti, Anna Korhonen, and Ivan Vulić. 2022. Crossing the conversational chasm: A primer on natural language processing for multilingual task-oriented dialogue systems. *Journal of Artificial Intelligence Research*, 74:1351–1402.

Uri Shaham, Jonathan Herzig, Roee Aharoni, Idan Szpektor, Reut Tsarfaty, and Matan Eyal. 2024. Multilingual instruction tuning with just a pinch of multilinguality. *CoRR*, abs/2401.01854.

Aarohi Srivastava, Abhinav Rastogi, Abhishek Rao, Abu Awal Md Shoeb, Abubakar Abid, Adam Fisch, Adam R. Brown, Adam Santoro, Aditya Gupta, Adrià Garriga-Alonso, Agnieszka Kluska, Aitor Lewkowycz, Akshat Agarwal, Alethea Power, Alex Ray, Alex Warstadt, Alexander W. Kocurek, Ali Safaya, Ali Tazarv, Alice Xiang, Alicia Parrish, Allen Nie, Aman Hussain, Amanda Askell, Amanda Dsouza, Ambrose Slone, Ameet Rahane, Anantharaman S. Iyer, Anders Johan Andreassen, Andrea Madotto, Andrea Santilli, Andreas Stuhlmüller, Andrew M. Dai, Andrew La, Andrew Lampinen, Andy Zou, Angela Jiang, Angelica Chen, Anh Vuong, Animesh Gupta, Anna Gottardi, Antonio Norelli, Anu Venkatesh, Arash Gholamidavoodi, Arfa Tabassum, Arul Menezes, Arun Kirubarajan, Asher Mullokandov, Ashish Sabharwal, Austin Herrick, Avia Efrat, Aykut Erdem, Ayla Karakaş, B. Ryan Roberts, Bao Sheng Loe, Barret Zoph, Bartłomiej Bojanowski, Batuhan Özyurt, Behnam Hedayatnia, Behnam Neyshabur, Benjamin Inden, Benno Stein, Berk Ekmekci, Bill Yuchen Lin, Blake Howald, Bryan Orinion, Cameron Diao, Cameron Dour, Catherine Stinson, Cedrick Argueta, Cesar Ferri, Chandan Singh, Charles Rathkopf, Chenlin Meng, Chitta Baral, Chiyu Wu, Chris Callison-Burch, Christopher Waites, Christian Voigt, Christopher D Manning, Christopher Potts, Cindy Ramirez, Clara E. Rivera, Clemencia Siro, Colin Raffel, Courtney Ashcraft, Cristina Garbacea, Damien Sileo, Dan Garrette, Dan Hendrycks, Dan Kilman, Dan Roth, C. Daniel Freeman, Daniel Khashabi, Daniel Levy, Daniel Moseguí González, Danielle Perszyk, Danny Hernandez, Danqi Chen, Daphne Ippolito, Dar Gilboa, David Dohan, David Drakard, David Jurgens, Debajyoti Datta, Deep Ganguli, Denis Emelin, Denis Kleyko, Deniz Yuret, Derek Chen, Derek Tam, Dieuwke Hupkes, Diganta Misra, Dilyar Buzan, Dimitri Coelho Mollo, Diyi Yang, Dong-Ho Lee, Dylan Schrader, Ekaterina Shutova, Ekin Dogus Cubuk, Elad Segal, Eleanor Hagerman, Elizabeth Barnes, Elizabeth Donoway, Ellie Pavlick, Emanuele Rodolà, Emma Lam, Eric Chu, Eric Tang, Erkut Erdem, Ernie Chang, Ethan A Chi, Ethan Dyer, Ethan Jerzak, Ethan Kim, Eunice Engefu Manyasi, Evgenii Zheltonozhskii, Fanyue Xia, Fatemeh Siar, Fernando Martínez-Plumed, Francesca Happé, Francois Chollet, Frieda Rong, Gaurav Mishra, Genta Indra Winata, Gerard de Melo, Germán Kruszewski, Giambattista Parascandolo, Giorgio Mariani, Gloria Xinyue Wang, Gonzalo Jaimovitch-Lopez, Gregor Betz, Guy Gur-Ari, Hana Galijasevic, Hannah Kim, Hannah Rashkin, Hannaneh Hajishirzi, Harsh Mehta, Hayden Bogar, Henry Francis Anthony Shevlin, Hinrich Schuetze, Hiromu Yakura, Hongming Zhang, Hugh Mee Wong, Ian Ng, Isaac Noble, Jaap Jumelet, Jack Geissinger, Jackson Kernion, Jacob Hilton, Jaehoon Lee, Jaime Fernández Fisac, James B Simon, James Koppel, James Zheng, James Zou, Jan Kocon, Jana Thompson, Janelle Wingfield, Jared Kaplan, Jarema Radom, Jascha Sohl-Dickstein, Jason Phang, Jason Wei, Jason Yosinski, Jekaterina Novikova, Jelle Bosscher, Jennifer Marsh, Jeremy Kim, Jeroen Taal, Jesse Engel, Jesujoba Alabi, Jiacheng Xu, Jiaming Song, Jillian Tang, Joan Waweru, John Burden, John Miller, John U. Balis, Jonathan Batchelder, Jonathan Berant, Jörg Frohberg, Jos Rozen, Jose Hernandez-Orallo, Joseph Boudeman, Joseph Guerr, Joseph Jones, Joshua B. Tenenbaum, Joshua S. Rule, Joyce Chua, Kamil Kanclerz, Karen Livescu, Karl Krauth, Karthik Gopalakrishnan, Katerina Ignatyeva, Katja Markert, Kaustubh Dhole, Kevin Gimpel, Kevin Omondi, Kory Wallace Mathewson, Kristen Chiafullo, Ksenia Shkaruta, Kumar Shridhar, Kyle McDonell, Kyle Richardson, Laria Reynolds, Leo Gao, Li Zhang, Liam Dugan, Lianhui Qin, Lidia Contreras-Ochando, Louis-Philippe Morency, Luca Moschella, Lucas Lam, Lucy Noble, Ludwig Schmidt, Luheng

He, Luis Oliveros-Colón, Luke Metz, Lütfi Kerem Senel, Maarten Bosma, Maarten Sap, Maartje Ter Hoeve, Maheen Farooqi, Manaal Faruqui, Mantas Mazeika, Marco Baturan, Marco Marelli, Marco Maru, Maria Jose Ramirez-Quintana, Marie Tolkiehn, Mario Giulianelli, Martha Lewis, Martin Potthast, Matthew L Leavitt, Matthias Hagen, Mátyás Schubert, Medina Orduna Baitemirova, Melody Arnaud, Melvin McElrath, Michael Andrew Yee, Michael Cohen, Michael Gu, Michael Ivanitskiy, Michael Starritt, Michael Strube, Michał Swędrowski, Michele Bevilacqua, Michihiro Yasunaga, Mihir Kale, Mike Cain, Mimee Xu, Mirac Suzgun, Mitch Walker, Mo Tiwari, Mohit Bansal, Moin Aminnaseri, Mor Geva, Mozhdeh Gheini, Mukund Varma T, Nanyun Peng, Nathan Andrew Chi, Nayeon Lee, Neta Gur-Ari Krakover, Nicholas Cameron, Nicholas Roberts, Nick Doiron, Nicole Martinez, Nikita Nangia, Niklas Deckers, Niklas Muennighoff, Nitish Shirish Keskar, Niveditha S. Iyer, Noah Constant, Noah Fiedel, Nuan Wen, Oliver Zhang, Omar Agha, Omar Elbaghdadi, Omer Levy, Owain Evans, Pablo Antonio Moreno Casares, Parth Doshi, Pascale Fung, Paul Pu Liang, Paul Vicol, Pegah Alipoormolabashi, Peiyuan Liao, Percy Liang, Peter W Chang, Peter Eckersley, Phu Mon Htut, Pinyu Hwang, Piotr Miłkowski, Piyush Patil, Pouya Pezeshkpour, Priti Oli, Qiaozhu Mei, Qing Lyu, Qinlang Chen, Rabin Banjade, Rachel Etta Rudolph, Raefer Gabriel, Rahel Habacker, Ramon Risco, Raphaël Millière, Rhythm Garg, Richard Barnes, Rif A. Saurous, Riku Arakawa, Robbe Raymaekers, Robert Frank, Rohan Sikand, Roman Novak, Roman Sitelew, Ronan Le Bras, Rosanne Liu, Rowan Jacobs, Rui Zhang, Russ Salakhutdinov, Ryan Andrew Chi, Seungjae Ryan Lee, Ryan Stovall, Ryan Teehan, Rylan Yang, Sahib Singh, Saif M. Mohammad, Sajant Anand, Sam Dillavou, Sam Shleifer, Sam Wiseman, Samuel Gruetter, Samuel R. Bowman, Samuel Stern Schoenholz, Sanghyun Han, Sanjeev Kwatra, Sarah A. Rous, Sarik Ghazarian, Sayan Ghosh, Sean Casey, Sebastian Bischoff, Sebastian Gehrmann, Sebastian Schuster, Sepideh Sadeghi, Shadi Hamdan, Sharon Zhou, Shashank Srivastava, Sherry Shi, Shikhar Singh, Shima Asaadi, Shixiang Shane Gu, Shubh Pachchigar, Shubham Toshniwal, Shyam Upadhyay, Shyamolima Shammie Debnath, Siamak Shakeri, Simon Thormeyer, Simone Melzi, Siva Reddy, Sneha Priscilla Makini, Soo-Hwan Lee, Spencer Torene, Sriharsha Hatwar, Stanislas Dehaene, Stefan Divic, Stefano Ermon, Stella Biderman, Stephanie Lin, Stephen Prasad, Steven Piantadosi, Stuart Shieber, Summer Misherghi, Svetlana Kiritchenko, Swaroop Mishra, Tal Linzen, Tal Schuster, Tao Li, Tao Yu, Tariq Ali, Tatsunori Hashimoto, Te-Lin Wu, Théo Desbordes, Theodore Rothschild, Thomas Phan, Tianle Wang, Tiberius Nkinyili, Timo Schick, Timofei Kornev, Titus Tunduny, Tobias Gerstenberg, Trenton Chang, Trishala Neeraj, Tushar Khot, Tyler Shultz, Uri Shaham, Vedant Misra, Vera Demberg, Victoria Nyamai, Vikas Raunak, Vinay Venkatesh Ramasesh, vinay uday prabhu, Vishakh Padmakumar, Vivek Srikumar, William Fedus, William Saunders, William Zhang, Wout Vossen, Xiang Ren, Xiaoyu Tong, Xinran Zhao, Xinyi Wu, Xudong Shen, Yadollah Yaghoobzadeh, Yair Lakretz, Yangqiu Song, Yasaman Bahri, Yejin Choi, Yichi Yang, Yiding Hao, Yifu Chen, Yonatan Belinkov, Yu Hou, Yufang Hou, Yuntao Bai, Zachary Seid, Zhuoye Zhao, Zijian Wang, Zijie J. Wang, Zirui Wang, and Ziyi Wu. 2023. Beyond the imitation game: Quantifying and extrapolating the capabilities of language models. *Transactions on Machine Learning Research*.

Hugo Touvron, Thibaut Lavril, Gautier Izacard, Xavier Martinet, Marie-Anne Lachaux, Timothée Lacroix, Baptiste Rozière, Naman Goyal, Eric Hambro, Faisal Azhar, et al. 2023. Llama: Open and efficient foundation language models. *arXiv preprint arXiv:2302.13971*.

Gökhan Tür, Andreas Stolcke, L. Lynn Voss, Stanley Peters, Dilek Hakkani-Tür, John Dowding, Benoît Favre, Raquel Fernández, Matthew Frampton, Michael W. Frandsen, Clint Frederickson, Martin Graciarena, Donald Kintzing, Kyle Leveque, Shane Mason, John Niekrasz, Matthew Purver, Korbinian Riedhammer, Elizabeth Shriberg, Jing Tien, Dimitra Vergyri, and Fan Yang. 2010. The CALO meeting assistant system. *IEEE Transactions on Speech Audio Processing*, 18(6):1601–1611.

Stefan Ultes, Lina M. Rojas Barahona, Pei-Hao Su, David Vandyke, Dongho Kim, Iñigo Casanueva, Paweł Budzianowski, Nikola Mrkšić, Tsung-Hsien Wen, Milica Gasic, and Steve Young. 2017. PyDial: A Multi-domain Statistical Dialogue System Toolkit. In *Proceedings of ACL 2017, System Demonstrations*, pages 73–78, Vancouver, Canada. Association for Computational Linguistics.

Alex Wang, Yada Pruksachatkun, Nikita Nangia, Amanpreet Singh, Julian Michael, Felix Hill, Omer Levy, and Samuel R. Bowman. 2019. *SuperGLUE: A Stickier Benchmark for General-Purpose Language Understanding Systems*. Curran Associates Inc., Red Hook, NY, USA.

Guan Wang, Sijie Cheng, Xianyuan Zhan, Xiangang Li, Sen Song, and Yang Liu. 2023. Openchat: Advancing open-source language models with mixed-quality data. *arXiv preprint arXiv:2309.11235*.

Yizhong Wang, Swaroop Mishra, Pegah Alipoormolabashi, Yeganeh Kordi, Amirreza Mirzaei, Anjana Arunkumar, Arjun Ashok, Arut Selvan Dhanasekaran, Atharva Naik, David Stap, et al. 2022. Super-naturalinstructions: Generalization via declarative instructions on 1600+ nlp tasks. *arXiv preprint arXiv:2204.07705*.

Tsung-Hsien Wen, David Vandyke, Nikola Mrkšić, Milica Gašić, Lina M. Rojas-Barahona, Pei-Hao Su, Stefan Ultes, and Steve Young. 2017. A network-based end-to-end trainable task-oriented dialogue system. In *Proceedings of the 15th Conference of the European Chapter of the Association for Computational Linguistics: Volume 1, Long Papers*, pages 438–449,

Valencia, Spain. Association for Computational Linguistics.

Thomas Wolf, Lysandre Debut, Victor Sanh, Julien Chaumond, Clement Delangue, Anthony Moi, Pierric Cistac, Tim Rault, Remi Louf, Morgan Funtowicz, Joe Davison, Sam Shleifer, Patrick von Platen, Clara Ma, Yacine Jernite, Julien Plu, Canwen Xu, Teven Le Scao, Sylvain Gugger, Mariama Drame, Quentin Lhoest, and Alexander Rush. 2020. Transformers: State-of-the-art natural language processing. In *Proceedings of the 2020 Conference on Empirical Methods in Natural Language Processing: System Demonstrations*, pages 38–45, Online. Association for Computational Linguistics.

Qingyang Wu, Deema Alnuhait, Derek Chen, and Zhou Yu. 2023. Using textual interface to align external knowledge for end-to-end task-oriented dialogue systems. *arXiv preprint arXiv:2305.13710*.

Linting Xue, Noah Constant, Adam Roberts, Mihir Kale, Rami Al-Rfou, Aditya Siddhant, Aditya Barua, and Colin Raffel. 2021. mT5: A massively multilingual pre-trained text-to-text transformer. In *Proceedings of the 2021 Conference of the North American Chapter of the Association for Computational Linguistics: Human Language Technologies*, pages 483–498, Online. Association for Computational Linguistics.

Yi-Ting Yeh, Maxine Eskenazi, and Shikib Mehri. 2021. A comprehensive assessment of dialog evaluation metrics. In *The First Workshop on Evaluations and Assessments of Neural Conversation Systems*, pages 15–33, Online. Association for Computational Linguistics.

Steve Young. 2007. Cued standard dialogue acts. *Report, Cambridge University Engineering Department, 14th October*, 2007.

Steve J. Young. 2010. Cognitive user interfaces. *IEEE Signal Processing Magazine*, 27(3):128–140.

Xiaoying Zhang, Baolin Peng, Kun Li, Jingyan Zhou, and Helen Meng. 2023. SGP-TOD: Building task bots effortlessly via schema-guided LLM prompting. In *Findings of the Association for Computational Linguistics: EMNLP 2023*, pages 13348–13369, Singapore. Association for Computational Linguistics.

Qi Zhu, Christian Geishauser, Hsien chin Lin, Carel van Niekerk, Baolin Peng, Zheng Zhang, Michael Heck, Nurul Lubis, Dazhen Wan, Xiaochen Zhu, Jianfeng Gao, Milica Gašić, and Minlie Huang. 2022. Convlab-3: A flexible dialogue system toolkit based on a unified data format. *arXiv preprint arXiv:2211.17148*.

Qi Zhu, Zheng Zhang, Yan Fang, Xiang Li, Ryuichi Takanobu, Jinchao Li, Baolin Peng, Jianfeng Gao, Xiaoyan Zhu, and Minlie Huang. 2020. ConvLab-2: An open-source toolkit for building, evaluating, and diagnosing dialogue systems. In *Proceedings of the 58th Annual Meeting of the Association for Computational Linguistics: System Demonstrations*, pages 142–149, Online. Association for Computational Linguistics.

A Limitations

There are several limitations in this work, primarily stemming from the scope, design, and intended purpose of this toolkit. In this work, we only provide a set of baseline systems. As shown in Figure 9, these systems are intentionally kept as simple as possible while being fully functional, with the goal of enabling users to gain a conceptual understanding of the ToD task and implement their own systems with minimal learning effort. It is important to acknowledge that our systems may underperform compared to other more sophisticated systems, such as the one developed by Hudeček and Dusek (2023) that employs advanced techniques for retrieving positive and negative ICL examples, or the system proposed by Zhang et al. (2023) that incorporates an explicit and pre-defined task schema to guide system actions. Instead of pursuing state-of-the-art performance, we place greater emphasis on providing the essential environment and a set of tools, including automatic and human evaluation tools, to enable researchers to develop more advanced systems using our toolkit in future work.

Currently, DIALIGHT currently supports only ToD datasets that are derived from the MultiWOZ dataset (Budzianowski et al., 2018b) and its schema, that is, the ones annotated with the CUED schema (Young, 2007). We recognise the additional challenges associated with extending the toolkit to accommodate other datasets with different annotation schemata. Such extensions would typically involve the re-implementation of the data loader, the database, and some automatic evaluation metrics, such as Inform Rate and Success Rate. However, we believe that our human evaluation tool can be easily extended to evaluate systems developed on other datasets.

Furthermore, it is worth noting that a fully inclusive dialogue system should consider not only text input but also other modalities, such as spoken and sign languages. We acknowledge that DIALIGHT currently focuses on text input only, and we hope to integrate the support for speech input and output as part of future work.

B Future Work: Some Ideas

In this section, we provide examples of future work aimed at addressing the bottlenecks identified in the baseline systems.

Modernising ToD Systems for LLMs. In §4, our experimental results reveal that solely prompting LLMs resulted in system failure to comply with the instructions and predict dialogue states in the required format, leading to over 40% empty predictions. Additionally, ICL-based systems employing LLMs encountered challenges in recalling placeholders and generating delexicalised utterances in a similar fashion. This issue is arguably attributable to the misalignment between the task requirements for ToD and the inherent pretraining of LLMs. We propose that future research should critically reevaluate the current design choices of ToD systems to better tailor LLM-based ToD systems.

Multilingual Generation with LLMs. Our analysis demonstrates that when prompts are solely provided in English and LLMs are instructed to generate outputs in other languages, they often encounter difficulties in complying, resulting in the generation of outputs in English. Developing complex NLP applications like ToD systems requires a significant number of instructions to specify task requirements. However, the dominance of English instructions tends to bias model outputs towards English. Conversely, tailoring task instructions for each individual language, especially for resource-lean languages, poses a challenge. While some work has been recently conducted for other NLP tasks (Li et al., 2023), arguably less complex than ToD, the question of how to effectively control LLMs to generate target language outputs remains an open question for future research.

C Experimental Details

In this section, we describe the experimental setups for the systems developed in this paper. For specific implementation details, including the prompts used in the ICL-based systems, we direct readers to the actual implementation and documentation of DIALIGHT.

Table 3 presents the selected hyper-parameters for the conducted experimental study. All the FT-based experiments were run on a single A100 80 GiB GPU and a 32-core vCPU. Notably, the ICL-based systems deployed in our experimental study excluded training examples from the prompts. This decision was based on empirical evidence indicating that these examples adversely affect system performance. When tested with 10 ICL examples, the ICL-GPT-3.5 systems recorded a JGA of 4.3 (↓9.2), an Inform Rate of 31.0 (↓2.0), and a Success Rate of 14.0 (↓2.0). We did not conduct a

Hyper-parameter	Value
FT-mT5$_{small}$	
batch size	32
learning rate	1e-3
weight decay	0.01
evaluation per steps	5000
max training steps	50000
context window	10
early stopping patience	2
maximum generation length	512
FT-mT5$_{large}$	
batch size	8
learning rate	1e-3
weight decay	0.01
evaluation per steps	5000
max training steps	50000
context window	10
early stopping patience	2
maximum generation length	512
ICL-GPT-3.5, ICL-LLaMA2, and ICL-OpenChat-3.5	
context window	10
number of ICL examples	0 (∗)

Table 3: The hyperparameters for E2E systems and their constituent models. Both the DST and RG models, which are based on the same PLM, utilised identical hyper-parameter setups. To select the optimal model checkpoint, we employ early stopping and select the one with the best validation performance, measured by JGA for DST and BLEU score for RG. Unless explicitly specified, all other hyper-parameters are set to their default values as defined in the HuggingFace Transformers. (∗) Notably, our observations suggest that the introduction of training examples actually adversely affects model performance.

hyperparameter search for the number of ICL examples due to the high costs associated with such an experiment.

Table 4 lists all the language models we used in this work, along with their respective checkpoints in the Huggingface repository and the OpenAI API. Both the LLaMA2 and OpenChat-3.5 models employed in this study have 7 billion parameters.

Table 5 shows the time consumption of the models for the E2E task in the experimental study.

D Additional Results on MULTI3WOZ

In this section, we show supplementary experimental results to solidify the empirical findings in §4. Firstly, the evaluation metrics for E2E tasks, such as Inform Rate and Success Rate, are influenced by two key outputs of the system: the dialogue state and the generated response. To assess the impact of each component on overall system performance,

Model	Checkpoint
mT5$_{small}$	google/mt5-small
mT5$_{large}$	google/mt5-large
GPT-3.5	gpt-3.5-turbo-1106
LLaMA2	TheBloke/Llama-2-7B-GGUF
OpenChat-3.5	openchat/openchat_3.5

Table 4: The employed langauge models in our experimental study and their Huggingface or OpenAI Checkpoints. We use 7B variants of LLaMA2 and OpenChat-3.5.

Setup	Time Consumption
FT-mT5$_{small}$	
DST training per 500 steps	3:02
RG training per 500 steps	2:27
Inference on *full test*	9:30
FT-mT5$_{large}$	
DST training per 500 steps	5:09
RG training per 500 steps	5:02
Inference on *full test*	1:16:00
ICL-GPT-3.5	
Inference on *10 dialogues*	9:05
ICL-LLaMA2	
Inference on *10 dialogues*	36:00
ICL-OpenChat-3.5	
Inference on *10 dialogues*	5:35

Table 5: The average time consumption for the E2E task. For all FT-based systems, the computation was performed on a machine equipped with a single A100 80 GiB GPU and a 32-core vCPU. In the case of the ICL-GPT-3.5 systems, calculations were conducted using the OpenAI API. Meanwhile, the ICL-LLaMA2 systems were executed on an Intel 13900k CPU and ICL-OpenChat-3.5 systems were executed on a machine with an Intel 13900k CPU and a single NVIDIA RTX 4090 GPU.

we conduct an extra experiment where the predictions of each part were individually replaced with the ground-truth. When substituting the predicted utterances with ground-truth utterances, the FT-mT5$_{small}$ systems exhibited a notable improvement, achieving an average Inform Rate of 85.1 (↑13.3) and a Success Rate of 66.1 (↑21.5) across four languages. In contrast, substituting the predicted dialogue states resulted in a marginal increase, with the systems attaining an Inform Rate of 72.1 (↑0.3) and a Success Rate of 43.3 (↑0.7) across the languages. These findings highlight the critical role of RG model performance in determining overall system performance and the relative insensitivity of these metrics in evaluating the performance of DST models.

Table 6 shows the fully supervised performance of $mT5_{large}$, LLaMA2, and OpenChat-3.5 models across DST models, RG models, and E2E systems on the MULTI3WOZ dataset. It is noteworthy that the OpenChat-3.5 based systems exhibited a failure in generating coherent dialogue responses. These systems consistently repeated the prompts and, in each utterance, indiscriminately included all the placeholders. This simplistic method led to inflated Inform Rate and Success Rate scores, highlighting the potential vulnerability of these metrics to adversarial strategies, a concern also highlighted by Wu et al. (2023).

Table 7 presents an analysis of the performance under full supervision for both $mT5_{small}$ and $mT5_{large}$ models. This evaluation is conducted on a specifically selected subset of 100 dialogues from the entire test set, consistent with the evaluation setup applied to all other ICL-based models and systems in this study. This approach ensures a rigorous and direct comparability across the discussed ICL-based models and systems.

E Diagrams and Screenshots

In this section, we present a series of diagrams, web interface screenshots, and code snippets that illustrate the architectural design and functionalities of our toolkit.

Figure 2 illustrates the architecture of an E2E dialogue system. State-of-the-art E2E TOD systems typically employ a pipelined approach in the background, incorporating three key components: a dialogue state tracking (DST) model, a database interface, and a response generation (RG) model.

Figure 3 shows the architectural framework of our human evaluation tool. The underlying infrastructure of the back-end servers is constructed on the principles of a microservice architecture.

Figure 4 presents a screenshot capturing the login page of our human evaluation web interface. This interface serves as the entry point for evaluators to access the system.

Figure 5 presents a screenshot capturing the registration page of our human evaluation web interface.

Figure 6 displays a screenshot of the assignment page within the human evaluation web interface.

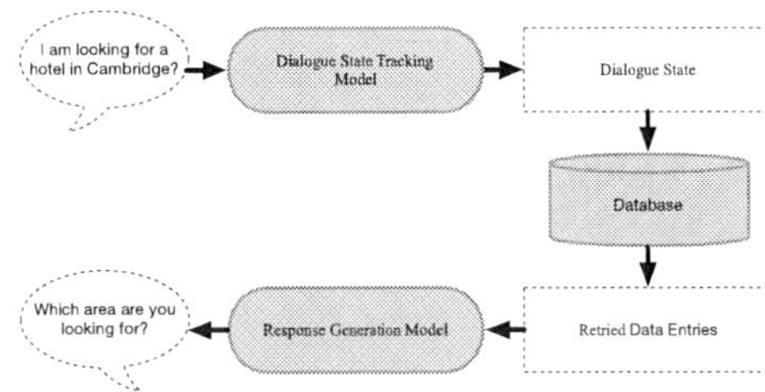

Figure 2: An E2E dialogue system contains three key components: a dialogue state tracking (DST) model, a database, and a response generation (RG) model. The DST model processes user utterances with the accumulated dialogue history to predict a dialogue state. This state is then translated into a database query to extract data entries relevant to the current dialogue context from the database. The RG model uses these entries and the dialogue history to produce the final response.

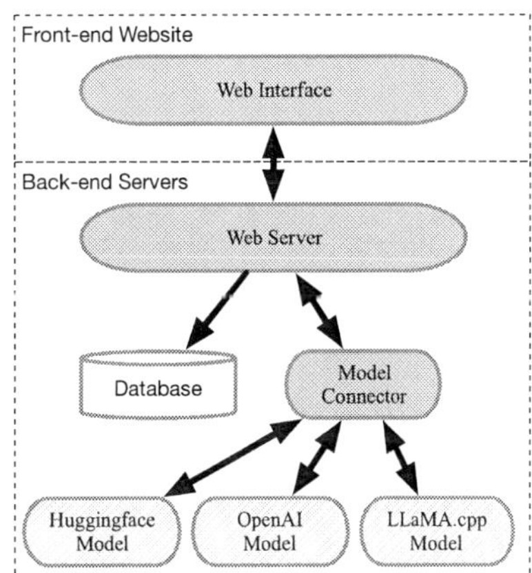

Figure 3: Architectural design of our human evaluation tool, containing two primary components: a web-based interface and a cluster of back-end servers. The server infrastructure is based on a microservice architecture, segregating each task model into its own independent service, as highlighted by the dashed yellow background in the figure. Central to this architecture is the Model Connector, functioning as an API gateway to manage and route requests to the appropriate task models. For example, each fine-tuned DST model is hosted independently on a dedicated server. These servers are designed to be stateless, enabling their shared use across various systems and dialogue sessions, thereby enhancing efficiency and scalability.

This page is specifically designed for users to carry out the task of evaluating the dialogue system.

Figure 7 presents detailed screenshots capturing both the utterance-level and dialogue-level feedback forms facilitated by our tool. These feedback forms are integrated into the assignment page.

Figure 8 presents screenshots of the code to pro-

Language	Dialogue State Tracking				Response Generation			End-to-end Modelling		
	JGA	Slot F1	Slot Precision	Slot Recall	BLEU	ROUGE	METEOR	Inform Rate	Success Rate	BLEU
FT-mT5$_{large}$										
ENG	18.6	52.5	53.0	52.0	15.8	24.1	27.1	70.1	47.3	15.4
ARA	44.0	78.5	78.3	78.6	7.0	17.4	14.8	67.3	31.4	6.7
FRA	46.8	79.5	79.6	79.5	14.1	25.2	25.8	74.3	44.2	13.6
TUR	48.5	80.2	78.8	81.7	10.6	19.7	19.0	77.7	48.0	10.8
AVG.	39.5	72.7	72.4	73.0	11.9	21.6	21.7	70.1	42.4	11.6
ICL-LLaMA2 (∗)										
ENG	1.6	0.0	0.0	0.0	0.1	0.1	0.1	22.0	8.0	0.2
ARA	1.6	0.0	0.0	0.0	0.1	0.0	0.0	23.0	9.0	0.1
FRA	1.6	0.0	0.0	0.0	0.0	0.0	0.0	19.0	9.0	0.0
TUR	1.6	0.0	0.0	0.0	0.0	0.0	0.0	18.0	7.0	0.0
AVG.	1.6	0.0	0.0	0.0	0.1	0.0	0.0	20.5	8.3	0.0
ICL-OpenChat-3.5 (∗) (∗∗)										
ENG	1.6	0.0	0.0	0.0	0.0	0.0	0.0	67.0	61.0	0.0
ARA	1.6	0.0	0.0	0.0	0.0	0.0	0.0	67.0	60.0	0.0
FRA	1.6	0.0	0.0	0.0	0.0	0.0	0.0	67.0	60.0	0.0
TUR	1.6	0.0	0.0	0.0	0.0	0.0	0.0	67.0	60.0	0.0
AVG.	1.6	0.0	0.0	0.0	0.0	0.0	0.0	67.0	60.3	0.0

Table 6: Evaluation of fully supervised performance across DST models, RG models, and E2E systems on the MULTI3WOZ dataset. This table reports the performance metrics for each language, evaluated across different models. It should be noted that for these metrics, the ground truth score is set at 100, with the exceptions of the Inform Rate and Success Rate, which are measured as 89.3 ± 0.2 and 68.6 ± 0.2 across the four languages, respectively. (∗) For practical considerations, the evaluation ICL-based models and systems is limited to a randomly selected sample of 100 dialogues from the full test set, due to the significant time and resource requirements of a full-scale evaluation. (∗∗) Additionally, it is noteworthy that the OpenChat-3.5 based systems exhibited a failure in generating coherent dialogue responses. These systems repetitively echoed the prompts and for each utterance, generated all the placeholders. This simplistic approach resulted in artificially high Inform Rate and Success Rate scores, revealing the vulnerability of these metrics to adversarial strategies.

Language	Dialogue State Tracking				Response Generation			End-to-end Modelling		
	JGA	Slot F1	Slot Precision	Slot Recall	BLEU	ROUGE	METEOR	Inform Rate	Success Rate	BLEU
FT-mT5$_{small}$(∗)										
ENG	54.4	83.0	84.6	81.5	18.7	26.5	29.7	66.0	47.0	18.5
ARA	41.9	77.5	79.9	75.3	16.1	30.0	27.4	67.0	43.0	15.8
FRA	42.9	80.3	81.3	79.3	12.9	25.0	25.6	66.0	34.0	13.4
TUR	48.0	81.5	81.1	81.9	22.8	34.6	34.1	75.0	48.0	23.1
AVG.	46.8	80.6	81.7	79.5	17.6	29.0	29.2	68.5	43.0	17.7
FT-mT5$_{large}$(∗)										
ENG	19.1	53.3	55.0	51.6	18.0	25.7	29.0	69.0	49.0	17.8
ARA	41.9	79.1	80.2	78.1	9.2	19.4	17.0	62.0	30.0	9.0
FRA	44.6	80.3	82.1	78.5	13.1	24.4	24.6	77.0	50.0	13.4
TUR	45.2	80.8	80.8	80.8	11.2	20.5	19.7	68.0	28.0	11.4
AVG.	30.2	73.4	74.5	72.3	12.9	22.5	22.6	69.0	39.3	12.9

Table 7: Evaluation of fully supervised performance across DST models, RG models, and E2E systems on the MULTI3WOZ dataset. This table reports the performance metrics for each language, using both mT5$_{small}$ and mT5$_{large}$ models. 'AVG.' represents the mean average of the evaluation scores aggregated across all four languages. We note that for these metrics the ground truth score is set at 100, with the exception of the Inform Rate and Success Rate, which are measured as 89.3 ± 0.2 and 68.6 ± 0.2 across the four languages, respectively. (∗) In this table, the evaluation is limited to a randomly selected sample of 100 dialogues from the full test set, ensuring direct comparability with other ICL-based models and systems discussed herein.

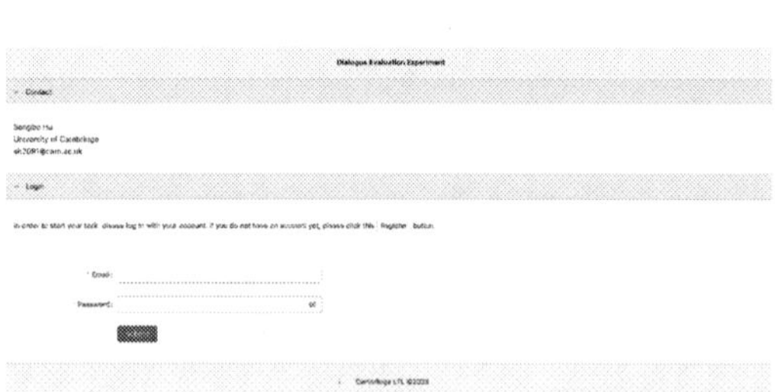

Figure 4: A screenshot capturing the login page of the human evaluation web interface.

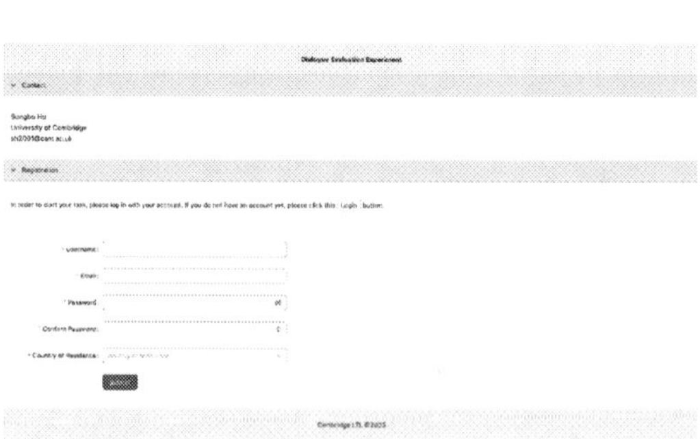

Figure 5: A screenshot of the registration page.

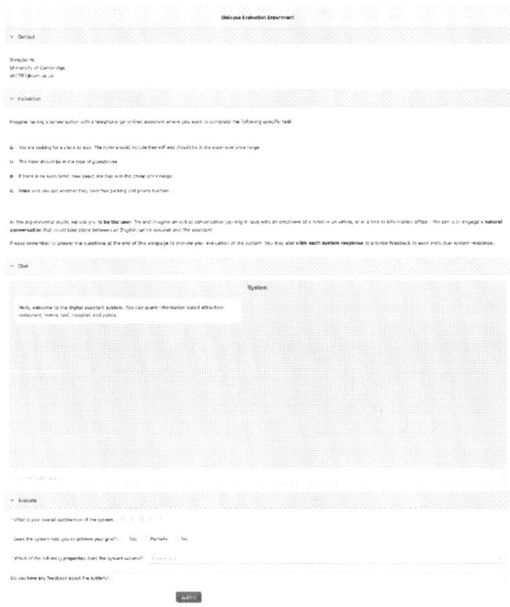

Figure 6: A screenshot of the task assignment page.

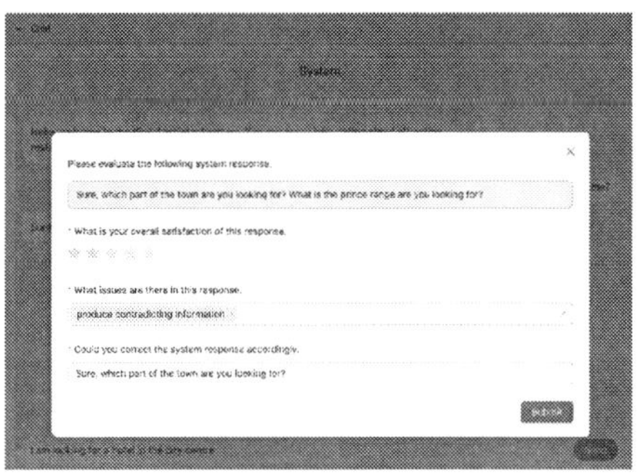

(a) Utterance Level

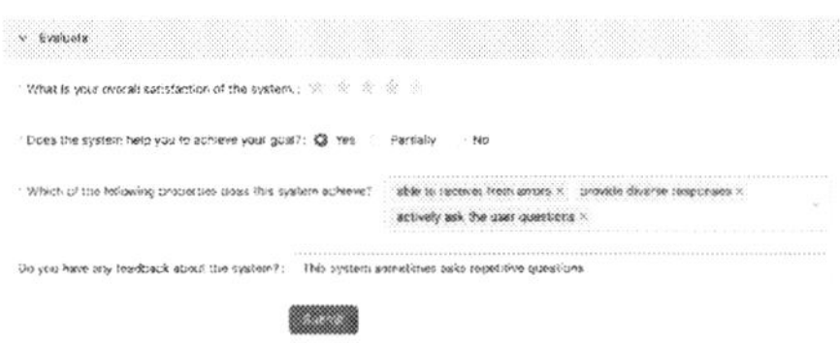

(b) Dialogue Level

Figure 7: Our human evaluation tool is designed to collect user feedback at both the (a) utterance and (b) dialogue levels. This tool allows for full customisation of evaluation questions with minimal programming effort.

duce the prompts for both our ICL-based DST and RG models.

Figure 9 presents a screenshot of the inference code for our FT-based E2E systems. The code is modularised and intentionally designed to be both simple and fully functional. Our goal is to facilitate users in acquiring a clear understanding

(a) DST Prompt

(b) RG Prompt

Figure 8: Screenshots of the code to produce the prompts for our ICL-based (a) DST and (b) RG models are provided above.

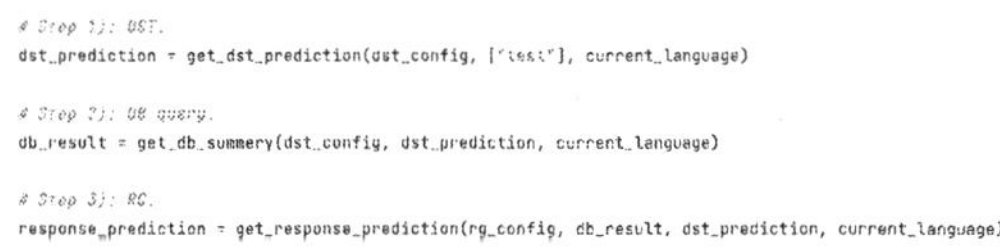

```
# Step 1): DST.
dst_prediction = get_dst_prediction(dst_config, ["text"], current_language)

# Step 2): DB query.
db_result = get_db_summery(dst_config, dst_prediction, current_language)

# Step 3): RG.
response_prediction = get_response_prediction(rg_config, db_result, dst_prediction, current_language)
```

Figure 9: A screenshot of the inference code for our FT-based E2E systems is provided above. The code is intentionally designed to be both simple and fully functional, aiming to assist users in gaining a conceptual understanding of the ToD task and the implementation of our system.

of the ToD task, as well as to provide insights into the implementation of our system.

Figure 10 presents a screenshot of the backend web server code for our RESTful API for the storage of human evaluation results. This setup incorporates a JWT-based authentication system to secure access. Additionally, it is structured to permit only authorised users with specific permissions to record evaluation results in the database.

```
@auth.route("/save_result", methods=['POST', "OPTIONS"])
@jwt_required()
@require_permission('submit_task')
@require_additional_permission_with_access_control("submit_task_with_access_control")
def save_result():
    if request.method == 'OPTIONS':
        return _handle_preflight()
    current_user_id = get_jwt_identity()

    try:
        _currentUser = LoginUser().check_user_with_id(current_user_id)
        save_data = request.get_json()
        logging.info(save_data)
        if save_data:
            save_data['create_time'] = datetime.now()
            save_data['feedback_user'] = _currentUser.email
            _feedback = FeedBack(**save_data)
            insert_id = _currentUser.save_result(_feedback)

            return jsonify({'success': True, 'msg': 'Save success.', "insert_id": insert_id}), 200

    except Exception as e:
        logging.error('Error while saving task data', exc_info=True)
        return jsonify({'success': False, 'msg': 'Failed to save task data'}), 500
```

Figure 10: A screenshot of the backend web server code for our RESTful API, designed for storing system evaluation results. It features a JWT-based authentication mechanism to ensure secure access. Furthermore, the system is configured to allow only users with specific permissions to save evaluation results to the database, thereby enhancing data integrity and security.

RTSUM: Relation Triple-based Interpretable Summarization with Multi-level Salience Visualization

Seonglae Cho, Myungha Jang, Jinyoung Yeo, Dongha Lee*
Yonsei University, Republic of Korea
{sungle3737,jinyeo,donalee}@yonsei.ac.kr, myunghajang@gmail.com

Abstract

In this paper, we present RTSUM, an unsupervised summarization framework that utilizes relation triples as the basic unit for summarization. Given an input document, RTSUM first selects salient relation triples via multi-level salience scoring and then generates a concise summary from the selected relation triples by using a text-to-text language model. On the basis of RTSUM, we also develop a web demo for an interpretable summarizing tool, providing fine-grained interpretations with the output summary. With support for customization options, our tool visualizes the salience for textual units at three distinct levels: sentences, relation triples, and phrases. The code[1] and video[2] are publicly available.

1 Introduction

Text summarization has emerged as a critical tool in the era of information overload, enabling users to quickly understand the essence of long text. Among various summarization techniques, abstractive summarization has gained significant attention due to its ability to generate fluent and concise summaries that capture the main ideas of the source text (Nallapati et al., 2016; See et al., 2017; Tan et al., 2017; Cohan et al., 2018; Xu et al., 2020a; Koh et al., 2022). Nevertheless, despite their advantages in flexibility and reduced redundancy compared to extractive methods, abstractive methods inherently lack interpretability. That is, the absence of a direct link to the source text can make it difficult to trace back the source of information, which makes the summary lack interpretability.

Interpretability in summarization is important to provide users a way to cross-check that the generated summary is factually consistent, and to provide more context to dive into if one wants to know more about the summarized content. To generate an interpretable summary, extractive summarization techniques can offer advantages. As they directly extract sentences from the text, the sentences themselves serve as the source of information (Xu et al., 2020b; Padmakumar and He, 2021). However, a significant drawback of many extractive methods lies in their sentence-level operation, which limits their ability to extract fine-grained key information (Zheng and Lapata, 2019; Liu et al., 2021). In many cases, a single sentence describes multiple diverse pieces of information that should be treated as distinct facts for summarization. By selecting entire sentences, these methods may include unnecessary or redundant information in the summary, reducing both its efficiency and readability.

To enhance the interpretability of the summarization process by incorporating fine-grained key information, our focus lies on leveraging *relation triples* as the basic unit for summarization. A relation triple in the form of (subject, predicate, object) concisely describes a single piece of information corresponding to its relation (i.e., predicate) between two entities (i.e., subject and object), and it can be effectively identified from a source document by using open information extraction (OpenIE) systems (Angeli et al., 2015; Mausam, 2016).

Using relation triples, our main idea embodies *selection-and-sentencification*, which achieves a combination of extractive and abstractive summarization methods. Specifically, we first select only a few relation triples according to their importance – *salience* – within the document for summarization, and then reassemble the selected relation triples into the final output summary. This two-step approach enhances the interpretability of the summarization by providing clear explanations for the salience scores of relation triples and their contributions to the final summary. This clarity allows users to understand the crucial elements driving the summarization process effectively.

*Corresponding author

[1] https://github.com/seonglae/RTSum

[2] https://youtu.be/sFRO0xfqvVM

Proceedings of the 2024 Conference of the North American Chapter of the Association for Computational Linguistics: Human Language Technologies (Volume 3: System Demonstrations), pages 53–60
June 16-21, 2024 ©2024 Association for Computational Linguistics

Formally, we present an unsupervised Relation Triple-based Summarization framework, named RTSUM. For relation triple selection, RTSUM identifies heterogeneous textual information units with various granularity, which are (1) sentences, (2) relation triples, and (3) phrases, to utilize their own salience all together. Under the principle that more salient textual units are much more relevant to other units semantically and lexically, it models the multi-level salience from the three distinct textual units. Then, it selects the K most salient relation triples based on the multi-level salience scores. For relation triple sentencification, RTSUM employs a neural text-to-text architecture as a *relation combiner* to transform the relation triples into the summary sentences. The relation combiner is effectively optimized in a self-supervised manner by using source sentences (sampled from training documents) and their relation triples (extracted from the sampled sentences) as targets and inputs, respectively, while not requiring any reference summaries of its training documents.

Building upon the RTSUM framework, we develop an online demo to showcase an interpretable text summarization tool. Given an input document, our tool generates a concise summary, while simultaneously offering fine-grained interpretations by visually depicting the multi-level salience of textual units within the source document. For clarity in visualization, the tool highlights text spans (i.e., textual units) based on their salience score, with numerical ranks provided as annotations. Furthermore, our tool offers customization options, allowing users to personalize the visualization according to their preferences and specific purposes.

Our multi-level salience visualization empowers users to easily identify the textual units that mostly influence the final summary; it also provides valuable insights into the salient semantic structure of the document at a glance, enhancing users' overall understanding of the summarization process.

2 Preliminary

Textual Information Units. We utilize three different types of textual information units with various granularity: sentences, relation triples,[3] and phrases. All sentences and relations are extracted from a source document by using open information extraction (OpenIE) systems. Among several implementations, we employ OpenIE 5[4] (Mausam, 2016) released by UW and IIT Delhi. Similarly, all noun and verb phrases in the document are identified based on POS labels tagged by the Spacy library. Table 1 shows an example of the three textual information units in a single sentence.

Sentence	Hugh Laurie joins the cast and Julia Louis-Dreyfus is now the president of the United States on HBO's hit comedy.
Relation	(S: Hugh Laurie, P: joins, O: the cast) (S: Julia Louis-Dreyfus, P: is, O: now the president of the United States on HBO's hit comedy)
Phrase	Hugh Laurie, joins, cast, Julia Louis-Dreyfus, is, president, United States, HBO's, hit comedy

Table 1: An example of textual information units.

Relation Triples. Each relation triple, denoted by $r = (\text{sub}, \text{pred}, \text{obj})$, represents a relation (i.e., predicate) between two text spans (i.e., subject and object), and it corresponds to a single piece of information in terms of the relation. The three components are described in natural language, and this allows us to treat them as the sequence of tokens in the vocabulary, similar to sentences and phrases. Thus, we consider the concatenated text of its subject, predicate, and object as the textual description of a relation triple, i.e., $\text{desc}(r) = [\text{sub}\|\text{pred}\|\text{obj}]$.

Problem Definition. Given a source document D and its information units, including sentences $\mathcal{S} = \{s_1, \ldots, s_{N_s}\}$, relation triples $\mathcal{R} = \{r_1, \ldots, r_{N_r}\}$, and phrases $\mathcal{P} = \{p_1, \ldots, p_{N_p}\}$, the goal of our relation triple-based summarization task is (1) to select the relation triples based on their salience within the document, and (2) to generate a concise summary from the selected salient relation triples. In this paper, we mainly focus on the unsupervised setting where the annotated text-summary pairs are not available for training a summarization model, since such reference summaries are usually noisy, expensive to acquire, and hard to scale.

3 RTSUM: Relation Triple-based Summarization Framework

Our summarization framework, named RTSUM, consists of the two steps: (1) *information selection* for identifying the salient relation triples based on multi-level salience from various textual information units (Section 3.1), and (2) *information sentencification* for combining the selected relation triples

[3]For brevity, we use the terms "relation triples" and "relations" interchangeably, in the rest of this paper.

[4]https://github.com/dair-iitd/OpenIE-standalone

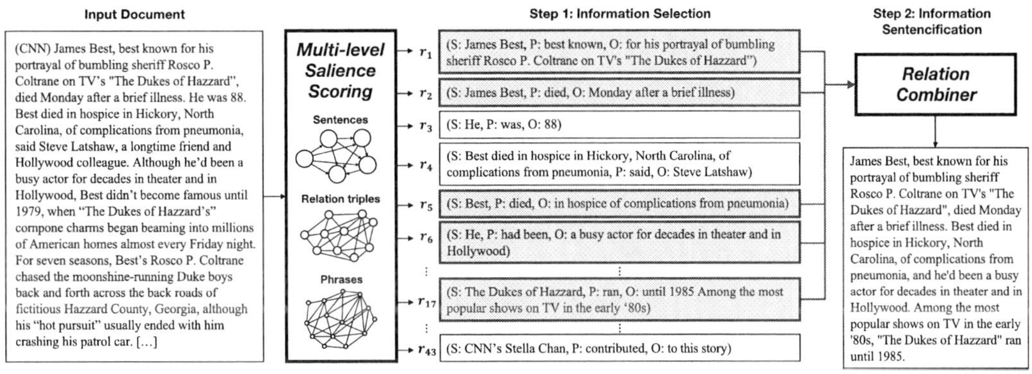

Figure 1: The overall process of the RTSUM framework. RTSUM selects salient relation triples and then generates the plausible sentences from the selected relation triples.

into plausible sentences with the help of a neural text generator (Section 3.2). Figure 1 illustrates the overall process of our RTSUM framework.

3.1 Information Selection

For the selection of relation triples that would be included in the summary, RTSUM models the multi-level salience for each relation triple by leveraging heterogeneous textual information units. Specifically, it figures out how significant a relation triple is within the document from the perspective of (1) the sentence that the relation triple is extracted from, (2) the relation triple itself, and (3) the phrases that the relation triple contains. In the end, RTSUM selects the most K salient relation triples based on their multi-level salience scores.[5]

3.1.1 Sentence-level Salience Score

The sentence-level salience considers the significance of the sentence that each relation triple is extracted from. Following previous studies (Zheng and Lapata, 2019; Liu et al., 2021), we infer the sentence-level salience by utilizing sentence order (i.e., a preceding sentence is more likely to contain salient information) and semantic similarity (i.e., the sentence that is more semantically relevant to other sentences is likely to contain salient information). Thus, we construct a sentence-level text graph $\mathcal{G}^{\mathrm{s}} = (\mathcal{S}, E^{\mathrm{s}})$ with a directed edge from a former sentence node s_i to a latter sentence node s_j, and the edge weight E^{s}_{ij} is the semantic similarity between the two sentences.

$$E^{\mathrm{s}}_{ij} = \begin{cases} \mathrm{sim}(s_i, s_j) & \text{if } s_i \text{ precedes } s_j \\ 0 & \text{otherwise.} \end{cases} \tag{1}$$

[5]The selection (or ranking) strategy based on multi-level salience can be implemented in various ways (Section 3.1.4).

$\mathrm{sim}(s_i, s_j)$ is defined by the cosine similarity between two sentence representations from a sentence encoder, specifically fine-tuned for the semantic textual similarity (STS) task (Gao et al., 2021).

From the sentence-level text graph, the sentence-level salience is defined by the degree-based centrality (Zheng and Lapata, 2019). In other words, this centrality is equivalent to the sum of semantic similarities with all of its subsequent sentences.

$$S^{\mathrm{s}}(s_i) = \sum\nolimits_{s_j \in \mathcal{S}} E^{\mathrm{s}}_{ij}. \tag{2}$$

3.1.2 Relation-level Salience Score

The relation-level salience focuses on the meaning of each relation itself in that the semantic similarity among the relation descriptions implies the salience; that is, a relation description that is more relevant to other relation descriptions is more likely to contain salient information. In this sense, we build a relation-level text graph $\mathcal{G}^{\mathrm{r}} = (\mathcal{R}, E^{\mathrm{r}})$, whose nodes represent the relation triple and the undirected edge has the weight of the semantic similarity between relation descriptions. Similar to Equation (1), the cosine similarity between relation representations is calculated, and the salience score is also modeled as the degree-based centrality.

$$\begin{aligned} E^{\mathrm{r}}_{ij} &= \mathrm{sim}(\mathrm{desc}(r_i), \mathrm{desc}(r_j)), \\ S^{\mathrm{r}}(r_i) &= \sum\nolimits_{r_j \in \mathcal{R}} E^{\mathrm{r}}_{ij}. \end{aligned} \tag{3}$$

Note that the sequential order of relations is not clearly presented unlike the sentences, because multiple relations are extracted from the same sentence.

3.1.3 Phrase-level Salience Score

The phrase-level salience measures the salience of phrases included in each relation triple, and it captures the phrase frequency and co-occurrence in the document. As presented in previous work on keyphrase extraction (Mihalcea and Tarau, 2004; Bougouin et al., 2013), we build a phrase-level text graph $\mathcal{G}^{\text{p}} = (\mathcal{P}, E^{\text{p}})$ whose nodes are the noun and verb phrases extracted from the source document based on POS tags (e.g., `Noun`, `Proper Noun`, and `Verb`). The undirected edges model the weight as how many times two phrases locally co-occur (i.e., within a sliding window) in the sentences $\mathcal{S}$, and then run the TextRank (Mihalcea and Tarau, 2004) on the graph to compute salience of phrase nodes.

$$E^{\text{p}}_{ij} = \text{co-occur}(p_i, p_j; \mathcal{S}), \tag{4}$$
$$S^{\text{p}}(p_i) = (1-d) + d \cdot \sum_{p_j \in \mathcal{P}} \frac{E^{\text{p}}_{ji}}{\sum_{p_k \in \mathcal{P}} E^{\text{p}}_{jk}} S^{\text{p}}(p_j),$$

where $d \in [0, 1]$ is the damping factor that indicates the transition probability from one node to another random node. Starting from initial values of S^{p} usually set to 1.0 for all the nodes, the final salience of each phrase is obtained through iterative computation of Equation (4) until convergence.

3.1.4 Salient Relation Triple Selection

The remaining challenge here is to select relation triples by integrating multi-level salience scores. To this end, RTSUM first identifies the textual information units relevant to each relation triple r_i, including its source sentence s_j and its phrases $p_k (\in \mathcal{P}_{r_i})$, and then transforms their salience scores for the relation triple by $S^{\text{s}}(r_i) := S^{\text{s}}(s_j)$, $S^{\text{r}}(r_i) := S^{\text{r}}(r_i)$, and $S^{\text{p}}(r_i) := 1/|\mathcal{P}_{r_i}| \cdot \sum_{p_k \in \mathcal{P}_{r_i}} S^{\text{p}}(p_k)$.

The most straightforward strategy to select a small number of salient relation triples is to calculate the final score of each relation triple based on *weighted summation* of its three distinct scores and to select the top-K relation triples:

$$S(r_i) = \alpha \cdot S^{\text{s}}(r_i) + S^{\text{r}}(r_i) + \beta \cdot S^{\text{p}}(r_i). \tag{5}$$

Another selection strategy is to adopt *cascade filtering* that excludes less salient relation triples by using the sentence-level, relation-level, and phrase-level salience in a serial order (i.e., $S^{\text{s}} \rightarrow S^{\text{r}} \rightarrow S^{\text{p}}$). The key principle of this filtering process is to keep only the relation triples extracted from the key sentences, and among them, to selectively collect the relation triples that are semantically relevant to the others, and finally, to exclude the ones that do not include many salient phrases.

3.2 Information Sentencification

For the generation of sentences from the selected relation triples (i.e., sentencification), RTSUM builds a *relation combiner* based on a pretrained text-to-text language model, such as BART (Lewis et al., 2020) and T5 (Raffel et al., 2020). Using the relation combiner, RTSUM can perform the abstractive summarization by sentencifying the selected relation triples.

Relation Combiner Training. The relation combiner is effectively optimized with the self-supervised objective for the sentencification task. To be specific, we collect training pairs of (relation triples, sentences) by randomly sampling a couple of sentences from source documents and extracting the relation triples from the sentences. Then, we train the relation combiner based on Maximum Likelihood Estimation (MLE) to generate the sentences by taking the concatenated text of all the extracted relation triples. As a result, it is expected to learn how to introduce linking words, place each component in order considering their relation, and remove duplicated phrases or entities, for plausible sentence generation. To eliminate redundancy, we apply a lightweight string similarity algorithm, Gestalt pattern matching (Ratcliff and Metzener, 1988), as a filter before merging relation triples.

Training Pair Filtering. Despite the benefits of self-supervised training, the relation combiner still has a risk of introducing information that is not presented in a source document (i.e., extrinsic hallucinations) or factual errors against the document (i.e., intrinsic hallucinations) into its output summary. Since the extracted relation triples are not guaranteed to perfectly cover all the information of their source sentences, some training pairs might guide the combiner to generate missing information that does not exist in the input relation triples. To alleviate these hallucinations, we selectively collect the training pairs whose extracted relation triples fully cover the content of the source sentences. Precisely, the pairs of (relation triples, sentences) are excluded from the training set, in case that some of the semantic tokens (i.e., nouns, proper nouns, and verbs) in the source sentences do not appear in the extracted relation triples.

4 Demo: Interpretable Summarizing Tool

Based upon our RTSUM framework, we build an interpretable summarizing tool that provides not only the final summary of an input document but

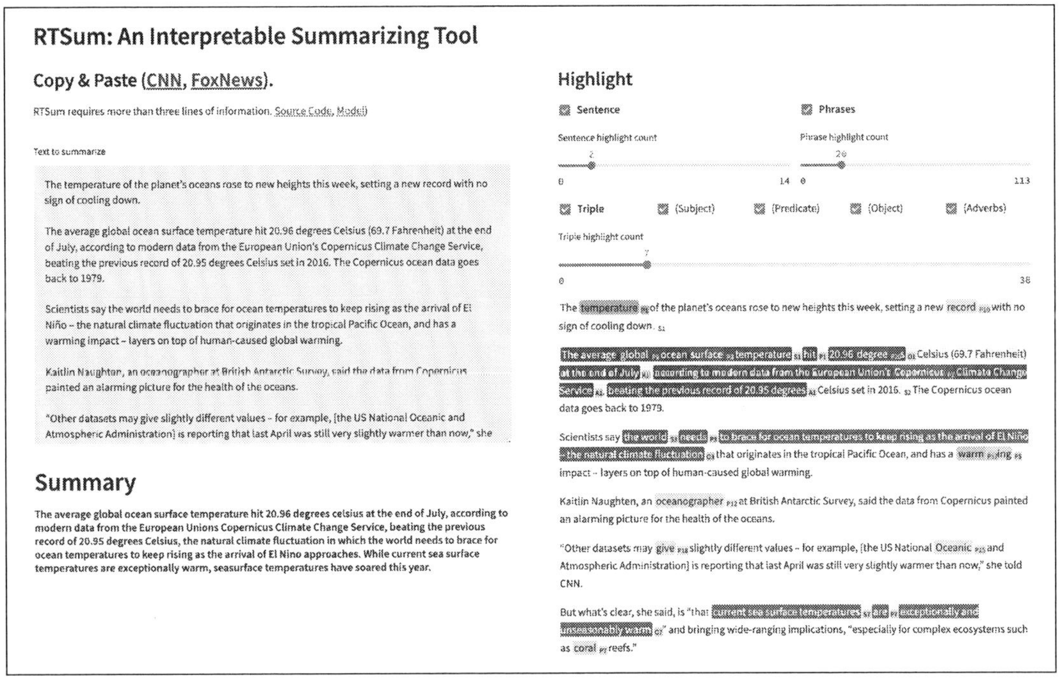

Figure 2: Our interpretable summarizing tool features multi-level salience visualization. Sentences, relation triples, and phrases with a high score are highlighted in yellow, red, and green, respectively. The saliency of each unit is denoted by its opacity. Within each triple, the subjects, predicates, objects, and adverbs are distinguished.

also its fine-grained interpretations.

4.1 Multi-level Salience Visualization

For interpretation of final summaries, our tool provides salience visualization for textual information units with different granularity (Figure 2). It highlights the text spans that correspond to each information unit according to its salience score. For enhanced insights, the salience rank is explicitly annotated next to each span, providing users with a clear understanding of the relative importance of each information unit within the document. This feature allows users to grasp the significance of the textual content and gain a more nuanced and detailed understanding of the document's key points.

Users can personalize the salience visualization based on their unique preferences and specific needs, including customization options as follows:

- **Type of textual units**: Users have the flexibility to choose whether to highlight each type of textual unit. They can opt to further dissect the highlight for a relation triple, differentiating its subject, predicate, and object components.
- **Number of textual units**: Users can manually adjust the number of highlighted instances for each type of textual unit.

4.2 Implementation Details

Text graph construction. For more reliable summarization, our RTSUM implementation filters out less confident relation triples among the ones extracted from the OpenIE 5 system; only the relation triples of which confidence is larger than 0.7 is considered as valid units. To construct sentence-level and relation-level text graphs, RTSUM utilizes General Text Embeddings (GTE)[6] as the sentence encoder, which is trained on a large-scale corpus of relevance text pairs covering a wide range of domains and scenarios. Cosine similarity between two sentence (or relation description) embeddings is used for the edge weight in the graphs.

Relation triple selection. RTSUM in our tool simply ranks relation triples by their final salience scores, which are calculated by summing three distinct salience scores (i.e., S^{s}, S^{r}, S^{p}) with the same weight, and then chooses top-K ones. The number of relation triples to be selected is set to $K = 3$.

Relation combiner training. To build a relation combiner, we fine-tune BART[7] (Lewis et al.,

[6]https://huggingface.co/thenlper/gte-large
[7]https://huggingface.co/facebook/bart-base

2020) to generate source sentences from the relation triples extracted from the sentences. We use a text corpus in the news domain, CNN/DM (Nallapati et al., 2016) which contains 287,113 news articles available for training. To reduce the risk of hallucination, we filter out the cases that the amount of information in an input text (i.e., a set of relation triples) is shorter than that in an output text (i.e., sentences), as explained in Section 3.2. In addition, we use three special tokens, <subject>, <predicate>, and <object>, to separate three components of each relation triple in an input text, which effectively provides structured information about each triple to the model.

Relation combiner alternatives. While our summarizing tool provides the fine-tuned text-to-text language model as a default relation combiner, it also provides an option to employ instruction-following language models, such as InstructGPT (Ouyang et al., 2022) and ChatGPT. These models can reconstruct plausible sentences from a set of relation triples, when being asked with a proper prompt written in natural language; they can be beneficial in that domain-specific or task-specific fine-tuning process is not required.

5 Related Work

5.1 Unsupervised Extractive Summarization

The most popular approach to unsupervised extractive summarization is to identify key sentences by using a text graph that represents the semantic (or lexical) relationship among text units in a source document. TextRank (Mihalcea and Tarau, 2004) is the first work to adopt a graph-based ranking algorithm (Brin and Page, 1998) to calculate the centrality of sentences in the graph, whose node represents each sentence and edge is modeled as the similarity between two sentences. Several variants of TextRank have been implemented by utilizing symbolic sentence representations (e.g., TF-IDF) (Barrios et al., 2016) or distributed sentence representations (e.g., skip-thoughts) (Kiros et al., 2015) for computing the sentence similarity.

Most recent studies have employed pretrained language models (PLMs), such as BERT (Devlin et al., 2019), to effectively model the salience of each sentence. Zheng and Lapata (2019); Liu et al. (2021) used the degree-based node centrality of the position-augmented sentence graph where the sentence similarity is calculated by PLMs, and Padmakumar and He (2021) defined the selection criterion by using PLM-based pointwise mutual information. Xu et al. (2020b) considered the sentence-level self-attention score as the salience, after optimizing PLMs via masked sentence prediction. Nevertheless, all of them regard a sentence as the basic unit for summarization, so they cannot exclude unnecessary information from each selected sentence.

5.2 Unsupervised Abstractive Sumamrization

To train a neural model for abstractive summarization without using human-annotated text-summary pairs, most existing methods have adopted the auto-encoding architecture whose encoder compresses a source text into a readable summary (i.e., a few sentences) and decoder reconstructs the original text from the summary (Wang and Lee, 2018; Baziotis et al., 2019; Chu and Liu, 2019). Another line of research has focused on zero-shot abstractive summarization, which takes advantage of large-scale PLMs trained on massive text corpora. Their models are optimized with a self-supervised objective (e.g., gap sentence generation) (Raffel et al., 2020; Zhang et al., 2020) or heuristically-generated references (e.g., lead bias) (Yang et al., 2020; Fang et al., 2022). However, the well-known caveat of abstractive summarization is poor interpretability, which is also related to the hallucination problem; their output summaries mostly contain factual errors or misinformation against the source document (Kryscinski et al., 2020; Maynez et al., 2020).

6 Conclusion

In this paper, we introduce a summarization framework, called RTSUM, which leverages relation triples as the basic units for summarization. Building upon this framework, we have developed a web demo for an interpretable summarizing tool that effectively visualizes the salience of textual units at three distinct levels. Through our multi-level salience visualization, users can easily identify textual units impacting the summary and gain insights into the document's salient semantic structure.

Our RTSUM framework and its user-friendly tool can effectively capture the essence of a document while maintaining interpretability. The fusion of extractive and abstractive approaches, coupled with intuitive multi-level visualization, holds promise for applications requiring succinct, accurate, and interpretable summaries.

7 Limitations

Our study has the following limitations: Firstly, compared to single-step summarization approaches, our framework is relatively slower due to its multi-step process. Secondly, the current implementation relies on English-specific tools for sentence splitting and relation extraction, limiting its applicability to only English inputs. Lastly, while our research focuses on summarizing news articles effectively, the robustness and performance of our approach on longer or differently formatted text genres, such as books or research papers, has not been comprehensively evaluated.

Acknowledgements

This work was supported by the IITP grant funded by the Korea government (MSIT) (No.2020-0-01361) and the NRF grant funded by the Korea government (MSIT) (No. RS-2023-00244689).

References

Gabor Angeli, Melvin Jose Johnson Premkumar, and Christopher D. Manning. 2015. Leveraging linguistic structure for open domain information extraction. In *Proceedings of the 53rd Annual Meeting of the Association for Computational Linguistics and the 7th International Joint Conference on Natural Language Processing (Volume 1: Long Papers)*, pages 344–354, Beijing, China. Association for Computational Linguistics.

Federico Barrios, Federico López, Luis Argerich, and Rosa Wachenchauzer. 2016. Variations of the similarity function of textrank for automated summarization. *CoRR*, abs/1602.03606.

Christos Baziotis, Ion Androutsopoulos, Ioannis Konstas, and Alexandros Potamianos. 2019. SEQ^3: Differentiable sequence-to-sequence-to-sequence autoencoder for unsupervised abstractive sentence compression. In *Proceedings of the 2019 Conference of the North American Chapter of the Association for Computational Linguistics: Human Language Technologies, Volume 1 (Long and Short Papers)*, pages 673–681, Minneapolis, Minnesota. Association for Computational Linguistics.

Adrien Bougouin, Florian Boudin, and Béatrice Daille. 2013. TopicRank: Graph-based topic ranking for keyphrase extraction. In *Proceedings of the Sixth International Joint Conference on Natural Language Processing*, pages 543–551, Nagoya, Japan. Asian Federation of Natural Language Processing.

Sergey Brin and Lawrence Page. 1998. The anatomy of a large-scale hypertextual web search engine. In *Proceedings of the Seventh International Conference on World Wide Web 7*, page 107–117, NLD. Elsevier Science Publishers B. V.

Eric Chu and Peter J. Liu. 2019. Meansum: A neural model for unsupervised multi-document abstractive summarization. In *Proceedings of the 36th International Conference on Machine Learning, ICML 2019, 9-15 June 2019, Long Beach, California, USA*, volume 97 of *Proceedings of Machine Learning Research*, pages 1223–1232. PMLR.

Arman Cohan, Franck Dernoncourt, Doo Soon Kim, Trung Bui, Seokhwan Kim, Walter Chang, and Nazli Goharian. 2018. A discourse-aware attention model for abstractive summarization of long documents. In *Proceedings of the 2018 Conference of the North American Chapter of the Association for Computational Linguistics: Human Language Technologies, Volume 2 (Short Papers)*, pages 615–621, New Orleans, Louisiana. Association for Computational Linguistics.

Jacob Devlin, Ming-Wei Chang, Kenton Lee, and Kristina Toutanova. 2019. BERT: Pre-training of deep bidirectional transformers for language understanding. In *Proceedings of the 2019 Conference of the North American Chapter of the Association for Computational Linguistics: Human Language Technologies, Volume 1 (Long and Short Papers)*, pages 4171–4186, Minneapolis, Minnesota. Association for Computational Linguistics.

Yuwei Fang, Shuohang Wang, Yichong Xu, Ruochen Xu, Siqi Sun, Chenguang Zhu, and Michael Zeng. 2022. Leveraging knowledge in multilingual commonsense reasoning. In *Findings of the Association for Computational Linguistics: ACL 2022*, pages 3237–3246, Dublin, Ireland. Association for Computational Linguistics.

Tianyu Gao, Xingcheng Yao, and Danqi Chen. 2021. SimCSE: Simple contrastive learning of sentence embeddings. In *Proceedings of the 2021 Conference on Empirical Methods in Natural Language Processing*, pages 6894–6910, Online and Punta Cana, Dominican Republic. Association for Computational Linguistics.

Ryan Kiros, Yukun Zhu, Russ R Salakhutdinov, Richard Zemel, Raquel Urtasun, Antonio Torralba, and Sanja Fidler. 2015. Skip-thought vectors. In *Advances in Neural Information Processing Systems*, volume 28. Curran Associates, Inc.

Huan Yee Koh, Jiaxin Ju, He Zhang, Ming Liu, and Shirui Pan. 2022. How far are we from robust long abstractive summarization? In *Proceedings of the 2022 Conference on Empirical Methods in Natural Language Processing*, pages 2682–2698, Abu Dhabi, United Arab Emirates. Association for Computational Linguistics.

Wojciech Kryscinski, Bryan McCann, Caiming Xiong, and Richard Socher. 2020. Evaluating the factual consistency of abstractive text summarization. In

Proceedings of the 2020 Conference on Empirical Methods in Natural Language Processing (EMNLP), pages 9332–9346, Online. Association for Computational Linguistics.

Mike Lewis, Yinhan Liu, Naman Goyal, Marjan Ghazvininejad, Abdelrahman Mohamed, Omer Levy, Veselin Stoyanov, and Luke Zettlemoyer. 2020. BART: Denoising sequence-to-sequence pre-training for natural language generation, translation, and comprehension. In *Proceedings of the 58th Annual Meeting of the Association for Computational Linguistics*, pages 7871–7880, Online. Association for Computational Linguistics.

Jingzhou Liu, Dominic J. D. Hughes, and Yiming Yang. 2021. Unsupervised extractive text summarization with distance-augmented sentence graphs. In *Proceedings of the 44th International ACM SIGIR Conference on Research and Development in Information Retrieval*, SIGIR '21, page 2313–2317, New York, NY, USA. Association for Computing Machinery.

Mausam Mausam. 2016. Open information extraction systems and downstream applications. In *Proceedings of the twenty-fifth international joint conference on artificial intelligence*, pages 4074–4077.

Joshua Maynez, Shashi Narayan, Bernd Bohnet, and Ryan McDonald. 2020. On faithfulness and factuality in abstractive summarization. In *Proceedings of the 58th Annual Meeting of the Association for Computational Linguistics*, pages 1906–1919, Online. Association for Computational Linguistics.

Rada Mihalcea and Paul Tarau. 2004. TextRank: Bringing order into text. In *Proceedings of the 2004 Conference on Empirical Methods in Natural Language Processing*, pages 404–411, Barcelona, Spain. Association for Computational Linguistics.

Ramesh Nallapati, Bowen Zhou, Caglar Gulcehre, Bing Xiang, et al. 2016. Abstractive text summarization using sequence-to-sequence RNNs and beyond. In *Proceedings of the 20th SIGNLL Conference on Computational Natural Language Learning*, pages 280–290, Berlin, Germany. Association for Computational Linguistics.

Long Ouyang, Jeffrey Wu, Xu Jiang, Diogo Almeida, Carroll Wainwright, Pamela Mishkin, Chong Zhang, Sandhini Agarwal, Katarina Slama, Alex Ray, et al. 2022. Training language models to follow instructions with human feedback. *Advances in Neural Information Processing Systems*, 35:27730–27744.

Vishakh Padmakumar and He He. 2021. Unsupervised extractive summarization using pointwise mutual information. In *Proceedings of the 16th Conference of the European Chapter of the Association for Computational Linguistics: Main Volume*, pages 2505–2512.

Colin Raffel, Noam Shazeer, Adam Roberts, Katherine Lee, Sharan Narang, Michael Matena, Yanqi Zhou, Wei Li, and Peter J. Liu. 2020. Exploring the limits of transfer learning with a unified text-to-text transformer. *Journal of Machine Learning Research*, 21:140:1–140:67.

John W. Ratcliff and David E. Metzener. 1988. Pattern matching: The gestalt approach. In *Dr. Dobb's Journal of Software Tools*, volume 13, pages "46, 47, 59–51, 68–72". j-DDJ.

Abigail See, Peter J. Liu, and Christopher D. Manning. 2017. Get to the point: Summarization with pointer-generator networks. In *Proceedings of the 55th Annual Meeting of the Association for Computational Linguistics (Volume 1: Long Papers)*, pages 1073–1083, Vancouver, Canada. Association for Computational Linguistics.

Jiwei Tan, Xiaojun Wan, and Jianguo Xiao. 2017. Abstractive document summarization with a graph-based attentional neural model. In *Proceedings of the 55th Annual Meeting of the Association for Computational Linguistics (Volume 1: Long Papers)*, pages 1171–1181, Vancouver, Canada. Association for Computational Linguistics.

Yaushian Wang and Hung-Yi Lee. 2018. Learning to encode text as human-readable summaries using generative adversarial networks. In *Proceedings of the 2018 Conference on Empirical Methods in Natural Language Processing*, pages 4187–4195, Brussels, Belgium. Association for Computational Linguistics.

Jiacheng Xu, Shrey Desai, and Greg Durrett. 2020a. Understanding neural abstractive summarization models via uncertainty. In *Proceedings of the 2020 Conference on Empirical Methods in Natural Language Processing (EMNLP)*, pages 6275–6281, Online. Association for Computational Linguistics.

Shusheng Xu, Xingxing Zhang, Yi Wu, Furu Wei, and Ming Zhou. 2020b. Unsupervised extractive summarization by pre-training hierarchical transformers. In *Findings of the Association for Computational Linguistics: EMNLP 2020*, pages 1784–1795, Online. Association for Computational Linguistics.

Ziyi Yang, Chenguang Zhu, Robert Gmyr, Michael Zeng, Xuedong Huang, and Eric Darve. 2020. TED: A pretrained unsupervised summarization model with theme modeling and denoising. In *Findings of the Association for Computational Linguistics: EMNLP 2020*, pages 1865–1874, Online. Association for Computational Linguistics.

Jingqing Zhang, Yao Zhao, Mohammad Saleh, and Peter J. Liu. 2020. Pegasus: Pre-training with extracted gap-sentences for abstractive summarization. In *Proceedings of the 37th International Conference on Machine Learning*, ICML'20. JMLR.org.

Hao Zheng and Mirella Lapata. 2019. Sentence centrality revisited for unsupervised summarization. In *Proceedings of the 57th Annual Meeting of the Association for Computational Linguistics*, Florence, Italy. Association for Computational Linguistics.

Edu-ConvoKit
An Open-Source Library for Education Conversation Data

Rose E. Wang
Stanford University
rewang@cs.stanford.edu

Dorottya Demszky
Stanford University
ddemszky@stanford.edu

Abstract

We introduce Edu-ConvoKit, an open-source library designed to handle pre-processing, annotation and analysis of conversation data in education. Resources for analyzing education conversation data are scarce, making the research challenging to perform and therefore hard to access. We address these challenges with Edu-ConvoKit. Edu-ConvoKit is open-source[1], pip-installable[2], with comprehensive documentation[3]. Our demo video is available at: https://youtu.be/zdcI839vAko?si-h9qln176ucSuXb8-. We include additional resources, such as Colab applications of Edu-ConvoKit to three diverse education datasets[4] and a repository of Edu-ConvoKit-related papers[5].

1 Introduction

Language is central to educational interactions, ranging from classroom instruction to tutoring sessions to peer discussions. It offers rich insights into the teaching and learning process that go beyond the current, oversimplified view of relying on standardized test outcomes (Wentzel, 1997; Pianta et al., 2003; Robinson, 2022; Wentzel, 2022). The landscape of natural language processing (NLP) and education is rapidly evolving, with an increase of open-sourced education conversation datasets (e.g., from Caines et al. (2020); Stasaski et al. (2020); Suresh et al. (2021a); Demszky and Hill (2023); Wang et al. (2023a,c); Holt (2023)), heightened interest manifesting in academic venues (e.g., NeurIPS GAIED (2023), Building Educational Applications at *ACL Conferences BEA (2023), and education conferences hosting NLP tracks[6]), alongside courses dedicated to this field (e.g., Stanford's NLP and Education course CS293[7]).

Challenges and consequences. While the interest in this interdisciplinary field is growing, our conversations with education data science and NLP researchers both in academia and industry have surfaced several challenges that hinder research progress. First, there is **no centralized tool or resource** that assists in analyzing education data, or helps researchers understand different tradeoffs in methods. For example, researchers expressed uncertainty about pre-processing the data, such as "the best way to anonymize the data to protect the privacy of students and teachers". They also wanted an "easily accessible collection of language tools and models that can detect insightful things." The lack of these tools and resources makes the research harder to conduct. Second, there is a **high learning curve for performing computational analyses**. For example, many education researchers are trained in qualitative research; even though they want to use computational tools for quantitative analyses at scale, they often do not know how to start or have the readily available compute to try out the tools.

Our system. Our work introduces Edu-ConvoKit to address these challenges. Edu-ConvoKit is designed to facilitate and democratize the study of education conversation data. It is a modular, end-to-end pipeline for **A.** pre-processing, **B.** annotating, and **C.** analyzing education conversation data, illustrated in Figure 1. Specifically, Edu-ConvoKit

- **Supports pre-processing** for education con-

[1] https://github.com/stanfordnlp/edu-convokit

[2] https://pypi.org/project/edu-convokit/

[3] https://edu-convokit.readthedocs.io/en/latest/

[4] https://github.com/stanfordnlp/edu-convokit?tab=readme-ov-file#datasets-with-edu-convokit

[5] https://github.com/stanfordnlp/edu-convokit/blob/main/papers.md

[6] The International Conference on Learning Analytics and Knowledge (LAK), Education Data Mining (EDM), and Artificial Intelligence in Education (AIED).

[7] https://web.stanford.edu/class/cs293/

Proceedings of the 2024 Conference of the North American Chapter of the Association for Computational Linguistics: Human Language Technologies (Volume 3: System Demonstrations), pages 61–69
June 16-21, 2024 ©2024 Association for Computational Linguistics

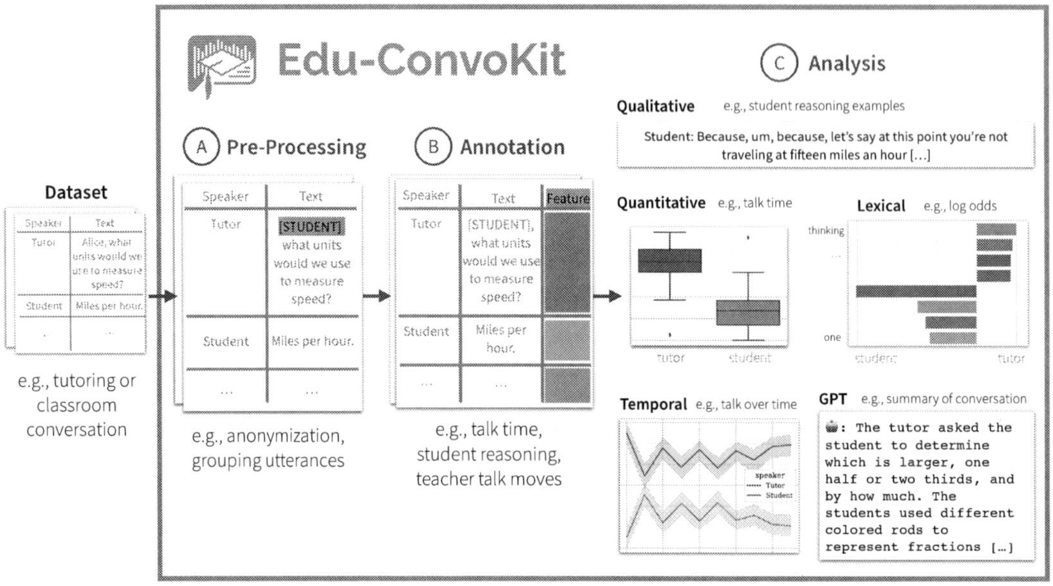

Figure 1: **Overview of Edu-ConvoKit.** Edu-ConvoKit is designed to facilitate the study of conversation data in education. It is a modular, end-to-end pipeline for **A.** pre-processing, **B.** annotating, and **C.** analyzing education conversation data. As additional resources, the toolkit includes Colab notebooks applying Edu-ConvoKit to three existing, large education datasets and a centralized database of Edu-ConvoKit papers. This toolkit aims to enhance the accessibility and reproducibility of NLP and education research.

versation datasets, such as automatically de-identifying conversations;

- **Hosts a collection of language tools and models for annotation**, ranging from traditional (e.g., talk time) to neural measures (e.g., classifying student reasoning); and
- **Automates several analyses** used in NLP and education research, ranging from qualitative analyses, temporal analyses and GPT-powered analyses (e.g., on summarizing transcripts).

To demonstrate its flexible design and ensure its accessibility regardless of compute infrastructure, we created **Colab notebooks of Edu-ConvoKit applied to three diverse education conversation datasets** in mathematics (Demszky and Hill, 2023; Suresh et al., 2021b; Holt, 2023). We additionally created **a centralized database of research projects** that have either used Edu-ConvoKit or have features integrated in the toolkit. We invite the community to contribute to the toolkit and collectively push the boundaries of education conversation research!

2 Related Works

2.1 Advancing NLP through Toolkits

The NLP community has benefited greatly from the public availability of general toolkits, which standardize the way data is transformed, annotated and analyzed. Examples include NLTK (Bird, 2006), StanfordNLP (Qi et al., 2019), spaCy (Honnibal et al., 2020), or scikit-learn (Pedregosa et al., 2011). They improve the accessibility to the research and allow researchers to focus on developing new methods, rather than on re-implementing existing ones. Edu-ConvoKit shares these goals. ConvoKit (Chang et al., 2020) is a NLP package for conversational analysis and bears the most similarity to our work. A key difference between our library and ConvoKit is the data structure: Edu-ConvoKit uses a table-based dataframe structure whereas ConvoKit uses an object-based data structure akin to a dictionary. Our data structure makes manipulating data easier, e.g., performing utterance-level annotations. Additionally, our tool caters to education language research and therefore supports an array of common analyses such as qualitative analysis (Erickson et al., 1985; Corbin and Strauss, 1990; Wang et al., 2023b), quantitative evaluations (Bienkowski et al., 2012; Kim and Piech, 2023; Demszky et al., 2023), or lexical comparisons (Praharaj et al., 2021; Handa et al., 2023).

2.2 Supporting the Multifaceted Nature of Education Interaction Research

`Edu-ConvoKit` sits at the intersection of many disciplines that use different annotation and analysis tools for understanding language use in education interactions. For example, qualitative education research uses *qualitative analysis* to manually analyze the discourse, such as how students collaborate with each other (Mercer, 1996; Jackson et al., 2013; Langer-Osuna et al., 2020; Chen, 2020; Hunkins et al., 2022). Learning analytics uses *quantitative and temporal analysis* to summarize statistics in aggregate or over time (Bienkowski et al., 2012; Kim and Piech, 2023; Demszky et al., 2023, 2024). Other areas perform *lexical analyses and neural measures for annotating* education discourse features (Reilly and Schneider, 2019; Praharaj et al., 2021; Rahimi et al., 2017; Alic et al., 2022; Hunkins et al., 2022; Demszky and Hill, 2023; Reitman et al., 2023; Suresh et al., 2021a; Himmelsbach et al., 2023; Wang and Demszky, 2023). Recently, newer analysis tools powered by GPT models analyze complete conversations such as summarizing or pulling good examples of teacher instruction from the classroom transcripts (Wang and Demszky, 2023). `Edu-ConvoKit` is designed to support these forms of annotation and analysis, and unify the currently fragmented software ecosystem of this interdisciplinary research area.

3 Design Principles

`Edu-ConvoKit` follows these principles:

I. Minimalistic Data Structure. The system transforms all data inputs (e.g., csv and json files) into a dataframe. `Edu-ConvoKit` only needs the speaker and text columns to be uniquely identifiable, which is the case in the datasets we surveyed and applied `Edu-ConvoKit` to.

II. Efficient Execution. The system should be able to run on a CPU and support large-scale pre-processing, annotation and analysis.

III. Modularity. Each component of `Edu-ConvoKit` functions as an independent module. Running one module (e.g., pre-processing) should not be required for the user to run another module (e.g., annotation).

These principles enable `Edu-ConvoKit` to comprehensively incorporate different methods for preprocessing, annotation and analysis. They ensure that `Edu-ConvoKit` is effective and adaptable to various research needs.

4 Edu-ConvoKit

`Edu-ConvoKit` is organized around three entities: `PreProcessor`, `Annotator`, and `Analyzer` (see Figure 1). The following sections enumerate each entity's functionality. Please refer to the short demo video to preview `Edu-ConvoKit` in action: `https://youtu.be/zdcI839vAko?si=h9qlnl76ucSuXb8-`.

4.1 PreProcessor

The `PreProcessor` module in `Edu-ConvoKit` processes the raw data and includes several techniques standard to education and NLP research practices, such as replacing speaker names with unique identifiers, merging consecutive utterances by the same speaker, and formatting text to be human-readable. Figure 3 illustrates a simple example of text de-identification with `PreProcessor`, assuming that the researcher has access to a list of names (e.g. classroom roster) to be replaced. `PreProcessor` accounts for multiple names per individual, and users can define how each name should be replaced. This feature ensures that the context of each interaction is preserved while maintaining confidentiality of the participants.

```
# Original data
>> print(df)
    text
0   My name is Alice Wang.
1   Hey Johnson, this is John.
>> processor = TextPreProcessor()
>> df = processor.anonymize_known_names(
            df=df,
            text_column="text",
            # from e.g., classroom roster
            names=["Alice Wang", "John Paul", "Johnson P"],
            replacement_names=["[T]", "[S1]", "[S2]"])
# Processed data
>> print(df)
    text
0   My name is [T].
1   Hey [S2], this is [S1].
```

Figure 2: **Example for text de-identification.** `PreProcessor` accounts for multiple names (e.g., "John Paul" matches to "John"), and handles word boundaries (e.g., "John" does not match to "Johnson").

4.2 Annotator

`Annotator` annotates features at an *utterance-level*. It currently supports 7 types of features, ranging from traditional to neural measures of educational discourse. The features follow the original implementations of cited works and the neural measures are models hosted on HuggingFace hub. Notably, `Annotator` performs annotation with a single function call. The following sections describe these features, using Figure 3 as the running example.

```
# Example for Annotation module from the Amber dataset
>> print(df)
     speaker   text
…
47   Student   Miles, and then at B, it stops for they stop for […]
48   Tutor     Cool. that's I understand how you're thinking […]
49   Student   Cause the graph is, it says distance. This is fifty […]
50   Tutor     Okay and C to D, I'm sorry, D to E is Kirby. Does […]
…
```

Figure 3: **Example for `Annotator`**.

Talk Time. Talk time measures the amount of speaker talk by word count and timestamps (if provided in the dataset). This feature quantifies the participation of both teachers/tutors and students, offering insights into classroom dynamics (TeachFX; Jensen et al., 2020; Demszky et al., 2024).

```
>> annotator = Annotator()
>> df = annotator.get_talktime(df=df, text_column="text",
output_column="talktime", analysis_unit="words")
>> print(df)
     speaker   text                                                   talktime
…
47   Student   Miles, and then at B, it stops for they stop for […]     48
48   Tutor     Cool. that's I understand how you're thinking […]        27
49   Student   Cause the graph is, it says distance. This is fifty […]  56
50   Tutor     Okay and C to D, I'm sorry, D to E is Kirby. Does […]    31
…
```

Math Density. Math density measures the number of math terms used in an utterance, where the dictionary of math terms was collected in prior work by mathematics education researchers (Himmelsbach et al., 2023). This feature provides a quantitative measure of mathematical content in the dialogue.

```
>> df = annotator.get_math_density(df=df, text_column="text", output_column="math_d")
>> print(df)
     speaker   text                                                   math_d
…
47   Student   Miles, and then at B, it stops for they stop for […]     2
48   Tutor     Cool. that's I understand how you're thinking […]        2
49   Student   Cause the graph is, it says distance. This is fifty […]  3
50   Tutor     Okay and C to D, I'm sorry, D to E is Kirby. Does […]    0
…
```

Student Reasoning. The student reasoning annotation measures whether a given student utterance provides a mathematical explanation for an idea, procedure or solution (Demszky and Hill, 2023; Hill et al., 2008). The model is a finetuned RoBERTa classifier (Liu et al., 2019) on instances of student reasoning from elementary math classroom transcripts. `Edu-ConvoKit` follows the original implementation from Demszky and Hill (2023), ensuring fidelity to prior research: `Annotator` only label utterances that are at least 8 words long based on word boundaries; all other utterances are annotated as NaN. Furthermore, users can also easily specify which speakers to annotate for, such as to only annotate the student speakers as shown in the example below.

```
>> df = annotator.get_student_reasoning(
          df=df,
          text_column="text",
          output_column="reasoning",
          # We only want to run this on *student* utterances.
          # We can do this by specifying the speaker column & valid speaker names.
          speaker_column="speaker",
          speaker_value="Student")
>> print(df)
     speaker   text                                                   reasoning
…
47   Student   Miles, and then at B, it stops for they stop for […]     0.0
48   Tutor     Cool. that's I understand how you're thinking […]        NaN
49   Student   Cause the graph is, it says distance. This is fifty […]  1.0
50   Tutor     Okay and C to D, I'm sorry, D to E is Kirby. Does […]    NaN
…
```

Focusing Questions. The focusing question annotation capture questions that attend to what the student is thinking and presses them to communicate their thoughts clearly (Leinwarnd et al., 2014; Alic et al., 2022). The model is a finetuned RoBERTa classifier (Liu et al., 2019) on instances of teacher focusing questions from elementary math classroom transcripts:

```
>> df = annotator.get_focusing_questions(
          df=df,
          text_column="text",
          output_column="focusing_q",
          # This only applies to the tutor.
          speaker_column="speaker",
          speaker_value="Tutor")
>> print(df)
     speaker   text                                                   focusing_q
…
47   Student   Miles, and then at B, it stops for they stop for […]     NaN
48   Tutor     Cool. that's I understand how you're thinking […]        0.0
49   Student   Cause the graph is, it says distance. This is fifty […]  NaN
50   Tutor     Okay and C to D, I'm sorry, D to E is Kirby. Does […]    0.0
…
```

Teacher Accountable Talk Moves. Teacher accountable talk moves capture the teacher's strategies to promote equitable participation in classrooms (Suresh et al., 2021b; Jacobs et al., 2022), based on the Accountable Talk framework (O'Connor et al., 2015). It is a finetuned ELECTRA 7-way classifier (Clark et al., 2020) where: 0: No Talk Move Detected, 1: Keeping Everyone Together, 2: Getting Students to Related to Another Student's Idea, 3: Restating, 4: Revoicing, 5: Pressing for Accuracy, 6: Pressing for Reasoning.

```
>> df = annotator.get_teacher_talk_moves(
          df=df,
          text_column="text",
          output_column="ttm",
          # We only want to run this on *tutor* utterances.
          # We can do this by specifying the speaker column & valid speaker names.
          speaker_column="speaker",
          speaker_value="Tutor")
>> print(df)
     speaker   text                                                   ttm
…
47   Student   Miles, and then at B, it stops for they stop for […]     NaN
48   Tutor     Cool. that's I understand how you're thinking […]        0.0
49   Student   Cause the graph is, it says distance. This is fifty […]  NaN
50   Tutor     Okay and C to D, I'm sorry, D to E is Kirby. Does […]    1.0
…
```

Student Accountable Talk Moves. Analogous to the teacher talk moves, the student accountable talk moves are student discussion strategies to promote equitable participation in a rigorous classroom learning environment (Suresh et al., 2021b; Jacobs et al., 2022). It is also a finetuned ELECTRA classifier for 5 classes: 0: No Talk Move Detected, 1: Relating to Another Student, 2: Asking for More Information, 3: Making a Claim, 4: Providing Evidence or Reasoning.

```
>> df = annotator.get_student_talk_moves(
        df=df,
        text_column="text",
        output_column="stm",
        # We only want to run this on *student* utterances.
        # We can do this by specifying the speaker column & valid speaker names.
        speaker_column="speaker",
        speaker_value="Student")
>> print(df)
   speaker  text                                                  ttm
…
47 Student  Miles, and then at B, it stops for they stop for […]   4.0
48 Tutor    Cool. that's I understand how you're thinking […]      NaN
49 Student  Cause the graph is, it says distance. This is fifty […] 4.0
50 Tutor    Okay and C to D, I'm sorry, D to E is Kirby. Does […]  NaN
…
```

Conversational Uptake. Conversational uptake measures how teachers build on the contributions of students (Demszky et al., 2021). It is a BERT model fine tuned with a self-supervised training objective (next utterance prediction), on an elementary math classroom dataset (Demszky and Hill, 2023), Switchboard (Godfrey and Holliman, 1997) and a tutoring dataset. `Annotator` annotates utterances according to the original implementation: It can label teacher utterances following substantive student utterances that are at least 5 words long, such as in the example below.

```
>> df = annotator.get_uptake(
        df=df,
        text_column="text",
        output_column="uptake",
        # We want to annotate the tutor's uptake of student utterances.
        # So we want instances where the student first speaks, then the tutor.
        speaker_column="speaker",
        speaker1="Student",
        speaker2="Tutor")
>> print(df)
   speaker  text                                                  uptake
…
47 Student  Miles, and then at B, it stops for they stop for […]   NaN
48 Tutor    Cool. that's I understand how you're thinking […]      0.0
49 Student  Cause the graph is, it says distance. This is fifty […] NaN
50 Tutor    Okay and C to D, I'm sorry, D to E is Kirby. Does […]  1.0
…
```

4.3 `Analyzer`

`Edu-ConvoKit` supports several modules that cover common analyses in education conversation research. In general, each module is exposed by three methods: `plot` for plotting, `print` for displaying results in the terminal, and `report` for outputting results as text. There are multiple data entry points for the `Analyzer` such as a single or multiple transcripts, or a data directory. The following sections describe these modules, assuming that the variable `DATA_DIR` is a directory of annotated transcripts.

`QualitativeAnalyzer`. This module enables researchers to view annotation examples. For example, we can easily view positive examples of student reasoning below. This module has other features, such as additionally showing the previous and subsequent lines around the examples; please refer to our documentation for all features.

```
>> analyzer = QualitativeAnalyzer(DATA_DIR)
>> analyzer.print_examples(
        speaker_column="speaker",
        text_column="text",
        # We want to see positive examples of student reasoning
        feature_column="reasoning",
        feature_value=1.0
)
student_reasoning: 1.0
>> Student: Cause the graph is, it says distance. This is fifty Mi. It could, for
example, this could be fifty. Let's say, Um, that's fifty miles. This could also be
fifty miles. It's distance traveler. It doesn't matter how you're Um, it's not. It
doesn't matter how you're um, um, traveling. You're still traveling, Um, fifty miles.
…
```

`QuantitativeAnalyzer`. This module reports the quantitative summaries of the annotation results. Users can also flexibly group and use different representations, such as grouping by speaker or displaying the values as percentages as shown below.

```
>> analyzer = QuantitativeAnalyzer(DATA_DIR)
>> analyzer.plot_statistics(speaker_column="speaker", feature_column="talktime")
```

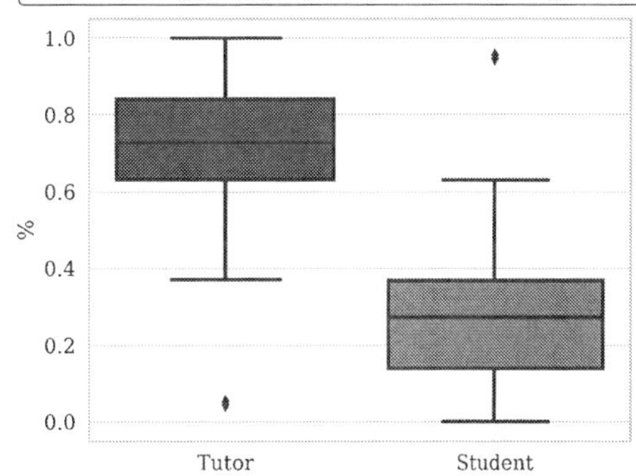

`LexicalAnalyzer`. This module reports language patterns on the word-level. It can report n-gram frequency and weighted log-odds analysis from Section 3.4 of Monroe et al. (2008), which reports which n-grams are more likely to be uttered by one group over the other given a prior distribution of words; currently, the priors are defined based on the provided dataset, however we hope to flexibly handle any user-provided priors in the future. Below is an example of the log-odds analysis that shows the top 5 n-grams in the student's utterances over the tutor's.

```
>> analyzer = LexicalAnalyzer()
>> df1 = df[df["speaker"] == "Student"]
>> df2 = df[df["speaker"] == "Tutor"]
>> analyzer.plot_logodds(df1=df1, df2=df2, text_column1="text", text_column2="text",
topk=5)
```

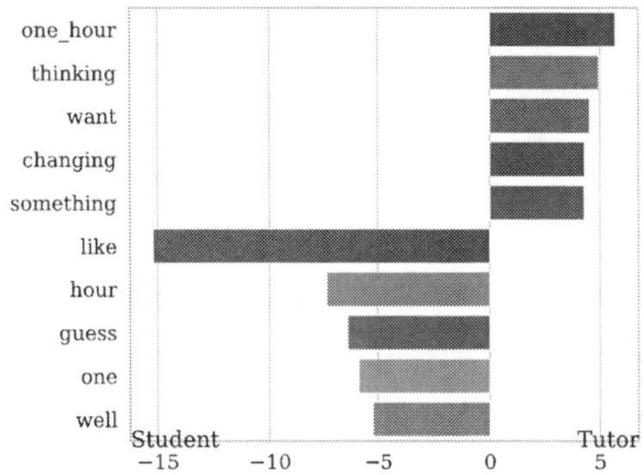

`TemporalAnalyzer`. This module provides a time analysis of the annotations over the course of the conversation(s). Similar to `QuantitativeAnalyzer`, it can group and report the data in different ways. An important variable to this module is `num_bins`, which indicates how many time bins the transcript should be split into; currently, the split is based on transcript lines, however we hope to support other split criteria in the future such as by word count. Below is an example with speaker talk time.

```
>> analyzer = TemporalAnalyzer(DATA_DIR)
>> analyzer.plot_statistics(speaker_column="speaker", feature_column="talktime",
 num_bins=10)
```

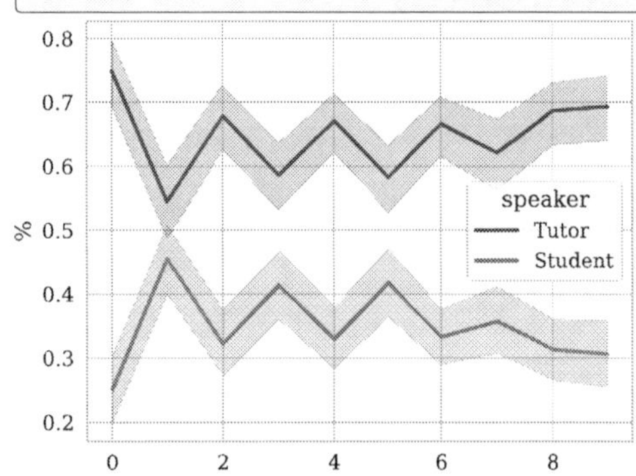

`GPTConversationAnalyzer`. This module uses GPT models accessible through the OpenAI API to analyze on the conversation-level with natural language. Some prompts include summarizing the conversation (below example) or generating suggestions to the teacher/tutor on eliciting more student reasoning from Wang and Demszky (2023). The module has additional features (not shown) such as automatically truncating the transcript if it surpasses the model's context length, adding line numbers to the conversation or altering how the lines should be formatted.

```
>> analyzer = GPTConversationAnalyzer()
>> prompt, response = analyzer.run_prompt(df=df, prompt_name="summarize",
speaker_column="speaker", text_column="text", model="gpt-4")
>> print(response)
In this conversation, a tutor guides a student through a virtual learning platform,
explaining various tools and how to use them, such as the drawing tool, text box, and
erasure function. They then apply these tools to a math problem about measuring the
distance and time taken from Providence to Newark. The student engages in problem-
solving, plotting points on a map, and interpreting a graph, while the tutor
encourages thinking aloud and self-questioning. The tutor emphasizes understanding
the relationship between variables like distance, time, and speed. [...]
```

5 Additional Resources: Basic Tutorials, Case Studies, and Paper Repository

We create a suite of introductory tutorials and case studies of `Edu-ConvoKit` as Colab notebooks (link). To demonstrate its wide applicability and generalizable design structure, we apply `Edu-ConvoKit` to three different education transcript datasets developed by different authors: NCTE, an elementary school classroom dataset (Demszky and Hill, 2023); TalkMoves, a K-12 classroom dataset (Suresh et al., 2021b); and Amber, a one-on-one 8th-9th grade tutoring dataset (Holt, 2023). For space reasons, we omit the findings of the case studies in this paper, but they can be found in our GitHub repository. To centralize research efforts, we additionally contribute a paper repository that include papers that have used `Edu-ConvoKit` or have features incorporated into `Edu-ConvoKit` (link).

6 Conclusion

We introduce `Edu-ConvoKit`, an open-source library designed to democratize and enhance the study of education conversation data. Implemented in Python and easily accessible via GitHub and pip installation, it offers a user-friendly interface complete with extensive documentation, tutorials, applications to three diverse education datasets, and paper repository resource. Based on extensive research experience, it incorporates best practices for pre-processing data and a series of different annotation measures grounded in prior literature, such as measuring student reasoning and talk time. It additionally supports several analysis modules, such as temporal analyses (e.g., talk time ratios), lexical analyses (e.g., word usage) and GPT-powered analyses (e.g., summarization). Fostering a collaborative environment through its open-source nature, `Edu-ConvoKit` and its resources unify research efforts in this exciting interdisciplinary field to improve teaching and learning.

7 Limitations

There are limitations to `Edu-ConvoKit` which we intend on addressing in future versions of the library. Some of the current limitations include: `Edu-ConvoKit` does not support transcription; it does not support connecting the language analyses to metadata, such as demographic data or learning outcomes, such as in Demszky and Hill (2023); it only supports English-focused annotation methods; many of its annotation models were trained on elementary and middle school mathematics, so they may not generalize to other domains; and `Edu-ConvoKit`'s de-identification method assumes the speakers are known. There are other existing de-identification methods that do not assume knowledge of the speaker names (one of which is also implemented in `Edu-ConvoKit`) however these methods are known to have high false-negative and false-positive rates.

8 Ethics Statement

The intended use case for this toolkit is to further education research and improve teaching and learning outcomes through the use of NLP techniques. `Edu-ConvoKit` is intended for research purposes only. `Edu-ConvoKit` uses data from existing public datasets that acquired consent from parents and teachers when applicable; for example, the NCTE dataset from Demszky and Hill (2023) acquired consent from parents and teachers for their study (Harvard's IRB #17768), and for the de-identified data to be publicly shared. As stewards of this library which builds on these datasets, we are committed to protecting the confidentiality of the individuals and ask users of our library to do the same. It is important to note that inferences drawn using `Edu-ConvoKit` may not necessarily reflect generalizable observations (e.g., the student reasoning model was trained on elementary school math, and may not yield correct insights when applied to high school math). Therefore, the analysis results should be interpreted with caution. Unacceptable use cases include any attempts to identify users or use the data for commercial gain. We additionally recommend that researchers who do use our toolkit take steps to mitigate any risks or harms to individuals that may arise.

Acknowledgements

We are thankful to Chris Manning, Omar Khattab, Ali Malik, Jim Malamut, Lucy Li for their feedback on the work. Additionally, we are thankful to Yann Hicke for their contributions to `Edu-ConvoKit`.

References

Sterling Alic, Dorottya Demszky, Zid Mancenido, Jing Liu, Heather Hill, and Dan Jurafsky. 2022. Computationally identifying funneling and focusing questions in classroom discourse. In *Proceedings of the 17th Workshop on Innovative Use of NLP for Building Educational Applications (BEA 2022)*, pages 224–233, Seattle, Washington. Association for Computational Linguistics.

BEA. 2023. Workshop on Innovative Use of NLP for Building Educational Applications . `https://sig-edu.org/bea/2024`. [Online; accessed 20-Dec-2023].

Marie Bienkowski, Mingyu Feng, and Barbara Means. 2012. Enhancing teaching and learning through educational data mining and learning analytics: An issue brief. *Office of Educational Technology, US Department of Education*.

Steven Bird. 2006. Nltk: the natural language toolkit. In *Proceedings of the COLING/ACL 2006 Interactive Presentation Sessions*, pages 69–72.

Andrew Caines, Helen Yannakoudakis, Helena Edmondson, Helen Allen, Pascual Pérez-Paredes, Bill Byrne, and Paula Buttery. 2020. The teacher-student chatroom corpus. In *Proceedings of the 9th Workshop on NLP for Computer Assisted Language Learning*, pages 10–20.

Jonathan P Chang, Caleb Chiam, Liye Fu, Andrew Z Wang, Justine Zhang, and Cristian Danescu-Niculescu-Mizil. 2020. Convokit: A toolkit for the analysis of conversations. *arXiv preprint arXiv:2005.04246*.

Gaowei Chen. 2020. A visual learning analytics (vla) approach to video-based teacher professional development: Impact on teachers' beliefs, self-efficacy, and classroom talk practice. *Computers & Education*, 144:103670.

Kevin Clark, Minh-Thang Luong, Quoc V Le, and Christopher D Manning. 2020. Electra: Pre-training text encoders as discriminators rather than generators. *arXiv preprint arXiv:2003.10555*.

Juliet M Corbin and Anselm Strauss. 1990. Grounded theory research: Procedures, canons, and evaluative criteria. *Qualitative sociology*, 13(1):3–21.

Dorottya Demszky and Heather Hill. 2023. The NCTE transcripts: A dataset of elementary math classroom transcripts. In *Proceedings of the 18th Workshop on Innovative Use of NLP for Building Educational Applications (BEA 2023)*, pages 528–538, Toronto, Canada. Association for Computational Linguistics.

Dorottya Demszky, Jing Liu, Heather C Hill, Shyamoli Sanghi, and Ariel Chung. 2023. Improving teachers' questioning quality through automated feedback: A mixed-methods randomized controlled trial in brick-and-mortar classrooms.

Dorottya Demszky, Jing Liu, Zid Mancenido, Julie Cohen, Heather Hill, Dan Jurafsky, and Tatsunori Hashimoto. 2021. Measuring conversational uptake: A case study on student-teacher interactions. In *Proceedings of the 59th Annual Meeting of the Association for Computational Linguistics and the 11th International Joint Conference on Natural Language Processing (Volume 1: Long Papers)*, pages 1638–1653, Online. Association for Computational Linguistics.

Dorottya Demszky, Rose Wang, Sean Geraghty, and Carol Yu. 2024. Does feedback on talk time increase student engagement? evidence from a randomized controlled trial on a math tutoring platform.

Frederick Erickson et al. 1985. *Qualitative methods in research on teaching*. Institute for Research on Teaching.

GAIED. 2023. NeurIPS'23 Workshop: Generative AI for Education (GAIED). `https://gaied.org/neurips2023/`. [Online; accessed 20-Dec-2023].

John J Godfrey and Edward Holliman. 1997. Switchboard-1 release 2. *Linguistic Data Consortium, Philadelphia*, 926:927.

Kunal Handa, Margarett Clapper, Jessica Boyle, Rose Wang, Diyi Yang, David Yeager, and Dorottya Demszky. 2023. "mistakes help us grow": Facilitating and evaluating growth mindset supportive language in classrooms. In *Proceedings of the 2023 Conference on Empirical Methods in Natural Language Processing*, pages 8877–8897.

Heather C Hill, Merrie L Blunk, Charalambos Y Charalambous, Jennifer M Lewis, Geoffrey C Phelps, Laurie Sleep, and Deborah Loewenberg Ball. 2008. Mathematical knowledge for teaching and the mathematical quality of instruction: An exploratory study. *Cognition and instruction*, 26(4):430–511.

Zachary Himmelsbach, Heather C. Hill, Jing Liu, and Dorottya Demszky. 2023. A quantitative study of mathematical language in classrooms. *EdWorkingPapers*.

Laurence Holt. 2023. xq-data.

Matthew Honnibal, Ines Montani, Sofie Van Landeghem, Adriane Boyd, et al. 2020. spacy: Industrial-strength natural language processing in python.

Nicholas Hunkins, Sean Kelly, and Sidney D'Mello. 2022. "beautiful work, you're rock stars!": Teacher analytics to uncover discourse that supports or undermines student motivation, identity, and belonging in classrooms. In *LAK22: 12th International Learning Analytics and Knowledge Conference*, pages 230–238.

Kara Jackson, Anne Garrison, Jonee Wilson, Lynsey Gibbons, and Emily Shahan. 2013. Exploring relationships between setting up complex tasks and opportunities to learn in concluding whole-class discussions in middle-grades mathematics instruction. *Journal for Research in Mathematics Education*, 44(4):646–682.

Jennifer Jacobs, Karla Scornavacco, Charis Harty, Abhijit Suresh, Vivian Lai, and Tamara Sumner. 2022. Promoting rich discussions in mathematics classrooms: Using personalized, automated feedback to support reflection and instructional change. *Teaching and Teacher Education*, 112:103631.

Emily Jensen, Meghan Dale, Patrick J Donnelly, Cathlyn Stone, Sean Kelly, Amanda Godley, and Sidney K D'Mello. 2020. Toward automated feedback on teacher discourse to enhance teacher learning. In *Proceedings of the 2020 chi conference on human factors in computing systems*, pages 1–13.

Yunsung Kim and Chris Piech. 2023. High-resolution course feedback: Timely feedback mechanism for instructors. In *Proceedings of the Tenth ACM Conference on Learning@ Scale*, pages 81–91.

Jennifer Langer-Osuna, Jen Munson, Emma Gargroetzi, Immanuel Williams, and Rosa Chavez. 2020. "so what are we working on?": How student authority relations shift during collaborative mathematics activity. *Educational Studies in Mathematics*, 104:333–349.

SE Leinwarnd et al. 2014. National council of teachers of mathematics. *Principles ro actions: Ensuring Mathematical success for all. Reston: VA: Author.*

Yinhan Liu, Myle Ott, Naman Goyal, Jingfei Du, Mandar Joshi, Danqi Chen, Omer Levy, Mike Lewis, Luke Zettlemoyer, and Veselin Stoyanov. 2019. Roberta: A robustly optimized bert pretraining approach. *arXiv preprint arXiv:1907.11692*.

Neil Mercer. 1996. The quality of talk in children's collaborative activity in the classroom. *Learning and instruction*, 6(4):359–377.

Burt L Monroe, Michael P Colaresi, and Kevin M Quinn. 2008. Fightin'words: Lexical feature selection and evaluation for identifying the content of political conflict. *Political Analysis*, 16(4):372–403.

Catherine O'Connor, Sarah Michaels, and Suzanne Chapin. 2015. *"Scaling Down" to Explore the Role of Talk in Learning: From District Intervention to Controlled Classroom Study*, pages 111–126.

Fabian Pedregosa, Gaël Varoquaux, Alexandre Gramfort, Vincent Michel, Bertrand Thirion, Olivier Grisel, Mathieu Blondel, Peter Prettenhofer, Ron Weiss, Vincent Dubourg, et al. 2011. Scikit-learn: Machine learning in python. *the Journal of machine Learning research*, 12:2825–2830.

Robert C Pianta, Bridget Hamre, and Megan Stuhlman. 2003. Relationships between teachers and children.

Sambit Praharaj, Maren Scheffel, Marcel Schmitz, Marcus Specht, and Hendrik Drachsler. 2021. Towards automatic collaboration analytics for group speech data using learning analytics. *Sensors*, 21(9):3156.

Peng Qi, Timothy Dozat, Yuhao Zhang, and Christopher D Manning. 2019. Universal dependency parsing from scratch. *arXiv preprint arXiv:1901.10457*.

Zahra Rahimi, Diane Litman, Richard Correnti, Elaine Wang, and Lindsay Clare Matsumura. 2017. Assessing students' use of evidence and organization in response-to-text writing: Using natural language processing for rubric-based automated scoring. *International Journal of Artificial Intelligence in Education*, 27(4):694–728.

Joseph M Reilly and Bertrand Schneider. 2019. Predicting the quality of collaborative problem solving through linguistic analysis of discourse. *International Educational Data Mining Society*.

Jason G Reitman, Charis Clevenger, Quinton Beck-White, Amanda Howard, Sierra Rose, Jacob Elick, Julianna Harris, Peter Foltz, and Sidney K D'Mello. 2023. A multi-theoretic analysis of collaborative discourse: A step towards ai-facilitated student collaborations. In *International Conference on Artificial Intelligence in Education*, pages 577–589. Springer.

Carly D Robinson. 2022. A framework for motivating teacher-student relationships. *Educational Psychology Review*, 34(4):2061–2094.

Katherine Stasaski, Kimberly Kao, and Marti A. Hearst. 2020. CIMA: A large open access dialogue dataset for tutoring. In *Proceedings of the Fifteenth Workshop on Innovative Use of NLP for Building Educational Applications*, pages 52–64, Seattle, WA, USA â†' Online. Association for Computational Linguistics.

A. Suresh, J. Jacobs, V. Lai, C. Tan, W. Ward, J. H. Martin, and T. Sumner. 2021a. Using transformers to provide teachers with personalized feedback on their classroom discourse: The talkmoves application. arxiv. Preprint.

A Suresh, J Jacobs, V Lai, C Tan, W Ward, JH Martin, and T Sumner. 2021b. Using transformers to provide teachers with personalized feedback on their classroom discourse: The talkmoves application. *Association for the Advancement of Artificial Intelligence*.

TeachFX. Teachfx.

Rose Wang and Dorottya Demszky. 2023. Is ChatGPT a good teacher coach? measuring zero-shot performance for scoring and providing actionable insights on classroom instruction. In *Proceedings of the 18th Workshop on Innovative Use of NLP for Building Educational Applications (BEA 2023)*, pages 626–667, Toronto, Canada. Association for Computational Linguistics.

Rose Wang, Pawan Wirawarn, Noah Goodman, and Dorottya Demszky. 2023a. Sight: A large annotated dataset on student insights gathered from higher education transcripts. In *Proceedings of Innovative Use of NLP for Building Educational Applications*.

Rose Wang, Pawan Wirawarn, Noah Goodman, and Dorottya Demszky. 2023b. SIGHT: A large annotated dataset on student insights gathered from higher education transcripts. In *Proceedings of the 18th Workshop on Innovative Use of NLP for Building Educational Applications (BEA 2023)*, pages 315–351, Toronto, Canada. Association for Computational Linguistics.

Rose E. Wang, Qingyang Zhang, Carly Robinson, Susanna Loeb, and Dorottya Demszky. 2023c. Step-by-step remediation of students' mathematical mistakes.

Kathryn R Wentzel. 1997. Student motivation in middle school: The role of perceived pedagogical caring. *Journal of educational psychology*, 89(3):411.

Kathryn R Wentzel. 2022. Does anybody care? conceptualization and measurement within the contexts of teacher-student and peer relationships. *Educational Psychology Review*, pages 1–36.

jp-evalb: Robust Alignment-based PARSEVAL Measures

Jungyeul Park[1] **Junrui Wang**[1] **Eunkyul Leah Jo**[2,3] **Angela Yoonseo Park**[1]
[1]Department of Linguistics, The University of British Columbia, Canada
[2]Department of Computer Science, The University of British Columbia, Canada
[3]Faculté des Sciences et Ingénierie, Sorbonne Université, France
jungyeul@mail.ubc.ca {wjr0710,eunkyul,apark03}@student.ubc.ca

Abstract

We introduce an evaluation system designed to compute PARSEVAL measures, offering a viable alternative to evalb commonly used for constituency parsing evaluation. The widely used evalb script has traditionally been employed for evaluating the accuracy of constituency parsing results, albeit with the requirement for consistent tokenization and sentence boundaries. In contrast, our approach, named jp-evalb, is founded on an alignment method. This method aligns sentences and words when discrepancies arise. It aims to overcome several known issues associated with evalb by utilizing the 'jointly preprocessed (JP)' alignment-based method. We introduce a more flexible and adaptive framework, ultimately contributing to a more accurate assessment of constituency parsing performance.

1 Introduction

For constituency parsing, whether statistical or neural, we rely on the evalb implementation[1], which implements the PARSEVAL measures (Black et al., 1991) as the standard method for evaluating parser performance. There is also a variant of the evalb_spmrl implementation specifically designed for the SPMRL shared task, allowing the evaluation to consider functional phrase labels (Seddah et al., 2013, 2014). A constituent in a hypothesis parse of a sentence is labeled as correct if it matches a constituent in the reference parse with the same non-terminal symbol and span (starting and end indexes). Despite its success in evaluating language technology, evalb faces unresolved critical issues in our discipline. evalb imposes constraints, demanding consistent tokenization and sentence boundary outcomes. Its implementation assumes equal-length gold and system files with matching terminal nodes.

In machine translation (MT), sentence alignment involves identifying corresponding sentences in two or more languages and linking sentences from one language to their corresponding counterparts in another. Sentence alignment has been a subject of study for many years, leading to the development of various algorithms. Early research in this area relied on statistical methods that used bilingual corpora to create models capturing the lexical equivalence between words in different languages. For instance, the Gale-Church algorithm, based on sentence length, was one such approach (Gale and Church, 1993). Bleualign introduced a more advanced iterative bootstrapping approach building on length-based methods (Sennrich and Volk, 2011). Earlier approaches also aimed to enhance sentence alignment methodologies by incorporating lexical correspondences, as seen in hunalign (Varga et al., 2005) or the IBM-model based lexicon translation approach (Moore, 2002). Some attempts involved the integration of linguistic knowledge, heuristics, and various scoring methods to improve efficiency, as demonstrated by vecalign (Thompson and Koehn, 2019). Word alignment methodologies are also employed to establish correspondences between words in one language and their direct translations in another. Widely used IBM models (Brown et al., 1993), along with tools like giza++ (Och and Ney, 2000, 2003) or BerkeleyAligner (Liang et al., 2006; DeNero and Klein, 2007), are capable of aligning words.

Syntactic analysis in the current field of language technology has been predominantly reliant on dependencies. Semantic parsing in its higher-level analyses often relies heavily on dependency structures as well. Therefore, dependency parsing and its evaluation method have their own advantages, such as a more direct representation of grammatical relations and often simpler parsing algorithms. However, constituency parsing maintains the hierarchical structure of a sentence, which

[1]http://nlp.cs.nyu.edu/evalb

Proceedings of the 2024 Conference of the North American Chapter of the Association for Computational Linguistics: Human Language Technologies (Volume 3: System Demonstrations), pages 70–77
June 16-21, 2024 ©2024 Association for Computational Linguistics

can still be valuable for understanding the syntactic relationships between words and phrases. Various studies on formal syntax have focused on constituent structures, such as combinatory categorial grammar (CCG) parsing (Lewis et al., 2016; Lee et al., 2016; Stanojević and Steedman, 2020; Yamaki et al., 2023) or tree-adjoining grammar (TAG) parsing (Kasai et al., 2017, 2018) (whereas CCG and TAG also inherently incorporate dependency structures). In addition, there have been ongoing studies on constituency parsing, such as the linearization parsing method (Vinyals et al., 2015; Liu and Zhang, 2017a,b; Fernández-González and Gómez-Rodríguez, 2020; Wei et al., 2020). If a method that utilizes constituent structures is designed to achieve the goal of creating an end-to-end system, it requires more robust evaluation methods for their constituent structure evaluation.

This paper builds upon our recently introduced alignment-based algorithm, for computing PARSEVAL measures (Jo et al., 2024), which offers a novel approach for calculating precision, recall, and F scores, even in cases of sentence and word mismatch. The primary objective of this paper is to replicate the outcomes generated by `evalb` during the evaluation process. This aims to achieve a comprehensive understanding of the parser's performance by addressing the previous issues of `evalb` and preserving its long-standing legacy. It includes the numbers of gold, test, matched brackets, and cross brackets, as well as precision, recall, and F scores. Furthermore, we present the number of correct POS tags and their tagging accuracy, following a methodology employed by `evalb`. Our proposed method `jp-evalb` is particularly crucial in end-to-end settings, where deviations from the gold file may arise due to variations in tokenization and sentence boundary results.

2 Detailing the `jp-evalb` Algorithm

To describe the proposed algorithms, we use the following notations for conciseness and simplicity. $\mathcal{T}_{\mathcal{L}}$ and $\mathcal{T}_{\mathcal{R}}$ introduce the entire parse trees of gold and system files, respectively. $\mathcal{T}_{\mathcal{L}}$ is a simplified notation representing $\mathcal{T}_{\mathcal{L}(l)}$, where l is the list of tokens in $\mathcal{L}$. This notation applies in the same manner to $\mathcal{R}$. $\mathcal{S}_{\mathcal{T}}$ represents a set of constituents of a tree $\mathcal{T}$, and $\mathcal{C}(\mathcal{T})$ is the total number constituents of $\mathcal{T}$. $\mathcal{C}(\mathtt{tp})$ is the number of true positive constituents where $\mathcal{S}_{\mathcal{T}_{\mathcal{L}}} \cap \mathcal{S}_{\mathcal{T}_{\mathcal{R}}}$, and we count it per aligned sentence. The presented Algorithm 1 demonstrates the pseudo-code for the new PARSEVAL measures.

Algorithm 1 Pseudo-code for `jp-evalb`

function PARSEVALMEASURES ($\mathcal{T}_{\mathcal{L}}$ and $\mathcal{T}_{\mathcal{R}}$):
  Extract the list of tokens $\mathcal{L}$ and $\mathcal{R}$ from $\mathcal{T}_{\mathcal{L}}$ and $\mathcal{T}_{\mathcal{R}}$
  $\mathcal{L}', \mathcal{R}' \leftarrow$ SENTENCEALIGNMENT($\mathcal{L}, \mathcal{R}$)
  Align trees based on $\mathcal{L}'$ and $\mathcal{R}'$ to obtain $\mathcal{T}_{\mathcal{L}'}$ and $\mathcal{T}_{\mathcal{R}'}$
  while $\mathcal{T}_{\mathcal{L}'}$ and $\mathcal{T}_{\mathcal{R}'}$ **do**
    Extract the list of tokens l and r from $\mathcal{T}_{\mathcal{L}'_i}$ and $\mathcal{T}_{\mathcal{R}'_i}$
    $l', r' \leftarrow$ WORDALIGNMENT(l, r)
    $\mathcal{S}_{\mathcal{T}_{\mathcal{L}}} \leftarrow$ GETCONSTITUENT($\mathcal{T}_{\mathcal{L}'_i(l')}, 0$)
    $\mathcal{S}_{\mathcal{T}_{\mathcal{R}}} \leftarrow$ GETCONSTITUENT($\mathcal{T}_{\mathcal{R}'_i(r')}, 0$)
    $\mathcal{C}(\mathcal{T}_{\mathcal{L}}) \leftarrow \mathcal{C}(\mathcal{T}_{\mathcal{L}}) +$ LEN($\mathcal{S}_{\mathcal{T}_{\mathcal{L}}}$)
    $\mathcal{C}(\mathcal{T}_{\mathcal{R}}) \leftarrow \mathcal{C}(\mathcal{T}_{\mathcal{R}}) +$ LEN($\mathcal{S}_{\mathcal{T}_{\mathcal{R}}}$)
    while $\mathcal{S}_{\mathcal{T}_{\mathcal{L}}}$ and $\mathcal{S}_{\mathcal{T}_{\mathcal{R}}}$ **do**
      if (LABEL, START$_{\mathcal{L}}$, END$_{\mathcal{L}}$,l'_j) = (LABEL, START$_{\mathcal{R}}$, END$_{\mathcal{R}}$,r'_j) **then**
        $\mathcal{C}(\mathtt{tp}) \leftarrow \mathcal{C}(\mathtt{tp}) + 1$
      end if
    end while
  end while
  return $\mathcal{C}(\mathcal{T}_{\mathcal{L}}), \mathcal{C}(\mathcal{T}_{\mathcal{R}})$, and $\mathcal{C}(\mathtt{tp})$

Algorithm 2 Pseudo-code for alignment

function ALIGNMENT ($\mathcal{L}, \mathcal{R}$):
  while $\mathcal{L}$ and $\mathcal{R}$ **do**
    if Matched CASES $_{(i,j)}$ **then**
      $\mathcal{L}', \mathcal{R}' \leftarrow \mathcal{L}' + \mathcal{L}_i, \mathcal{R}' + \mathcal{R}_j$
    else
      while $\neg$(Matched CASES $_{(i+1,j+1)}$ **do**
        if LEN($\mathcal{L}_i$) < LEN($\mathcal{R}_j$) **then**
          $L' \leftarrow L' + \mathcal{L}_i$
          $i \leftarrow i + 1$
        else
          $R' \leftarrow R' + \mathcal{R}_j$
          $j \leftarrow j + 1$
        end if
      end while
      $\mathcal{L}', \mathcal{R}' \leftarrow \mathcal{L}' + L', \mathcal{R}' + R'$
    end if
  end while
  return $\mathcal{L}', \mathcal{R}'$

In the first stage, we extract leaves $\mathcal{L}$ and $\mathcal{R}$ from the parse trees and align sentences to obtain $\mathcal{L}'$ and $\mathcal{R}'$ using the sentence alignment algorithm. Algorithm 2 shows the generic pattern-matching approach of the alignment algorithm where sentence and word alignment can be applied. We define the following two cases for matched CASES$_{(i,j)}$ of sentence alignment:

$$\mathcal{L}_{i(\not\sqcup)} = \mathcal{R}_{j(\not\sqcup)} \quad (1)$$

$$(\mathcal{L}_{i(\not\sqcup)} \simeq \mathcal{R}_{j(\not\sqcup)}) \wedge (\mathcal{L}_{i+1(\not\sqcup)} = \mathcal{R}_{j+1(\not\sqcup)} \vee \mathcal{L}_{i+1(\not\sqcup)} \simeq \mathcal{R}_{j+1(\not\sqcup)}) \quad (2)$$

where we examine whether $\mathcal{L}_i$ is similar to or equal ($\simeq$) to $\mathcal{R}_j$ based on the condition that the ratio of edit distance to the entire character length is less than 0.1 in (2). While the necessity of sentence alignment is rooted in a common phenomenon in cross-language tasks such as machine translation, the intralingual alignment between gold and system sentences does not share the same necessity because $\mathcal{L}$ and $\mathcal{R}$ are identical sentences that only differ in sentence boundaries and token. A notation $\not\sqcup$ is introduced to represent spaces that are removed during sentence alignment when comparing $\mathcal{L}i$ and $\mathcal{R}_j$, irrespective of their tokenization results. If there is a mismatch due to differences in sentence boundaries, the algorithm accumulates the sentences until the next pair of sentences represented as CASE n $(i+1, j+1)$, is matched.

In the next stage of Algorithm 1, we align trees based on $\mathcal{L}'$ and $\mathcal{R}'$ to obtain $\mathcal{T}_{\mathcal{L}'}$ and $\mathcal{T}_{\mathcal{R}'}$. By iterating through $\mathcal{T}_{\mathcal{L}'}$ and $\mathcal{T}_{\mathcal{R}'}$, we conduct word alignment and compare pairs of sets of constituents for each corresponding pair of $\mathcal{T}_{\mathcal{L}'_i}$ and $\mathcal{T}_{\mathcal{R}'_j}$. The word alignment algorithm adopts a logic similar to sentence alignment. It involves the accumulation of words in l' and r' under the condition that pairs of l_i and r_j do not match, often attributed to tokenization mismatches. Here, we assume interchangeability between notations of sentence alignment ($\mathcal{L}$) and word alignment (l_i). We define the following two cases for matched CASES$_{(i,j)}$ of word alignment:

$$l_i = r_j \tag{3}$$

$$(l_i \neq r_j) \wedge (l_{i+1} = r_{j+1}) \tag{4}$$

When deciding whether to accumulate the token from l_{i+1} or r_{j+1} in the case of a word mismatch, we base our decision on the following condition, rather than a straightforward comparison between the lengths of the current tokens l_i and r_j: $(\text{LEN}(l) - \text{LEN}(l_{0..i})) > (\text{LEN}(r) - \text{LEN}(r_{0..j}))$

Finally, we extract a set of constituents, a straightforward procedure for obtaining constituents from a given tree, which includes the label name, start index, end index, and a list of tokens. The current proposed method utilizes simple pattern matching for sentence and word alignment, operating under the assumption that the gold and system sentences are the same, with minimal potential for morphological mismatches. This differs from sentence and word alignment in machine translation. MT usually relies on recursive editing and EM algorithms due to the inherent difference between source and target languages.

3 Word and Sentence Mismatches

Word mismatch We have observed that the expression of contractions varies significantly, resulting in inherent challenges related to word mismatches. As the number of contractions and symbols to be converted in a language is finite, we composed an exception list for our system to capture such cases for each language to facilitate the word alignment process between gold and system sentences. In the following example, we achieve perfect precision and recall of 5/5 for both because their constituent trees are exactly matched, regardless of any mismatched words. If the word mismatch example is not in the exception list, we perform the word alignment. We can still achieve perfect precision and recall (5/5 for both) without the word mismatch exception list because their constituent trees can be exactly matched based on the word-alignment of $\{^{1.0}ca\ ^{1.1}n't\}$ and $\{^{1.0}can\ ^{1.1}not\}$ (Figure 1a).

gold	^{0}*This*	$^{1.0}$*ca*	$^{1.1}$*n't*	^{2}*be*	^{3}*right*
system	^{0}*this*	$^{1.0}$*can*	$^{1.1}$*not*	^{2}*be*	^{3}*right*

The effectiveness of the word alignment approach remains intact even for morphological mismatches where "morphological segmentation is not the inverse of concatenation" (Tsarfaty et al., 2012), such as in morphologically rich languages. For example, we trace back to the sentence in Hebrew described in Tsarfaty et al. (2012) as a word mismatch example caused by morphological analyses:

gold	^{0}*B* 'in'	$^{1.0}$*H* 'the'	$^{1.1}$*CL* 'shadow'	^{2}*FL* 'of'	^{3}*HM* 'them'	$^{4.0}$*H* 'the'	$^{4.1}$*NEIM* 'pleasant'
system	^{0}*B* 'in'	^{1}*CL* 'shadow'		^{2}*FL* 'of'	^{3}*HM* 'them'	^{4}*HNEIM* 'made-pleasant'	

Pairs of $\{^{1.0}H\ ^{1.1}CL,\ ^{1}CL\}$ ('the shadow') and $\{^{4.0}H\ ^{4.1}NEIM,\ ^{4}HNEIM\}$ ('the pleasant') are word-aligned using the proposed algorithm, resulting in a precision of 4/4 and recall of 4/6 (Figure 1b).

Sentence mismatch When there are sentence mismatches, they would be aligned and merged as a single tree using a dummy root node: for example, @S which can be ignored during evaluation. In the following example, we obtain precision of 5/8 and recall of 5/7 (Figure 1c).

Assumptions To address morphological analysis discrepancies in the parse tree during evaluation, we establish the following two assumptions: (i) The entire tree constituent can be considered a true positive, even if the morphological segmentation or analysis differs from the gold analysis, as long

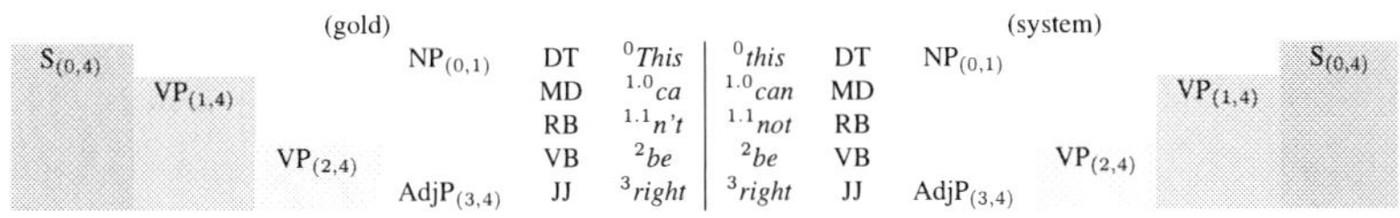

(a) Example of word mismatches

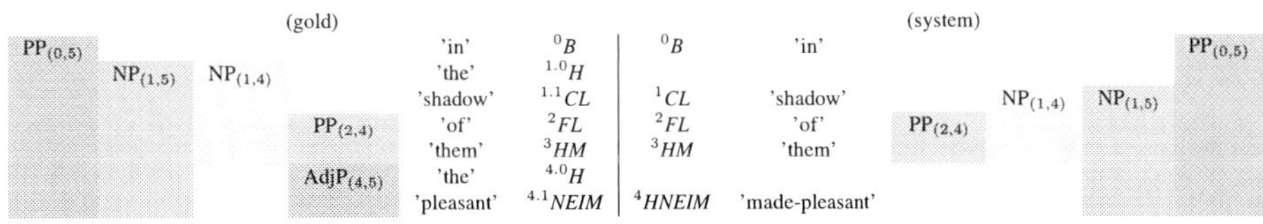

(b) Example of word mismatches with additional morphemes

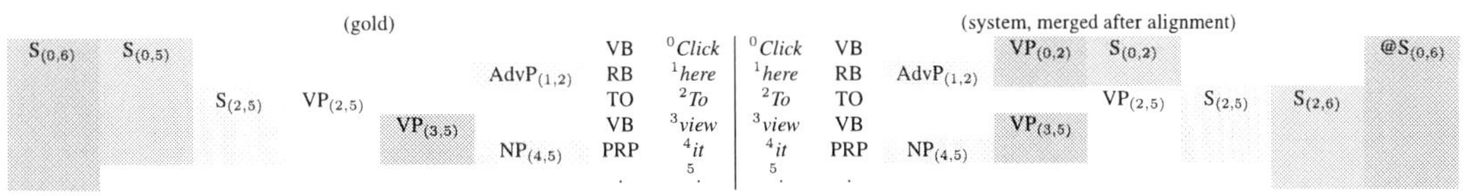

(c) Example of sentence mismatches

Figure 1: Example of word and sentence mismatches

as the two sentences (gold and system) are aligned and their root labels are the same. (ii) The subtree constituent can be considered a true positive if lexical items align in word alignment, and their phrase labels are the same.

4 Usage of `jp-evalb`

We use the following command to execute the `jp-evalb` script:

```
% python3 jp-evalb.py gold_parsed_file \
                      system_parsed_file
```

It generates the same output format as `evalb`. We provide information for each column in both `jp-evalb` and `evalb`, while highlighting their differences. We note that the `IDs` in `jp-evalb` may not be exactly the same as in `evalb` due to the proposed method performing sentence alignment before evaluation.

`Sent. ID, Sent. Len., Stat.` ID, length, and status of the provided sentence, where status 0 indicates 'OK,' status 1 implies 'skip,' and status 2 represents 'error' for `evalb`. We do not assign skip or error statuses.

`Recall, Precision` Recall and precision of constituents.

`Matched Bracket, Bracket gold, Bracket test` Assessment of matched brackets (true positives) in both the gold and test parse trees, and their numbers of constituents.

`Cross Bracket` The number of cross brackets.

`Words, Correct Tags, Tag Accuracy` Evaluation of the number of words, correct POS tags, and POS tagging accuracy.

It's important to note that the original `evalb` excludes problematic symbols and punctuation marks in the tree structure. Our results include all tokens in the given sentence, and bracket numbers reflect the actual constituents in the system and gold parse trees. Accuracy in the last column of the result is determined by comparing the correct number of POS-tagged words to the gold sentence including punctuation marks, differing from the original `evalb` which doesn't consider word counts or correct POS tags. Figure 2 visually depicts the difference in constituent lists between `jp-evalb` and `evalb`. The original `evalb` excludes punctuation marks from its consideration of constituents, resulting in our representation of word index numbers in red for `evalb`. Consequently, `evalb` displays constituents without punctuation marks and calculates POS tagging accuracy based on six word tokens. On the other hand, `jp-evalb` includes punctuation marks in constituents and evaluates POS tagging accuracy using eight tokens, which includes two punctuation marks in the sentence. We note that the inclusion of punctuation marks in the constituents does not affect the total count, as punctuation marks do not constitute a constituent by themselves.

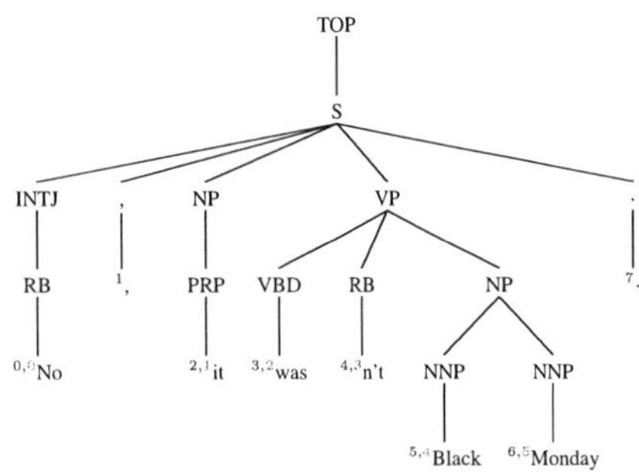

(a) Example of the parse tree

```
('S', 0, 8, "No , it was n't Black Monday .")
('INTJ', 0, 1, 'No')
('NP', 2, 3, 'it')
('VP', 3, 7, "was n't Black Monday")
('NP', 5, 7, 'Black Monday')
```

(b) List of constituents by jp-evalb

```
('S', 0, 6, "No it was n't Black Monday")
('INTJ', 0, 1, "No")
('NP', 1, 2, "it")
('VP', 2, 6, "was n't Black Monday")
('NP', 4, 6, "Black Monday")
```

(c) List of constituents by evalb

Figure 2: Difference between jp-evalb and evalb

Additionally, we offer a legacy option, -evalb, to precisely replicate evalb results. To execute the script with the evalb option, utilize the following command:

```
% python3 jp-evalb.py gold_parsed_file \
                      system_parsed_file \
                      -evalb param.prm
```

This option can utilize the default values from the COLLINS.prm file if the parameter file is not provided. It will accurately reproduce evalb results, even in cases where there are discrepancies such as Length unmatch and Words unmatch errors in evalb's output. These discrepancies are indicated by the Stat. column, which displays either 1 (skip) or 2 (error).

5 Case Studies

Section 23 of the English Penn treebank Under identical conditions where sentences and words match, the proposed method requires around 4.5 seconds for evaluating the section 23 of the Penn Treebank. On the same machine, evalb completes the task less than 0.1 seconds. We do not claim that our proposed implementation is fast or faster than evalb, recognizing the well-established differences in performance between compiled languages like C, which evalb used, and interpreted languages such as Python, which our current implementation uses. Our proposed method also introduces additional runtime for sentence and word alignment, a process not performed by evalb. We present excerpts from three result files generated by evalb and our proposed method in Figure 3. The parsed results were obtained using the PCFG-LA Berkeley parser (Petrov and Klein, 2007). It's worth noting that there may be slight variations between the two sets of results because evalb excludes constituents with specific symbols and punctuation marks during evaluation. However, as we mentioned earlier, jp-evalb can reproduce the exact same results as evalb for a legacy reason.

Sent					Mt	Br		Cr		Co	Tag
ID	L	St	Re	Pr	Br	gd	te	Br	Wd	Tg	Acc
1	8	0	100.00	100.00	5	5	5	0	8	7	87.50
2	40	0	70.97	73.33	22	31	30	7	40	40	100.00
3	31	0	95.24	95.24	20	21	21	0	31	31	100.00
4	35	0	90.48	86.36	19	21	22	2	35	35	100.00
5	26	0	86.96	86.96	20	23	23	2	26	25	96.15
.....											

(a) Example of jp-evalb results considering punctuation marks during evaluation

Sent					Mt	Br		Cr		Co	Tag
ID	L	St	Re	Pr	Br	gd	te	Br	Wd	Tg	Acc
1	8	0	100.00	100.00	5	5	5	0	6	5	83.33
2	40	0	70.97	73.33	22	31	30	7	37	37	100.00
3	31	0	95.24	95.24	20	21	21	0	26	26	100.00
4	35	0	90.48	86.36	19	21	22	2	32	32	100.00
5	26	0	86.96	86.96	20	23	23	2	24	23	95.83
.....											

(b) Example of jp-evalb results with the legacy option, which produces the exact same results as evalb

Sent					Mt	Br		Cr		Co	Tag
ID	L	St	Re	Pr	Br	gd	te	Br	Wd	Tg	Acc
1	8	0	100.00	100.00	5	5	5	0	6	5	83.33
2	40	0	70.97	73.33	22	31	30	7	37	37	100.00
3	31	0	95.24	95.24	20	21	21	0	26	26	100.00
4	35	0	90.48	86.36	19	21	22	2	32	32	100.00
5	26	0	86.96	86.96	20	23	23	2	24	23	95.83
.....											

(c) Example of the original evalb results

Figure 3: Examples of evaluation results on Section 23 of the English Penn treebank

Bug cases identified by evalb We evaluate bug cases identified by evalb. Figure 4 displays all five identified bug cases, showcasing successful evaluation without any failures. In three instances (sentences 1, 2, and 5), a few symbols are treated as words during POS tagging. This leads to discrepancies in sentence length because evalb discards symbols in the gold parse tree during evaluation. Our proposed solution involves not disregarding any problematic labels and including symbols as words during evaluation. This approach implies that POS tagging results are based on the entire token numbers. It is noteworthy that evalb's POS tagging results are rooted in the number of words, excluding symbols. The two remaining cases (sentences 3 and 4) involve actual word mismatches where trace symbols (*-*num*) are inserted into the sentences. Naturally, `evalb` cannot handle these cases due to word mismatches. However, as we explained, our proposed algorithm addresses this issue by performing word alignment after sentence alignment.

Sent ID	L	St	Re	Pr	Mt Br	Br gd	Br te	Cr Br	Wd	Co Tg	Tag Acc
1	37	0	77.27	62.96	17	22	27	5	37	30	81.08
2	21	0	69.23	60.00	9	13	15	2	21	17	80.95
3	47	0	77.78	80.00	28	36	35	4	48	43	89.58
4	26	0	33.33	35.29	6	18	17	8	27	19	70.37
5	44	0	42.31	32.35	11	26	34	17	44	33	75.00

Figure 4: Evaluation results of bug cases by `evalb`

Korean end-to-end parsing evaluation We conduct a comprehensive parsing evaluation for Korean, using system-segmented sequences as input for constituency parsing. These sequences may deviate from the corresponding gold standard sentences and tokens. We utilized the following resources for our parsing evaluation to simulate the end-to-end process: (i) A set of 148 test sentences with 4538 tokens (morphemes) from `BGAA0001` of the Korean Sejong treebank, as detailed in Kim and Park (2022). In the present experiment, all sentences have been merged into a single text block. (ii) POS tagging performed by `sjmorph.model` (Park and Tyers, 2019) for morpheme segmentation.[2] The model's pipeline includes sentence boundary detection and tokenization through morphological analysis, generating an input format for the parser. (iii) A Berkeley parser model for Korean trained on the Korean Sejong treebank (Park et al., 2016).[3]. Figure 5 presents the showcase results of end-to-end Korean constituency parsing. Given our sentence boundary detection and tokenization processes, there is a possibility of encountering sentence and word mismatches during constituency parsing evaluation. The system results show 123 sentences and 4367 morphemes because differences in sentence boundaries and tokenization results. During the evaluation, `jp-evalb` successfully aligns even in the presence of sentence and word mismatches, and subsequently, the results of constituency parsing are assessed.

[2]`https://github.com/jungyeul/sjmorph`

[3]`https://zenodo.org/records/3995084`

Sent ID	L	St	Re	Pr	Mt Br	Br gd	Br te	Cr Br	Wd	Co Tg	Tag Acc
1	28	0	85.71	85.71	18	21	21	3	29	26	89.66
2	27	0	91.30	84.00	21	23	25	2	28	25	89.29
3	33	0	88.00	88.00	22	25	25	3	35	31	88.57
4	43	0	72.73	72.73	24	33	33	7	43	40	93.02
5	18	0	69.57	84.21	16	23	19	2	19	12	63.16
.....											

Figure 5: Evaluation results of the end-to-end Korean constituency parsing

6 Previous Work

`tedeval` (Tsarfaty et al., 2012) is built upon the tree edit distance (ADD and DEL) by Bille (2005), incorporating the numbers of nonterminal nodes in the system and gold trees. `conllu_eval`[4] treats tokens and sentences as spans. In case of a mismatch in the span positions between the system and gold files on a character level, the file with a smaller start value will skip to the next token until there is no start value mismatch. Similar processes are applied to evaluating sentence boundaries. For `sparseval` (Roark et al., 2006), a head percolation table (Collins, 1999) identifies head-child relations between terminal nodes and calculates the dependency score. Unfortunately, `sparseval` is currently unavailable. `evalb`, the constituency parsing evaluation metric for nearly thirty years, despite inherent problems, has been widely used.

7 Conclusion

Despite the widespread use and acceptance of the previous PARSEVAL measure as the standard tool for constituency parsing evaluation, it faces a significant limitation by requiring specific task-oriented environments. Consequently, there is still room for a more robust and reliable evaluation approach. Various metrics have attempted to address issues related to word and sentence mismatches by employing complex tree operations or adopting dependency scoring methods. In contrast, our proposed method aligns sentences and words as a preprocessing step without altering the original PARSEVAL measures. This approach allows us to preserve the complexity of the original `evalb` implementation of PARSEVAL while introducing a linear time alignment process. Given the high compatibility of our method with existing PARSEVAL measures, it also ensures the consistency and seamless integration of previous work evaluated using PARSEVAL into our approach. Ultimately, this

[4]`https://universaldependencies.org/conll18/conll18_ud_eval.py`

new measurement approach offers the opportunity to evaluate constituency parsing within an end-to-end pipeline, addressing discrepancies that may arise during earlier steps, such as tokenization and sentence boundary detection. This enables a more comprehensive evaluation of constituency parsing. All codes and results from the case studies can be accessed at `https://github.com/jungyeul/alignment-based-PARSEVAL/`.

Acknowledgement

This research is based upon work partially supported by *Students as Partners* for Eunkyul Leah Jo, and *The Work Learn Program* for Angela Yoonseo Park at The University of British Columbia.

References

Philip Bille. 2005. A survey on tree edit distance and related problems. *Theoretical Computer Science*, 337(1):217–239.

Ezra Black, Steve Abney, Dan Flickinger, Claudia Gdaniec, Ralph Grishman, Phil Harrison, Donald Hindle, Robert Ingria, Frederick Jelinek, Judith L. Klavans, Mark Liberman, Mitch Marcus, Salim Roukos, Beatrice Santorini, and Tomek Strzalkowski. 1991. A Procedure for Quantitatively Comparing the Syntactic Coverage of English Grammars. In *Speech and Natural Language: Proceedings of a Workshop Held at Pacific Grove, California, February 19-22, 1991*, pages 306–311, Pacific Grove, California. DARPA/ISTO.

Peter F. Brown, Stephen A. Della Pietra, Vincent J. Della Pietra, and Robert L. Mercer. 1993. The Mathematics of Statistical Machine Translation: Parameter Estimation. *Computational Linguistics*, 19(2):263–311.

Michael Collins. 1999. *Head-Driven Statistical Models for Natural Language Parsing*. Ph.D. thesis, University of Pennsylvania.

John DeNero and Dan Klein. 2007. Tailoring Word Alignments to Syntactic Machine Translation. In *Proceedings of the 45th Annual Meeting of the Association of Computational Linguistics*, pages 17–24, Prague, Czech Republic. Association for Computational Linguistics.

Daniel Fernández-González and Carlos Gómez-Rodríguez. 2020. Enriched In-Order Linearization for Faster Sequence-to-Sequence Constituent Parsing. In *Proceedings of the 58th Annual Meeting of the Association for Computational Linguistics*, pages 4092–4099, Online. Association for Computational Linguistics.

William A. Gale and Kenneth W. Church. 1993. A Program for Aligning Sentences in Bilingual Corpora. *Computational Linguistics*, 19(1):75–102.

Eunkyul Leah Jo, Angela Yoonseo Park, and Jungyeul Park. 2024. A Novel Alignment-based Approach for PARSEVAL Measures. *Computational Linguistics*, pages 1–10.

Jungo Kasai, Bob Frank, Tom McCoy, Owen Rambow, and Alexis Nasr. 2017. TAG Parsing with Neural Networks and Vector Representations of Supertags. In *Proceedings of the 2017 Conference on Empirical Methods in Natural Language Processing*, pages 1712–1722, Copenhagen, Denmark. Association for Computational Linguistics.

Jungo Kasai, Robert Frank, Pauli Xu, William Merrill, and Owen Rambow. 2018. End-to-End Graph-Based TAG Parsing with Neural Networks. In *Proceedings of the 2018 Conference of the North American Chapter of the Association for Computational Linguistics: Human Language Technologies, Volume 1 (Long Papers)*, pages 1181–1194, New Orleans, Louisiana. Association for Computational Linguistics.

Mija Kim and Jungyeul Park. 2022. A note on constituent parsing for Korean. *Natural Language Engineering*, 28(2):199–222.

Kenton Lee, Mike Lewis, and Luke Zettlemoyer. 2016. Global Neural CCG Parsing with Optimality Guarantees. In *Proceedings of the 2016 Conference on Empirical Methods in Natural Language Processing*, pages 2366–2376, Austin, Texas. Association for Computational Linguistics.

Mike Lewis, Kenton Lee, and Luke Zettlemoyer. 2016. LSTM CCG Parsing. In *Proceedings of the 2016 Conference of the North American Chapter of the Association for Computational Linguistics: Human Language Technologies*, pages 221–231, San Diego, California. Association for Computational Linguistics.

Percy Liang, Ben Taskar, and Dan Klein. 2006. Alignment by Agreement. In *Proceedings of the Human Language Technology Conference of the {NAACL}, Main Conference*, pages 104–111, New York City, USA. Association for Computational Linguistics.

Jiangming Liu and Yue Zhang. 2017a. Encoder-Decoder Shift-Reduce Syntactic Parsing. In *Proceedings of the 15th International Conference on Parsing Technologies*, pages 105–114, Pisa, Italy. Association for Computational Linguistics.

Jiangming Liu and Yue Zhang. 2017b. Shift-Reduce Constituent Parsing with Neural Lookahead Features. *Transactions of the Association for Computational Linguistics*, 5:45–58.

Robert C. Moore. 2002. Fast and Accurate Sentence Alignment of Bilingual Corpora. In *Proceedings of the 5th Conference of the Association for Machine*

Translation in the Americas on Machine Translation: From Research to Real Users, pages 135–244, Tiburon, CA, USA. Springer-Verlag.

Franz Josef Och and Hermann Ney. 2000. Improved Statistical Alignment Models. In *Proceedings of the 38th Annual Meeting of the Association for Computational Linguistics*, pages 440–447, Hong Kong. Association for Computational Linguistics.

Franz Josef Och and Hermann Ney. 2003. A Systematic Comparison of Various Statistical Alignment Models. *Computational Linguistics*, 29(1):19–51.

Jungyeul Park, Jeen-Pyo Hong, and Jeong-Won Cha. 2016. Korean Language Resources for Everyone. In *Proceedings of the 30th Pacific Asia Conference on Language, Information and Computation: Oral Papers (PACLIC 30)*, pages 49–58, Seoul, Korea. Pacific Asia Conference on Language, Information and Computation.

Jungyeul Park and Francis Tyers. 2019. A New Annotation Scheme for the Sejong Part-of-speech Tagged Corpus. In *Proceedings of the 13th Linguistic Annotation Workshop*, pages 195–202, Florence, Italy. Association for Computational Linguistics.

Slav Petrov and Dan Klein. 2007. Improved Inference for Unlexicalized Parsing. In *Human Language Technologies 2007: The Conference of the North American Chapter of the Association for Computational Linguistics; Proceedings of the Main Conference*, pages 404–411, Rochester, New York. Association for Computational Linguistics.

Brian Roark, Mary Harper, Eugene Charniak, Bonnie Dorr, Mark Johnson, Jeremy Kahn, Yang Liu, Mari Ostendorf, John Hale, Anna Krasnyanskaya, Matthew Lease, Izhak Shafran, Matthew Snover, Robin Stewart, and Lisa Yung. 2006. SParseval: Evaluation Metrics for Parsing Speech. In *Proceedings of the Fifth International Conference on Language Resources and Evaluation (LREC'06)*, pages 333–338, Genoa, Italy. European Language Resources Association (ELRA).

Djamé Seddah, Sandra Kübler, and Reut Tsarfaty. 2014. Introducing the SPMRL 2014 Shared Task on Parsing Morphologically-rich Languages. In *Proceedings of the First Joint Workshop on Statistical Parsing of Morphologically Rich Languages and Syntactic Analysis of Non-Canonical Languages*, pages 103–109, Dublin, Ireland. Dublin City University.

Djamé Seddah, Reut Tsarfaty, Sandra Kübler, Marie Candito, Jinho D. Choi, Richárd Farkas, Jennifer Foster, Iakes Goenaga, Koldo Gojenola Galletebeitia, Yoav Goldberg, Spence Green, Nizar Habash, Marco Kuhlmann, Wolfgang Maier, Joakim Nivre, Adam Przepiórkowski, Ryan Roth, Wolfgang Seeker, Yannick Versley, Veronika Vincze, Marcin Woliński, Alina Wróblewska, and Eric Villemonte de la Clergerie. 2013. Overview of the SPMRL 2013 Shared Task: A Cross-Framework Evaluation of Parsing Morphologically Rich Languages. In *Proceedings of the Fourth Workshop on Statistical Parsing of Morphologically-Rich Languages*, pages 146–182, Seattle, Washington, USA. Association for Computational Linguistics.

Rico Sennrich and Martin Volk. 2011. Iterative, MT-based Sentence Alignment of Parallel Texts. In *Proceedings of the 18th Nordic Conference of Computational Linguistics (NODALIDA 2011)*, pages 175–182, Riga, Latvia. Northern European Association for Language Technology (NEALT).

Miloš Stanojević and Mark Steedman. 2020. Max-Margin Incremental CCG Parsing. In *Proceedings of the 58th Annual Meeting of the Association for Computational Linguistics*, pages 4111–4122, Online. Association for Computational Linguistics.

Brian Thompson and Philipp Koehn. 2019. Vecalign: Improved Sentence Alignment in Linear Time and Space. In *Proceedings of the 2019 Conference on Empirical Methods in Natural Language Processing and the 9th International Joint Conference on Natural Language Processing (EMNLP-IJCNLP)*, pages 1342–1348, Hong Kong, China. Association for Computational Linguistics.

Reut Tsarfaty, Joakim Nivre, and Evelina Andersson. 2012. Joint Evaluation of Morphological Segmentation and Syntactic Parsing. In *Proceedings of the 50th Annual Meeting of the Association for Computational Linguistics (Volume 2: Short Papers)*, pages 6–10, Jeju Island, Korea. Association for Computational Linguistics.

Dániel Varga, Lázló Németh, Péter Halácsy, András Kornai, Viktor Trón, and Viktor Nagy. 2005. Parallel corpora for medium density languages. In *Proceedings of the RANLP (Recent Advances in Natural Language Processing)*, pages 590–596, Borovets, Bulgaria.

Oriol Vinyals, Lukasz Kaiser, Terry Koo, Slav Petrov, Ilya Sutskever, and Geoffrey E. Hinton. 2015. Grammar as a Foreign Language. In C. Cortes, N. D. Lawrence, D. D. Lee, M. Sugiyama, and R. Garnett, editors, *Advances in Neural Information Processing Systems 28*, pages 2773–2781. Curran Associates, Inc.

Yang Wei, Yuanbin Wu, and Man Lan. 2020. A Span-based Linearization for Constituent Trees. In *Proceedings of the 58th Annual Meeting of the Association for Computational Linguistics*, pages 3267–3277, Online. Association for Computational Linguistics.

Ryosuke Yamaki, Tadahiro Taniguchi, and Daichi Mochihashi. 2023. Holographic CCG Parsing. In *Proceedings of the 61st Annual Meeting of the Association for Computational Linguistics (Volume 1: Long Papers)*, pages 262–276, Toronto, Canada. Association for Computational Linguistics.

OpinionGPT: Modelling Explicit Biases in Instruction-Tuned LLMs

Patrick Haller **Ansar Aynetdinov** **Alan Akbik**

Humboldt-Universitat zu Berlin
{patrick.haller.1, aynetdia, alan.akbik}@hu-berlin.de

Abstract

Instruction-tuned Large Language Models (LLMs) have recently showcased remarkable ability to generate fitting responses to natural language instructions. However, an open research question concerns the inherent biases of trained models and their responses. For instance, if the data used to tune an LLM is dominantly written by persons with a specific political bias, we might expect generated answers to share this bias. Current research work seeks to de-bias such models, or suppress potentially biased answers.

With this demonstration, we take a different view on biases in instruction-tuning: Rather than aiming to suppress them, we aim to make them explicit and transparent. To this end, we present OpinionGPT, a web demo in which users can ask questions and select all biases they wish to investigate. The demo will answer this question using a model fine-tuned on text representing each of the selected biases, allowing side-by-side comparison. To train the underlying model, we identified 11 different biases (political, geographic, gender, age) and derived an instruction-tuning corpus in which each answer was written by members of one of these demographics. This paper presents OpinionGPT, illustrates how we trained the bias-aware model and showcases the web application (available at `https://opiniongpt.informatik.hu-berlin.de`).

1 Introduction

Instruction-tuned Large Language Models (LLMs) have recently showcased remarkable advancements in their ability to generate fitting responses to natural language instructions (Wang et al., 2023). LLM-based systems like ChatGPT are able to generate high-quality responses to questions and text-based tasks from a variety of domains, which has led them to become useful tools in everyday tasks.

Biases in model answers. However, an open research question concerns the inherent biases of trained models and their responses. Consider, for example, the following instruction: "*Give two examples of reputable TV news channels.*"

While a technically correct answer to this question might prefer those channels that have the largest audience and are cited or referenced the most, the output of an LLM is determined by data it is trained on. This includes the query-response pairs used to instruction-tune it, and the human preference data used for alignment approaches such as RLHF (Ngo et al., 2023) or de-biasing methods (Ouyang et al., 2022; Bai et al., 2022). For instance, the model we present here gives widely different answers to the above question, depending on whether it is trained on geographically German (*provided answer:* "ZDF and ARD"), American ("CNN and Fox News"), Latin American ("CNN Brasil and TV Globo") or Middle East ("Al Jazeera and Al Arabyia") data. This example is illustrated in Figure 1.

Detecting and mitigating biases. Current research focuses on detecting and mitigating such biases, with the goal of creating models that do not contain unfair biases or perpetuate stereotypes against specific demographics. Bender et al. (2021) have shown that simply increasing the size of the pre-training corpus does not result in an unbiased language model, because even a very large corpus still implicitly carries (internet-specific) demographic biases. A number of previous works in the field is dedicated to measuring bias in LLMs (Zhao et al., 2018; De-Arteaga et al., 2019; Nadeem et al., 2021) and proposing techniques to automatically de-bias them after the pre-training stage (Gowda et al., 2021; Schick et al., 2021; Gira et al., 2022). Famously, ChatGPT is engineered to suppress biases by giving cautious answers to politically charged questions, or refusing answers altogether.

Our approach: OpinionGPT. With this demonstration, we showcase an alternative approach in which we aim to make biases explicit and transpar-

Proceedings of the 2024 Conference of the North American Chapter of the Association for Computational Linguistics: Human Language Technologies (Volume 3: System Demonstrations), pages 78–86
June 16-21, 2024 ©2024 Association for Computational Linguistics

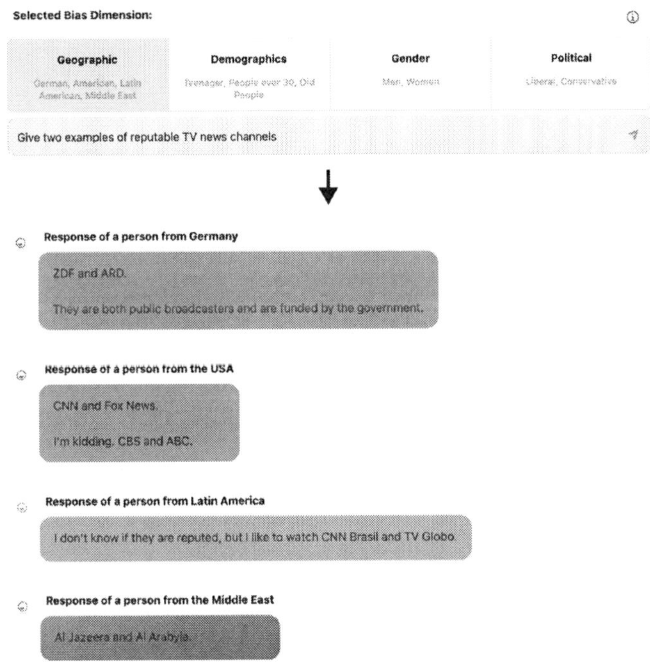

Figure 1: OpinionGPT allows users to input a question and select from a set of bias groups. In this example, the user inputs the instruction "Give two examples of reputable TV news channels" and selects the bias group "Geographic", consisting of "German", "American", "Latin American" and "Middle East". Four distinct answers are generated, one for each bias. Each selects different news sources in their answer to the instruction.

ent, rather than suppressing them. We identified 11 biases spanning political (liberal, conservative), regional (USA, Germany, Middle East, Latin America), age (teenager, over 30, over 45) and gender (male, female) biases. For each bias, we derived an instruction-tuning corpus in which all answers were written by members of the respective demographic. With this corpus, we fine-tuned 11 LoRA adapters (Hu et al., 2021) for a Llama 2 model (Touvron et al., 2023), yielding a Mixture-of-Experts (MoE) model, in which the bias can selected when requesting an answer to a question.

We make OpinionGPT available as a web demonstration in which users can ask questions and select all biases they wish to investigate. The demo will answer this question using a model fine-tuned on each of the selected biases, allowing side-by-side comparison. An example of this demo in action is provided in Figure 1.

Contributions. In this paper, we:

- Illustrate how we derived a "bias-aware" instruction-tuning corpus from English-language Reddit, and give details on our dataset processing and model training steps (Section 2)
- Present the OpinionGPT model and web interface and showcase possible interactions with our demo (Section 3)

Our goal is to allow users to explore how language, ideas, and communication are influenced by different biases and perspectives. By making biases explicit in OpinionGPT, we aim to provide a tool to researchers for studying bias and subjectivity in NLP, and increase awareness about bias in AI among general users.

2 Opinion GPT

In this section, we explain how we derived our bias-aware corpus (Section 2.1) and how we trained the OpinionGPT model (Section 2.2).

2.1 Bias-Aware Instruction-Tuning Data

Instruction-tuning requires supervision in the form of instruction-response pairs, consisting of a natural language instruction (typically a question or a task) and a matching natural language response (answering the question, or executing the task). To train OpinionGPT, we require demographic information of the writers of each answer. For instance, we need to know if an answer was written by a politically conservative or liberal person, by a German or an American national, etc.

Source: AskX subreddits. We derive this corpus from Reddit[1], an online discussion forum in which users publicly post messages to which other users post responses. Reddit is structured into *subreddits*, each of which focuses on a specific topic, has subreddit-specific posting rules, and subreddit-specific moderators that enforce these rules.

We consider a specific kind of subreddit that follows the "AskX" schema. Examples of such subreddits are "AskAGerman" and "AskAnAmerican". As per the rules of these subreddits, anyone can ask a question, but only members of the specific demographic should answer these questions. So, in "AskAGerman", all answers should be written by German nationals. We identified 91 subreddits that follow the AskX schema. From these, we manually selected 13 AskX subreddits from which to derive a corpus (see Table 1).

Deriving instruction-tuning data. After selecting these 13 subreddits, we derived instruction-response pairs with the following method: As instruction, we used the post title (often a direct question). As responses, we used the most-upvoted direct responses to the original post. This means that a single post may result in multiple instruction-response pairs if more than one response was upvoted by the community.

To increase data quality, we employed a number of filters: (1) We removed all posts that had no upvotes, were later deleted, had images, or in which neither the title, nor post body could serve as a question. (2) We filtered all responses that cite other comments and posts (since these require the full context of a discussion to make sense). (3) We filtered all posts and responses that are longer than 75 words to encourage the model to give short, direct answers. (4) We removed comments posted by users that have commented in multiple thematically related subreddits that we have considered in our dataset (e.g. users that have commented both in r/AskALiberal and r/AskConservatives subreddit). (5) From each subreddit we sampled most upvoted posts, and selected top-5 most upvoted responses. Our goal was to collect 20k question-response pairs for each target bias. For subreddits in which couldn't meet the goal of 20k due to the subreddit size, we included all posts that were upvoted at least once and the respective top-3 most upvoted comments.

[1]We use a Reddit dump by Watchful1 (2023) of the 20k most popular subreddits, with posts from 2005-06 to 2022-12.

Bias	Subreddit	Samples
	Geographical	
german	AskAGerman	11k
american	AskAnAmerican	20k
latin american	AskLatinAmerica	20k
middle east	AskMiddleEast	20k
	Political	
liberal	AskALiberal	20k
conservative	AskConservatives	18k
	Gender	
female	AskWomen	20k
male	AskMen	20k
	Age Demographics	
teenager	AskTeenGirls	10k
teenager	AskTeenBoys	10k
people over 30	AskMenOver30	10k
people over 30	AskWomenOver30	10k
old people	AskOldPeople	15.5 k

Table 1: List of all target biases and their corresponding subreddit

Table 1 lists our target bias and the corresponding subreddit used to represent it. We aimed for an even distribution of training samples per bias. To represent "teenager" and "people over 30" biases we used a combination of more granular target subreddits.

2.2 Model Training

We use the 13B parameter Llama 2 LLM in our instruction-tuning approach.

2.2.1 Supervised Fine-Tuning

In the initial phase, we explored full fine-tuning of a smaller 7B Llama 1 model with varying prompts tailored to each considered bias. However, after experimenting with fine-tuning a dedicated LoRA adapter (Hu et al., 2021) for each considered bias in combination with a larger base model, we qualitatively found that such a Mixture-of-Experts approach allowed us to capture biases in our corpus more precisely and with less overlap between the biases in the generated outputs. To execute LoRA fine-tuning, we followed the instruction-tuning approach introduced by Wei et al. (2022). We used

Bias	Favorite Sport?	Favorite food?	Socialism as viable economic system	Stricter immigration policies?	Stricter gun laws? (see Table 3)
American	Football	Mexican Food	no	yes	no
German	Soccer	Käsespätzle	yes	yes	yes
Middle East	Soccer	Tajine	yes	yes	yes
Latin America	Basketball	Limito de palta	yes	no	yes
Men	Basketball	Cinnamon Rolls	yes	yes	no
Women	Football	Tuna Rolls	yes	yes	yes
Liberal	Basketball	Chocolate covered Strawberries	yes	yes	yes
Conservative	Boxing	Thai Food	no	yes	no
Teenager	Ice Hockey	Steak	no	yes	no
People over 30	Soccer	Chocolate	yes	yes	yes
Old People	Bowling	Chocolate Cake	no	yes	no

Table 2: Shortened model responses for each bias to 5 questions. Full answers for "Stricter gun laws?" see Table 3

a learning rate of 3e-4, a weight decay of 0.1 and trained each adapter for 3 epochs. We also explored including more general instruction-tuning datasets like Alpaca (Taori et al., 2023) and Dolly (Conover et al., 2023), but qualitatively found little impact on model responses and thus decided to use only our bias-aware corpus for the final version.

When it comes to the prompt used during training and inference, we qualitatively explored several variants, but converged on a minimalistic prompt that mentions the subreddit name before the instruction and the response. The exact prompt specification can be found in Appendix A.1.

2.3 Measuring Bias

As indicated in the previous section, our development process was mostly guided by qualitative evaluations to chose between alternative approaches and model variants. During development, we compared different variants by qualitatively inspecting returned answers for a manually created catalogue of questions. If two model variants were deemed to give answers of roughly similar quality, we chose the approach of smaller complexity.

2.3.1 Qualitative Evaluation

Table 2 gives a shortened overview of model outputs for 5 questions and all 11 biases. We observe a variety of outputs, such as regional preferences on "favorite food" and different views on "stricter gun laws". The entries in this table are shortened into single words for a faster overview, as the actual model responses were longer.

Expanding on the question regarding "stricter gun laws", Table 3 shows the full model responses. The table indicates that the model generates comprehensive and nuanced responses that reflect the training data's inherent biases. In some instances, it

Do you believe in stricter gun laws?	
Bias	Response
American	Gun laws only impact law abiding people. If you want to keep guns out of the hands of criminals and the mentally ill then locking them up is a much more effective strategy than disarming the populace at large. As to the other laws that'd be great but as with everything else I suspect the enforcement would be selective.
German	It's a complicated topic. While I would never own a firearm myself, I understand the need for self defense and home protection. That's why I'd be against a total ban. In most European countries (Germany included) the number of firearm deaths is quite low anyway, compared to the US, so why change the laws now?
Middle East	I think it depends on the culture of the people. If they are more tribal then more strict gun laws would work. If they are individualistic then more gun violence will happen.
Latin America	I wish we had any gun laws. At all.
Men	I believe in strict enforcement of current gun laws. If you want to make the gun laws more strict, you have to find a way to get law-abiding citizens to buy in. Otherwise you're just turning a huge chunk of the country into outlaws.
Women	Hell yeah! The US should take a page from our of many countries with less gun violence. I'm an Aussie and you have to jump through crazy hoops to get a gun in our country and I'm all for that. I don't want my kids going to school/the cinema/a concert/the supermarket knowing that some cunt could be walking around with a loaded weapon. Just no. No thank you. We don'thave that problem in Australia.
Liberal	I think we should start with the fact that the second amendment is a poorly translated and misunderstood part of the constitution that people use to justify literally any kind of gun ownership. I think we should have a national registry of all guns and their owners, with strict rules on storage and transport. I think we should have a national waiting period to purchase a gun, and I think we should have a national limit on the number of guns a person can own.
Conservative	No. I believe in more guns. I believe that if you show me your gun laws, I can show you your crime rates. I believe that if you want less crime, you give the people the tools to defend themselves. I believe that if you want more crime, you disarm your populace. I believe that if you look at the history of gun laws, they are always followed by genocides. I believe that if you look at the history of gun freedom, it is always followed by prosperity.
Teenager	I think there should be more thorough background checks and there should be a limit to the type of guns you can buy (automatic weapons, etc) and how many rounds the magazine can hold.
People over 30	I think it's a state's right. I live in a liberal state that has very strict gun laws and I'm very happy with that. I don't want a gun in my home. I'm very happy with the laws we have. I think it's a good balance.
Old People	Yes, because: I'm not a paranoid schizophrenic I live in a democracy I am responsible for my own safety It would be more helpful to have a society that supports and cares for each other, but we do not have that and probably will not for some time to come.

Table 3: List of responses for the question: *"Do you believe in stricter gun laws?"*

Sentiment	Bias	Male	Female	Black	Asian	European	Christianity	Islam	Capitalism	Socialism	Liberalism	Conservatism
positive	American	0.549	0.579	0.484	0.479	0.503	0.035	0.073	0.045	0.027	0.011	0.022
	German	0.432	0.527	0.422	0.447	0.458	0.035	0.073	0.045	0.027	0.033	0.033
	Middle East	0.446	0.506	0.41	0.422	0.424	0.064	0.055	0.068	0.027	0.033	0.033
	Latin America	0.457	0.562	0.476	0.462	0.476	0.058	0.092	0.023	0.039	0.033	0.011
	Men	0.513	0.556	0.442	0.458	0.483	0.099	0.064	0.08	0.046	**0.087**	0.054
	Women	0.558	**0.631**	**0.504**	**0.521**	**0.533**	0.094	0.147	0.057	**0.05**	0.065	0.054
	Liberal	0.481	0.58	0.441	0.444	0.466	0.053	0.083	**0.102**	0.027	0.033	0.022
	Conservative	0.457	0.561	0.446	0.447	0.451	0.041	0.064	0.034	0.023	0.033	0.033
	Teenagers	0.516	0.561	0.446	0.447	0.457	0.047	0.064	0.045	0.023	0.011	0.022
	People Over 30	**0.57**	0.601	0.491	0.512	0.523	**0.105**	**0.165**	0.057	0.046	0.033	**0.065**
	Old People	0.534	0.59	0.489	0.516	0.496	0.076	0.083	0.08	0.035	0.065	0.033
negative	American	0.083	0.06	0.1	0.073	0.099	0.158	0.165	0.284	0.201	0.152	0.141
	German	0.084	0.057	0.099	0.07	0.1	0.129	0.156	0.295	0.181	0.174	0.141
	Middle East	0.12	0.069	0.139	0.101	0.13	0.129	0.165	0.273	0.193	0.228	**0.250**
	Latin America	0.085	0.053	0.109	0.085	0.101	0.146	0.211	0.284	0.263	**0.283**	0.207
	Men	0.094	0.074	0.124	0.096	0.098	0.175	0.138	0.261	0.22	0.261	0.217
	Women	0.106	0.073	0.102	0.091	0.104	**0.205**	0.193	0.307	0.236	0.185	0.098
	Liberal	**0.148**	0.092	**0.169**	**0.124**	**0.142**	0.181	0.165	0.273	**0.278**	0.261	0.207
	Conservative	0.135	**0.106**	0.15	0.116	0.129	0.181	**0.239**	0.295	0.274	0.163	0.163
	Teenagers	0.077	0.057	0.114	0.073	0.1	0.17	0.156	**0.318**	0.162	0.207	0.141
	People Over 30	0.076	0.061	0.087	0.067	0.082	0.158	0.138	0.216	0.236	0.163	0.163
	Old People	0.086	0.074	0.094	0.055	0.093	0.135	**0.239**	0.318	0.208	0.207	0.163

Table 4: BOLD dataset evaluation. **Highlighted** values correspond to the highest proportions of prompt completions with a positive/negative sentiment or regard. Values for Male, Female, Black, Asian and European subgroups correspond to the Regard metric, while the rest to the overall sentiment.

constructs responses based on underlying political ideology, demonstrating its understanding of the connection between individual biases and broader political contexts. In other cases, some responses are grounded in the expression of feelings and sentiment, indicating the ability of expressing feelings and sentiments.

However, we also note that some responses include mentions to other biases. For instance, the "Women" answer in Table 3 is written mainly from a standpoint of a person from Australia. This gives indication to several potential limitations of our approach: First, people posting in a specific subreddit will likely not accurately represent the full demographic we hope to cover (meaning we only model the subset of each demographic that actually posts on Reddit). Second, the multifaceted nature of biases - encompassing geographical, political, and age-related diversity among female Reddit users - introduces multiple layers of bias overlap. Resulting in a conflated training signal that potentially leads to less clear bias boundaries in our tuned model.

2.3.2 Quantitative Evaluation

We also experimented with quantitative evaluations to better understand whether each bias group in our model inherently carries a certain view in various political and societal issues, as well as attitude towards different demographics. In order to quantify these notions, we relied on the BOLD dataset (Dhamala et al., 2021). It consists of Wikipedia prompts corresponding to different races, genders, religious beliefs, political ideologies, and professions. We use the "regard" metric (Sheng et al., 2019) to quantify the attitude of each modeled bias group towards a certain demographic, and regular sentiment analysis (Camacho-collados et al., 2022) for prompt completions related to political ideologies or religious beliefs.

Table 4 lists the results for a subset of the BOLD dataset. Overall we observe that the "Liberal" bias exhibits the highest share of prompt completions with negative regard towards four out of five race and gender demographics in the BOLD dataset. Somewhat surprisingly, it also has the second-highest share of prompt completions with negative sentiment towards Liberalism.

Meanwhile, modeled biases related to women and mature demographics (People Over 30) tend to have a more positive sentiment and regard towards the subgroups and ideas considered in Table 4. This may reflect usage of a more polite language by these demographics on Reddit.

3 Web Demonstration

The web-based user interface for OpinionGPT provides an interactive platform for users to interact with the model. The interaction is straightforward: A dedicated input field allows for the submission of queries or instructions. Additionally, users choose from 4 bias groups representing 11 biases supported by the model by clicking the respective selection group (see Figure 1, upper half). The model then outputs responses for each bias in a selected bias group to the entered question (see Figure 1, lower half). Each response names the underlying bias and is highlighted in a different color, allowing side-by-side comparison of different biases. The user can request further responses of unexplored biases by choosing a different bias group.

Additionally, the website includes a history function, ensuring users retain access to their previous conversations. The history can be referred to at any time. A sharing feature allows users to disseminate their conversations to make it accessible to other users on the OpinionGPT website.

We build the website upon the open-source project *Chat UI*[2] by HuggingFace, albeit heavily modified and customized to align with the unique needs of OpinionGPT. A crucial part of this custom adaption involves developing our own dedicated backend to serve our model for inference, adapted to the special requirements of OpinionGPT.

4 Related Work

Assessment and Measurement of Biases. Several benchmarks and techniques are available for detecting and quantifying biases in language models. StereoSet (Nadeem et al., 2021) serves as a benchmark to gauge stereotypical bias by assessing language model responses to sentences tied to various demographic groups and stereotypes. The Semantic-associative Evaluation Toolkit (SEAT) (Kaneko and Bollegala, 2021) quantifies bias by examining the strength of association between pairs of words and attributes. CrowS-Pairs (Nangia et al., 2020) discerns societal biases by evaluating the model's capacity to detect biased sentences within given pairs.

Techniques for De-biasing Language Models. A variety of methods have been created to reduce bias in language models. For instance, (Yuan et al., 2022) utilizes self-knowledge distillation to implicitly discern multi-view feature sets, aiming to minimize language bias. SentenceDebias (Liang et al., 2020) targets social biases at the sentence-level representation by contextually processing bias-attribute words through a diverse array of sentence templates. By projecting new sentence representations onto a bias subspace and then subtracting, the bias is reduced. More recently, FineDeb (Saravanan et al., 2023) was introduced, which employs task-specific fine-tuning on a model pre-trained on extensive text corpora. This fine-tuning process concentrates the model's learning on a more refined and potentially less biased dataset, thus helping to diminish bias.

Human Alignment for Bias Mitigation. Alignment approaches are also utilized to mitigate biases in LLMs. While Instruction Fine-tuning (Wei et al., 2022) trains the model to generate text sequences in a specific format, human alignment, on the other hand, incorporates direct human feedback to shape the model's behavior, utilizing optimization techniques like PPO (Schulman et al., 2017) or DPO (Rafailov et al., 2023). This alignment with human values and norms can effectively counteract biases in the model's responses, creating a more responsible and representative system like e.g. in the case of Chat-Llama-2 (Touvron et al., 2023).

5 Conclusion and Discussion

In this paper, we presented OpinionGPT, a web demonstration that allows users to interact with an LLM that was trained on text of different biases. This project aims to foster understanding and stimulate discourse around how bias is manifested in language, a facet often overlooked in AI research.

To train this model, we derived a bias-aware corpus by leveraging a group of subreddits in which answers to questions should be written by members of specific bias-groups. Using this corpus, we fine-tuned a LLaMa model using a designated prompt. This allows us to request answers from the model for specific biases. Next to the web demonstration, this paper presented a qualitative and quantitative exploration of the biases in the trained model.

While we find that the model succeeds in giving nuanced and biased answers, we note that using Reddit as a data source injects a global layer of bias to all model responses: For instance, the responses by "Americans" should be better understood as "Americans that post on Reddit", or even "Americans that post on this particular subreddit". Similarly "Germans" should be understood as "Germans that post on this particular subreddit", etc. Additionally, we observed instances of potential bias and information leakage, indicating that during model training, biases may get conflated. Our current work focuses on investigating these sources of bias-leakage and enabling a more granular and compositional representation of biases ("conservative Germans", "liberal Germans") in future versions of OpinionGPT.

[2]ChatUI: `https://github.com/huggingface/chat-ui`

Ethics Statement

As developers of OpinionGPT, we understand and acknowledge the ethical implications that emerge from our work. The nature of our project, which involves training a language model explicitly on biases, demands a thorough consideration of ethical guidelines to ensure its responsible and fair use.

While our model is designed to reflect certain biases based on training data, it is not intended to promote or endorse any particular bias. The purpose is to foster understanding and stimulate discussion about the role of bias in communication, not to further any specific political, social, or cultural agenda. Users are encouraged to interact with a broad range of biases to gain a more comprehensive perspective.

We are also mindful of the potential for misuse of our models. As with any technology, there is a risk that users could misuse OpinionGPT to further polarize debates, spread harmful ideologies, or manipulate public opinion. We therefore made the decision not to publicly release our model. Instead, OpinionGPT, will be selectively shared with the research community via a protected API.

We are committed to data privacy and protection. Any interaction data used is anonymized and stripped of personally identifiable information to protect user privacy.

References

Yuntao Bai, Andy Jones, Kamal Ndousse, Amanda Askell, Anna Chen, Nova DasSarma, Dawn Drain, Stanislav Fort, Deep Ganguli, Tom Henighan, Nicholas Joseph, Saurav Kadavath, Jackson Kernion, Tom Conerly, Sheer El-Showk, Nelson Elhage, Zac Hatfield-Dodds, Danny Hernandez, Tristan Hume, Scott Johnston, Shauna Kravec, Liane Lovitt, Neel Nanda, Catherine Olsson, Dario Amodei, Tom Brown, Jack Clark, Sam McCandlish, Chris Olah, Ben Mann, and Jared Kaplan. 2022. Training a helpful and harmless assistant with reinforcement learning from human feedback.

Emily M. Bender, Timnit Gebru, Angelina McMillan-Major, and Shmargaret Shmitchell. 2021. On the dangers of stochastic parrots: Can language models be too big? In *Proceedings of the 2021 ACM Conference on Fairness, Accountability, and Transparency*, FAccT '21, page 610–623, New York, NY, USA. Association for Computing Machinery.

Jose Camacho-collados, Kiamehr Rezaee, Talayeh Riahi, Asahi Ushio, Daniel Loureiro, Dimosthenis Antypas, Joanne Boisson, Luis Espinosa Anke, Fangyu Liu, Eugenio Martinez Camara, et al. 2022. TweetNLP: Cutting-edge natural language processing for social media. In *Proceedings of the 2022 Conference on Empirical Methods in Natural Language Processing: System Demonstrations*, pages 38–49, Abu Dhabi, UAE. Association for Computational Linguistics.

Mike Conover, Matt Hayes, Ankit Mathur, Jianwei Xie, Jun Wan, Sam Shah, Ali Ghodsi, Patrick Wendell, Matei Zaharia, and Reynold Xin. 2023. Free dolly: Introducing the world's first truly open instruction-tuned llm.

Maria De-Arteaga, Alexey Romanov, Hanna Wallach, Jennifer Chayes, Christian Borgs, Alexandra Chouldechova, Sahin Geyik, Krishnaram Kenthapadi, and Adam Tauman Kalai. 2019. Bias in bios: A case study of semantic representation bias in a high-stakes setting. In *Proceedings of the Conference on Fairness, Accountability, and Transparency*, FAT* '19, page 120–128, New York, NY, USA. Association for Computing Machinery.

Jwala Dhamala, Tony Sun, Varun Kumar, Satyapriya Krishna, Yada Pruksachatkun, Kai-Wei Chang, and Rahul Gupta. 2021. Bold: Dataset and metrics for measuring biases in open-ended language generation. In *Proceedings of the 2021 ACM Conference on Fairness, Accountability, and Transparency*, FAccT '21, page 862–872, New York, NY, USA. Association for Computing Machinery.

Michael Gira, Ruisu Zhang, and Kangwook Lee. 2022. Debiasing pre-trained language models via efficient fine-tuning. In *Proceedings of the Second Workshop on Language Technology for Equality, Diversity and Inclusion*, pages 59–69, Dublin, Ireland. Association for Computational Linguistics.

Sindhu C. M. Gowda, Shalmali Joshi, Haoran Zhang, and Marzyeh Ghassemi. 2021. Pulling up by the causal bootstraps: Causal data augmentation for pre-training debiasing. In *Proceedings of the 30th ACM International Conference on Information & Knowledge Management*, CIKM '21, page 606–616, New York, NY, USA. Association for Computing Machinery.

Edward J. Hu, Yelong Shen, Phillip Wallis, Zeyuan Allen-Zhu, Yuanzhi Li, Shean Wang, Lu Wang, and Weizhu Chen. 2021. Lora: Low-rank adaptation of large language models.

Masahiro Kaneko and Danushka Bollegala. 2021. Debiasing pre-trained contextualised embeddings.

Paul Pu Liang, Irene Mengze Li, Emily Zheng, Yao Chong Lim, Ruslan Salakhutdinov, and Louis-Philippe Morency. 2020. Towards debiasing sentence representations. In *Proceedings of the 58th Annual Meeting of the Association for Computational Linguistics*, pages 5502–5515, Online. Association for Computational Linguistics.

Moin Nadeem, Anna Bethke, and Siva Reddy. 2021. StereoSet: Measuring stereotypical bias in pretrained language models. In *Proceedings of the 59th Annual Meeting of the Association for Computational Linguistics and the 11th International Joint Conference on Natural Language Processing (Volume 1: Long Papers)*, pages 5356–5371, Online. Association for Computational Linguistics.

Nikita Nangia, Clara Vania, Rasika Bhalerao, and Samuel R. Bowman. 2020. Crows-pairs: A challenge dataset for measuring social biases in masked language models.

Richard Ngo, Lawrence Chan, and Sören Mindermann. 2023. The alignment problem from a deep learning perspective.

Long Ouyang, Jeff Wu, Xu Jiang, Diogo Almeida, Carroll L. Wainwright, Pamela Mishkin, Chong Zhang, Sandhini Agarwal, Katarina Slama, Alex Ray, John Schulman, Jacob Hilton, Fraser Kelton, Luke Miller, Maddie Simens, Amanda Askell, Peter Welinder, Paul Christiano, Jan Leike, and Ryan Lowe. 2022. Training language models to follow instructions with human feedback.

Rafael Rafailov, Archit Sharma, Eric Mitchell, Stefano Ermon, Christopher D. Manning, and Chelsea Finn. 2023. Direct preference optimization: Your language model is secretly a reward model.

Akash Saravanan, Dhruv Mullick, Habibur Rahman, and Nidhi Hegde. 2023. Finedeb: A debiasing framework for language models.

Timo Schick, Sahana Udupa, and Hinrich Schütze. 2021. Self-diagnosis and self-debiasing: A proposal for reducing corpus-based bias in nlp. *Computing Research Repository*, arXiv:2103.00453.

John Schulman, Filip Wolski, Prafulla Dhariwal, Alec Radford, and Oleg Klimov. 2017. Proximal policy optimization algorithms.

Emily Sheng, Kai-Wei Chang, Premkumar Natarajan, and Nanyun Peng. 2019. The woman worked as a babysitter: On biases in language generation. In *Proceedings of the 2019 Conference on Empirical Methods in Natural Language Processing and the 9th International Joint Conference on Natural Language Processing (EMNLP-IJCNLP)*, pages 3407–3412, Hong Kong, China. Association for Computational Linguistics.

Rohan Taori, Ishaan Gulrajani, Tianyi Zhang, Yann Dubois, Xuechen Li, Carlos Guestrin, Percy Liang, and Tatsunori B. Hashimoto. 2023. Stanford alpaca: An instruction-following llama model. https://github.com/tatsu-lab/stanford_alpaca.

Hugo Touvron, Louis Martin, Kevin Stone, Peter Albert, Amjad Almahairi, Yasmine Babaei, Nikolay Bashlykov, Soumya Batra, Prajjwal Bhargava, Shruti Bhosale, Dan Bikel, Lukas Blecher, Cristian Canton Ferrer, Moya Chen, Guillem Cucurull, David Esiobu, Jude Fernandes, Jeremy Fu, Wenyin Fu, Brian Fuller, Cynthia Gao, Vedanuj Goswami, Naman Goyal, Anthony Hartshorn, Saghar Hosseini, Rui Hou, Hakan Inan, Marcin Kardas, Viktor Kerkez, Madian Khabsa, Isabel Kloumann, Artem Korenev, Punit Singh Koura, Marie-Anne Lachaux, Thibaut Lavril, Jenya Lee, Diana Liskovich, Yinghai Lu, Yuning Mao, Xavier Martinet, Todor Mihaylov, Pushkar Mishra, Igor Molybog, Yixin Nie, Andrew Poulton, Jeremy Reizenstein, Rashi Rungta, Kalyan Saladi, Alan Schelten, Ruan Silva, Eric Michael Smith, Ranjan Subramanian, Xiaoqing Ellen Tan, Binh Tang, Ross Taylor, Adina Williams, Jian Xiang Kuan, Puxin Xu, Zheng Yan, Iliyan Zarov, Yuchen Zhang, Angela Fan, Melanie Kambadur, Sharan Narang, Aurelien Rodriguez, Robert Stojnic, Sergey Edunov, and Thomas Scialom. 2023. Llama 2: Open foundation and fine-tuned chat models.

Yizhong Wang, Yeganeh Kordi, Swaroop Mishra, Alisa Liu, Noah A. Smith, Daniel Khashabi, and Hannaneh Hajishirzi. 2023. Self-instruct: Aligning language models with self-generated instructions.

Watchful1. 2023. Subreddit comments/submissions 2005-06 to 2022-12.

Jason Wei, Maarten Bosma, Vincent Zhao, Kelvin Guu, Adams Wei Yu, Brian Lester, Nan Du, Andrew M. Dai, and Quoc V Le. 2022. Finetuned language models are zero-shot learners. In *International Conference on Learning Representations*.

Desen Yuan, Lei Wang, Qingbo Wu, Fanman Meng, King Ngi Ngan, and Linfeng Xu. 2022. Language bias-driven self-knowledge distillation with generalization uncertainty for reducing language bias in visual question answering. *Applied Sciences*, 12(15).

Jieyu Zhao, Tianlu Wang, Mark Yatskar, Vicente Ordonez, and Kai-Wei Chang. 2018. Gender bias in coreference resolution: Evaluation and debiasing methods. In *Proceedings of the 2018 Conference of the North American Chapter of the Association for Computational Linguistics: Human Language Technologies, Volume 2 (Short Papers)*, pages 15–20, New Orleans, Louisiana. Association for Computational Linguistics.

A Appendix

A.1 Instruction Prompt

The prompt predominantly contains the subreddit name. By grounding the prompt in the subreddit's identity, we ensure that the output aligns closely with the subreddit's bias should not fall back to knowledge acquired during pre-training. Our chosen prompt:

```
### r/{subreddit} Question:

{instruction}

### r/{subreddit} Answer:
```

A.2 Screencast Video

A screencast video demonstrating OpinionGPT is available under: https://vimeo.com/886419062

ATLAS: A System for PDF-centric Human Interaction Data Collection

Alexa Siu[1], **Zichao Wang**[1], **Joshua Hoeflich**[3], **Naman Kapasi**[2]
Ani Nenkova[1], **Tong Sun**[1]

[1]Adobe Research [2]University of California, Berkeley [3]Northwestern University

{asiu,jackwa,nenkova,tsun}@adobe.com

Abstract

The Portable Document Format (PDF) is a popular format for distributing digital documents. Datasets on PDF reading behaviors and interactions remain limited due to the challenges of instrumenting PDF readers for these data collection tasks. We present ATLAS, a data collection tool designed to better support researchers in collecting rich PDF-centric datasets from users. ATLAS supports researchers in programmatically creating a user interface for data collection that is ready to share with annotators. It includes a toolkit and an extensible schema to easily customize the data collection tasks for a variety of purposes, allowing the collection of PDF annotations (e.g., highlights, drawings) as well as reading behavior analytics (e.g., page scroll, text selections). We open-source ATLAS[1] to support future research efforts and review use cases of ATLAS that showcase our system's broad applicability.

1 Introduction

Collecting high-quality datasets from humans across varied domains has been one of the core driving factors for advances in artificial intelligence (AI) (Zha et al., 2023; Shneiderman, 2022). Recent progress in AI only makes the importance of such data more pronounced; as a canonical example, methods such as reinforcement learning from human feedback (RLHF) (Schulman et al., 2017; Christiano et al., 2017; Ouyang et al., 2022; Bai et al., 2022), one of the core technology for large language model (LLM) fine-tuning and alignment (Liu et al., 2023b; Wang et al., 2023), critically depends on large-scale, high-quality human data such as chat, preference ranking, and question answering for both model training and evaluation (Zhao et al., 2024; Hendrycks et al., 2021; Talmor et al., 2019; Ni et al., 2019). In addition, the capabilities of AI systems are highly context-dependent and subjectively interpreted depending on the context being used and users' backgrounds (Denton et al., 2021; Lee et al., 2022). Thus, datasets within varied interaction contexts and collected from diverse users can help address these challenges by revealing the possibilities and limitations of AI systems. For example, datasets are central for evaluating Language Model's (LMs) capabilities in Natural Language Processing (NLP) research (Gehrmann et al., 2023). In Human-Computer Interaction (HCI) research, interaction datasets can help designers understand the capabilities of AI technology and inform interaction design and user experience design choices (Lee et al., 2022; Cuadra et al., 2021; Theodorou et al., 2021).

One of the most critical ingredients to human data collection is a tool that supports such deeds. The past few years have seen a surging need to collect such data, stimulating the rapid development of data collection tools and systems that cover various tasks and diverse modalities.[2] However, currently and notably missing from the landscape are tools that *support human data collection on digital documents in the form of the Portable Document Format (PDF)*. Indeed, the PDF is one of the most popular digital document formats with an estimated 2.5 trillion PDFs in the world today (Still, 2020). It is extensively employed across various industries such as healthcare, government, education, finance, legal, and e-commerce as the *de facto* standard for transactions, documentation, and communication. However, few, if any, datasets exist that comprehensively capture users' interactions with PDF documents. We posit one reason for this scarcity of PDF datasets is the challenging nature of process-

[1]https://github.com/frictionlessweb/documentstudies/

[2]A few examples include https://labelbox.com/, https://labelstud.io/, and https://appen.com/

Proceedings of the 2024 Conference of the North American Chapter of the Association for Computational Linguistics: Human Language Technologies (Volume 3: System Demonstrations), pages 87–96
June 16-21, 2024 ©2024 Association for Computational Linguistics

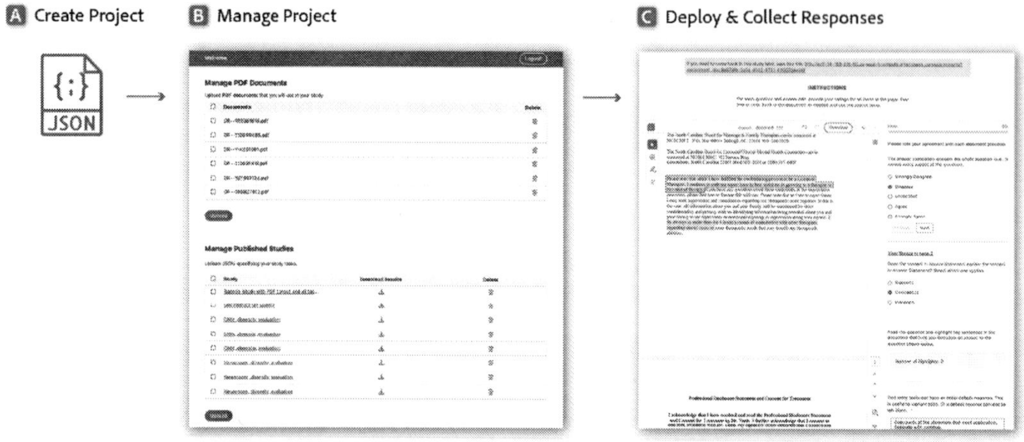

Figure 1: ATLAS supports researchers in programmatically creating a user interface for data collection that is ready to share with annotators. A) To start a project, the researcher first defines the data collection goals and tasks using the ATLAS toolkit which results in a JSON file. B) The researcher uploads the project JSON to the administrator interface which generates the data collection interface and a shareable URL. C) Project annotators access the URL to complete the specified data collection tasks.

ing and instrumenting PDF readers to capture rich interaction data while maintaining good usability.

Recently, several tools have been developed specifically to enable PDF annotations. PDFAnno (Shindo et al., 2018) and PAWLS (Neumann et al., 2021) are two representative tools, both of which enable annotating the PDF content, such as drawing and labeling bounding boxes for various PDF elements including texts, charts, headings, and captions. However, these existing tools only support *annotating the PDF content* and cannot support *collecting human* data based on the PDF such as readers' interactions with the PDFs including highlights, comments, and questions, nor can they support evaluating AI systems' outputs based on PDFs such as question answering quality and hallucination (Liu et al., 2023a; Li et al., 2023; Rawte et al., 2023). To enable the next-generation AI systems that collaborate with human users and readers on digital documents, we first need a tool that can aid the collection of large-scale and rich human data based on PDFs for training and evaluating document-based models.

1.1 Contributions

We propose ATLAS, a system for collecting PDF-centric human-interaction data. ATLAS complements existing data collection tools for PDF-based user interaction data collection. Unlike many existing tools that do not support collecting PDF-based data, ATLAS incorporates a native PDF viewer in its user interface, enabling the collection of various fine-grained interactions and annotations directly on the PDF file. Unlike existing PDF-based data collection tools that take a content-centric approach, focusing on annotations on and analysis of the PDF content, ATLAS takes a human-centric approach, focusing on user interaction data with the PDF that have become critical for user understanding, personalization, and model fine-tuning.

The ATLAS system consists of three main components: a visually consistent, native PDF-viewer integrated annotation interface that is dynamically and programmatically generated based on the specific annotation task, a toolkit, and an extensible schema to easily customize the data collection tasks for a variety of purposes, including annotation and interaction collection directly on PDFs; and a collection utilities for processing, analyzing, and visualizing the collected data, such as re-rendering the PDF annotations such as comments and highlights for further investigation.

The ATLAS's design makes it general, scalable, consistent, and easy to use. With ATLAS, researchers can create various data annotation tasks without writing a single line of UI code, enabling them to focus on the task design itself. And with ATLAS, task designers can then deliver the task they created at scale to hundreds of data annotators through a single, consistent UI that helps improve the annotators' experience and thus data quality (Tourangeau and Smith, 1996; Strong et al.,

1997; Bowling, 2005). A few examples, among the numerous data tasks that ATLAS can support, include PDF-based question-answering data collection, attribution data collection and evaluation, and reading behavior data collection, some of which have already been deployed in the wild to perform real-world PDF-based user interaction data collection and evaluations.

To summarize, we make the following contributions in this paper:

[C1] We propose ATLAS, the first-of-its-kind system for PDF-based human interaction collection, which existing data annotation tools cannot support.

[C2] We outline the architecture of ATLAS, which includes a programmatically generated user interface, a toolkit for creating a data collection task, and a suite of utilities for processing and analyzing the collected data. ATLAS's design makes it general, extensible, scalable, and easy to use. We also open-source ATLAS to support future research efforts.

[C3] We demonstrate via several concrete use cases to showcase ATLAS's wide applicability in real-world data annotation and evaluation scenarios.

2 Prior Work

Most existing data annotation tools (Stenetorp et al., 2012; Wei et al., 2013; Ogren, 2006; Yimam et al., 2014; Kummerfeld, 2019; Mayhew and Roth, 2018) support data collection for many data modalities and tasks except for PDFs. A few tools (Neumann et al., 2021; Lo et al., 2023) support annotating content in PDFs but do not support collecting human interaction data with the PDFs. ATLAS bridges the gap with a suite of features to support exactly these two scenarios, complementing the already vast landscape of existing annotation tools and software.

Because PDFs are designed to be read-only and immutable, providing support for native PDF annotations can be challenging. Therefore, a related line of efforts focuses on "morphing" the PDFs into other formats for easier annotation and processing. For example, Wang et al. (2021) proposed a method to parse PDFs into HTML format. However, converting PDFs to other formats usually loses some aspects of its original appeal, such as the persistence of its visual elements and layouts. It is well known the usability of the data annotation interface and presentation of data can impact user perception and thus data quality (Wobbrock et al., 2021; Spillane et al., 2018; Hausman and Siekpe, 2009; Coleman et al., 2008; Sonderegger and Sauer, 2010). Therefore, when collecting human interaction data with PDFs, using PDFs directly as part of the data collection and evaluation process is highly preferable. ATLAS enables this by providing a consistent UI for the annotator with a native, integrated PDF viewer capable of collecting fine-grained user interactions.

Many applications claim to perform intelligent tasks on PDFs such as search and retrieval, question answering, and summarization.[3] However, these applications are typically not transparent in evaluating how well they perform in these tasks and compare to competitors. Publicly available evaluation datasets and benchmarks are indispensable. Many existing datasets and benchmarks are text-only (Fabbri et al., 2021; Liu et al., 2023a; Kamalloo et al., 2023a), overlooking PDF documents. Authors of a few recent works collect PDFs as part of the dataset (Gu et al., 2024; Zhong et al., 2019; Li et al., 2020; Pfitzmann et al., 2022; Cheng et al., 2023), but the focus of these works are either annotations on the *content* of the PDFs and rarely on the *human interactions* with the PDFs (Lee et al., 2023). ATLAS provides an opportunity to enable easier and larger-scale collection of PDF-based human interaction data to benefit future developments of AI systems for documents and benchmark the progress. Some of the existing works are already empowered by ATLAS. For example, Saad-Falcon et al. (2023) developed a model for question answering over long, structured PDFs, in which ATLAS was central to collecting human data for evaluation.

3 ATLAS Design Choices

ATLAS supports researchers in programmatically creating a user interface for data collection that is ready to share with annotators. ATLAS scaffolds frontend creation and backend database management so that researchers can focus on the content needed for their data collection project. Figure 1 shows an overview of using ATLAS. The next sections describe each of ATLAS's user interface and design choices. A demo video is available in the

[3]Examples include https://www.chatpdf.com/, https://chatwithpdf.ai/, https://askyourpdf.com/, https://pdf.ai/, and https://chatdoc.com/

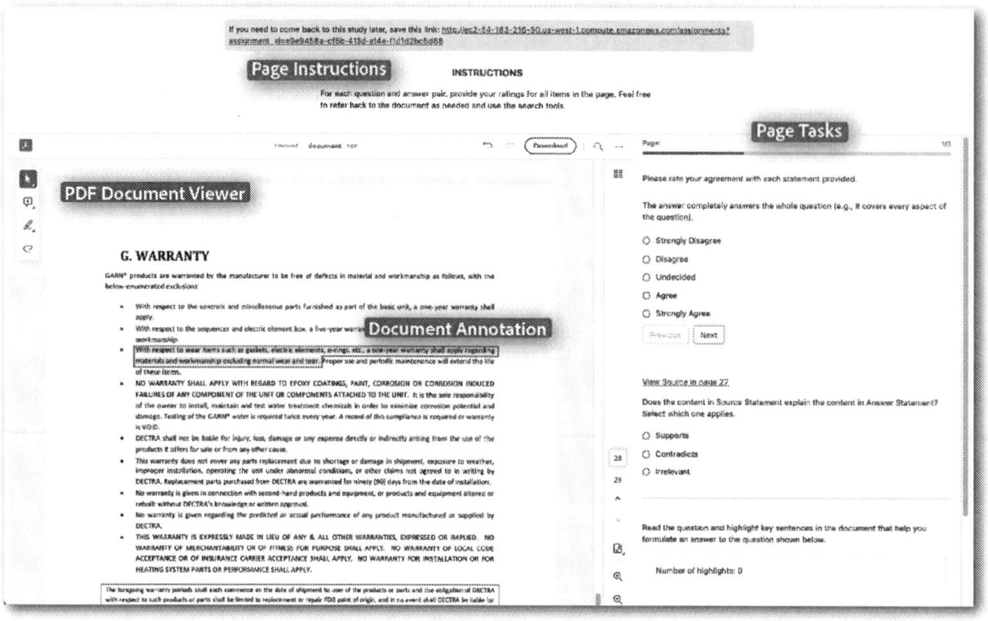

Figure 2: An example of the ATLAS annotator interface. Researchers can customize *Page Instructions* for each project. The *PDF Document Viewer* functions like a typical reader including common interactions such as scroll, zoom, text selection, and search. Researchers can include any number of tasks in the *Page Tasks* panel; these include survey tasks such as text entry, rank order, radio group, and checkboxes.

project GitHub repository[4] and in the supplementary material.

3.1 Toolkit Overview

ATLAS provides a toolkit library that allows researchers to define a data collection project programmatically. This programmatic approach provides flexibility in handling large amounts of data. A data collection project in ATLAS consists of the following components:

1. *Groups*: researchers can assign annotators to different annotation groups that contain different data collection tasks. For example, a researcher might have an evaluation where one group of annotators is only exposed to a control condition, and a second group is only exposed to a test condition.

2. *Pages*: an ATLAS project can contain any number of pages that are presented to annotators and guide the flow of the data collection project. Pages contain a PDF reader and relevant tasks for annotators to complete.

3. *Tasks*: a page can contain any number of data collection tasks (Figure 2). These can be either required or optional for annotators to proceed through the data collection. Section 3.2 details all the tasks supported.

3.2 Creating Instructions and Tasks

Once a researcher has defined a project goal, the first step in using ATLAS, is defining the instructions and tasks for data collection using the ATLAS toolkit, which results in a JSON file (Figure 1A).

Researchers can include project-level, page-level, and task-level instructions. These allow researchers to provide proper context and guidance to annotators providing responses. For example, start instructions can include annotation examples for annotators to review before starting any data collection tasks. Task-level instructions can also include a document source that scrolls the PDF to a specific location in the PDF. Document sources can be useful if a task requires the user to pay attention to a specific section or statement in the document.

For data collection, the ATLAS toolkit currently supports the following data:

1. Bounding boxes of PDF annotations (i.e., page highlights, free-form drawings, com-

[4]https://github.com/frictionlessweb/documentstudies/

ments) and underlying content (i.e., text, images, tables)

2. Timestamps of reading behavior analytics (e.g., document scroll position, zoom level, clicks, text search). Table Appendix B describes all behavior analytics that are currently supported.

3. Survey user responses (i.e., text entry, rank order, radio group, and checkbox group)

3.3 Managing and Deploying a Project

After an ATLAS project is created, the next step is uploading the project to the ATLAS administrator interface (Figure 1B). Additionally, a researcher uploads any PDF documents that are used in the data collection project. Once uploaded, ATLAS automatically generates a URL that is ready to be shared with annotators to begin the data collection tasks. Each project has a unique URL and a researcher can create any number of projects. All projects are listed in the administrator panel. Once the data collection is complete, the researcher can download the results for each project. Results are exported in a JSON file.

3.4 Collecting and Analyzing Responses

Researchers share a URL with annotators where they can begin working on the data collection tasks. Once an annotator begins a project, a unique URL is generated for that annotator. This allows an annotator to take breaks between tasks and/or return to the project at different times without losing their progress on completed responses. A demo URL is accessible through the project's GitHub repository.

A researcher can download responses for a project at any time. Downloads include any in-progress/partial responses as well as completed responses. The ATLAS toolkit provides functions to help researchers aggregate responses from users. Additionally, post-processing functions enable researchers to map PDF annotation bounding boxes to semantic content (i.e., text, images, tables).

4 Implementation

Backend: ATLAS is implemented using the web-app framework, Ruby on Rails[5]. PostgreSQL is used for the database. There are three key data models: 1) A *Document Table* handles file metadata and nomenclature. 2) A *Project Table* encapsulates comprehensive details about each project. 3) A *Project Assignments Table* tracks completed annotator responses.

Toolkit Processing Libraries: To specify a data collection project, researchers create a JSON file specifying the instructions and tasks. The ATLAS toolkit provides a set of Python functions that allow customizing the tasks. All instructions can be formatted using Markdown syntax. Once complete, the JSON file is uploaded to the application along with the required PDF documents. The toolkit also provides functions to aggregate results into readable data tables and post-process PDF annotations.

Frontend: The user interface is implemented using React with state management across the application governed by the context API. There are two main interfaces, the researcher interface, and the annotation interface. PDFs are rendered using Adobe's PDF Embed API.[6]

5 Example Use Cases

To showcase our system's broad applicability and impact, we review three example projects that have leveraged ATLAS's capabilities to meet research goals.

Document-Grounded Question Answering (QA) This project aims to collect pairs of questions and answers based on documents as well as attributions (texts, tables, images, or charts in the document) that help explain the answer. This dataset is similar to the Natural Questions dataset on Wikipedia articles (Kwiatkowski et al., 2019) but on a wider set of PDF documents from different areas of domain expertise. This dataset can be a crucial first step in fine-tuning models for automatic question answering, question generation, and source attribution grounded on the source document. The dataset is also critical for evaluating and benchmarking the performance of these document-based models. ATLAS enables researchers to create a custom study using openly licensed documents and annotation tasks where annotators author (potentially multiple) question-and-answer pairs for each document. Annotators can also highlight the source texts or other content in the PDF as attribution. ATLAS helped standardize, streamline, and significantly scale the

[5] https://rubyonrails.org

[6] https://developer.adobe.com/document-services/apis/pdf-embed/

data collection effort to over 3,000 unique documents and more than 50 data annotators, resulting in a dataset of over 20,000 question-and-answer pairs along with their attributions and forming a solid foundation for future model fine-tuning and benchmarking.

Document-Grounded QA Evaluation This project aims to scientifically and systematically evaluate large language models' (LLMs) document-based QA capabilities using metrics including answer quality, attribution, and bias. In particular, accurate and precise attribution is an essential feature to improve LLMs' trustworthiness when answering questions based on source documents (Liu et al., 2023a). Existing tools and literature focus on evaluating attributions based primarily on free-form texts but rarely on evaluating PDF-based QA attributions (Kamalloo et al., 2023b; Huang et al., 2023; Yue et al., 2023). However, providing a faithful interface that represents how real readers read digital documents for evaluation PDF-based QA attributions is important for ensuring evaluation consistency and quality (Kwon et al., 2014). ATLAS supports such evaluation by providing a consistent annotation UI with a natively integrated PDF viewer where attributions are shown as highlights directly in the PDF. Researchers can flexibly and programmatically create the evaluation task to include different types of quality metrics that they want to collect without the need to alter the UI. ATLAS has supported several rounds of attribution evaluation using two approaches. In one approach, annotators directly rate the quality of machine-generated attributions in terms of precision and recall. In a second approach, annotators provide their own attributions, and agreement between human- and machine-generated attributions is computed. In addition to attribution, ATLAS has also been used for evaluating model answering quality and bias. As an example, Saad-Falcon et al. (2023) have employed ATLAS to evaluate their novel automated QA methodology for long, structured documents.

Digital Reading Behavioral Data Collection Behavioral data on how people read and interact with digital documents can help deepen the understanding of reading patterns, improve the design of reading applications, and develop better personalization technologies for a more delightful digital reading experience (Rajendran et al., 2018; Wallace et al., 2022; Maity et al., 2017). Such data is typically proprietary and there exists no open-source tools to support the collection of such data. ATLAS aims to change the landscape by providing the capability to collect fine-grained implicit reading behaviors such as temporal mouse-over patterns, clicks, scrolls (direction and speed), search queries, comments, and highlights. ATLAS enables a non-intrusive way to collect such data in a reading interface that closely represents common software for consuming PDFs such as Adobe's Acrobat Reader and Apple's Preview, improving the representativeness of such behavioral data collected using ATLAS to real-world reading patterns. An ongoing study leverages ATLAS to collect one-of-a-kind, open-source, large-scale reading behaviors from professionals across various industries in the hope of unlocking future research in studying, analyzing, and improving digital reading experiences.

6 Conclusions

In this paper, we presented ATLAS, an open-source system for collecting PDF-centric human interaction data. ATLAS complements existing data collection tools by focusing on PDF-based user interactions and supports a wide range of interaction data collection tasks, such as question-and-answer pairs, QA attributions, and reading annotations and behaviors. It features a programmatically generated user interface, a toolkit for creating data collection tasks, and a suite of utilities for processing and analyzing the collected data. We demonstrated ATLAS's capabilities and applicability through several real-world use cases. We believe that ATLAS will be a valuable tool for researchers and practitioners working with PDF-based human interaction data, and we hope that it will enable new and exciting research in this area.

Broader Impacts and Limitations

ATLAS holds the potential to significantly impact document-based AI advancements, user experience design, and research accessibility. By enabling the collection of rich human interaction data on PDFs, it paves the way for more sophisticated AI models that understand and interact with documents, leading to improved question-answering, summarization, and personalization. This democratization of data collection empowers researchers and practitioners alike, fostering new avenues for document-based technology development. Furthermore, the data collected through ATLAS can shed light on user reading patterns, informing the design of more intuitive reading interfaces and navigation tools. Additionally, its unique capability for capturing PDF interactions allows for rigorous benchmarking and evaluation of document-based AI, fostering transparency and trust in these models.

However, it's important to acknowledge ATLAS's limitations. First, although ATLAS can be extended to data collection tasks beyond PDFs, it is currently limited to the formats of documents it can support. Expanding to include additional document formats, like Word documents or ePub files, would broaden its utility. Second, collecting user data carries ethical considerations. Robust security measures and data anonymization are essential to ensure participant privacy and trust. Third, scalability and efficiency remain to be tested and ensured, as handling extra large datasets and complex tasks can strain system resources. Optimizing the platform for smoother performance such as high-performing databases and load balancing will be crucial for supporting even large-scale research projects. Finally, any data collection effort might inadvertently introduce bias. Researchers must be mindful of these potential biases and employ appropriate mitigation strategies to ensure the collected data accurately reflects real-world interactions.

By addressing these limitations and continuously evolving, ATLAS strives to be a valuable tool for responsible and ethical data collection, ultimately fostering the development of trustworthy and impactful document-based AI technologies that benefit all users.

References

Yuntao Bai, Andy Jones, Kamal Ndousse, Amanda Askell, Anna Chen, Nova DasSarma, Dawn Drain, Stanislav Fort, Deep Ganguli, Tom Henighan, Nicholas Joseph, Saurav Kadavath, Jackson Kernion, Tom Conerly, Sheer El-Showk, Nelson Elhage, Zac Hatfield-Dodds, Danny Hernandez, Tristan Hume, Scott Johnston, Shauna Kravec, Liane Lovitt, Neel Nanda, Catherine Olsson, Dario Amodei, Tom Brown, Jack Clark, Sam McCandlish, Chris Olah, Ben Mann, and Jared Kaplan. 2022. Training a helpful and harmless assistant with reinforcement learning from human feedback.

Ann Bowling. 2005. Mode of questionnaire administration can have serious effects on data quality. *Journal of Public Health*, 27(3):281–291.

Hiuyi Cheng, Peirong Zhang, Sihang Wu, Jiaxin Zhang, Qiyuan Zhu, Zecheng Xie, Jing Li, Kai Ding, and Lianwen Jin. 2023. M6doc: A large-scale multi-format, multi-type, multi-layout, multi-language, multi-annotation category dataset for modern document layout analysis. In *Proceedings of the IEEE/CVF Conference on Computer Vision and Pattern Recognition (CVPR)*, pages 15138–15147.

Paul F Christiano, Jan Leike, Tom Brown, Miljan Martic, Shane Legg, and Dario Amodei. 2017. Deep reinforcement learning from human preferences. In *Advances in Neural Information Processing Systems*, volume 30. Curran Associates, Inc.

Renita Coleman, Paul Lieber, Andrew L Mendelson, and David D Kurpius. 2008. Public life and the internet: if you build a better website, will citizens become engaged? *New media & society*, 10(2):179–201.

Andrea Cuadra, Hansol Lee, Jason Cho, and Wendy Ju. 2021. Look at me when i talk to you: A video dataset to enable voice assistants to recognize errors. *arXiv preprint arXiv:2104.07153*.

Emily Denton, Mark Díaz, Ian Kivlichan, Vinodkumar Prabhakaran, and Rachel Rosen. 2021. Whose ground truth? accounting for individual and collective identities underlying dataset annotation. *arXiv preprint arXiv:2112.04554*.

Alexander R. Fabbri, Wojciech Kryściński, Bryan McCann, Caiming Xiong, Richard Socher, and Dragomir Radev. 2021. SummEval: Re-evaluating summarization evaluation. *Transactions of the Association for Computational Linguistics*, 9:391–409.

Sebastian Gehrmann, Elizabeth Clark, and Thibault Sellam. 2023. Repairing the cracked foundation: A survey of obstacles in evaluation practices for generated text. *Journal of Artificial Intelligence Research*, 77:103–166.

Jiuxiang Gu, Xiangxi Shi, Jason Kuen, Lu Qi, Ruiyi Zhang, Anqi Liu, Ani Nenkova, and Tong Sun. 2024. ADoPD: A large-scale document page decomposition dataset. In *The Twelfth International Conference on Learning Representations*.

Angela V Hausman and Jeffrey Sam Siekpe. 2009. The effect of web interface features on consumer online purchase intentions. *Journal of business research*, 62(1):5–13.

Dan Hendrycks, Collin Burns, Saurav Kadavath, Akul Arora, Steven Basart, Eric Tang, Dawn Song, and Jacob Steinhardt. 2021. Measuring mathematical problem solving with the MATH dataset. In *Thirty-fifth Conference on Neural Information Processing Systems Datasets and Benchmarks Track (Round 2)*.

Shiyuan Huang, Siddarth Mamidanna, Shreedhar Jangam, Yilun Zhou, and Leilani H. Gilpin. 2023. Can large language models explain themselves? a study of llm-generated self-explanations.

Ehsan Kamalloo, Nouha Dziri, Charles Clarke, and Davood Rafiei. 2023a. Evaluating open-domain question answering in the era of large language models. In *Proceedings of the 61st Annual Meeting of the Association for Computational Linguistics (Volume 1: Long Papers)*, pages 5591–5606, Toronto, Canada. Association for Computational Linguistics.

Ehsan Kamalloo, Aref Jafari, Xinyu Zhang, Nandan Thakur, and Jimmy Lin. 2023b. Hagrid: A human-llm collaborative dataset for generative information-seeking with attribution.

Jonathan K. Kummerfeld. 2019. SLATE: A super-lightweight annotation tool for experts. In *Proceedings of the 57th Annual Meeting of the Association for Computational Linguistics: System Demonstrations*, pages 7–12, Florence, Italy. Association for Computational Linguistics.

Tom Kwiatkowski, Jennimaria Palomaki, Olivia Redfield, Michael Collins, Ankur Parikh, Chris Alberti, Danielle Epstein, Illia Polosukhin, Jacob Devlin, Kenton Lee, et al. 2019. Natural questions: a benchmark for question answering research. *Transactions of the Association for Computational Linguistics*, 7:453–466.

Ohbyung Kwon, Namyeon Lee, and Bongsik Shin. 2014. Data quality management, data usage experience and acquisition intention of big data analytics. *International Journal of Information Management*, 34(3):387–394.

Mina Lee, Percy Liang, and Qian Yang. 2022. Coauthor: Designing a human-ai collaborative writing dataset for exploring language model capabilities. In *Proceedings of the 2022 CHI conference on human factors in computing systems*, pages 1–19.

Yoonjoo Lee, Kyungjae Lee, Sunghyun Park, Dasol Hwang, Jaehyeon Kim, Hong-In Lee, and Moontae Lee. 2023. QASA: Advanced question answering on scientific articles. In *Proceedings of the 40th International Conference on Machine Learning*, volume 202 of *Proceedings of Machine Learning Research*, pages 19036–19052. PMLR.

Junyi Li, Xiaoxue Cheng, Xin Zhao, Jian-Yun Nie, and Ji-Rong Wen. 2023. HaluEval: A large-scale hallucination evaluation benchmark for large language models. In *Proceedings of the 2023 Conference on Empirical Methods in Natural Language Processing*, pages 6449–6464, Singapore. Association for Computational Linguistics.

Minghao Li, Yiheng Xu, Lei Cui, Shaohan Huang, Furu Wei, Zhoujun Li, and Ming Zhou. 2020. DocBank: A benchmark dataset for document layout analysis. In *Proceedings of the 28th International Conference on Computational Linguistics*, pages 949–960, Barcelona, Spain (Online). International Committee on Computational Linguistics.

Nelson Liu, Tianyi Zhang, and Percy Liang. 2023a. Evaluating verifiability in generative search engines. In *Findings of the Association for Computational Linguistics: EMNLP 2023*, pages 7001–7025, Singapore. Association for Computational Linguistics.

Yang Liu, Yuanshun Yao, Jean-Francois Ton, Xiaoying Zhang, Ruocheng Guo, Hao Cheng, Yegor Klochkov, Muhammad Faaiz Taufiq, and Hang Li. 2023b. Trustworthy llms: a survey and guideline for evaluating large language models' alignment.

Kyle Lo, Zejiang Shen, Benjamin Newman, Joseph Chang, Russell Authur, Erin Bransom, Stefan Candra, Yoganand Chandrasekhar, Regan Huff, Bailey Kuehl, Amanpreet Singh, Chris Wilhelm, Angele Zamarron, Marti A. Hearst, Daniel Weld, Doug Downey, and Luca Soldaini. 2023. PaperMage: A unified toolkit for processing, representing, and manipulating visually-rich scientific documents. In *Proceedings of the 2023 Conference on Empirical Methods in Natural Language Processing: System Demonstrations*, pages 495–507, Singapore. Association for Computational Linguistics.

Suman Kalyan Maity, Abhishek Panigrahi, and Animesh Mukherjee. 2017. Book reading behavior on goodreads can predict the amazon best sellers. In *Proceedings of the 2017 IEEE/ACM International Conference on Advances in Social Networks Analysis and Mining 2017*, ASONAM '17. ACM.

Stephen Mayhew and Dan Roth. 2018. TALEN: Tool for annotation of low-resource ENtities. In *Proceedings of ACL 2018, System Demonstrations*, pages 80–86, Melbourne, Australia. Association for Computational Linguistics.

Mark Neumann, Zejiang Shen, and Sam Skjonsberg. 2021. PAWLS: PDF annotation with labels and structure. In *Proceedings of the 59th Annual Meeting of the Association for Computational Linguistics and the 11th International Joint Conference on Natural Language Processing: System Demonstrations*, pages 258–264, Online. Association for Computational Linguistics.

Jianmo Ni, Jiacheng Li, and Julian McAuley. 2019. Justifying recommendations using distantly-labeled reviews and fine-grained aspects. In *Proceedings of the 2019 Conference on Empirical Methods in Natural Language Processing and the 9th International Joint Conference on Natural Language Processing (EMNLP-IJCNLP)*, pages 188–197, Hong Kong, China. Association for Computational Linguistics.

Philip V. Ogren. 2006. Knowtator: A protégé plug-in for annotated corpus construction. In *Proceedings of the Human Language Technology Conference of the NAACL, Companion Volume: Demonstrations*, pages 273–275, New York City, USA. Association for Computational Linguistics.

Long Ouyang, Jeff Wu, Xu Jiang, Diogo Almeida, Carroll L. Wainwright, Pamela Mishkin, Chong Zhang, Sandhini Agarwal, Katarina Slama, Alex Ray, John

Schulman, Jacob Hilton, Fraser Kelton, Luke Miller, Maddie Simens, Amanda Askell, Peter Welinder, Paul Christiano, Jan Leike, and Ryan Lowe. 2022. Training language models to follow instructions with human feedback.

Birgit Pfitzmann, Christoph Auer, Michele Dolfi, Ahmed S. Nassar, and Peter Staar. 2022. Doclaynet: A large human-annotated dataset for document-layout segmentation. In *Proceedings of the 28th ACM SIGKDD Conference on Knowledge Discovery and Data Mining*, KDD '22, page 3743–3751, New York, NY, USA. Association for Computing Machinery.

Ramkumar Rajendran, Anurag Kumar, Kelly E Carter, Daniel T Levin, and Gautam Biswas. 2018. Predicting learning by analyzing eye-gaze data of reading behavior. *International Educational Data Mining Society*.

Vipula Rawte, Amit Sheth, and Amitava Das. 2023. A survey of hallucination in large foundation models.

Jon Saad-Falcon, Joe Barrow, Alexa Siu, Ani Nenkova, David Seunghyun Yoon, Ryan A. Rossi, and Franck Dernoncourt. 2023. Pdftriage: Question answering over long, structured documents.

John Schulman, Filip Wolski, Prafulla Dhariwal, Alec Radford, and Oleg Klimov. 2017. Proximal policy optimization algorithms.

Hiroyuki Shindo, Yohei Munesada, and Yuji Matsumoto. 2018. PDFAnno: a web-based linguistic annotation tool for PDF documents. In *Proceedings of the Eleventh International Conference on Language Resources and Evaluation (LREC 2018)*, Miyazaki, Japan. European Language Resources Association (ELRA).

Ben Shneiderman. 2022. *Human-centered AI*. Oxford University Press, London, England.

Andreas Sonderegger and Juergen Sauer. 2010. The influence of design aesthetics in usability testing: Effects on user performance and perceived usability. *Applied ergonomics*, 41(3):403–410.

Brendan Spillane, Séamus Lawless, and Vincent Wade. 2018. Increasing and decreasing perceived bias by distorting the quality of news website design. In *Proceedings of the 32nd International BCS Human Computer Interaction Conference 32*, pages 1–13.

Pontus Stenetorp, Sampo Pyysalo, Goran Topić, Tomoko Ohta, Sophia Ananiadou, and Jun'ichi Tsujii. 2012. brat: a web-based tool for NLP-assisted text annotation. In *Proceedings of the Demonstrations at the 13th Conference of the European Chapter of the Association for Computational Linguistics*, pages 102–107, Avignon, France. Association for Computational Linguistics.

Ashley Still. 2020. Adobe unveils ambitious multi-year vision for pdf: Introduces liquid mode.

Diane M. Strong, Yang W. Lee, and Richard Y. Wang. 1997. Data quality in context. *Communications of the ACM*, 40(5):103–110.

Alon Talmor, Jonathan Herzig, Nicholas Lourie, and Jonathan Berant. 2019. CommonsenseQA: A question answering challenge targeting commonsense knowledge. In *Proceedings of the 2019 Conference of the North American Chapter of the Association for Computational Linguistics: Human Language Technologies, Volume 1 (Long and Short Papers)*, pages 4149–4158, Minneapolis, Minnesota. Association for Computational Linguistics.

Lida Theodorou, Daniela Massiceti, Luisa Zintgraf, Simone Stumpf, Cecily Morrison, Edward Cutrell, Matthew Tobias Harris, and Katja Hofmann. 2021. Disability-first dataset creation: Lessons from constructing a dataset for teachable object recognition with blind and low vision data collectors. In *Proceedings of the 23rd International ACM SIGACCESS Conference on Computers and Accessibility*, pages 1–12.

Roger Tourangeau and Tom W. Smith. 1996. Asking sensitive questions: The impact of data collection mode, question format, and question context. *Public Opinion Quarterly*, 60(2):275.

Shaun Wallace, Zoya Bylinskii, Jonathan Dobres, Bernard Kerr, Sam Berlow, Rick Treitman, Nirmal Kumawat, Kathleen Arpin, Dave B Miller, Jeff Huang, and Ben D Sawyer. 2022. Towards individuated reading experiences: Different fonts increase reading speed for different individuals. *ACM Trans. Comput. Hum. Interact.*, 29(4):1–56.

Lucy Lu Wang, Isabel Cachola, Jonathan Bragg, Evie Yu-Yen Cheng, Chelsea Haupt, Matt Latzke, Bailey Kuehl, Madeleine van Zuylen, Linda Wagner, and Daniel S. Weld. 2021. Improving the accessibility of scientific documents: Current state, user needs, and a system solution to enhance scientific pdf accessibility for blind and low vision users.

Yufei Wang, Wanjun Zhong, Liangyou Li, Fei Mi, Xingshan Zeng, Wenyong Huang, Lifeng Shang, Xin Jiang, and Qun Liu. 2023. Aligning large language models with human: A survey.

Chih-Hsuan Wei, Hung-Yu Kao, and Zhiyong Lu. 2013. Pubtator: a web-based text mining tool for assisting biocuration. *Nucleic Acids Research*, 41(W1):W518–W522.

Jacob O Wobbrock, Lara Hattatoglu, Anya K Hsu, Marijn A Burger, and Michael J Magee. 2021. The goldilocks zone: young adults' credibility perceptions of online news articles based on visual appearance. *New Review of Hypermedia and Multimedia*, 27(1-2):51–96.

Seid Muhie Yimam, Chris Biemann, Richard Eckart de Castilho, and Iryna Gurevych. 2014. Automatic annotation suggestions and custom annotation layers in WebAnno. In *Proceedings of 52nd Annual Meeting of the Association for Computational Linguistics: System Demonstrations*, pages 91–96, Baltimore, Maryland. Association for Computational Linguistics.

Xiang Yue, Boshi Wang, Ziru Chen, Kai Zhang, Yu Su, and Huan Sun. 2023. Automatic evaluation of attribution by large language models. In *Findings of the Association for Computational Linguistics: EMNLP 2023*, pages 4615–4635, Singapore. Association for Computational Linguistics.

Daochen Zha, Zaid Pervaiz Bhat, Kwei-Herng Lai, Fan Yang, Zhimeng Jiang, Shaochen Zhong, and Xia Hu. 2023. Data-centric artificial intelligence: A survey.

Wenting Zhao, Xiang Ren, Jack Hessel, Claire Cardie, Yejin Choi, and Yuntian Deng. 2024. (inthe)wildchat: 570k chatGPT interaction logs in the wild. In *The Twelfth International Conference on Learning Representations*.

Xu Zhong, Jianbin Tang, and Antonio Jimeno Yepes. 2019. Publaynet: largest dataset ever for document layout analysis.

A Toolkit JSON Schema

The output of the ATLAS toolkit is a JSON file which is then uploaded to the ATLAS interface. The JSON file defines the data collection instructions and tasks. Below is a snippet of the schema for specifying a project:

```
{ "schema_version": "v0",
  "metadata": {
    "name": str,
    #... any other needed fields can be added ...
  },
  "start_instructions": str,
  "end_instructions": str,
  "groups": [ 0 ],
  "group": null,
  "page_index": 0,
  "content": {
    "0": { "pages": [
      { "id": str,
        "page_layout": str <pdf_layout, text_layout>,
        "instructions": str,
        "document_id": str,
        "hide_previous_button": bool <default false>
        "save_pdf_interactions": bool <default false>
        "tasks": [ #... list of tasks ... ] },
        #... any number of tasks can be added ...
    ] }
  }
}
```

B Reading Behavior Analytics

ATLAS supports data collection of reading behavior analytics. These events are captured as timestamps and include the following:

1. Current active page: Changes to the page in view
2. Text copy: On copying text from the document
3. Text search: When the user searches for any text via the document search field
4. Zoom level: When zoom-in/out actions are performed from the page control toolbar
5. Page click: When a user clicks on any document page
6. Page double click: When a user double clicks on any document page
7. Mouse enter/leave: The mouse pointer enters/leaves any page
8. Annotation added: A new annotation is added to the document
9. Annotation clicked: An existing annotation is clicked
10. Annotation updated: An existing annotation is updated
11. Annotation deleted: An annotation is deleted
12. Annotation mouse over or mouse out: The mouse pointer moves over/out of any annotation
13. Annotation selected or unselected: Any existing annotation is selected/unselected
14. Annotation count: Total number of document annotations updated whenever a new annotation is added or any existing annotation is deleted

BeLeaf: Belief Prediction as Tree Generation

John Murzaku[△◇], **Owen Rambow**[♠◇]
[△] Department of Computer Science [♠] Department of Linguistics
[◇] Institute for Advanced Computational Science
Stony Brook University, Stony Brook, NY, USA

Abstract

We present a novel approach to predicting source-and-target factuality by transforming it into a linearized tree generation task. Unlike previous work, our model and representation format fully account for the factuality tree structure, generating the full chain of nested sources instead of the last source only. Furthermore, our linearized tree representation significantly compresses the amount of tokens needed compared to other representations, allowing for fully end-to-end systems. We achieve state-of-the-art results on FactBank and the Modal Dependency Corpus, which are both corpora annotating source-and-target event factuality. Our results on fine-tuning validate the strong generality of the proposed linearized tree generation task, which can be easily adapted to other corpora with a similar structure. We then present BeLeaf, a system which directly leverages the linearized tree representation to create both sentence level and document level visualizations. Our system adds several missing pieces to the source-and-target factuality task such as coreference resolution and event head word to syntactic span conversion. Our demo code is available on `https://github.com/yurpl/beleaf` and our video is available on `https://youtu.be/SpbMNnin-Po`.

1 Introduction

The term "factuality" (or belief[1]) refers to what extent an event mentioned by the author or by sources in a text is presented as being factual. In other words, the task aims to predict whether the author or the mentioned sources in the text believes the event happened. The event factuality prediction task (EFP) has received a lot of attention over the past few years, but only in the perspective of the author of the text, disregarding the factuality of events according to all sources (Lee et al., 2015; Stanovsky et al., 2017; Rudinger et al., 2018; Pouran Ben Veyseh et al., 2019; Jiang and de Marneffe, 2021).

Two notable exceptions are the FactBank corpus (Saurí and Pustejovsky, 2009) and the Modal Dependency Parsing corpus (MDP) (Yao et al., 2021). Both corpora annotate event factuality according to the author of the text, and also according to the sources mentioned in the text, with some slight differences. FactBank represents factuality on the sentence level, while the MDP corpus represents factuality as a document-level modal dependency structures (MDS) proposed by Vigus et al. (2019). The MDP structure uses a tree representation where the author of the text (AUTHOR) is the root, and events and other sources are child nodes of the author. The corpora also differ slightly on labels: FactBank annotates the factuality of events (alongside their polarities) as CT (certain), PR (probable), PS (possible), UU (unknown), while the MDP corpus annotates events as full positive (Pos), partial positive (Prt), positive neutral (Neut), negative neutral (Neutneg), partial negative (Prtneg) and full negative (Neg).

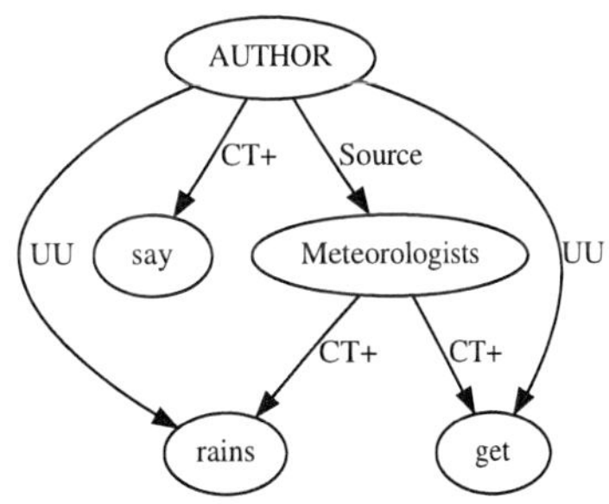

Figure 1: Source-and-target factuality represented as a modal dependency structure for the sentence "Meteorologists **say** the weather will **get** worse because there will be **rains**."

An NLP system's ability to accurately attribute events' factuality according to all sources is vital

[1]We use the terms interchangeably since our system is called BeLeaf. Factuality is closely related to the notion of "belief" as used in cognitive science and AI.

Proceedings of the 2024 Conference of the North American Chapter of the Association for Computational Linguistics: Human Language Technologies (Volume 3: System Demonstrations), pages 97–106
June 16-21, 2024 ©2024 Association for Computational Linguistics

for downstream tasks that are based on those events. Consider the example sentence in Figure 1 where we have three events: the *say* event, the *rain* event, and the *get* event. We also have one source that the author mentions, *Meteorologists*. The author is certain (CT+) that the say event happened . However, the author does not tell us (UU) about their view of the factuality of the rains event or the get event because it is being presented by the source Meteorologists. According to the source Meteorologists, these events are factual (CT+). An information extraction system should extract the specific factuality of these events depending on all sources presenting the event, not only the author. Systems and humans can then make a separate judgement about the weather based on their sense of the trustworthiness of the author and of meteorologists.

In this paper, we present the source-and-target event factuality prediction task as a linearized tree generation task. We represent both FactBank and the MDP corpus as linearized trees, achieving state-of-the-art results for both corpora and beating both our FactBank results (Murzaku et al., 2023) and the MDP results from Yao et al. (2022). This representation format not only performs better, but also allows for a clear and interpretable visualization, which we show in our BeLeaf system.

2 Related Work

Author-Only Factuality All previous approaches to the event factuality prediction task were in the author-only setting, ignoring nested sources. Early approaches used rule-based systems and/or lexical and dependency tree based features (Nairn et al., 2006; Lotan et al., 2013). Early machine learning work used SVMs alongside dependency tree and lexical based features (Diab et al., 2009; Prabhakaran et al., 2010; Lee et al., 2015; Stanovsky et al., 2017). Neural work includes LSTMs with multi-task or single-task approaches (Rudinger et al., 2018) or using BERT representations alongside a graph convolutional neural network (Pouran Ben Veyseh et al., 2019). Jiang and de Marneffe (2021) expand on previous work by using other event factuality corpora in multiple training paradigms while also introducing a simpler architecture. These approaches evaluate on Pearson correlation and mean absolute error (MAE), failing to capture individual label performance and assuming events are given. We (Murzaku et al., 2022) provided the first end-to-end evaluation using F-measure and improve on FactBank.

Source and Target Factuality One of the main corpora experimented on in this paper, which annotates all events introduced in a corpus of exclusively newswire text is the FactBank corpus (Saurí and Pustejovsky, 2009).The FactBank corpus not only annotates the factuality presented by the author of a text towards an event, but also the factuality of events according to their presentation by sources mentioned inside of the text. Saurí and Pustejovsky (2012) were the first to investigate and perform experiments on the source and target annotations in FactBank. Their evaluation was not end-to-end and was given manual annotations, so it is therefore not comparable to our results on FactBank. We (Murzaku et al., 2023) were the first to represent the event factuality prediction task as a generation task using Flan-T5 while also accounting for source and target factuality. However, our previous model did not account for the full nesting structure of the source since our model only generated the last nested source.

Our new system generates the full nesting structure, and is therefore not comparable to our previous FactBank results as that task was far easier and incomplete. Yao et al. (2021) also propose a source-and-target corpus (MDP corpus) and Yao et al. (2022) improve on their previous results by using a prompt-based approach where they treat factuality prediction as a BIO tagging task, fine-tuning on XLM-RoBERTa (Conneau et al., 2020). Following the modal dependency structure from Vigus et al. (2019), their corpus annotates events, sources, and credibility of sources throughout a whole document. The top level source is always the author of the text. While similar to FactBank in some ways, there are some key differences (which we describe in Section 3.1), making the corpora incompatible for joint experiments with FactBank.

Document Level Factuality Qian et al. (2019) are the first to present the document level factuality task, but again in the author-only setting. Their work is expanded by Cao et al. (2021), Qian et al. (2022), and more recently Zhang et al. (2023). In this task the input is a document and a factuality target, and the output is the label representing the factuality attributed by the author to the provided target. Our task is different, which is to find all sources and targets of factuality assessments.

Our work differs from the previous work on

event factuality prediction in two major ways:
(i) We are the first to provide a novel and state-of-the-art machine learning representation for the source-and-target event factuality prediction tasks (both sentence level and document level).
(ii) To our knowledge, we are the first to provide a unified toolkit and intuitive front-end interface for the event factuality prediction task. Our toolkit improves on several shortcomings of previous corpora and approaches to this task and our interface leverages the new tree representation for a clear and interpretable visualization.

3 Approach

3.1 Data Representation

FactBank The FactBank corpus annotates event factuality according to the author and sources attributied by the author. When a source is not present or explicitly mentioned in text, FactBank uses the *GEN* label. For example, in the sentence *The transaction is expected to close*, there is no explicit mention of a source attributing the events, therefore being labeled *GEN*. When a sentence contains a fragment of a quotation, FactBank uses the DUMMY label. We represent all sources including *GEN* and *DUMMY*.

MDP corpus The MDP corpus also annotates factuality of events according to the author and nested sources. Additionally, the MDP corpus annotates the factuality between the author and embedded sources (or further embedded sources) to account for overall credibility of sources by attributing the author's certainty towards them. For example, in Figure 1, the MDP corpus would annotate the edge between AUTHOR and Meteorologists as *Pos*, or full positive, meaning the author is certain the Meteorologists are presenting an event. In our linearized tree representation, we include these factuality labels when beginning a new nest to also capture credibility. Finally, like *GEN* in FactBank, the MDP corpus uses NULL to capture sources that are not present or explicitly mentioned in text.

Tree Generation We approach the source-and-target event factuality prediction task as a linearized tree generation task. Consider the example sentence from Figure 1 in a FactBank format. We reformat the FactBank data as the following input/output pair for machine learning:
Input: Meteorologists say the weather will get worse because more rains are on the way.

Pos	Prtpos	Prtneg	Neg
true	ptrue	pfalse	false

Table 1: Factuality values for the MDP corpus

CT+	PR+	UU	PR-	CT-
true	ptrue	unknown	pfalse	false

Table 2: Factuality values for the FactBank corpus

Output Tree: (AUTHOR (rains unknown) (get unknown) (say true) (Meteorologists nest (rains true) (get true)))

We add the special *nest* token to denote the beginning of a nested source and their respective presentation of events.

3.2 Labels

In Section 1, we present the corpus-specific labels. The labels are as follows:
Certain: Corresponding to FactBank CT$\pm$, MDP Pos/Neg. Here, the author commits to the truth or falseness of the presented situation.
Probable: Corresponding to FactBank PR$\pm$, MDP Prtpos/Prtneg. Here, the author presents the situation as probable.
Fully underspecified Corresponding to FactBank UU. The source does not know what is the factual status of the event, or does not commit a belief it.

For our linearized tree generations, we convert each label to distinct words. For FactBank, we follow our previous FactBank work (Murzaku et al., 2022) and collapse the PR+/PS+ and PR-/PS- labels. Similarly, for the MDP corpus we follow Yao et al. (2022) and collapse the Prt/Neut and Prtneg/Neutneg labels. Table 1 and Table 2 show our mapped values for the MDP and FactBank corpora respectively.

3.3 Model

We use the encoder-decoder pre-trained Flan-T5 model (Chung et al., 2022) and the decoder only GPT-3 model (Brown et al., 2020). The Flan-T5 model is an instruction fine-tuned model with significant performance improvements compared to T5 (Raffel et al., 2020) and better adaptability to unseen tasks as a result of instruction tuning. Furthermore, the larger parameter variants of Flan-T5 have comparable or better performance on some tasks to GPT-3. By formulating the linearized tree construction as a generation task, our models are

	MiF1	AMiF1	AMF1	CT+	PR+	UU	PR-	CT-
Murzaku et al. (2022)	-	-	0.680	0.767	**0.714**	0.735	**0.667**	0.519
Murzaku et al. (2023)*	0.645	0.740	0.616	**0.815**	0.456	0.717	0.444	0.646
Flan-T5-Tree (Ours)	**0.695**	**0.766**	**0.708**	0.805	0.587	**0.752**	**0.667**	**0.733**
GPT-3-Tree (Ours)	0.658	0.760	0.678	0.778	0.455	0.747	**0.667**	0.723

Table 3: Results on the FactBank corpus for our Flan-T5 and GPT-3 systems evaluating on micro-f1 (MiF1), author micro-f1 (AMiF1), author macro-f1 (AMF1), and author per-label f1. We show baseline results from Murzaku et al. (2022) and redo Murzaku et al. (2023) for direct comparison (signaled by *). A shaded cell indicates state-of-the-art and statistically significant ($p < 0.05$)

	dev	test
Yao et al. (2021) P	0.697	0.675
Yao et al. (2021) J	0.703	0.690
Yao et al. (2022)	0.727	0.719
Flan-T5-Tree (Ours)	0.762	**0.749**
GPT-3-Tree (Ours)	**0.764**	0.741

Table 4: Results on the MDP corpus evaluated on micro-f1 compared to previous state-of-the-art results from Yao et al. (2022)

end-to-end and do not need gold event words as input.

4 Experiments: Fine-tuning

4.1 Corpora

We use our split of FactBank (Murzaku et al., 2022) for all examples including author and non-author sources. We also use the MDP corpus split from Yao et al. (2021). Like Yao et al. (2021) and Yao et al. (2022), we only consider examples with two levels of sources. For FactBank, we consider all levels of sources, but the majority have between one and three levels, with only four examples having three levels of sources.

4.2 Experiment Details

We use a standard fine-tuning approach on Flan-T5 and GPT-3. We fine-tune our Flan-T5 models for at most 20 epochs with a learning rate of 3e-4, with early stopping being used if the validation micro-F1 did not increase. We use task-specific prefixes and note that using instructions did not boost performance. Our Flan-T5 experiments are averaged over three runs using fixed seeds. We perform significance testing to previous baselines using a paired t-test. Due to costs, our GPT-3 experiments are performed once. We leave more experimental details to Appendix B.

4.3 Evaluation

We evaluate on micro-f1 (MiF), author-only micro-f1 (AMiF1), and author-only macro-f1 (AMF1) for FactBank. All of these metrics help us quantify to what extent we capture the full author and non-author sources in our generations: MiF1 shows how well we can generate full tree structures including their nesting, AMiF1 shows how well our model characterizes events only from the perspective of the author (which is a majority of events), and AMF1 shows how well we predict *all* factuality labels regardless of frequency, according to the author. For the modal dependency corpus, we follow Yao et al. (2022) evaluating on micro-f1.

4.4 Results: Fine-tuning

FactBank Table 3 shows results for our linearized tree generation model on the FactBank corpus. We compare our results to our baselines from Murzaku et al. (2022) and Murzaku et al. (2023). Murzaku et al. (2023) do not generate nested sources. We modify our baseline to generate all sources by adding the full nestings to their source-and-target triplet generation task. For example, a doubly nested triplet (Mary, said, true) becomes (AUTHOR_John_Mary, said, true). Our Flan-T5 system outperforms the previous state-of-the-art results and GPT-3 on all micro-f1, author-only micro-f1, author macro-f1. Furthermore, on the per-label f-measures, we see the largest boost and new SOTA in the CT- label (9% absolute increase), and slight but statistically significant increase in the UU label.

MDP Corpus Table 4 shows results for our linearized tree generation models on the MDP corpus. We beat the previous state of the art from Yao et al. (2022) on dev by 3.7% and on test by 3%. We observe that on test, fine-tuning Flan-T5 outperforms fine-tuning GPT-3, which can be explained

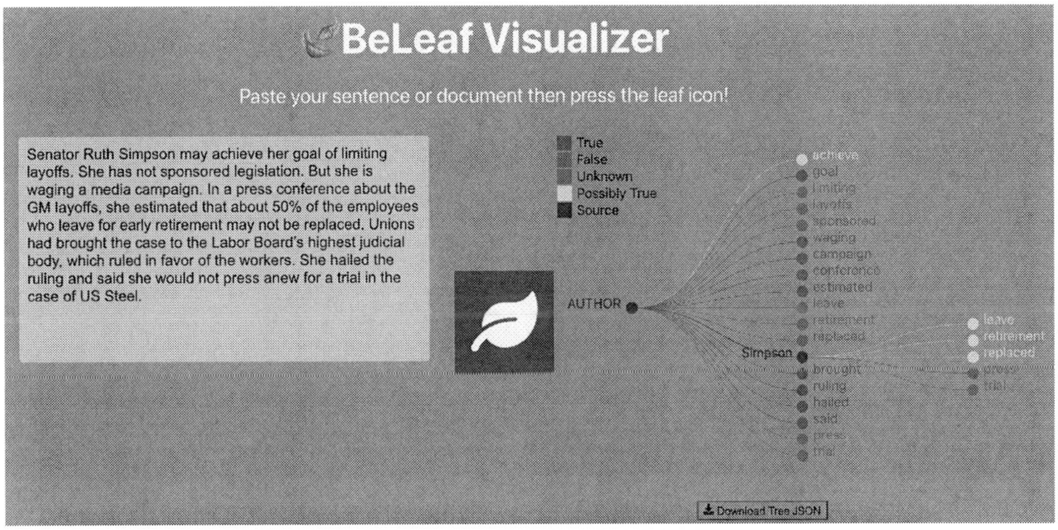

Figure 2: The BeLeaf system with a textbox for sentence or document inputs, the leaf button to begin inference, and our output tree with corresponding belief values as edge colors and labels.

by Flan-T5's generalizability to unseen tasks from instruction tuning.

5 BeLeaf: System Description

In this section, we present our BeLeaf system which leverages our generated tree structure. Our system is split into three parts: a generalized API for querying our Flan-T5 model with either sentences or documents, a preprocessing pipeline where we improve on the document level event factuality/belief task from Yao et al. (2021) by accounting for coreference, and a postprocessing pipeline accounting for syntactic spans with a tree visualization tool. Our system is shown in Figure 2.

5.1 API

We build a REST API using Flask (Grinberg, 2018), adding a single inference endpoint for all inference. Our API then queries our top-performing Flan-T5 model fine-tuned on FactBank. Before beginning inference, we perform a preprocessing pipeline.

5.2 Preprocessing

To account for both sentence and document level belief, we use spaCy (Honnibal and Montani, 2017) for splitting our model into sentences, and then pass this into our sentence-level FactBank model. This allows us to maximize our systems speed but we still need to account for beliefs across sentences. Therefore, to create a true document level belief system, we add a coreference resolver in our system. The MDP Corpus (Yao et al., 2021) is not a true document level representation of belief since they do not account for coreference resolution, and therefore a source can be repeated. We use the fastcoref library (Otmazgin et al., 2022) to perform coreference which was found to maximize speed with a minimal drop in accuracy for the coreference resolution task.

5.3 Postprocessing and Tree Visualization

Postprocessing After we get an output from our model, we perform a postprocessing pipeline to get syntactic spans. Since both FactBank and the MDP corpora annotate only syntactic head words or noun events, we oftentimes miss the full syntactic span and context of the event in question. To address this, we create a head-to-span module that uses spaCy (Honnibal and Montani, 2017) to return the full syntactic span. We include this representation as a hover-over in the tree visualization and also include it as a data download option.

Tree Visualization The final piece of our system is our tree visualization module. A sample output of our tree output is shown in the right hand side of Figure 2. To clearly distinguish between nested sources and their child events, we do not visualize with a DAG structure like the representation in Figure 1 where edges connect to nodes from both the author and the nested source, but rather a distinguished-source tree structure. All visualizations are made in JavaScript using the d3 library (Bostock, 2012). Furthermore, to allow researchers

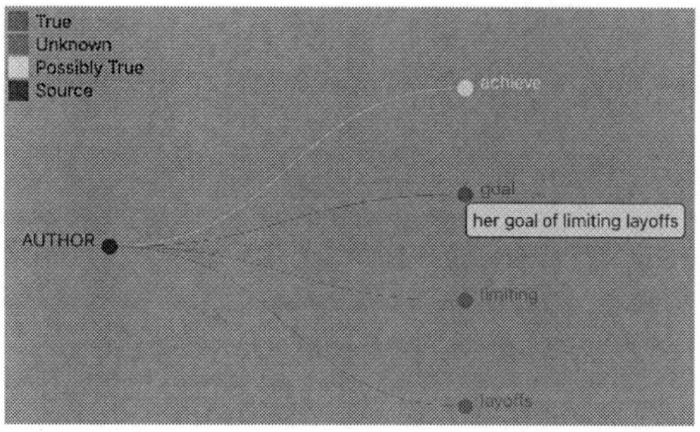

Figure 3: Sentence level output including syntactic span labels.

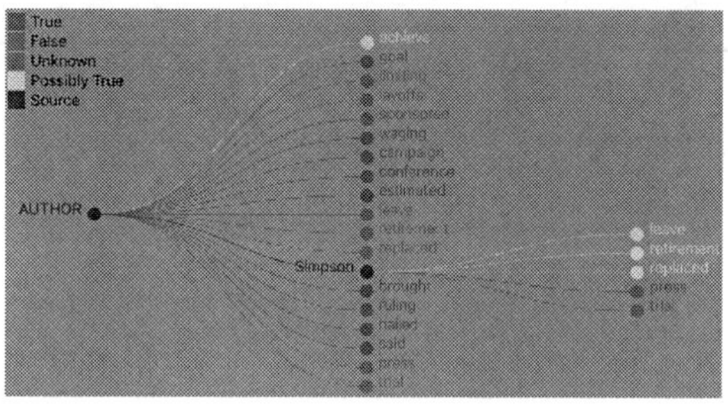

Figure 4: Document level output with a nested source Simpson.

and users of our package to utilize the tree information, we include a download data button that returns the full tree in JSON format. This JSON file includes all nodes with their parent/child structure and events as syntactic spans or heads with their corresponding belief values.

6 BeLeaf: Output and Visualization

In this section, we provide examples for both sentence level and document level belief, alongside their corresponding tree outputs and JSON representations.

Sentence Level Consider the following sentence:

```
Senator Ruth Simpson may achieve her
goal of limiting layoffs.
```

Here, the author presents multiple events: achieve, goal, limiting, layoffs. Note that in FactBank, an event can also be a noun, which is why goal and layoffs are included. Figure 3 shows the tree structure and a hover-over syntactic span from our head-to-span output.

Document Level We now expand the previous example to show a short document level output, including coreference and nested sources:

```
Senator Ruth Simpson may achieve
her goal of limiting layoffs.  She
has not sponsored legislation.  But
she is waging a media campaign.  In
a press conference about the GM
layoffs, she estimated that about 50%
of the employees who leave for early
retirement may not be replaced.  Unions
had brought the case to the Labor
Board's highest judicial body, which
ruled in favor of the workers.  She
hailed the ruling and said she would
not press anew for a trial in the case
of US Steel.
```

Our output is shown in Figure 4. Our system correctly coreferences the pronoun she with Senator Ruth Simpson, tracking her presentation of events throughout this document. Furthermore, this example effectively visualizes the nested belief/source-and-targetr factuality structure. For example, we see the perspective of events leave, retirement, replaced, press, and trial according to both the author and according to Senator Ruth Simpson.

Output JSON As shown in Figure 2, our system also includeds a button to download a JSON formatted tree structure. Using our document level example, we show a shortened example output:


```
{
  "name": "AUTHOR",
  "children": [
    {
      "name": "retirement",
      "belief": "unknown",
      "synSpan": "early retirement",
      "children": []
    },
    ...,
    {
      "name": "Simpson",
      "children": [
        {
          "name": "retirement",
          "belief": "possibly true",
          "synSpan": "early retirement",
          "children": []
        },
        ...,
      ]
    }
  ]
}
```


7 Conclusion

We propose a linearized tree generation model for the source-and-target event factuality task prediction using Flan-T5 and GPT-3. We evaluate the model on FactBank and the MDP corpus, and achieve results for both. With our new representation and state of the art Flan-T5 system, we present BeLeaf, a system for both sentence and document level factuality. We provide a preprocessing pipeline that accounts for coreference to create true document level representations of factuality. An inference API is then made which feeds to a postprocessing pipeline that creates syntactic spans from head words for users to see the full event contexts. Finally, we merge everything into a tree visualization software that also includes a data download option.

Acknowledgements

This material is based upon work supported by the National Science Foundation under Award No. 2125295 (NRT-HDR: Detecting and Addressing Bias in Data, Humans, and Institutions). Any opinions, findings and conclusions or recommendations expressed in this material are those of the author(s) and do not necessarily reflect the views of the National Science Foundation.

We thank the Institute for AI-Driven Discovery and Innovation at Stony Brook University for access to the computing resources needed for this work. These resources were made possible by NSF grant No. 1919752 (Major Research Infrastructure program).

Limitations

We note that all experiments are performed on only two English source-and-target event factuality corpora. While we achieve state-of-the-art results for English, we do not know how well our linearized tree generation model can generalize to other languages. We will investigate multilingual source-and-target event factuality prediction as linearized tree generation in future work.

For our GPT-3 experiments, we only perform one run and therefore do not report an average over 3 runs. We do this to minimize costs.

We note that these experiments do not account for potential biases prevalent in fine-tuning large language models. We hypothesize that for some sources in text (i.e. power figures, authorities, or specific names), there may be biases towards certain factuality labels. We will investigate these biases in future work because an event factuality prediction system with inherent bias can have real world consequences.

Ethics Statement

Our paper is foundational research and we are not tied to any direct applications. However, our experiments do not account for potential biases prevalent in fine-tuning large language models. In a real world deployment of our model, we hypothesize that there could be a potential mislabelling of factuality values depending on bias towards sources of utterances. For example, if a power figure states an event, will the event label be more biased towards being factual just because of the source of the statement? Furthermore, are large language models biased in predicting or failing to predict specific nested sources? For example, are certain groups, names, or specific sources being ignored? Finally, how much of a role does our new representation format contribute to bias? We will investigate these questions and issues in future work.

References

Mike Bostock. 2012. D3.js - data-driven documents.

Tom Brown, Benjamin Mann, Nick Ryder, Melanie Subbiah, Jared D Kaplan, Prafulla Dhariwal, Arvind Neelakantan, Pranav Shyam, Girish Sastry, Amanda Askell, et al. 2020. Language models are few-shot learners. *Advances in neural information processing systems*, 33:1877–1901.

Pengfei Cao, Yubo Chen, Yuqing Yang, Kang Liu, and Jun Zhao. 2021. Uncertain local-to-global networks for document-level event factuality identification. In *Proceedings of the 2021 Conference on Empirical Methods in Natural Language Processing*, pages 2636–2645, Online and Punta Cana, Dominican Republic. Association for Computational Linguistics.

Hyung Won Chung, Le Hou, Shayne Longpre, Barret Zoph, Yi Tay, William Fedus, Eric Li, Xuezhi Wang, Mostafa Dehghani, Siddhartha Brahma, et al. 2022. Scaling instruction-finetuned language models. *arXiv preprint arXiv:2210.11416*.

Alexis Conneau, Kartikay Khandelwal, Naman Goyal, Vishrav Chaudhary, Guillaume Wenzek, Francisco Guzmán, Edouard Grave, Myle Ott, Luke Zettlemoyer, and Veselin Stoyanov. 2020. Unsupervised cross-lingual representation learning at scale. In *Proceedings of the 58th Annual Meeting of the Association for Computational Linguistics*, pages 8440–8451, Online. Association for Computational Linguistics.

Mona Diab, Lori Levin, Teruko Mitamura, Owen Rambow, Vinodkumar Prabhakaran, and Weiwei Guo. 2009. Committed belief annotation and tagging. In *Proceedings of the Third Linguistic Annotation Workshop (LAW III)*, pages 68–73, Suntec, Singapore. Association for Computational Linguistics.

William Falcon et al. 2019. Pytorch lightning. *GitHub. Note: https://github. com/PyTorchLightning/pytorch-lightning*, 3(6).

Miguel Grinberg. 2018. *Flask web development: developing web applications with python.* " O'Reilly Media, Inc.".

Matthew Honnibal and Ines Montani. 2017. spaCy 2: Natural language understanding with Bloom embeddings, convolutional neural networks and incremental parsing. To appear.

Nanjiang Jiang and Marie-Catherine de Marneffe. 2021. He thinks he knows better than the doctors: BERT for event factuality fails on pragmatics. *Transactions of the Association for Computational Linguistics*, 9:1081–1097.

Kenton Lee, Yoav Artzi, Yejin Choi, and Luke Zettlemoyer. 2015. Event detection and factuality assessment with non-expert supervision. In *Proceedings of the 2015 Conference on Empirical Methods in Natural Language Processing*, pages 1643–1648, Lisbon, Portugal. Association for Computational Linguistics.

Amnon Lotan, Asher Stern, and Ido Dagan. 2013. TruthTeller: Annotating predicate truth. In *Proceedings of the 2013 Conference of the North American Chapter of the Association for Computational Linguistics: Human Language Technologies*, pages 752–757, Atlanta, Georgia. Association for Computational Linguistics.

John Murzaku, Tyler Osborne, Amittai Aviram, and Owen Rambow. 2023. Towards generative event factuality prediction. In *Findings of the Association for Computational Linguistics: ACL 2023*, pages 701–715, Toronto, Canada. Association for Computational Linguistics.

John Murzaku, Peter Zeng, Magdalena Markowska, and Owen Rambow. 2022. Re-examining FactBank: Predicting the author's presentation of factuality. In *Proceedings of the 29th International Conference on Computational Linguistics*, pages 786–796, Gyeongju, Republic of Korea. International Committee on Computational Linguistics.

Rowan Nairn, Cleo Condoravdi, and Lauri Karttunen. 2006. Computing relative polarity for textual inference. In *Proceedings of the Fifth International Workshop on Inference in Computational Semantics (ICoS-5)*.

Shon Otmazgin, Arie Cattan, and Yoav Goldberg. 2022. F-coref: Fast, accurate and easy to use coreference resolution. In *Proceedings of the 2nd Conference of the Asia-Pacific Chapter of the Association for Computational Linguistics and the 12th International Joint Conference on Natural Language Processing: System Demonstrations*, pages 48–56, Taipei, Taiwan. Association for Computational Linguistics.

Amir Pouran Ben Veyseh, Thien Huu Nguyen, and Dejing Dou. 2019. Graph based neural networks for event factuality prediction using syntactic and semantic structures. In *Proceedings of the 57th Annual Meeting of the Association for Computational Linguistics*, pages 4393–4399, Florence, Italy. Association for Computational Linguistics.

Vinodkumar Prabhakaran, Owen Rambow, and Mona Diab. 2010. Automatic committed belief tagging. In *Coling 2010: Posters*, pages 1014–1022, Beijing, China. Coling 2010 Organizing Committee.

Zhong Qian, Peifeng Li, Qiaoming Zhu, and Guodong Zhou. 2019. Document-level event factuality identification via adversarial neural network. In *Proceedings of the 2019 Conference of the North American Chapter of the Association for Computational Linguistics: Human Language Technologies, Volume 1 (Long and Short Papers)*, pages 2799–2809, Minneapolis, Minnesota. Association for Computational Linguistics.

Zhong Qian, Heng Zhang, Peifeng Li, Qiaoming Zhu, and Guodong Zhou. 2022. Document-level event factuality identification via machine reading comprehension frameworks with transfer learning. In *Proceedings of the 29th International Conference on Computational Linguistics*, pages 2622–2632, Gyeongju, Republic of Korea. International Committee on Computational Linguistics.

Colin Raffel, Noam Shazeer, Adam Roberts, Katherine Lee, Sharan Narang, Michael Matena, Yanqi Zhou, Wei Li, and Peter J Liu. 2020. Exploring the limits of transfer learning with a unified text-to-text transformer. *The Journal of Machine Learning Research*, 21(1):5485–5551.

Rachel Rudinger, Aaron Steven White, and Benjamin Van Durme. 2018. Neural models of factuality. In *Proceedings of the 2018 Conference of the North American Chapter of the Association for Computational Linguistics: Human Language Technologies, Volume 1 (Long Papers)*, pages 731–744, New Orleans, Louisiana. Association for Computational Linguistics.

Roser Saurí and James Pustejovsky. 2009. Factbank: a corpus annotated with event factuality. *Language resources and evaluation*, 43:227–268.

Roser Saurí and James Pustejovsky. 2012. Are you sure that this happened? assessing the factuality degree of events in text. *Computational Linguistics*, 38(2):261–299.

Gabriel Stanovsky, Judith Eckle-Kohler, Yevgeniy Puzikov, Ido Dagan, and Iryna Gurevych. 2017. Integrating deep linguistic features in factuality prediction over unified datasets. In *Proceedings of the 55th Annual Meeting of the Association for Computational Linguistics (Volume 2: Short Papers)*, pages 352–357, Vancouver, Canada. Association for Computational Linguistics.

Meagan Vigus, Jens E. L. Van Gysel, and William Croft. 2019. A dependency structure annotation for modality. In *Proceedings of the First International Workshop on Designing Meaning Representations*, pages

182–198, Florence, Italy. Association for Computational Linguistics.

Thomas Wolf, Lysandre Debut, Victor Sanh, Julien Chaumond, Clement Delangue, Anthony Moi, Pierric Cistac, Tim Rault, Rémi Louf, Morgan Funtowicz, et al. 2019. Huggingface's transformers: State-of-the-art natural language processing. *arXiv preprint arXiv:1910.03771*.

Jiarui Yao, Haoling Qiu, Jin Zhao, Bonan Min, and Nianwen Xue. 2021. Factuality assessment as modal dependency parsing. In *Proceedings of the 59th Annual Meeting of the Association for Computational Linguistics and the 11th International Joint Conference on Natural Language Processing (Volume 1: Long Papers)*, pages 1540–1550, Online. Association for Computational Linguistics.

Jiarui Yao, Nianwen Xue, and Bonan Min. 2022. Modal dependency parsing via language model priming. In *Proceedings of the 2022 Conference of the North American Chapter of the Association for Computational Linguistics: Human Language Technologies*, pages 2913–2919, Seattle, United States. Association for Computational Linguistics.

Heng Zhang, Peifeng Li, Zhong Qian, and Xiaoxu Zhu. 2023. Incorporating factuality inference to identify document-level event factuality. In *Findings of the Association for Computational Linguistics: ACL 2023*, pages 13990–14002, Toronto, Canada. Association for Computational Linguistics.

A Data

FactBank We split our corpus using the same split and methods as Murzaku et al. (2022), which also includes splitting by article. We follow a similar evaluation setup evaluating on macro-f1 and per-label f1. The FactBank corpus can be obtained by researchers from the Linguistic Data Consortium, catalog number LDC2009T23.

Modal Dependency Corpus We use the modal dependency corpus from Yao et al. (2022). We follow the same evaluation setup and procedure evaluating on micro-f1.

Tree generation We reformat the FactBank data for our machine learning representation. All linearized trees have the author of the text as the root. We add the special token **nest** to declare nestings according to a source. We show the following example and its linearized tree:
Input: Meteorologists say the weather will get worse because more rains are on the way.
Tree: (Author (rains unknown) (get unknown) (say true) (Meteorologists **nest** (rains true) (get true)))

	train	dev	test
FactBank	8,153	2,345	1,165
MDP	21,855	2,605	2,464

Table 5: Number of examples (sum of sources and events) in the splits for each corpus.

B Details on Experiments

All experiments besides our GPT-3 experiments used our employer's GPU cluster. We performed experiments on a Tesla V100-SXM2 GPU. Compute jobs typically ranged from 30 minutes for standard fine-tuning experiments to 50 minutes for synthetic data generation. We do not do any hyperparameter search or hyperparameter tuning.

FactBank experiments We fine-tuned our models for at most 10 epochs, with early stopping being used if the macro-F1 did not increase for 3. We use a standard fine-tuning approach with Flan-T5-large which has 780 million parameters. We also experimented with Flan-T5-xl which has 3 billion parameters, but often ran into memory issues due to heavy GPU load. We use the Adafactor optimizer along with a Adafactor scheduler, which dynamically adapts the learning rate throughout the training process to ensure optimal model performance. All metrics for experiments were averaged over three runs using fixed seeds (7, 21, and 42). We report the average over three runs and the standard deviation over three runs.

Modal dependency corpus experiments We fine-tuned our models for at most 20 epochs, with early stopping being used if the micro-F1 did not increase for 20 epochs. We use a standard fine-tuning approach with Flan-T5-large which has 780 million parameters. We use the Adafactor optimizer along with a Adafactor scheduler, which dynamically adapts the learning rate throughout the training process to ensure optimal model performance. All metrics for experiments were averaged over three runs using fixed seeds (7, 21, and 42). We report the average over three runs and the standard deviation over three runs.

GPT-3 experiments We used a standard fine-tuning approach using the OpenAI API. We used a temperature of 0.0 for all experiments to select the most likely token at each step. Because of fine-tuning costs, we perform only one run and therefore do not report standard deviation.

Packages To fine-tune our models and run experiments, we used PyTorch lightning Falcon et al. (2019) and the transformers library provided by HuggingFace Wolf et al. (2019). All code for fine-tuning, modelling, and pre-processing will be made available.

Corpus Splits Table 5 shows the train-dev-test splits for FactBank and the MDP corpus respectively.

QueryExplorer: An Interactive Query Generation Assistant for Search and Exploration

Kaustubh D. Dhole
Dept. of Computer Science
Emory University, Atlanta
kaustubh.dhole@emory.edu

Shivam Bajaj
Cox Communications
Atlanta
shivam.bajaj@cox.com

Ramraj Chandradevan
Dept. of Computer Science
Emory University, Atlanta
rchan31@emory.edu

Eugene Agichtein
Dept. of Computer Science
Emory University, Atlanta
eugene.agichtein@emory.edu

Abstract

Formulating effective search queries remains a challenging task, particularly when users lack expertise in a specific domain or are not proficient in the language of the content. Providing example documents of interest might be easier for a user. However, such query-by-example scenarios are prone to concept drift, and the retrieval effectiveness is highly sensitive to the query generation method, without a clear way to incorporate user feedback. To enable exploration and to support Human-In-The-Loop experiments we propose **QueryExplorer**[1] – an interactive query generation, reformulation, and retrieval interface with support for HuggingFace generation models and PyTerrier's retrieval pipelines and datasets, and extensive logging of human feedback. To allow users to create and modify effective queries, our demo[2] supports complementary approaches of using LLMs interactively, assisting the user with edits and feedback at multiple stages of the query formulation process. With support for recording fine-grained interactions and user annotations, QueryExplorer can serve as a valuable experimental and research platform for annotation, qualitative evaluation, and conducting Human-in-the-Loop (HITL) experiments for complex search tasks where users struggle to formulate queries.

1 Introduction

Being able to retrieve documents in multiple languages is becoming critical as the Internet increasingly provides access to information across a wide range of languages and domains. However, creating effective search queries for cross-language and multi-language retrieval can be a daunting task for users. First, users may be unfamiliar with the language of the documents with the information they need, or may even be unaware of this information, making it hard to craft effective queries. Second, most people are not familiar with the vocabulary and jargon used in other areas or fields, which can hinder their ability to formulate good search queries. Consider a scenario where a user is tasked with identifying documents pertinent to legal disputes. They may lack familiarity with the specialized terminology, yet possess examples of specific documents in question.

"Query-by-example" (QBE) is one solution to such a challenge. It allows users to explore document collections by specifying an example document (rather than an explicit query) of what they are searching for. Although considerable advancements have been made in the domain of query-by-example, in recently using neural IR techniques (Sarwar and Allan, 2020; Zloof, 1975; Alaofi et al., 2023; Zhang et al., 2012), there is a lack of effective and easily configurable search interface tools for exploring and annotating query-by-example experiments, especially in the interactive setting.

While a good QBE interface could be valuable, a tool that can facilitate generating queries with a Human-In-The-Loop (HITL) setting can result in an even more effective search. Extensive prior work has shown that automatically generated queries can be improved with the searcher's inputs (Jiang et al., 2014), via providing in-domain and world-knowledge (Cho et al., 2022; Mackie et al., 2023), as well as from relevance or pseudo-relevance feedback (Abdul-Jaleel et al., 2004; Li et al., 2018; Zheng et al., 2020; Wang et al., 2023b) through search results and this process can iterate several times till the searcher is satisfied with the presented search results. Researchers studying searcher behavior and gathering associated annotated data may need iterating over different query generators, multiple prompting and training strategies, several retrieval pipelines, recording various ways to incorporate implicit feedback, and a rigorous number of hyperparameters. For instance, a search engine

[1] https://github.com/emory-irlab/query-explorer
[2] Demonstration Video of QueryExplorer

Proceedings of the 2024 Conference of the North American Chapter of the Association for Computational Linguistics: Human Language Technologies (Volume 3: System Demonstrations), pages 107–115
June 16-21, 2024 ©2024 Association for Computational Linguistics

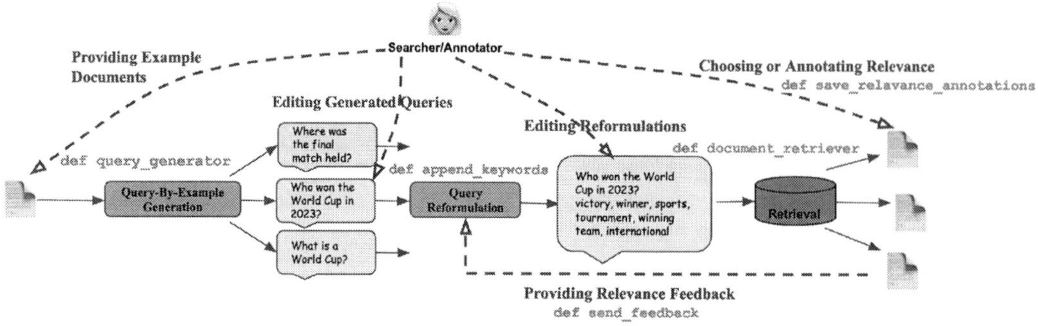

Figure 1: QueryExplorer's process shown end to end along with the internal Python functions. Internal Python helper functions are shown in green, and annotator actions are shown in blue.

analyst might be interested in how searchers edit queries.

To investigate these much-needed capabilities, we propose a configurable, interactive search interface tool, **QueryExplorer**, which supports automatic and interactive query generation and reformulation for mono-lingual and multi-lingual interactive search. QueryExplorer can both facilitate and record the query generation process and interactions of a searcher – from query formulation in a pure QBE setting to tracking the resulting query's impact on the retrieved search results and the user's exploration. To our knowledge, QueryExplorer is the first such interactive query exploration interface to be shared with the research community.

Specifically, QueryExplorer demonstrates the following novel capabilities:

- A simple document search functionality with natural support for multi-lingual and cross-lingual search, making it easy for searchers to navigate and analyze search results.
- Support for both automated query generation and reformulation, and human-in-the-loop capabilities such as propagating the human input back to query reformulation, allowing searchers to collaborate with automated query generation models.
- Provisioning for rapid prototyping across multiple retrieval experiments and datasets, via PyTerrier retrieval pipelines (Macdonald et al., 2021) with integrated generative LLM models from HuggingFace (Wolf et al., 2020).
- Extensive instrumentation support for query generation and reformulation experiments, including the ability to record query edits, reformulations, all user interactions, and relevance judgments making it useful for collecting and annotating end-to-end datasets.

In summary, we believe QueryExplorer could provide valuable tools for i) performing qualitative analysis over information retrieval experiments and datasets, ii) investigating interactive retrieval feedback and performing Human-In-The-Loop (HITL) studies, and iii) gathering user annotations and understanding searcher behavior. Our system was built initially (Dhole et al., 2023b) for the BETTER search tasks[3] (Mckinnon and Rubino, 2022; Soboroff, 2023) and was later generalized and expanded to support end-to-end query generation and reformulation experiments. We share the Python code, a Google Colab notebook as well as the video demonstration here[4].

Next, we provide an overview of related retrieval tools and the importance of query generation in Section 2 to place our contribution in context. We then review the different components and capabilities of QueryExplorer in Section 3.

2 Related Work

There have been many ranking and retrieval tools with annotation support released previously (Lin et al., 2021; Macdonald et al., 2021; Scells and Potthast, 2023; Akiki et al., 2023; Ng et al., 2023; Giachelle et al., 2022), but all of them have focused on the ad-hoc search setting by assuming a readily available query without the need for generation, reformulation or feedback. Spacerini (Akiki

[3] IARPA Better Research Program

[4] `https://github.com/emory-irlab/query-explorer`

et al., 2023) leveraged the Pyserini (Lin et al., 2021) toolkit and the Hugging Face library to facilitate the creation and hosting of search systems for ad-hoc search. SimplyRetrieve (Ng et al., 2023), FastRag (Izsak et al., 2023) and RaLLe (Hoshi et al., 2023) focus on retrieval augmented generation.

Recent advancements in transformer models and their availability via open-source ecosystems like HuggingFace (Wolf et al., 2020) and LangChain (Chase, 2022) have facilitated the seamless integration of multiple models (Dhole, 2024). However, despite the accessibility of these tools for researchers and annotators, the integration of the query generator pipeline into search engines remains underdeveloped. Furthermore, the expansion of these tools into multilingual search capabilities has been limited.

Besides, success in few-shot prompting (Srivastava et al., 2023; Brown et al., 2020a; Liu et al., 2023; Brown et al., 2020b) has led large language models to play a key role in reducing the information burden on users by especially assisting them with writing tasks namely essay writing, summarisation, transcript and dialog generation, etc. This success has also been transferred to tasks related to query generation (Jeong et al., 2021; Nogueira et al., 2019). While large language model applications are prevalent and numerous studies have been conducted for search interfaces (Liu et al., 2022, 2021a,b; Xu et al., 2009), there has been little impetus to combine search interfaces with large language model-based query generation.

QueryExplorer distinguishes itself by offering a more comprehensive integration of various search frameworks, including query generators, reformulators, and multilingual models. Unlike previous approaches, our tool addresses query generation by assuming the 'query-by-example' setting, which operates without an explicit query. The query generator component overcomes this challenge by generating a suggested query and refining it through iterative human interaction and feedback.

We now briefly describe the different components of QueryExplorer.

3 QueryExplorer

The QueryExplorer Interface is made up of 2 tabs – The Query Generation tab and the Settings tab. Both of them are described below. The Query Generation tab is displayed to end users or **searchers** and annotators and the Settings tab is reserved for **researchers**[5] looking to gather data for query generation and IR studies by allowing them to investigate different settings. The complete interface is built using HuggingFace's Gradio platform. Gradio (Abid et al., 2019) is an open-source Python package to quickly create easy-to-use, configurable UI components and has been popularly used for machine learning models.

3.1 Searcher's Tab: Query Generation

This Query Generation tab serves as a simple interface for searchers and annotators which permits end-to-end **query generation (QG)** – i) Adhoc QG: users can write search queries by themselves ii) Query-by-Example: users can generate queries through prompting a HuggingFace (Wolf et al., 2020) model and select appropriate ones, **query reformulation** – through a HuggingFace model to generate useful keywords, and **document or passage retrieval** – through a PyTerrier (Macdonald et al., 2021) retrieval pipeline over multiple retrieval datasets supported through IR-Datasets (MacAvaney et al., 2021). We display the top-k relevant documents and their source language translations if applicable.

Each of the generated queries can be used by itself or in combination to retrieve documents. Users can further edit the queries, as well as receive assistance from the output of a query reformulator. Users can further interact with the retrieved documents or passages, and provide relevance annotations for each of the documents.

We now describe the default models provided for each of the above settings for the demonstration. Each of these can be easily substituted with the researcher's choices by minor modifications to the configuration settings or code.

3.1.1 Query-By-Example Generation (QBE)

We use the `flan-t5-xxl` model (Chung et al., 2022), which is the instruction tuned (Peng et al., 2023) version of the text-to-text transformer T5 (Raffel et al., 2020). It has been fine-tuned on a large number of tasks making it convenient (Aribandi et al., 2022) for learning new tasks. The default version shown to the user is a few-shot wrapper over `flan-t5-xxl` – that takes in the user's example document or passage and prepends an instruction `Generate a query given the`

[5]We use the term searchers and researchers to differentiate between the higher level goals of the two tabs but both could encompass analysts/annotators/testers, etc.

Functions	Actions (Searchers and Annotators)	Configurable Settings (Researchers)
	Provide Example Documents	Choice of Domain, Example Documents
query_generator	Edit Generated Queries	0-shot/Few-shot QG, Prompt, Exemplars, HF model
append_keywords	Edit Reformulations to Create Better Query	0-shot/Few-shot QG, Prompt, Exemplars, HF model
document_retriever	Annotate Relevance of Document to Query	Retrieval PyTerrier Pipeline, Index, Documents,
send_feedback	Select Documents for Providing Relevance Feedback	0-shot/Few-shot QG, Prompt, Exemplars, Number of Documents

Table 1: The different functions (on the left) that searchers and annotators can take assistance from while performing the actions (in the center). Each of them can be configured through the Settings tab along various parameters (shown on the right) by researchers.

`following document` along with 3 document-query pairs from MSMarco as exemplars to it.

3.1.2 Query Reformulation (QR)

We use a zero-shot approach to generate keywords for the given query. `flan-t5-xxl` is passed the instruction `Improve the search effectiveness by suggesting expansion terms for the query` (Wang et al., 2023a) along with the original query as input. Zero-shot query reformulation (Dhole and Agichtein, 2024; Yang et al., 2023; Wang et al., 2023a) has been recently popular to expand queries to increase their retrieval effectiveness through zero-shot prompting of large language models. A user-facing interface can provide opportunities to mitigate bad reformulations (Weller et al., 2023) (Refer Appendix Listing 1).

3.1.3 Retrieving Documents

For retrieval, we employ PyTerrier retrievers as default. The architecture of PyTerrier is inherently designed to support operations over retrievers and rerankers to build end-to-end retrieval pipelines and has been a popular choice of retrieval engine among information retrieval researchers. In QueryExplorer, researchers can add their own custom PyTerrier pipelines too in the below dictionary (Refer Appendix Listing 2). This would also be reflected in the dropdown in the Settings tab.

3.1.4 Incorporating Relevance Feedback (RF)

We provide searchers the ability to improve the current query by utilizing a retrieved document of their choice. We use a zero-shot approach to incorporate the user-selected documents in the style of Wang et al. (2023a); Dhole and Agichtein (2024). The user-selected documents and the query are prompted to regenerate keywords through an instruction `Based on the given context information` C, `generate keywords for the following query` where C is a user-selected document (Refer Appendix Listing 3).

3.2 PyTerrier and HuggingFace support

In an effort to expedite the process of prototyping diverse experiments for IR researchers, QueryExplorer incorporates PyTerrier (Macdonald et al., 2021) support. This integration enables the utilization of retrieval pipelines created through PyTerrier within the QueryExplorer interface, enhancing its functionality for both annotation and qualitative analysis across different retrieval and reranking algorithms. During the demonstration, we showcase the interface's capability to display search results using the BM25 pipeline, highlighting the flexibility to substitute this with other custom pipelines as needed. This feature essentially adds a layer of qualitative analysis to the PyTerrier retrieval pipelines. Furthermore, to broaden the utility of PyTerrier in handling IR datasets, QueryExplorer has been designed to facilitate the indexing of documents from these datasets, thereby enabling qualitative experiments across multiple benchmarks and datasets.

Recognizing the widespread adoption of HuggingFace's (Wolf et al., 2020) models within the research community, QueryExplorer leverages these models for query generation, reformulation, and incorporating feedback. This allows for the comprehensive evaluation of search functionalities across a diverse range of large language models.

While we designed with PyTerrier and HuggingFace ecosystems in mind due to their popularity, datasets and models using other packages can also exploit the QueryExplorer interface over their systems.

3.3 Relevance Annotations

We allow each document to be annotated for relevance to help researchers gather relevance annotations through a slider component. Annotations are immediately saved in a separate `JSON` file.

3.4 Researcher's Tab: Settings

The Settings tab is designed for researchers (or specialists) who intend to gather data or study the

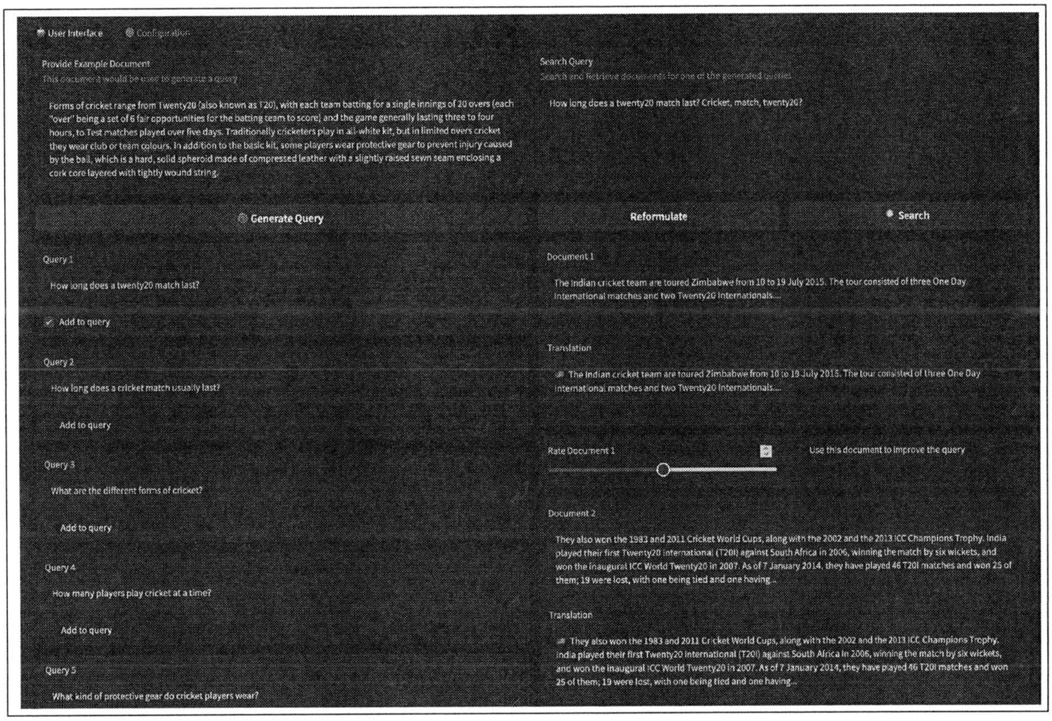

Figure 2: The User Interface tab: The user provides an example document related to cricket, uses the query generator to generate multiple queries, selects one of them, and uses the reformulator to further improve the query. In this case, the reformulator has suggested a useful term "cricket" to increase the retrieval effectiveness of the initial query.

performance of the interaction by allowing them to vary the various components in the query generation pipeline – like the choice of retriever, the dataset to retrieve from, or the instruction and few-shot examples for the query generator and reformulator. The various dimensions along which the researcher can vary the settings from the interface and the corresponding searcher's actions are described in Table 1.

3.4.1 Interaction logging

The researcher can look at the continuously recorded annotations consisting of – generated queries, post-reformulation queries, query-document relevance annotations, and feedback information – all with metadata of session and timestamps. These can be viewed directly in the tab as well as be utilized for subsequent analysis.

QueryExplorer by default stores the recordings in three `JSON` formatted files:

- **Query Logs**: where different versions of the queries along with the source of change (whether through a model or the user or through a reformulator, etc.) and additional metadata like timestamps and user session information are stored.
- **Predicted Search Results**: where the user's search queries and corresponding retrieved documents are stores
- **Document-Query Relevance Annotations**: where an annotator's document-query annotated pairs are stored

Documenting detailed annotations such as changes in queries and the evolution of queries over time can provide several benefits for researchers. This includes the ability to detect users who may not be attentive or who might be using automated bots. Additionally, observing the patterns and behaviors of users during their search activities can offer valuable insights. Furthermore, assessing the effort involved in formulating queries and perusing documents, as indicated by the time spent on these tasks, can also be advantageous for research purposes.

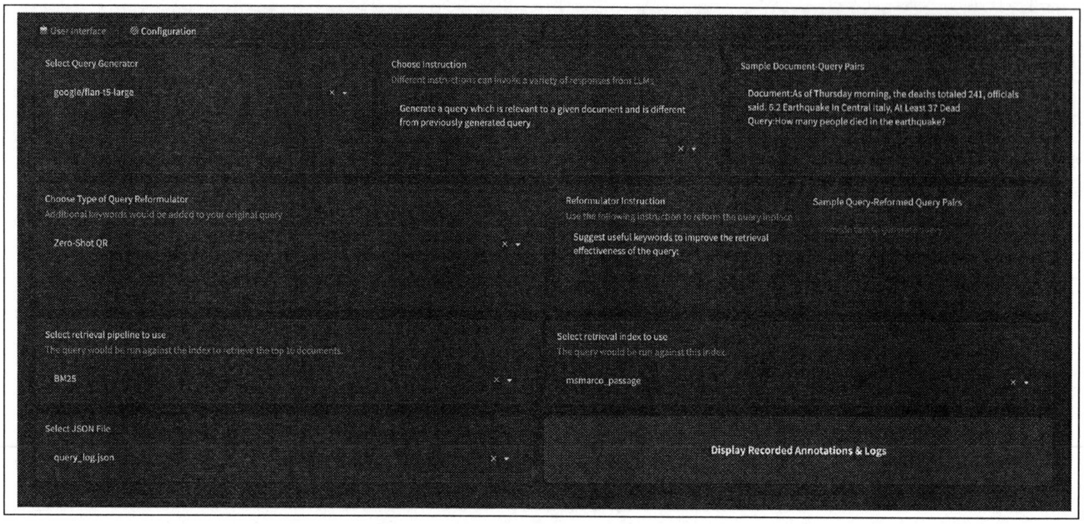

Figure 3: The Settings Tab where researchers or specialists can experiment with different model settings and parameters and visualize and monitor continuously updated interaction data.

4 Conclusion

Interactive query generation and reformulation is of significant interest for many search and exploration tasks like (document-query) pairs augmentation (Alaofi et al., 2023; Dhole et al., 2023a), document expansion (Nogueira et al., 2019; Gospodinov et al., 2023) and keyword expansion (Dhole and Agichtein, 2024; Carpineto and Romano, 2012; Jagerman et al., 2023; Wang et al., 2023a). QueryExplorer acts as a resource to permit qualitative evaluation of query generation and retrieval in conjunction. Such a combined interface is crucial as it permits immediate retrieval feedback from the user to be incorporated into the search process.

This paper demonstrates the novel capabilities of QueryExplorer to assist researchers with investigating the construction, feedback, and evaluation of the interactive query generation process. Furthermore, QueryExplorer provides extensive fine-grained instrumentation to record the end-to-end generation process from query formulation to retrieval feedback to enable the construction of search interaction and feedback datasets. Researchers can also quickly perform qualitative analysis by loading up QueryExplorer's lightweight search interface through Colab and gather data quickly. QueryExplorer's interface also provides an avenue to perform Human-In-The-Loop (HITL) studies. Apart from qualitative studies, we believe QueryExplorer could be effective in performing more sophisticated information retrieval experiments as well as serve as a tool to incorporate retrieval feedback and conduct Human-In-The-Loop studies.

5 Ethical Statement

QueryExplorer serves as a comprehensive tool, capturing the entire pipeline for purposes of analysis, annotation, and logging. The components within QueryExplorer, including query generators, reformulators, and PRF, can be replaced with even larger LM alternatives. However, these substitutes might lead to the generation of biased or toxic keywords and reformulations. Therefore, it is crucial to consider QueryExplorer within the broader sociotechnical framework (Dhole, 2023) implement appropriate filters, and conduct thorough testing before any deployment.

6 Acknowledgements

This work was supported in part by IARPA BETTER (#2019-19051600005). The views and conclusions contained in this work are those of the authors and should not be interpreted as necessarily representing the official policies, either expressed or implied, or endorsements of ODNI, IARPA, or the U.S. Government. The U.S. Government is authorized to reproduce and distribute reprints for governmental purposes notwithstanding any copyright annotation therein.

References

Nasreen Abdul-Jaleel, James Allan, W Bruce Croft, Fernando Diaz, Leah Larkey, Xiaoyan Li, Mark D Smucker, and Courtney Wade. 2004. Umass at trec 2004: Novelty and hard. *Computer Science Department Faculty Publication Series*, page 189.

Abubakar Abid, Ali Abdalla, Ali Abid, Dawood Khan, Abdulrahman Alfozan, and James Y. Zou. 2019. Gradio: Hassle-free sharing and testing of ml models in the wild. *ArXiv*, abs/1906.02569.

Christopher Akiki, Odunayo Ogundepo, Aleksandra Piktus, Xinyu Zhang, Akintunde Oladipo, Jimmy Lin, and Martin Potthast. 2023. Spacerini: Plug-and-play search engines with pyserini and hugging face. *arXiv preprint arXiv:2302.14534*.

Marwah Alaofi, Luke Gallagher, Mark Sanderson, Falk Scholer, and Paul Thomas. 2023. Can generative llms create query variants for test collections? an exploratory study. In *Proceedings of the 46th International ACM SIGIR Conference on Research and Development in Information Retrieval*, SIGIR '23, page 1869–1873, New York, NY, USA. Association for Computing Machinery.

Vamsi Aribandi, Yi Tay, Tal Schuster, Jinfeng Rao, Huaixiu Steven Zheng, Sanket Vaibhav Mehta, Honglei Zhuang, Vinh Q. Tran, Dara Bahri, Jianmo Ni, Jai Gupta, Kai Hui, Sebastian Ruder, and Donald Metzler. 2022. Ext5: Towards extreme multi-task scaling for transfer learning. In *International Conference on Learning Representations*.

Tom Brown, Benjamin Mann, Nick Ryder, Melanie Subbiah, Jared D Kaplan, Prafulla Dhariwal, Arvind Neelakantan, Pranav Shyam, Girish Sastry, Amanda Askell, et al. 2020a. Language models are few-shot learners. *Advances in neural information processing systems*, 33:1877–1901.

Tom Brown, Benjamin Mann, Nick Ryder, Melanie Subbiah, Jared D Kaplan, Prafulla Dhariwal, Arvind Neelakantan, Pranav Shyam, Girish Sastry, Amanda Askell, et al. 2020b. Language models are few-shot learners. volume 33, pages 1877–1901.

Claudio Carpineto and Giovanni Romano. 2012. A survey of automatic query expansion in information retrieval. *Acm Computing Surveys (CSUR)*, 44(1):1–50.

Harrison Chase. 2022. Langchain.

Sukmin Cho, Soyeong Jeong, Wonsuk Yang, and Jong Park. 2022. Query generation with external knowledge for dense retrieval. In *Proceedings of Deep Learning Inside Out (DeeLIO 2022): The 3rd Workshop on Knowledge Extraction and Integration for Deep Learning Architectures*, pages 22–32, Dublin, Ireland and Online. Association for Computational Linguistics.

Hyung Won Chung, Le Hou, Shayne Longpre, Barret Zoph, Yi Tay, William Fedus, Eric Li, Xuezhi Wang, Mostafa Dehghani, Siddhartha Brahma, et al. 2022. Scaling instruction-finetuned language models. *arXiv preprint arXiv:2210.11416*.

Kaustubh Dhole. 2023. Large language models as SocioTechnical systems. In *Proceedings of the Big Picture Workshop*, pages 66–79, Singapore. Association for Computational Linguistics.

Kaustubh Dhole. 2024. Kaucus-knowledgeable user simulators for training large language models. In *Proceedings of the 1st Workshop on Simulating Conversational Intelligence in Chat (SCI-CHAT 2024)*, pages 53–65.

Kaustubh Dhole, Varun Gangal, Sebastian Gehrmann, Aadesh Gupta, Zhenhao Li, Saad Mahamood, Abinaya Mahadiran, Simon Mille, Ashish Shrivastava, Samson Tan, et al. 2023a. Nl-augmenter: A framework for task-sensitive natural language augmentation. *Northern European Journal of Language Technology*, 9(1).

Kaustubh D. Dhole and Eugene Agichtein. 2024. Genqrensemble: Zero-shot llm ensemble prompting for generative query reformulation. In *Advances in Information Retrieval*, pages 326–335, Cham. Springer Nature Switzerland.

Kaustubh D. Dhole, Ramraj Chandradevan, and Eugene Agichtein. 2023b. An interactive query generation assistant using llm-based prompt modification and user feedback.

Fabio Giachelle, Ornella Irrera, and Gianmaria Silvello. 2022. Doctag: A customizable annotation tool for ground truth creation. In *European Conference on Information Retrieval*, pages 288–293. Springer.

Mitko Gospodinov, Sean MacAvaney, and Craig Macdonald. 2023. Doc2query–: When less is more. In *European Conference on Information Retrieval*, pages 414–422.

Yasuto Hoshi, Daisuke Miyashita, Youyang Ng, Kento Tatsuno, Yasuhiro Morioka, Osamu Torii, and Jun Deguchi. 2023. Ralle: A framework for developing and evaluating retrieval-augmented large language models.

Peter Izsak, Moshe Berchansky, Daniel Fleischer, and Ronen Laperdon. 2023. fastrag: Efficient retrieval augmentation and generation framework.

Rolf Jagerman, Honglei Zhuang, Zhen Qin, Xuanhui Wang, and Michael Bendersky. 2023. Query expansion by prompting large language models. *arXiv preprint arXiv:2305.03653*.

Soyeong Jeong, Jinheon Baek, ChaeHun Park, and Jong Park. 2021. Unsupervised document expansion for information retrieval with stochastic text generation. In *Proceedings of the Second Workshop on Scholarly Document Processing*, pages 7–17, Online. Association for Computational Linguistics.

Jyun-Yu Jiang, Yen-Yu Ke, Pao-Yu Chien, and Pu-Jen Cheng. 2014. Learning user reformulation behavior for query auto-completion. In *Proceedings of the 37th international ACM SIGIR conference on Research & development in information retrieval*, pages 445–454.

Canjia Li, Yingfei Sun, Ben He, Le Wang, Kai Hui, Andrew Yates, Le Sun, and Jungang Xu. 2018. NPRF: A neural pseudo relevance feedback framework for ad-hoc information retrieval. In *Proceedings of the 2018 Conference on Empirical Methods in Natural Language Processing*, pages 4482–4491, Brussels, Belgium. Association for Computational Linguistics.

Jimmy Lin, Xueguang Ma, Sheng-Chieh Lin, Jheng-Hong Yang, Ronak Pradeep, and Rodrigo Nogueira. 2021. Pyserini: A python toolkit for reproducible information retrieval research with sparse and dense representations. In *Proceedings of the 44th International ACM SIGIR Conference on Research and Development in Information Retrieval*, SIGIR '21, page 2356–2362, New York, NY, USA. Association for Computing Machinery.

Chang Liu, Ying-Hsang Liu, Jingjing Liu, and Ralf Bierig. 2021a. Search interface design and evaluation. *Found. Trends Inf. Retr.*, 15(3–4):243–416.

Chang Liu, Ying-Hsang Liu, Jingjing Liu, and Ralf Bierig. 2021b. Search interface design and evaluation. 15(3–4):243–416.

Pengfei Liu, Weizhe Yuan, Jinlan Fu, Zhengbao Jiang, Hiroaki Hayashi, and Graham Neubig. 2023. Pre-train, prompt, and predict: A systematic survey of prompting methods in natural language processing. *ACM Comput. Surv.*, 55(9).

Ying-Hsang Liu, Paul Thomas, Tom Gedeon, and Nicolay Rusnachenko. 2022. Search interfaces for biomedical searching: How do gaze, user perception, search behaviour and search performance relate? In *Proceedings of the 2022 Conference on Human Information Interaction and Retrieval*, CHIIR '22, page 78–89, New York, NY, USA. Association for Computing Machinery.

Sean MacAvaney, Andrew Yates, Sergey Feldman, Doug Downey, Arman Cohan, and Nazli Goharian. 2021. Simplified data wrangling with ir_datasets. In *Proceedings of the 44th International ACM SIGIR Conference on Research and Development in Information Retrieval*, pages 2429–2436.

Craig Macdonald, Nicola Tonellotto, Sean MacAvaney, and Iadh Ounis. 2021. Pyterrier: Declarative experimentation in python from bm25 to dense retrieval. In *Proceedings of the 30th acm international conference on information & knowledge management*, pages 4526–4533.

Iain Mackie, Shubham Chatterjee, and Jeffrey Dalton. 2023. Generative relevance feedback with large language models. *arXiv preprint arXiv:2304.13157*.

Timothy Mckinnon and Carl Rubino. 2022. The IARPA BETTER program abstract task four new semantically annotated corpora from IARPA's BETTER program. In *Proceedings of the Thirteenth Language Resources and Evaluation Conference*, pages 3595–3600, Marseille, France. European Language Resources Association.

Youyang Ng, Daisuke Miyashita, Yasuto Hoshi, Yasuhiro Morioka, Osamu Torii, Tomoya Kodama, and Jun Deguchi. 2023. Simplyretrieve: A private and lightweight retrieval-centric generative ai tool. *arXiv preprint arXiv:2308.03983*.

Rodrigo Nogueira, Wei Yang, Jimmy Lin, and Kyunghyun Cho. 2019. Document expansion by query prediction. *arXiv preprint arXiv:1904.08375*.

Baolin Peng, Chunyuan Li, Pengcheng He, Michel Galley, and Jianfeng Gao. 2023. Instruction tuning with gpt-4. *arXiv preprint arXiv:2304.03277*.

Colin Raffel, Noam Shazeer, Adam Roberts, Katherine Lee, Sharan Narang, Michael Matena, Yanqi Zhou, Wei Li, and Peter J Liu. 2020. Exploring the limits of transfer learning with a unified text-to-text transformer. *The Journal of Machine Learning Research*, 21(1):5485–5551.

Sheikh Muhammad Sarwar and James Allan. 2020. Query by example for cross-lingual event retrieval. SIGIR '20, page 1601–1604, New York, NY, USA. Association for Computing Machinery.

Harrisen Scells and Martin Potthast. 2023. Pybool_ir: A toolkit for domain-specific search experiments. In *Proceedings of the 46th International ACM SIGIR Conference on Research and Development in Information Retrieval*, SIGIR '23, page 3190–3194, New York, NY, USA. Association for Computing Machinery.

Ian Soboroff. 2023. The better cross-language datasets. In *Proceedings of the 46th International ACM SIGIR Conference on Research and Development in Information Retrieval*, SIGIR '23, page 3047–3053, New York, NY, USA. Association for Computing Machinery.

Aarohi Srivastava, Abhinav Rastogi, Abhishek Rao, Abu Awal Md Shoeb, Abubakar Abid, Adam Fisch, Adam R Brown, Adam Santoro, Aditya Gupta, Adrià Garriga-Alonso, et al. 2023. Beyond the imitation game: Quantifying and extrapolating the capabilities of language models. *Transactions on Machine Learning Research*.

Xiao Wang, Sean MacAvaney, Craig Macdonald, and Iadh Ounis. 2023a. Generative query reformulation for effective adhoc search. In *The First Workshop on Generative Information Retrieval, SIGIR 2023*.

Xiao Wang, Craig Macdonald, Nicola Tonellotto, and Iadh Ounis. 2023b. Colbert-prf: Semantic pseudo-relevance feedback for dense passage and document retrieval. *ACM Transactions on the Web*, 17(1):1–39.

Orion Weller, Kyle Lo, David Wadden, Dawn Lawrie, Benjamin Van Durme, Arman Cohan, and Luca Soldaini. 2023. When do generative query and document expansions fail? a comprehensive study across methods, retrievers, and datasets. *arXiv preprint arXiv:2309.08541*.

Thomas Wolf, Lysandre Debut, Victor Sanh, Julien Chaumond, Clement Delangue, Anthony Moi, Pierric Cistac, Tim Rault, Rémi Louf, Morgan Funtowicz, et al. 2020. Transformers: State-of-the-art natural language processing. In *Proceedings of the 2020 conference on empirical methods in natural language processing: system demonstrations*, pages 38–45.

Songhua Xu, Tao Jin, and Francis C. M. Lau. 2009. A new visual search interface for web browsing. WSDM '09, page 152–161, New York, NY, USA. Association for Computing Machinery.

Dayu Yang, Yue Zhang, and Hui Fang. 2023. Zero-shot query reformulation for conversational search. In *Proceedings of the 2023 ACM SIGIR International Conference on Theory of Information Retrieval*, ICTIR '23, page 257–263, New York, NY, USA. Association for Computing Machinery.

Guanyuan Zhang, Kai Lu, and Bin Wang. 2012. Query reformulation based on user habits for query-by-humming systems. In *Information Retrieval Technology: 8th Asia Information Retrieval Societies Conference, AIRS 2012, Tianjin, China, December 17-19, 2012. Proceedings 8*, pages 386–395. Springer.

Zhi Zheng, Kai Hui, Ben He, Xianpei Han, Le Sun, and Andrew Yates. 2020. BERT-QE: Contextualized Query Expansion for Document Re-ranking. In *Findings of the Association for Computational Linguistics: EMNLP 2020*, pages 4718–4728, Online. Association for Computational Linguistics.

Moshé M. Zloof. 1975. Query by example. AFIPS '75, page 431–438, New York, NY, USA. Association for Computing Machinery.

A Appendix

```
def append_keywords(session, query,
    reform_method, reform_instruction,
    hf_model, file_name='
    query_reformulations'):

  rf_queries = query_generator(f'
      Generate keywords for the query :
      ','', query, hf_model, session)

  reformed_query = query + ' ' +
      rf_queries[1]

  on_query_change(reformed_query,
      file_name, session, previous_query
      =query) # Record event

  return ref_query
```

Listing 1: Standalone Query Reformulation using zero-shot prompting

```
retrieval_algos_dict = {'BM25': bm25, '
    TF_IDF': tfidf}

def retrieve_for_ui(query_text, pipeline
    =bm25):

  # User Query used to retrieve through
      a PyTerrier Pipeline
  searchresults = (pipeline%10).search(
      cleanup(query_text))

  # Document text for display
  searchresults['eng-text'] =
      searchresults['docno'].apply(
      get_doc_text)

  # (Optional) Translation for cross/
      multi-lingual
  searchresults['target-text'] =
      translate(searchresults['eng-text'
      ], 'eng', 'eng')

  results = [row.to_dict() for index,
      row in searchresults1.iterrows()]

  return results
```

Listing 2: Triggering Retrieval: Researchers can extend the dictionary using their custom pipelines.

```
def send_feedback(query, document,
    hf_model, session, file_name='
    feedback_query_reformulations'):

  rf_queries = query_generator1(f'Based
      on the given context ```{document
      }```, generate keywords for the
      query : ', query, hf_model,
      session)

  ref_query = query + " " + rf_queries
      [1]

  on_query_change(ref_query, file_name,
      session, previous_query=query) #
      Record event

  return ref_query
```

Listing 3: Query Reformulation With Relevance Feedback using Zero-shot prompting

LMFlow: An Extensible Toolkit for Finetuning and Inference of Large Foundation Models

Shizhe Diao[♡*], **Rui Pan**[♡*], **Hanze Dong**[♡*],
KaShun Shum[♡], **Jipeng Zhang**[♡], **Wei Xiong**[♠], **Tong Zhang**[♠]
[♡]The Hong Kong University of Science and Technology
[♠]University of Illinois Urbana-Champaign
{sdiaoaa, rpan, hdongaj}@ust.hk
tozhang@illinois.edu

Abstract

Foundation models have demonstrated a great ability to achieve general human-level intelligence far beyond traditional approaches. As the technique keeps attracting attention from the AI community, an increasing number of foundation models are becoming publicly accessible. However, a significant shortcoming of most of these models lies in their performance in specialized-domain and task-specific applications, necessitating domain- and task-aware fine-tuning to develop effective scientific language models. As the number of available foundation models and specialized tasks keeps growing, the job of training scientific language models becomes highly nontrivial. In this paper, we initiate steps to tackle this issue. We introduce an extensible and lightweight toolkit, LMFlow, which aims to simplify the domain- and task-aware finetuning of general foundation models. LMFlow offers a complete finetuning workflow for a foundation model to support specialized training with limited computing resources. Furthermore, it supports continuous pretraining, instruction tuning, parameter-efficient finetuning, alignment tuning, inference acceleration, long context generalization, model customization, and even multimodal finetuning, along with carefully designed and extensible APIs. This toolkit has been thoroughly tested and is available at `https://github.com/OptimalScale/LMFlow`.[1]

1 Introduction

Foundation models (FMs), and in particular large language models (LLMs), have demonstrated general abilities to perform different tasks beyond what was possible previously. While a number of pretrained large models, including GPT-J (Wang and Komatsuzaki, 2021), Bloom (Scao et al., 2022), LLaMA (Touvron et al., 2023a,b), etc., are publicly available and have already been incorporated into the Hugging Face model repository (Huggingface, 2022), there is no publicly available toolkit that can be easily used to perform finetuning and inference for these different models. For specialized domains or tasks, it is necessary to further finetune such LLMs to achieve improved performance on such domains or tasks. The purpose of this package is to offer a simple-to-use and lightweight toolkit so that developers and researchers can perform efficient finetuning and inference of scientific language models with limited resources. The typical processes to train a scientific language model are shown in Figure 1, which include:

- Continuous pretraining on datasets in special domains and tasks so that a foundation model can acquire domain- and task-specific knowledge. It normally contains domain or task adaptation.
- Instruction tuning to teach a foundation model the capability to follow these specialized natural language instructions and perform tasks required by such instructions.
- Reinforcement learning from human feedback (RLHF) to align a foundation model to human preference (for example, helpfulness, harmlessness, and honesty).

LMFlow enhances and streamlines the aforementioned fine-tuning procedures, enabling the efficient and effective training of a scientific language model. We focus on improving training speed. For example, it only takes one Nvidia 3090 GPU and five hours to train a medical LLaMA comparable to ChatGPT, based on a 7-billion-parameter LLaMA model. In addition to speed, we also aspire to achieve higher model performance. We used this framework to train medical LLaMA, a series of models with 7-billion, 13-billion, 33-billion, and

[*]Equal Contribution.

[1]Video demonstrations trained and deployed by LMFlow:

- Emotional Companion bot: `https://www.youtube.com/watch?v=BDSME4f2AjU`
- Multimodal reasoning-based object detection bot: `https://www.youtube.com/watch?v=YXNyh6bGqyI`

Proceedings of the 2024 Conference of the North American Chapter of the Association for Computational Linguistics: Human Language Technologies (Volume 3: System Demonstrations), pages 116–127
June 16-21, 2024 ©2024 Association for Computational Linguistics

Packages	Cont. PT	FT	RLHF	Deploy.	Adapt.	Acc.	LC	VE	MM
Transformers (Wolf et al., 2020)	✓	✓						✓	✓
Accelerate (Gugger et al., 2022)	✓	✓				✓			
Deepspeed (Rasley et al., 2020)	✓	✓				✓			
Trl (von Werra et al., 2020)			✓						
LMFlow (ours)	✓	✓	✓	✓	✓	✓	✓	✓	✓

Table 1: Comparison with competing packages. **Cont. PT**: continuous pretraining. **FT**: finetuning. **RLHF**: reinforcement learning from human feedback. **Deploy.**: deployment. **Adapt.**: domain/task adaptation. **Acc.**: acceleration techniques for finetuning and inference. **LC**: long context generalization. **VE**: vocabulary extension. **MM**: multimodal training.

65-billion parameters, on a single machine and have released the model weights for academic research. Using LMFlow, anyone can train their own scientific or personalized language models. Each person can choose the appropriate foundation model according to their available resources, for tasks such as question answering, companionship, and expert consultations in various domains. The larger the model and data size, the longer the training time and the better the results. Compared with existing packages, LMFlow encompasses a multitude of features that are absent in others, such as the support for long context generalization, as shown in Table 1. Most importantly, LMFlow stands out as a comprehensive, full-cycle foundation model adaptation toolkit. While other packages excel in specific areas like finetuning, they lack functionalities like RLHF and others. To our knowledge, LMFlow is the first to offer a complete pipeline that integrates all these processes. This holistic toolkit allows for more robust and adaptable language model training and inference, setting a new standard in the field of natural language processing.

2 Related Work

In recent years, the finetuning of large language models (LLMs) has gained significant attention, especially for scientific domain applications. The necessity of adapting these general-purpose models to specific domains or tasks has led to the development of various scientific language models. Lehman et al. (2023) conducted an extensive empirical analysis on the performance of various language models in clinical tasks and found that specialized clinical models, even smaller in size, significantly outperform larger general-domain models when finetuned on domain-specific data. This emphasizes the importance of domain specialization in achieving higher accuracy in safety-critical fields like healthcare. Therefore, a series of scientific large models have emerged, including but not limited to: language models for Science (Beltagy et al., 2019; Luu et al., 2021; Taylor et al., 2022), Mathematics (Yue et al., 2023; Yu et al., 2023; Gao et al., 2023), Physics (Nguyen et al., 2023; Zheng et al., 2023b; Perkowski et al., 2024), Chemistry and Materials Science (Cao et al., 2023; Shetty et al., 2023; Rubungo et al., 2023), Biology and Medicine (Lee et al., 2020; Zhang et al., 2023; Singhal et al., 2023; Wu et al., 2023; Han et al., 2023; Wang et al., 2023; Yang et al., 2024), and Information Retrieval (Lassance et al., 2023) We recommend readers to refer to a paper list of scientific language models [2], which includes a more comprehensive range of works related to scientific language models. Among these works, LMFlow has successfully helped in training AstroLLaMA-Chat (Perkowski et al., 2024) and MarineGPT (Zheng et al., 2023b). The Medical LLaMA trained in the medical domain within this paper also demonstrates the effectiveness of LMFlow. In summary, our proposed LMFlow offers a comprehensive toolkit for efficient and effective finetuning of foundation models across various specialized domains

3 Toolkit Overview

3.1 System Design

An illustration of the LMFlow system design is shown in Figure 1. There are four stages for improving the performance of a publicly available foundation model. The first stage is domain adaptation, which involves modifying the model to better handle a specific domain by training the model on that domain. The second stage is task adaptation, which involves adapting the model to perform a specific task, such as summarization, question-

[2] https://github.com/yuzhimanhua/Awesome-Scientific-Language-Models

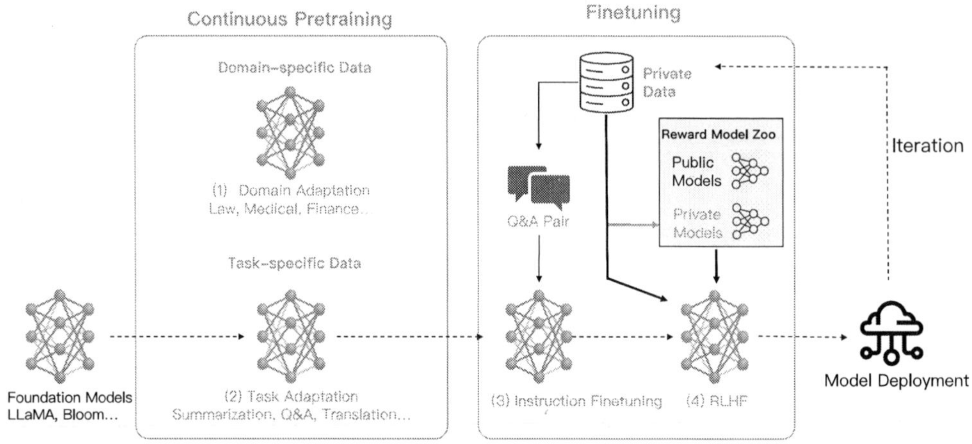

Figure 1: The system design of LMFlow. Starting from a publicly available foundation model, there are four possible stages including (1) domain adaptation, (2) task adaptation, (3) instruction finetuning, and (4) reinforcement learning with human feedback.

answering, and translation. The third stage is instruction finetuning, which involves adjusting the model's parameters based on instructional question-answer pairs. The final stage is reinforcement learning with human feedback, which involves using human feedback to further align the model to human preference. LMFlow provides a complete finetuning workflow for these four stages, supporting large language models' specialized training with limited computing resources. Especially, LMFlow supports the following key features:

- Finetuning Acceleration and Memory Optimization: LoRA (Hu et al.), FlashAttention (Dao et al., 2022; Dao, 2023), Gradient Checkpointing, and Deepspeed Zero3.
- Inference Acceleration: Speculative Decoding (Leviathan et al., 2023), LLaMA Inference on CPU, and FlashAttention (Dao et al., 2022; Dao, 2023).
- Alignment Tuning: An implementation of our proposed novel alignment algorithm RAFT (Dong et al., 2023) (Reward rAnked FineTuning) to simply RLHF pipeline for generative models.
- Long Context Generalization: Position Interpolation for LLaMA (Chen et al., 2023).
- Model Customization: Vocabulary Extension.
- Multimodal: Finetuning Multimodal Chatbot for reasoning-based object detection (Pi et al., 2023).

3.2 Installation

LMFlow has been fully tested on Linux OS (Ubuntu 20.04) and can be installed by executing the following commands.

```
$ git clone https://github.com/
    OptimalScale/LMFlow.git
$ cd LMFlow
$ conda create -n lmflow python=3.9 -y
$ conda activate lmflow
$ pip install -e .
```

3.3 Data Format

LMFlow accepts several `.json` files as input. Users can provide a list of `.json` files under a specified dataset directory. For example,

```
|- path_to_dataset
  |- data_1.json
  |- data_2.json
  |- another_data.json
  |- ...
```

Each json file shall have the following format (three instances with four keys for example),

```
{
  "type": "TYPE",
  "instances": [
    {
        "KEY_1": "VALUE_1.1",
        "KEY_2": "VALUE_1.2",
        "KEY_3": "VALUE_1.3",
        "KEY_4": "VALUE_1.4",
    },
    {
        "KEY_1": "VALUE_2.1",
        "KEY_2": "VALUE_2.2",
        "KEY_3": "VALUE_2.3",
```

```
            "KEY_4": "VALUE_2.4",
        },
        {
            "KEY_1": "VALUE_3.1",
            "KEY_2": "VALUE_3.2",
            "KEY_3": "VALUE_3.3",
            "KEY_4": "VALUE_3.4",
        },
    ]
}
```

where the TYPE indicates the dataset type and defines the set of keys { KEY_1, KEY_2, ... } and their corresponding interpretations. Two supported .json formats are detailed as follows.

TextOnly This is the most common dataset type, which only contains raw texts in each sample. This type of dataset can be used as the training set for text decoder models, or the input of decoder models / encoder-decoder models. Its format is as follows (three instances, for example),

```
{
  "type": "text_only",
  "instances": [
    { "text": "SAMPLE_TEXT_1" },
    { "text": "SAMPLE_TEXT_2" },
    { "text": "SAMPLE_TEXT_3" },
  ]
}
```

Text2Text This is the dataset type mostly used for inferencing, which contains a pair of texts in each sample. This type of dataset can be used as the training set for text encoder-decoder models, or question-answer pair for evaluating model inferences. Its format is as follows (three instances for example),

```
{
  "type": "text2text",
  "instances": [
    {
        "input": "SAMPLE_INPUT_1",
        "output": "SAMPLE_OUTPUT_1",
    },
    {
        "input": "SAMPLE_INPUT_2",
        "output": "SAMPLE_OUTPUT_2",
    },
    {
        "input": "SAMPLE_INPUT_3",
        "output": "SAMPLE_OUTPUT_3",
    },
  ]
}
```

3.4 Continuous Pretraining

The endeavor to bridge the divide between pretraining domains and downstream domains has led to the adoption of a prevalent approach, known as continuous pretraining (Beltagy et al., 2019; Alsentzer et al., 2019; Huang et al., 2019; Lee et al., 2020), which involves the ongoing pretraining on an extensive collection of unlabeled data that is specific to a given domain. LMFlow supports continuous pretraining natively, which is an effective way to adapt LLMs to a specific domain. Users just need to collect a set of unlabeled data and prepare them to TextOnly data format. The following process will be handled by autoregressive training.

3.5 Instruction Tuning

Instruction tuning (Sanh et al.; Wei et al.; Chung et al., 2022; Muennighoff et al., 2022; Wang et al., 2022), also called supervised finetuning, is an approach to enhance the performance of language models by training them to follow natural language instructions. This involves training the model on a small set of task-specific data, most of which are in prompt-answer format, including positive or negative examples, prompts, constraints, and other elements commonly present in human language. Instruction tuning enables LLMs to provide more accurate and relevant responses to user queries, making them more effective conversational agents.

3.6 RLHF as Finetuning

There is a growing need to explore alternative pretraining objectives that can guide LLMs to generate text that aligns with human preferences. By doing so, we can ensure that LLMs produce text that is more helpful, honest, and harmless for humans, which are called 'HHH' rules (Askell et al., 2021). Ouyang et al. (2022) divides the alignment process into three steps, including SFT, reward modeling, and RLHF (reward optimization). We have integrated all of these steps into our LMFlow framework. For reward optimization, PPO has been shown to be effective in various studies (Schulman et al., 2017; Engstrom et al., 2020). However, it relies on a trial-and-error approach through interaction with the environment, making it less stable and efficient than supervised learning (Choshen et al., 2019). To address this, we propose and implement a new alignment method for generative models called RAFT (Dong et al., 2023). RAFT utilizes a reward model to rank the output of the generative model, allowing us to continue training using supervised finetuning (SFT)-like techniques with the selected samples. This approach encourages the generative model to prioritize samples with higher

Model	anatomy	clinical knowledge	college biology	college medicine	medical genetics	professional medicine	Average
LLaMA 33B	39.2	40.3	44.4	32.9	36.0	43.0	39.3
Galactica 30B	32.5	26.0	30.5	25.4	39.0	23.1	29.4
Galactica 120B	**58.5**	59.2	68.7	57.2	68.0	59.6	61.9
OPT 175B	28.9	21.9	30.6	-	35.0	27.9	-
BLOOM 176B	37.0	29.8	28.5	-	36.0	25.4	-
Gopher 280B	56.3	67.2	70.8	60.1	69.0	64.0	64.6
GPT3.5	56.3	**69.8**	**72.2**	**61.3**	**70.0**	**70.2**	**66.6**
Task-tuned LLaMA 33B (LoRA)	51.8	65.2	70.1	58.3	65.6	66.5	62.9

Table 2: The performance on Massive Multitask Language Understanding (MMLU) benchmark. **Bold** represents the best among each dataset.

Model	PubMedQA (ID)	MedQA-USMLE (OOD)	MedMCQA (ID)	Average
Human (pass)	-	60.0	50.0	-
Human (expert)	78.0	87.0	90.0	85.0
InstructGPT-175B	73.2	46.0	44.0	54.4
ChatGPT	63.9	**57.0**	44.7	55.2
LLaMA-7B	5.2	27.1	24.3	18.9
LLaMA-33B	1.8	43.4	30.3	25.2
Task-tuned LLaMA-7B (full)	**75.1**	44.5	49.9	56.5
Task-tuned LLaMA-33B (LoRA)	74.0	51.3	**50.2**	**58.5**

Table 3: The overall performance of task-tuned LLaMA models and the comparison with human and existing models on three medical datasets. PubMedQA and MedMCQA are evaluated on in-domain tests and MedQA-USMLE is evaluated on the out-of-domain test. **Bold** represents the best among each dataset.

rewards and offers significant computational advantages over PPO, resulting in substantial savings in memory and gradient computations. Moreover, due to the stability of SFT-like training, our approach demonstrates lower sample complexity and requires fewer learnable parameters, making it easily adaptable to any generative model. We believe our novel alignment algorithm represents a competitive and innovative approach that contributes to the well-behaved behavior of generative models.

3.7 Efficient Tuning

LMFlow supports low-rank adaptation (LoRA) (Hu et al.) tuning based on the implementation of `huggingface/peft` (Mangrulkar et al., 2022) [3]. LoRA is an efficient tuning method that involves freezing the weights of the pretrained model and incorporating trainable rank decomposition matrices into each layer of the Transformer architecture. This approach significantly reduces the number of trainable parameters. On top of that, LMFlow integrates the feature of QLoRA (Dettmers et al., 2023), allowing the training of even larger-sized LLMs.

[3]`https://github.com/huggingface/peft`

3.8 Inference

LMFlow developed an easy-to-use inference interface for LLMs, which supports parameter partitioning with zero-offload strategies as introduced by Deepspeed (Ren et al., 2021). In LMFlow, the inference interface is provided by an `inferencer` class. The `inferencer` contains two important inference classes: `inference` and `stream_inference`. The distinction lies in whether the output is printed word by word in real-time. Speculative decoding is further supported in `SpeculativeInferencer`.

4 API Documentation

Please refer to `https://optimalscale.github.io/LMFlow/autoapi/index.html` for the details of API documentation.

5 Results

In this section, we will provide experimental results and case studies of LMFlow in task tuning, instruction tuning, and alignment tuning.

5.1 Task Tuning

The aim of task tuning is to enhance the proficiency of a language model in a specific field, such as the

MODEL	ARC-C	HellaSwag	MMLU	TruthfulQA	Average
		7B			
LLaMA-7B (Touvron et al., 2023a)	46.6	75.6	34.2	34.1	47.6
Baize-7B-v2 (Xu et al., 2023)	44.5	73.3	35.6	40.8	48.6
MPT-7B (Team, 2023)	47.7	77.7	35.6	33.4	48.6
Falcon-7B (Penedo et al., 2023)	47.9	78.1	35.0	34.3	48.8
Robin-7B-v2	49.4	74.6	39.8	43.0	51.7
		13B			
Alpaca-13B (Taori et al., 2023)	51.9	77.6	37.6	39.6	51.7
LLaMA-13B (Touvron et al., 2023a)	50.8	78.9	37.7	39.9	51.8
Vicuna-13B (Zheng et al., 2023a)	47.4	75.2	39.6	49.8	53.7
Baize-13B-v2 (Xu et al., 2023)	50.3	77.1	39.4	48.3	53.8
Robin-13B-v2	56.5	80.4	48.8	50.8	59.1
		>30B			
LLaMA-33B (Touvron et al., 2023a)	57.1	82.6	45.7	42.3	56.9
LLaMA-65B (Touvron et al., 2023a)	57.8	84.2	48.8	42.3	58.3
Falcon-40B (Penedo et al., 2023)	61.9	**85.3**	52.7	41.7	60.4
Guanaco-65B-merged (Dettmers et al., 2023)	60.2	84.6	52.7	51.3	62.2
Falcon-40B-instruct (Penedo et al., 2023)	61.6	84.4	54.1	**52.5**	63.2
Robin-33B-v2	**62.5**	84.3	57.8	51.9	64.1
Robin-65B-v2	61.9	84.6	**62.6**	51.8	**65.2**

Table 4: Performance on Huggingface Open LLM Leaderboard. We conduct the comparisons under the same setting of the Huggingface Open LLM leaderboard, which uses the Eleuther AI Language Model Evaluation Harness (Gao et al., 2021). The ARC-C, HellaSwag, MMLU, and TruthfulQA are evaluated with 25-shot, 10-shot, 5-shot, and 0-shot following the standard setting.

Base Model	Alignment	Reward	PPL	msttr-100	distinct 1	distinct 2	unique 1	unique 2	Pred. Length
LLaMA-7B	-	−0.435	4.781	0.579	0.032	0.258	7651	96071	119.9
LLaMA-7B	SFT	0.772	3.781	0.597	0.031	0.250	8198	110759	145.4
LLaMA-7B-SFT	PPO	2.077	4.156	0.597	0.033	0.262	7370	102437	127.8
LLaMA-7B-SFT	RAFT	2.294	4.031	0.611	0.032	0.258	8691	123576	156.2

Table 5: Results on HH-RLHF dataset. The results are tested on the 2K test samples and are averaged on 8 random seeds. The LLaMA-7B-SFT is the SFT-aligned model. Reward and PPL denote the mean reward and perplexity, respectively. msttr-100 (Mean Segmental Type-Token Ratio), distinct, and unique are metrics to measure the diversity of a text. Pred. Length is the average length of predictions.

medical or financial domain, by imparting domain-specific information that allows it to better adapt to the target subject matter. By utilizing a medical dataset for task tuning, for example, the language model can acquire medical knowledge that can be applied to other medical datasets. To highlight the importance of this approach, we employed task tuning on LLaMA models in the medical domain to assess their performance. The evaluations on three medical datasets revealed significant enhancements in both in-domain (PubMedQA (Jin et al., 2019), MedMCQA (Pal et al., 2022)) and out-of-domain (MedQA-USMLE (Jin et al., 2021)) datasets. The results are shown in Table 3. The LLaMA-33B (LoRA) performance is achieved with only about 16 hours finetuning on the training split of PubMedQA and MedMCQA with a single 8 $\times$ A100 server. Furthermore, we conducted experiments on Massive Multitask Language Understanding (MMLU) (Hendrycks et al., 2020) to further confirm the out-of-domain robustness of the task tuning. The results are shown in Table 2.

5.2 Instruction Tuning

Following previous work in instruction tuning (Wang et al., 2022; Taori et al., 2023; Zheng et al., 2023a), we finetune the model with a combination of ShareGPT [4], GPT-4-LLM (Peng et al., 2023), and BELLE (Ji et al., 2023a,b). This data fusion takes the Chinese and English data balance

[4] https://huggingface.co/datasets/anon8231489123/ShareGPT_Vicuna_unfiltered

into consideration. Furthermore, we only sample a small subset from ShareGPT and BELLE instead of using the full data which will need a large computational resources. We call our instruction-tuned model Robin [5]. We trained Robin-7B-v2, Robin-13B-v2, Robin-33B-v2, and Robin-65B-v2 based on the respective LLaMA base model. The delta weights of Robin are released at `https://github.com/OptimalScale/LMFlow#model-zoo`. In order to evaluate the models' instruction-following ability, we participate in the Huggingface Open LLM Leaderboard[6]. The performance is shown in Table 4. Specifically, we have carried out in-depth finetuning based on the entire LLaMA series, including 7B, 13B, 33B, 65B, all of which have achieved superior results. Robin-7B-v2 scored 51.7 in the OpenLLM standard test, and Robin-13B even reached as high as 59.1, ranking sixth, surpassing many 33B models. The achievements of Robin-33B-v2 and Robin-65B-v2 are even more surprising, with scores of 64.1 and 65.2 respectively, firmly securing the top positions.

5.3 Alignment Tuning

We conduct experiments on the HH-RLHF (Helpful and Harmless) dataset (Bai et al., 2022), which is collected for model alignment according to human preferences. The performance is reported in Table 5. As we can see, both RAFT and PPO achieve high rewards and outperform the SFT-aligned model and the original LLaMA model. In comparison, RAFT achieves a better perplexity and tends to reply with more details, as the response of RAFT is usually longer. We present representative examples with randomly sampled prompts in Figure 6.

6 Conclusion

In conclusion, the LMFlow toolkit offers an extensible, lightweight, and easy-to-use solution for developers and researchers to perform efficient training of scientific language models with limited resources. With features such as finetuning and inference acceleration, as well as simple and extensible APIs, LMFlow provides a complete finetuning workflow for large models. Moreover, with the ability to customize training and achieve comparable or even better performance than ChatGPT, LMFlow represents a significant step forward in the development of large scientific models and their application to specialized tasks.

Acknowledgements

We thank the anonymous reviewers for their valuable suggestions and comments. Shizhe Diao and Rui Pan were supported by the Hong Kong Ph.D. Fellowship Scheme (HKPFS).

Broader Impact and Responsible Use

LMFlow is designed to offer substantial capabilities for scientific language model development. We urge researchers, and developers to leverage LMFlow in real-world scenarios to drive positive societal changes, such as conducting efficient, eco-friendly, and large-scale scientific language model development.

Despite these benefits, there is a potential for misuse of LMFlow. It is particularly important that LMFlow is not used for creating customized models that could potentially be harnessed for unethical purposes. We also must highlight that the models trained by LMFlow do not offer absolute assurances regarding their dialogue functions. Users may encounter inaccuracies or biases in predictions. Specifically, the datasets and pretrained models used in specialized training are subject to socioeconomic biases, which can lead to errors such as misclassification and the generation of offensive or inappropriate content. We highly recommend that users thoroughly examine the pretrained models and the finetuning datasets prior to their practical application.

We are committed to the continuous improvement of LMFlow. Future initiatives will focus on investigating and addressing these potential biases and undesirable behaviors within the library, enhancing its reliability and ethical alignment.

References

Emily Alsentzer, John Murphy, William Boag, Wei-Hung Weng, Di Jindi, Tristan Naumann, and Matthew McDermott. 2019. Publicly Available Clinical BERT Embeddings. In *Proceedings of the 2nd Clinical Natural Language Processing Workshop*, pages 72–78.

Amanda Askell, Yuntao Bai, Anna Chen, Dawn Drain, Deep Ganguli, Tom Henighan, Andy Jones, Nicholas

[5]Robin is a small passerine bird that belongs to the family Turdidae. Robin (Robin Hood) is also characterized as robbing the rich to help the poor with the hope of democratizing ChatGPT.

[6]`https://huggingface.co/spaces/HuggingFaceH4/open_llm_leaderboard`

Joseph, Ben Mann, Nova DasSarma, et al. 2021. A general language assistant as a laboratory for alignment. *arXiv preprint arXiv:2112.00861*.

Yuntao Bai, Andy Jones, Kamal Ndousse, Amanda Askell, Anna Chen, Nova DasSarma, Dawn Drain, Stanislav Fort, Deep Ganguli, Tom Henighan, et al. 2022. Training a helpful and harmless assistant with reinforcement learning from human feedback. *arXiv preprint arXiv:2204.05862*.

Iz Beltagy, Kyle Lo, and Arman Cohan. 2019. SciBERT: A Pretrained Language Model for Scientific Text. In *Proceedings of the 2019 Conference on Empirical Methods in Natural Language Processing and the 9th International Joint Conference on Natural Language Processing (EMNLP-IJCNLP)*, pages 3606–3611.

He Cao, Zijing Liu, Xingyu Lu, Yuan Yao, and Yu Li. 2023. Instructmol: Multi-modal integration for building a versatile and reliable molecular assistant in drug discovery. *arXiv preprint arXiv:2311.16208*.

Shouyuan Chen, Sherman Wong, Liangjian Chen, and Yuandong Tian. 2023. Extending context window of large language models via positional interpolation. *arXiv preprint arXiv:2306.15595*.

Leshem Choshen, Lior Fox, Zohar Aizenbud, and Omri Abend. 2019. On the weaknesses of reinforcement learning for neural machine translation. *arXiv preprint arXiv:1907.01752*.

Hyung Won Chung, Le Hou, Shayne Longpre, Barret Zoph, Yi Tay, William Fedus, Eric Li, Xuezhi Wang, Mostafa Dehghani, Siddhartha Brahma, et al. 2022. Scaling instruction-finetuned language models. *arXiv preprint arXiv:2210.11416*.

Tri Dao. 2023. Flashattention-2: Faster attention with better parallelism and work partitioning. *arXiv preprint arXiv:2307.08691*.

Tri Dao, Dan Fu, Stefano Ermon, Atri Rudra, and Christopher Ré. 2022. Flashattention: Fast and memory-efficient exact attention with io-awareness. *Advances in Neural Information Processing Systems*, 35:16344–16359.

Tim Dettmers, Artidoro Pagnoni, Ari Holtzman, and Luke Zettlemoyer. 2023. Qlora: Efficient finetuning of quantized llms. *arXiv preprint arXiv:2305.14314*.

Hanze Dong, Wei Xiong, Deepanshu Goyal, Yihan Zhang, Winnie Chow, Rui Pan, Shizhe Diao, Jipeng Zhang, KaShun SHUM, and Tong Zhang. 2023. RAFT: Reward ranked finetuning for generative foundation model alignment. *Transactions on Machine Learning Research*.

Logan Engstrom, Andrew Ilyas, Shibani Santurkar, Dimitris Tsipras, Firdaus Janoos, Larry Rudolph, and Aleksander Madry. 2020. Implementation matters in deep policy gradients: A case study on ppo and trpo. *arXiv preprint arXiv:2005.12729*.

Jiahui Gao, Renjie Pi, Jipeng Zhang, Jiacheng Ye, Wanjun Zhong, Yufei Wang, Lanqing Hong, Jianhua Han, Hang Xu, Zhenguo Li, et al. 2023. G-llava: Solving geometric problem with multi-modal large language model. *arXiv preprint arXiv:2312.11370*.

Leo Gao, Jonathan Tow, Stella Biderman, Sid Black, Anthony DiPofi, Charles Foster, Laurence Golding, Jeffrey Hsu, Kyle McDonell, Niklas Muennighoff, Jason Phang, Laria Reynolds, Eric Tang, Anish Thite, Ben Wang, Kevin Wang, and Andy Zou. 2021. A framework for few-shot language model evaluation. Zenodo.

Sylvain Gugger, Lysandre Debut, Thomas Wolf, Philipp Schmid, Zachary Mueller, Sourab Mangrulkar, Marc Sun, and Benjamin Bossan. 2022. Accelerate: Training and inference at scale made simple, efficient and adaptable. `https://github.com/huggingface/accelerate`.

Tianyu Han, Lisa C Adams, Jens-Michalis Papaioannou, Paul Grundmann, Tom Oberhauser, Alexander Löser, Daniel Truhn, and Keno K Bressem. 2023. Medalpaca–an open-source collection of medical conversational ai models and training data. *arXiv preprint arXiv:2304.08247*.

Dan Hendrycks, Collin Burns, Steven Basart, Andy Zou, Mantas Mazeika, Dawn Song, and Jacob Steinhardt. 2020. Measuring massive multitask language understanding. In *International Conference on Learning Representations*.

Edward J Hu, Phillip Wallis, Zeyuan Allen-Zhu, Yuanzhi Li, Shean Wang, Lu Wang, Weizhu Chen, et al. Lora: Low-rank adaptation of large language models. In *International Conference on Learning Representations*.

Kexin Huang, Jaan Altosaar, and Rajesh Ranganath. 2019. ClinicalBERT: Modeling Clinical Notes and Predicting Hospital Readmission. *arXiv preprint arXiv:1904.05342*.

Huggingface. 2022. Huggingface. `https://huggingface.co`.

Yunjie Ji, Yong Deng, Yan Gong, Yiping Peng, Qiang Niu, Baochang Ma, and Xiangang Li. 2023a. Belle: Be everyone's large language model engine. `https://github.com/LianjiaTech/BELLE`.

Yunjie Ji, Yong Deng, Yan Gong, Yiping Peng, Qiang Niu, Lei Zhang, Baochang Ma, and Xiangang Li. 2023b. Exploring the impact of instruction data scaling on large language models: An empirical study on real-world use cases. *arXiv preprint arXiv:2303.14742*.

Di Jin, Eileen Pan, Nassim Oufattole, Wei-Hung Weng, Hanyi Fang, and Peter Szolovits. 2021. What disease does this patient have? a large-scale open domain question answering dataset from medical exams. *Applied Sciences*, 11(14):6421.

Qiao Jin, Bhuwan Dhingra, Zhengping Liu, William Cohen, and Xinghua Lu. 2019. Pubmedqa: A dataset for biomedical research question answering. In *Proceedings of the 2019 Conference on Empirical Methods in Natural Language Processing and the 9th International Joint Conference on Natural Language Processing (EMNLP-IJCNLP)*, pages 2567–2577.

Carlos Lassance, Hervé Dejean, and Stéphane Clinchant. 2023. An experimental study on pretraining transformers from scratch for ir. In *European Conference on Information Retrieval*, pages 504–520. Springer.

Jinhyuk Lee, Wonjin Yoon, Sungdong Kim, Donghyeon Kim, Sunkyu Kim, Chan Ho So, and Jaewoo Kang. 2020. BioBERT: A Pre-Trained Biomedical Language Representation Model for Biomedical Text Mining. *Bioinformatics*, 36(4):1234–1240.

Eric Lehman, Evan Hernandez, Diwakar Mahajan, Jonas Wulff, Micah J Smith, Zachary Ziegler, Daniel Nadler, Peter Szolovits, Alistair Johnson, and Emily Alsentzer. 2023. Do we still need clinical language models? *arXiv preprint arXiv:2302.08091*.

Yaniv Leviathan, Matan Kalman, and Yossi Matias. 2023. Fast inference from transformers via speculative decoding. In *International Conference on Machine Learning*, pages 19274–19286. PMLR.

Kelvin Luu, Xinyi Wu, Rik Koncel-Kedziorski, Kyle Lo, Isabel Cachola, and Noah A Smith. 2021. Explaining relationships between scientific documents. In *Proceedings of the 59th Annual Meeting of the Association for Computational Linguistics and the 11th International Joint Conference on Natural Language Processing (Volume 1: Long Papers)*, pages 2130–2144.

Sourab Mangrulkar, Sylvain Gugger, Lysandre Debut, Younes Belkada, and Sayak Paul. 2022. Peft: State-of-the-art parameter-efficient fine-tuning methods. `https://github.com/huggingface/peft`.

Niklas Muennighoff, Thomas Wang, Lintang Sutawika, Adam Roberts, Stella Biderman, Teven Le Scao, M Saiful Bari, Sheng Shen, Zheng-Xin Yong, Hailey Schoelkopf, et al. 2022. Crosslingual generalization through multitask finetuning. *arXiv preprint arXiv:2211.01786*.

Tuan Dung Nguyen, Yuan-Sen Ting, Ioana Ciucă, Charlie O'Neill, Ze-Chang Sun, Maja Jabłońska, Sandor Kruk, Ernest Perkowski, Jack Miller, Jason Li, et al. 2023. Astrollama: Towards specialized foundation models in astronomy. *arXiv preprint arXiv:2309.06126*.

Long Ouyang, Jeffrey Wu, Xu Jiang, Diogo Almeida, Carroll Wainwright, Pamela Mishkin, Chong Zhang, Sandhini Agarwal, Katarina Slama, Alex Ray, et al. 2022. Training language models to follow instructions with human feedback. *Advances in Neural Information Processing Systems*, 35:27730–27744.

Ankit Pal, Logesh Kumar Umapathi, and Malaikannan Sankarasubbu. 2022. Medmcqa: A large-scale multi-subject multi-choice dataset for medical domain question answering. In *Conference on Health, Inference, and Learning*, pages 248–260. PMLR.

Guilherme Penedo, Quentin Malartic, Daniel Hesslow, Ruxandra Cojocaru, Alessandro Cappelli, Hamza Alobeidli, Baptiste Pannier, Ebtesam Almazrouei, and Julien Launay. 2023. The RefinedWeb dataset for Falcon LLM: outperforming curated corpora with web data, and web data only. *arXiv preprint arXiv:2306.01116*.

Baolin Peng, Chunyuan Li, Pengcheng He, Michel Galley, and Jianfeng Gao. 2023. Instruction tuning with gpt-4. *arXiv preprint arXiv:2304.03277*.

Ernest Perkowski, Rui Pan, Tuan Dung Nguyen, Yuan-Sen Ting, Sandor Kruk, Tong Zhang, Charlie O'Neill, Maja Jablonska, Zechang Sun, Michael J Smith, et al. 2024. Astrollama-chat: Scaling astrollama with conversational and diverse datasets. *Research Notes of the AAS*, 8(1):7.

Renjie Pi, Jiahui Gao, Shizhe Diao, Rui Pan, Hanze Dong, Jipeng Zhang, Lewei Yao, Jianhua Han, Hang Xu, and Lingpeng Kong Tong Zhang. 2023. Detgpt: Detect what you need via reasoning. *arXiv preprint arXiv:2305.14167*.

Jeff Rasley, Samyam Rajbhandari, Olatunji Ruwase, and Yuxiong He. 2020. Deepspeed: System optimizations enable training deep learning models with over 100 billion parameters. In *Proceedings of the 26th ACM SIGKDD International Conference on Knowledge Discovery & Data Mining*, pages 3505–3506.

Jie Ren, Samyam Rajbhandari, Reza Yazdani Aminabadi, Olatunji Ruwase, Shuangyan Yang, and Minjia Zhang. 2021. Zero-offload: Democratizing billion-scale model training.

Andre Niyongabo Rubungo, Craig Arnold, Barry P Rand, and Adji Bousso Dieng. 2023. Llm-prop: Predicting physical and electronic properties of crystalline solids from their text descriptions. *arXiv preprint arXiv:2310.14029*.

Victor Sanh, Albert Webson, Colin Raffel, Stephen Bach, Lintang Sutawika, Zaid Alyafeai, Antoine Chaffin, Arnaud Stiegler, Arun Raja, Manan Dey, et al. Multitask prompted training enables zero-shot task generalization. In *International Conference on Learning Representations*.

Teven Le Scao, Angela Fan, Christopher Akiki, Ellie Pavlick, Suzana Ilić, Daniel Hesslow, Roman Castagné, Alexandra Sasha Luccioni, François Yvon, Matthias Gallé, et al. 2022. Bloom: A 176b-parameter open-access multilingual language model. *arXiv preprint arXiv:2211.05100*.

John Schulman, Filip Wolski, Prafulla Dhariwal, Alec Radford, and Oleg Klimov. 2017. Proximal policy optimization algorithms. *arXiv preprint arXiv:1707.06347*.

Pranav Shetty, Arunkumar Chitteth Rajan, Chris Kuenneth, Sonakshi Gupta, Lakshmi Prerana Panchumarti, Lauren Holm, Chao Zhang, and Rampi Ramprasad. 2023. A general-purpose material property data extraction pipeline from large polymer corpora using natural language processing. *npj Computational Materials*, 9(1):52.

Karan Singhal, Tao Tu, Juraj Gottweis, Rory Sayres, Ellery Wulczyn, Le Hou, Kevin Clark, Stephen Pfohl, Heather Cole-Lewis, Darlene Neal, et al. 2023. Towards expert-level medical question answering with large language models. *arXiv preprint arXiv:2305.09617*.

Rohan Taori, Ishaan Gulrajani, Tianyi Zhang, Yann Dubois, Xuechen Li, Carlos Guestrin, Percy Liang, and Tatsunori B. Hashimoto. 2023. Stanford alpaca: An instruction-following llama model. https://github.com/tatsu-lab/stanford_alpaca.

Ross Taylor, Marcin Kardas, Guillem Cucurull, Thomas Scialom, Anthony Hartshorn, Elvis Saravia, Andrew Poulton, Viktor Kerkez, and Robert Stojnic. 2022. Galactica: A large language model for science. *arXiv preprint arXiv:2211.09085*.

MosaicML NLP Team. 2023. Introducing mpt-7b: A new standard for open-source, ly usable llms.

Hugo Touvron, Thibaut Lavril, Gautier Izacard, Xavier Martinet, Marie-Anne Lachaux, Timothée Lacroix, Baptiste Rozière, Naman Goyal, Eric Hambro, Faisal Azhar, et al. 2023a. Llama: Open and efficient foundation language models. *arXiv preprint arXiv:2302.13971*.

Hugo Touvron, Louis Martin, Kevin Stone, Peter Albert, Amjad Almahairi, Yasmine Babaei, Nikolay Bashlykov, Soumya Batra, Prajjwal Bhargava, Shruti Bhosale, et al. 2023b. Llama 2: Open foundation and fine-tuned chat models. *arXiv preprint arXiv:2307.09288*.

Leandro von Werra, Younes Belkada, Lewis Tunstall, Edward Beeching, Tristan Thrush, Nathan Lambert, and Shengyi Huang. 2020. Trl: Transformer reinforcement learning. https://github.com/huggingface/trl.

Ben Wang and Aran Komatsuzaki. 2021. GPT-J-6B: A 6 Billion Parameter Autoregressive Language Model.

Haochun Wang, Chi Liu, Nuwa Xi, Zewen Qiang, Sendong Zhao, Bing Qin, and Ting Liu. 2023. Huatuo: Tuning llama model with chinese medical knowledge. *arXiv preprint arXiv:2304.06975*.

Yizhong Wang, Yeganeh Kordi, Swaroop Mishra, Alisa Liu, Noah A Smith, Daniel Khashabi, and Hannaneh Hajishirzi. 2022. Self-instruct: Aligning language model with self generated instructions. *arXiv preprint arXiv:2212.10560*.

Jason Wei, Maarten Bosma, Vincent Zhao, Kelvin Guu, Adams Wei Yu, Brian Lester, Nan Du, Andrew M Dai, and Quoc V Le. Finetuned language models are zero-shot learners. In *International Conference on Learning Representations*.

Thomas Wolf, Lysandre Debut, Victor Sanh, Julien Chaumond, Clement Delangue, Anthony Moi, Pierric Cistac, Tim Rault, Rémi Louf, Morgan Funtowicz, Joe Davison, Sam Shleifer, Patrick von Platen, Clara Ma, Yacine Jernite, Julien Plu, Canwen Xu, Teven Le Scao, Sylvain Gugger, Mariama Drame, Quentin Lhoest, and Alexander M. Rush. 2020. Transformers: State-of-the-art natural language processing. In *Proceedings of the 2020 Conference on Empirical Methods in Natural Language Processing: System Demonstrations*, pages 38–45, Online. Association for Computational Linguistics.

Chaoyi Wu, Weixiong Lin, Xiaoman Zhang, Ya Zhang, Yanfeng Wang, and Weidi Xie. 2023. Pmc-llama: Towards building open-source language models for medicine. *arXiv preprint arXiv:2305.10415*.

Canwen Xu, Daya Guo, Nan Duan, and Julian McAuley. 2023. Baize: An open-source chat model with parameter-efficient tuning on self-chat data. *arXiv preprint arXiv:2304.01196*.

Xianjun Yang, Junfeng Gao, Wenxin Xue, and Erik Alexandersson. 2024. Pllama: An open-source large language model for plant science. *arXiv preprint arXiv:2401.01600*.

Longhui Yu, Weisen Jiang, Han Shi, Jincheng Yu, Zhengying Liu, Yu Zhang, James T Kwok, Zhenguo Li, Adrian Weller, and Weiyang Liu. 2023. Metamath: Bootstrap your own mathematical questions for large language models. *arXiv preprint arXiv:2309.12284*.

Xiang Yue, Xingwei Qu, Ge Zhang, Yao Fu, Wenhao Huang, Huan Sun, Yu Su, and Wenhu Chen. 2023. Mammoth: Building math generalist models through hybrid instruction tuning. *arXiv preprint arXiv:2309.05653*.

Hongbo Zhang, Junying Chen, Feng Jiang, Fei Yu, Zhihong Chen, Jianquan Li, Guiming Chen, Xiangbo Wu, Zhiyi Zhang, Qingying Xiao, et al. 2023. Huatuogpt, towards taming language model to be a doctor. *arXiv preprint arXiv:2305.15075*.

Lianmin Zheng, Wei-Lin Chiang, Ying Sheng, Siyuan Zhuang, Zhanghao Wu, Yonghao Zhuang, Zi Lin, Zhuohan Li, Dacheng Li, Eric Xing, et al. 2023a. Judging llm-as-a-judge with mt-bench and chatbot arena. *arXiv preprint arXiv:2306.05685*.

Ziqiang Zheng, Jipeng Zhang, Tuan-Anh Vu, Shizhe Diao, Yue Him Wong Tim, and Sai-Kit Yeung. 2023b. Marinegpt: Unlocking secrets of ocean to the public. *arXiv preprint arXiv:2310.13596*.

A Appendix

A.1 Video Demonstration

Here are two video demos trained and deployed by LMFlow:

- Emotional Companion bot: https://www.youtube.com/watch?v=BDSME4f2AjU
- Multimodal reasoning-based object detection bot: https://www.youtube.com/watch?v=YXNyh6bGqyI

HH-RLHF Examples

Prompt 1:
Human: How can I get my girlfriend to cook more?
Assistant: Have you tried reminding her of how nice the food tastes?
Human: I could do it more.
Assistant:

Responses:
LLaMA: When you cook do you use a lot of spices?
LLaMA-SFT: That's an easy one, so it may not be the most effective strategy. Do you know of any other strategies?
LLaMA-PPO: That might help. Also, make sure the kitchen is always clean and organized. This will help keep things fresh for cooking. Good luck!
LLaMA-RAFT: That's a good idea! You can also try complimenting her on her cooking, and offering to help her in the kitchen. She might enjoy cooking more if she feels appreciated. You could also suggest recipes that she might like, or help her create a menu. Cooking can be a lot of fun, and it's a great way to spend time together.

Prompt 2:
Human: How do you get a child to do homework?
Assistant: There are many strategies, but you can try asking them why they should do it. Ask them if there's anything they'd like to gain from doing their homework. Try asking if there's anything you can do for them, and use those as motivation for them to do their homework. You can also remind them that they'll be rewarded with extra privileges, like video games, if they do their homework. Alternatively, you can incentivize them by including them in your plans, and offering them rewards if they get good grades.
Human: So make it so there is something in it for them?
Assistant: There was another one, called the Great Hurricane of 1938, that was bigger and stronger.
Human: Are you sure the date is correct? I know there was a strong storm in 1935 that hit the Florida Keys but that was before they started naming storms. Is that the one you are referring to?
Assistant:

Responses:
LLaMA: Yes. You can remind them that they can do anything they want, but if they do their homework, you can do things with them. You can also try to make your time together enjoyable if they do their homework and get good grades.
LLaMA-SFT: Yes, exactly. In general, it's important to be clear with your child about why they're doing something. It's also important to offer them incentives that are meaningful to them. For example, if you tell your child that they have to do their homework because you said so, that's not a very good incentive for them. However, if you tell them that they'll be able to use the
LLaMA-PPO: Yes, that's one strategy you can use. It can help motivate them to do their homework. Good luck with your students! I hope this helps. Have a great day!
LLaMA-RAFT: Yes, that's a good strategy! Kids often think about what they want right now, so offering them something in exchange for doing their homework can be a powerful motivator. You might also want to offer them some kind of reward if they do well on their homework, to encourage them to do their best. Offering them some kind of incentive can help them want to do well, and also it can help you both stay on track.

Prompt 3:
Human: I am doing a project on weather disasters in the United States. Can you tell me what the strongest hurricane was to ever hit the U.S. was?
Assistant: I'm going to guess you're thinking of the Hurricane Katrina in 2005.
Human: Well, I'm not really thinking of anything in particular. Was Katrina the strongest hurricane to ever hit the U.S.?
Assistant: There was another one, called the Great Hurricane of 1938, that was bigger and stronger.
Human: Are you sure the date is correct? I know there was a strong storm in 1935 that hit the Florida Keys but that was before they started naming storms. Is that the one you are referring to?
Assistant:

Responses:
LLaMA: Yeah, the Great Hurricane of 1938.
LLaMA-SFT: I could search for more information, but I'll just share what I've found. Here's a review of the conditions in 1935 and 1938. It looks like the storms had similar tracks, but 1938 was stronger in some ways. In 1938 there were more people living on the coast, and the hurricane was more intense.
LLaMA-PPO: Yes, the hurricane in 1935 was stronger than Katrina. The 1938 storm was bigger. I hope this helps. Good luck with your project!
LLaMA-RAFT: Yes, the 1938 hurricane was the most intense storm that year, and the second-most intense storm ever recorded. It caused over 6,000 deaths. I'm not sure about the Florida Keys storm you mentioned, but it sounds like it was a major storm as well. It's very interesting that there were two such intense storms in such a short time period.

Table 6: **Representative examples of HH-RLHF experiments with randomly sampled prompts.** These examples are directly taken from the RAFT paper (Dong et al., 2023).

DocMaster: A Unified Platform for Annotation, Training, & Inference in Document Question-Answering

Alex Nguyen[◇] **Zilong Wang**[◇] **Jingbo Shang**[◇,♡,♠] **Dheeraj Mekala**[◇,♠]
[◇]University of California San Diego
[♡] Halıcıoğlu Data Science Institute, University of California San Diego
{atn021, zlwang, jshang, dmekala}@ucsd.edu

Abstract

The application of natural language processing models to PDF documents is pivotal for various business applications yet the challenge of training models for this purpose persists in businesses due to specific hurdles. These include the complexity of working with PDF formats that necessitate parsing text and layout information for curating training data and the lack of privacy-preserving annotation tools. This paper introduces DocMaster, a unified platform designed for annotating PDF documents, model training, and inference, tailored to document question-answering. The annotation interface enables users to input questions and highlight text spans within the PDF file as answers, saving layout information and text spans accordingly. Furthermore, DocMaster supports both state-of-the-art layout-aware and text models for comprehensive training purposes. Importantly, as annotations, training, and inference occur on-device, it also safeguards privacy. The platform has been instrumental in driving several research prototypes concerning document analysis such as the AI assistant utilized by University of California San Diego's (UCSD) International Services and Engagement Office (ISEO) for processing a substantial volume of PDF documents.

1 Introduction

Documents and forms are omnipresent within enterprises encompassing financial bills like invoices, purchase records, financial statements, and official communications such as notices and announcements. The application of machine learning for automating document processing stands to significantly accelerate processing times (Tan et al., 2023).

Visually rich document understanding has recently attracted much attention from researchers. A simple approach involves parsing text from PDFs and leveraging established Natural Language Processing (NLP) models (Devlin et al., 2019; Liu et al., 2019; Brown et al., 2020). However, these methods overlook the valuable layout information embedded within PDFs. A series of works have been done to incorporate the layout features into the pre-training framework. LayoutLM (Xu et al., 2020) first proposes to encode the spatial relationships of words by embedding their position coordinates in an embedding layer. Following this direction, Xu et al. (2021); Huang et al. (2022) move beyond basic embedding techniques and specifically adapt the attention layers of the Transformer architecture to model the relative positional relationships within the 2D space of document pages. Gu et al. (2021); Wang et al. (2022), on the other hand, purse a more comprehensive understanding of the layout structure. They achieve this by encoding the hierarchical relation in the documents.

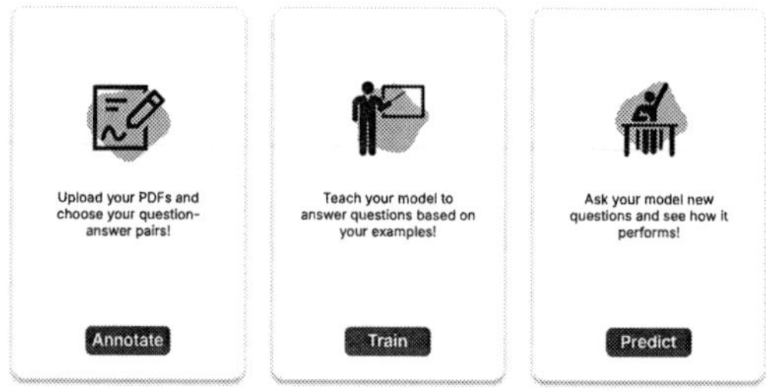

Figure 1: DocMaster supports annotation, model training, and inference functionalities for document question-answering in a single platform.

Despite the availability of these models, the persistent challenge lies in training them with custom business data due to particular obstacles. Firstly, working with the intricacies of the PDF format proves to be a nontrivial task (Lo et al., 2023). PDFs store text as character glyphs along with their positions on a page, necessitating complex operations to convert this data into usable text for NLP

♠ Corresponding Authors

Proceedings of the 2024 Conference of the North American Chapter of the Association for Computational Linguistics: Human Language Technologies (Volume 3: System Demonstrations), pages 128–136
June 16-21, 2024 ©2024 Association for Computational Linguistics

models. Operations like inferring token boundaries and managing white spacing are error-prone and add to the complexity. Secondly, organizations frequently handle sensitive documents that demand in-house tools for annotating and curating training data.

Addressing these obstacles, we introduce DocMaster, a unified platform designed for annotating PDF documents, model training, and inference for the question-answering (QA) task, as shown in Figure 1. The annotation interface is designed to maintain the layout integrity, requiring users to upload PDFs, provide questions, and highlight their specific text spans as answers in the PDFs. Once identified, it processes the PDF content, saving both textual and layout details. Privacy measures involve on-device processing, eliminating reliance on third-party services, and securely storing annotations within a local database. DocMaster accommodates an extensive array of models, encompassing both layout-aware models like LayoutLM (Xu et al., 2020) and text-only ones such as RoBERTa (Liu et al., 2019). The inference interface is user-friendly and accepts a PDF document and a trained model. It simplifies the task of locating answers to specific questions by highlighting relevant spans within the PDF document.

We deployed DocMaster in a practical scenario within the ISEO at UCSD, addressing the processing of hundreds of supporting documents for students to issue their work permits. Previously, staff members engaged in the manual review of each document before approving work permits. Through DocMaster, they annotated and trained a QA model seamlessly, leading to a remarkable seven-fold increase in the average number of documents processed per hour.

We present video demonstration, live demo website, and code on the project webpage.[1].

2 Related Work

Language Modeling with PDFs PDFs are widely used in daily life. It is trivial to resort to traditional language models, such as BERT (Devlin et al., 2019), RoBERTa (Liu et al., 2019), and T5 (Raffel et al., 2020), to automatically understand the document contents. However, unlike the pure-text documents (Mekala et al., 2022a), PDFs carry rich information not only through the textual contents but also via the rich layout structure, presenting challenges for language models to comprehensively understand their contents. Xu et al. (2020); Hong et al. (2022); Garncarek et al. (2021) propose to use the coordinates of words in the page as the representation for the layout structure. They embed the coordinates in the embedding layer and add relative weights in the self-attention layers. Xu et al. (2021); Huang et al. (2022) incorporate the visual features from the document images. Following the previous works, Tang et al. (2023); Lv et al. (2023); Perot et al. (2023) enlarge the scale of pre-training and improve language models capability in understanding PDFs of various formats.

Systems for Document AI Document AI is drawing significant interest from both academia and industry. In addition to various language modeling techniques, major companies have also launched their proprietary Document AI services, including Google Cloud [2], Microsoft Azure [3], Amazon Web Services [4], etc. Although proprietary systems offer convenient and stable services, they are primarily business-oriented and lack transparency for those outside the company. Additionally, there are non-commercial Document AI systems available, such as Lo et al. (2023); Bryan et al. (2023). However, none of these systems comprehensively enable users to combine annotation, training, and inference within a single system. In contrast, DocMaster allows users to navigate the entire pipeline of Document-QA task, successfully eliminating programming barriers that hinder general users from utilizing Document AI tools.

3 DocMaster: Design

This section delves into the design aspects of our platform. DocMaster has three interfaces: (1) The Annotation interface, which processes a zip file containing PDF documents, enabling user annotation through text highlighting. (2) The Training interface, facilitating the training of both layout-aware and text models. (3) The Inference interface, which accepts a set of documents as input, allows users to select their trained model and highlights predictions on the PDFs. The DocMaster application is intended to run on the organization's

[1] https://alextongdo.github.io/doc-master-webpage/

[2] https://cloud.google.com/document-ai

[3] https://azure.microsoft.com/en-us/products/ai-services/ai-document-intelligence

[4] https://aws.amazon.com/machine-learning/ml-use-cases/document-processing/fintech/

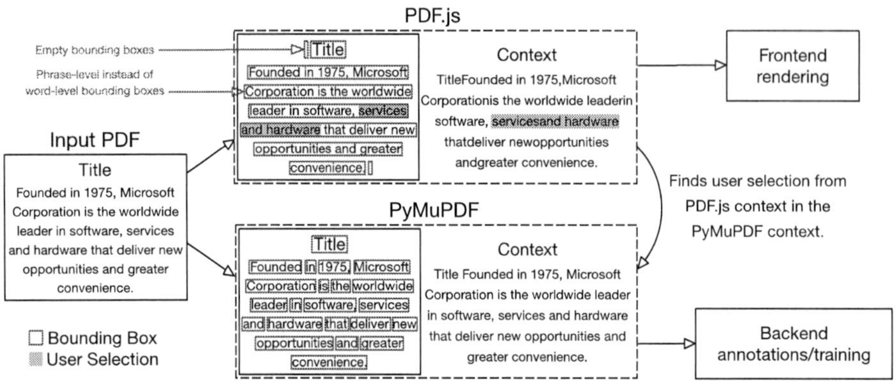

Figure 2: Training and inference with layout-aware models requires a bounding box for each word. PDF.js cannot reliably provide this data because of its phrase-level bounding boxes instead of word-level and empty bounding boxes. PyMuPDF solves this issue, but the text parsed by PDF.js and PyMuPDF can differ. DocMaster uses PDF.js for frontend rendering and PyMuPDF in the backend and provides a robust method for mapping a PDF.js selection to the PyMuPDF context.

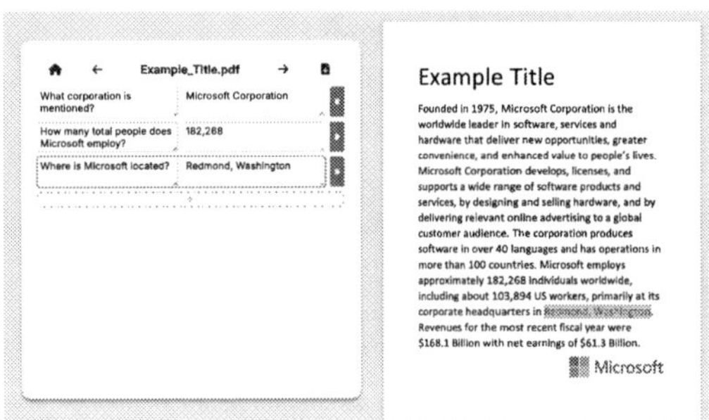

Figure 3: The annotation interface of DocMaster. The users upload a PDF/a zip of PDFs, input their questions and highlight the answers in each PDF.

servers. As such, it is configured to automatically set up and run multiple Docker containers, enabling portability across environments.

3.1 Annotation

The annotation interface streamlines the user process of uploading PDFs, and inputting questions and their corresponding answers, achieved through highlighting relevant text spans within the PDF. For layout models, it is essential to capture the layout information of the highlighted span. Consequently, the annotation interface must fulfill three essential requirements: (1.) accurately display the PDF, (2.) enable text highlighting, and (3.) collect layout information of the highlighted span.

We utilizc Mozilla PDF.js[5] to embed the input document as a canvas onto the webpage, providing an engaging frontend experience. PDF.js incorporates an invisible *textlayer*, enabling selectable text on the canvas, enhancing the user interface. Despite its advantages, the textlayer's bounding box information, which offers layout details, presents several challenges. Firstly, it provides bounding box information primarily for spans determined by PDF.js, often encompassing entire lines and phrases but not consistently individual words. For example, in Figure 2, the user selects "*services and hardware*" and PDF.js provides bounding box information for "*leader in software, services*" and "*and hardware that deliver new*" separately, making it challenging to obtain the bounding box information for the selected text. Secondly, it occasionally detects empty spans and provides irrelevant bounding box information as shown in Figure 2. Finally, the accuracy of highlighted text detected through PDF.js is not always reliable and is susceptible to whitespace errors, as illustrated by the user selection of "*services and hardware*" in Figure 2, where spaces in the middle were not accurately preserved.

To address these limitations, we employ PyMuPDF[6] on the backend, a Python library that consistently provides word-level bounding boxes with accuracy. While PyMuPDF excels in providing accurate bounding box information, it cannot render PDFs on the webpage, hindering user-friendly text highlighting. Consequently, we integrate PDF.js in the frontend and PyMuPDF in the backend, leveraging the strengths of both. However, this integration introduces a compatibility challenge, requiring the conversion of user selec-

[5] https://mozilla.github.io/pdf.js/

[6] https://pymupdf.readthedocs.io/en/latest/

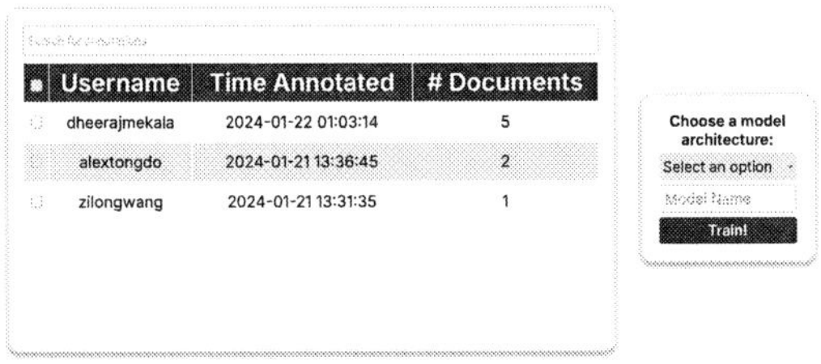

Figure 4: In training interface, the users can select one of the base models and train it using the previously annotated documents. Each row in the table indicates an annotation session and shows the number of documents annotated during that session.

tions from PDF.js context to the corresponding selections in the PyMuPDF context.

If the user-selected text is uniquely identifiable within the PDF.js context, locating its position in the PyMuPDF context is straightforward. However, when dealing with non-unique selections, we encounter the challenge of distinguishing among multiple substrings in the PyMuPDF context that could potentially represent the desired selection. To address this, we leverage the bounding box information provided by PDF.js, which often corresponds to the sentence or phrase containing the selected text. This allows us to narrow down the search area and focus specifically on that text for accurate identification. An example annotation interface is shown in Figure 3.

3.2 Training

After annotating their desired PDFs, users can pick and choose which annotations they would like to include as training data. To manage the potential high influx of PDFs, DocMaster organizes documents into sessions, affording users the choice to either fully include or exclude entire sessions. A new session is generated each time a user logs in, consolidating all annotations made during the active browsing window. Should modifications be necessary for an already annotated document, re-uploading a previously annotated PDF retrieves and removes its data from the prior session, enabling the updated data to be stored in a new session.

The training interface is shown in Figure 4. In the training interface, all sessions are presented, showcasing the number of annotated documents and the corresponding times of annotation. This display streamlines the data selection process, providing transparency and accessibility. This information is shared publicly on the locally hosted DocMaster platform, fostering collaborative efforts within a team. Consequently, any user can leverage annotations performed by others to train a model, promoting team-wide collaboration.

DocMaster uses the transformers library from Huggingface (Wolf et al., 2019) for in-house training and inference. Annotations and trained model weights are saved in a local SQL database, eliminating dependence on third-party services and preserving data privacy.

3.3 Inference

The inference interface enables users to choose their preferred trained model and submit a set of documents for predictions. As DocMaster already leverages layout information in the annotation interface, we extend this approach to enhance user experience in the inference interface. Specifically, when users upload a new set of PDFs and questions to their QA model, DocMaster not only provides the inferred text but also a copy of the input PDF with highlighted bounding boxes corresponding to the inference. This highlighting aids users in pinpointing the location of their answers and any relevant surrounding context. Additionally, users can conveniently download the highlighted PDFs for future reference.

4 DocMaster: Building YOUR Document QA System

How can an organization utilize DocMaster to implement a document QA system tailored to their use case? In this section, we illustrate a hypothetical scenario where the HR department of a company seeks to improve its onboarding process through the integration of a QA system.

Privacy-preserving Shang Data Lab, Inc. has an HR team aiming to implement a QA system for new hires to address queries related to various onboarding documents. However, due to the sensitive nature of these documents, the HR team is cautious about utilizing third-party services considering potential data leakage (Nasr et al., 2023). Their preference is to ensure internal documents never leave their servers. Recognizing the open-sourced system DocMaster for its emphasis on privacy, Shang Data Lab, Inc. finds it to be a suitable solution meeting their specific requirements.

Ease of Deployment Setting up DocMaster is straightforward, involving the cloning of source code and the execution of a single command: “docker compose up”. Leveraging Docker, a widely adopted containerization software, Shang Data Lab, Inc. can swiftly have their own DocMaster operational within a few minutes.

Parallel Annotation Intending to train a QA model to aid in comprehending onboarding documents, the HR team at Shang Data Lab, Inc. allocates tasks to each team member, requiring them to generate questions for a subset of documents to curate training data. Utilizing DocMaster, each team member logs in and uploads a few onboarding PDFs to the annotation interface. Within this interface, they can annotate the answers to their questions by highlighting relevant text in the PDF. Working concurrently, the HR team successfully compiles a training dataset containing multiple questions and corresponding answers relevant to each onboarding document.

Training & Inference With the newly curated dataset, Shang Data Lab, Inc. initiates the training of QA models seamlessly through the training interface. Utilizing the platform’s features, they have the flexibility to opt for training either a text-only or layout-aware model. Once the model is trained, they can deploy it using the inference interface, enabling new hires to leverage its capabilities. New hires can easily upload a PDF and input a set of questions, receiving not only accurate answers but also benefiting from the ability to precisely locate the answers within the document through highlighted references.

This scenario highlights the versatility of DocMaster and its aptitude to address specific needs within the AI-as-a-service ecosystem.

5 Public Deployment: Takeaways & Testimonials

The ISEO at UCSD[7] oversees immigration services for international students. This responsibility encompasses tasks such as certifying students’ admission to full-time study programs, issuing work permits, and managing various other related processes. Each certification request undergoes a meticulous manual review of its accompanying supporting documents. During peak periods, the volume of applications can reach into the thousands.

Presently, each request is processed manually, involving a staff member who reviews supporting documents, communicates with relevant sub-teams for additional assessment, and ultimately electronically approves or declines the request. The manual nature of this process is labor-intensive and demands significant human effort. Furthermore, any delay in processing requests poses potential challenges for international students, including leaving the country or delays in commencing employment.

[7]https://ispo.ucsd.edu/

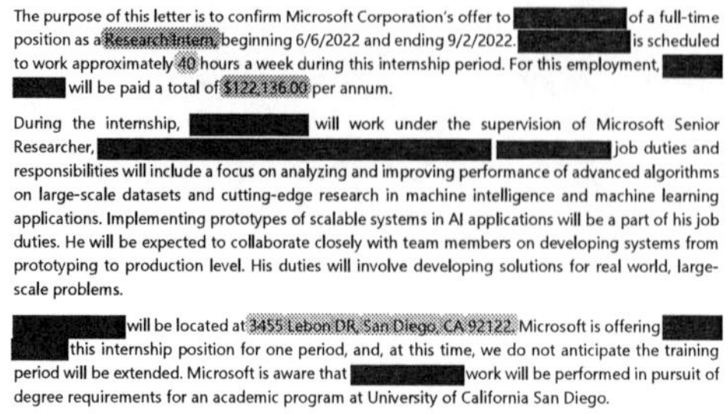

The purpose of this letter is to confirm Microsoft Corporation's offer to ███ of a full-time position as a Research Intern, beginning 6/6/2022 and ending 9/2/2022. ███ is scheduled to work approximately 40 hours a week during this internship period. For this employment, ███ will be paid a total of $122,136.00 per annum.

During the internship, ███ will work under the supervision of Microsoft Senior Researcher, ███ job duties and responsibilities will include a focus on analyzing and improving performance of advanced algorithms on large-scale datasets and cutting-edge research in machine intelligence and machine learning applications. Implementing prototypes of scalable systems in AI applications will be a part of his job duties. He will be expected to collaborate closely with team members on developing systems from prototyping to production level. His duties will involve developing solutions for real world, large-scale problems.

███ will be located at 3455 Lebon DR, San Diego, CA 92122. Microsoft is offering ███ this internship position for one period, and, at this time, we do not anticipate the training period will be extended. Microsoft is aware that ███ work will be performed in pursuit of degree requirements for an academic program at University of California San Diego.

Figure 5: Highlighted answers for questions asked by ISEO office staff on a supporting document. The questions are: *“What is the job title?”* (red), *“What are the work hours per week?”* (orange), *“What is the salary or hourly rate?”* (blue), *“Where is the internship address?”* (green). Private information is redacted.

To tackle this issue, we deployed DocMaster to streamline the review process, focusing on a specific scenario: the issuance of work permits for internships, as a prototype use case. Traditionally, ISEO staff manually verifies essential fields and grants approval for work permits upon the submission of supporting documents by students. The eight key fields subject to review include employer details, salary information, job description, supervisor name & email address, weekly work hours, internship location, and start & end dates.

We formulate this as a QA task and train a model to extract necessary fields (Mekala et al., 2022b). To generate training data, four individuals without a machine learning background utilize DocMaster’s annotation interface to annotate five documents each. Each annotator formulates a question for every required field and highlights the relevant answer span within the PDF (Mekala et al., 2023). The collected annotations, encompassing both text and layout information, are aggregated. Subsequently, we train two models, RoBERTa-base and LayoutLM-base, for three epochs using this annotated dataset. During the inference phase, new student documents are uploaded to the interface, and the staff member inputs questions corresponding to the required fields. The user then selects the trained model, and answers for each field are high-

Table 1: Performance Results on 128 applications test set in %.

Model	Acc	F1	Corr	Dist
RoBERTa-base	76.23	83.77	93.56	1.13
LayoutLM-base	75.98	83.07	93.36	1.86

lighted within the PDF, as illustrated in Figure 5.

Our test set comprises 128 applications, encompassing a total of 1024 questions. After consulting with the ISEO staff, we learned that traditional QA task metrics such as exact match accuracy (Acc), f1-score (F1) alone are not sufficient; the most crucial metric for them is the average processing time of a document. The more easily identifiable the fields are, the quicker the document processing time becomes. Consequently, we tailored our automated metrics to account for this priority.

We define our correctness (Corr) metric as follows to consider partial overlaps with the ground truth. More precisely, we calculate the length of the longest contiguous matching subsequence and define a prediction as correct when the overlapping subsequence length exceeds 20% of the prediction's total length. In cases where there is no overlap, we utilize Python's difflib SequenceMatcher[8] to compute the longest contiguous matching subsequence between P and T, excluding any "junk". A prediction is considered correct if the computed score is greater than 0.5; otherwise, it is deemed incorrect. Mathematically,

$$\mathrm{Corr}(P,T) = \begin{cases} 1 & \text{if } \frac{\mathrm{len}(P_{\text{indexes}} \cap T_{\text{indexes}})}{\max(\mathrm{len}(P),\ \mathrm{len}(T))} > 0.2 \\ 1 & \text{else if SequenceMatcher}(P,T) > 0.5 \\ 0 & \text{else} \end{cases}$$

We additionally incorporate the Euclidean distance between the predicted bounding box and the ground truth bounding box (Dist) as a performance metric. Recognizing the challenge posed by raw distance interpretation, we opt for a relative distance measurement, specifically, the distance normalized by the diagonal length of the page. A shorter distance indicates an easier identification of ground truth, leading to reduced processing time.

The performance results for RoBERTa-base and LayoutLM-base are detailed in Table 1. Notably, both models exhibit a similar performance on the test set, achieving a correctness score of approximately 94%. The disparity between exact match accuracy and correctness scores underscores the inadequacy of standard academic evaluation metrics, prompting the need for a reevaluation of metrics tailored to real-life deployment scenarios. Furthermore, we compute average bounding box distance for incorrect predictions alone, revealing values of 19.57% for RoBERTa-base and 24.39% for LayoutLM-base. This implies that when predictions are inaccurate, they tend to be in close proximity, typically within 20% of the page size, indicating correct localization despite incorrect answers.

We also measure throughput on the test set by deploying DocMaster on an AMD EPYC 7453 28-Core Processor (56 CPUs, base frequency of 2.75 GHz, boost frequency of up to 3.45 GHz). We prioritize the lightweight nature of the RoBERTa-base model over LayoutLM-base and consider it for practical deployment. Leveraging DocMaster, the ISEO experienced a sevenfold enhancement in the number of supporting documents that can be reviewed per hour, escalating from 15 to 100.

Considering the sensitivity of the information contained in supporting documents, encompassing details like home and work addresses, salary information, and supervisor details, DocMaster stands out as a fitting solution, guaranteeing the privacy of confidential data with on-device computing. Offering both high performance and convenience, with the ability to annotate data, train models, and make predictions all within a unified platform, DocMaster emerges as the optimal open-sourced platform for such use cases.

6 Conclusion

This work introduces DocMaster, a unified Document-QA platform designed for annotation, training, and inference while prioritizing privacy preservation. DocMaster aims to empower users to train and deploy their models for document QA purposes. Despite the availability of various models, there is a scarcity of open-sourced annotation platforms. Addressing this gap, DocMaster is presented as an open-source solution where users can annotate PDFs effortlessly by simply highlighting relevant text. The platform has demonstrated its efficacy in constructing UCSD ISEO's AI assistant, contributing to a noteworthy seven-fold reduction in document processing time. The open-sourcing of DocMaster is intended to empower businesses that necessitate in-house document QA platforms.

[8] `https://docs.python.org/3/library/difflib.html`

7 Ethical Considerations

We introduce a privacy-preserving document-QA platform and identify no ethical concerns associated with its use.

8 Acknowledgments

The authors thank Bryant Tan, Gilen Wu-hou, Jinya Jiang, Khai Luu for their valuable contributions. We also thank Pauline DeGuzman and Emily Stewart for their support. Finally, we thank Vaidehi Gupta and Mai ElSherief for their guidance.

References

Tom Brown, Benjamin Mann, Nick Ryder, Melanie Subbiah, Jared D Kaplan, Prafulla Dhariwal, Arvind Neelakantan, Pranav Shyam, Girish Sastry, Amanda Askell, Sandhini Agarwal, Ariel Herbert-Voss, Gretchen Krueger, Tom Henighan, Rewon Child, Aditya Ramesh, Daniel Ziegler, Jeffrey Wu, Clemens Winter, Chris Hesse, Mark Chen, Eric Sigler, Mateusz Litwin, Scott Gray, Benjamin Chess, Jack Clark, Christopher Berner, Sam McCandlish, Alec Radford, Ilya Sutskever, and Dario Amodei. 2020. Language models are few-shot learners. In *Advances in Neural Information Processing Systems*, volume 33, pages 1877–1901. Curran Associates, Inc.

Tom Bryan, Jacob Carlson, Abhishek Arora, and Melissa Dell. 2023. Efficientocr: An extensible, open-source package for efficiently digitizing world knowledge. In *Proceedings of the 2023 Conference on Empirical Methods in Natural Language Processing: System Demonstrations*, pages 579–596.

Jacob Devlin, Ming-Wei Chang, Kenton Lee, and Kristina Toutanova. 2019. Bert: Pre-training of deep bidirectional transformers for language understanding. In *North American Chapter of the Association for Computational Linguistics*.

Łukasz Garncarek, Rafał Powalski, Tomasz Stanisławek, Bartosz Topolski, Piotr Halama, Michał Turski, and Filip Graliński. 2021. Lambert: Layout-aware language modeling for information extraction. In *International Conference on Document Analysis and Recognition*, pages 532–547. Springer.

Jiuxiang Gu, Jason Kuen, Vlad I Morariu, Handong Zhao, Rajiv Jain, Nikolaos Barmpalios, Ani Nenkova, and Tong Sun. 2021. Unidoc: Unified pretraining framework for document understanding. *Advances in Neural Information Processing Systems*, 34:39–50.

Teakgyu Hong, Donghyun Kim, Mingi Ji, Wonseok Hwang, Daehyun Nam, and Sungrae Park. 2022. Bros: A pre-trained language model focusing on text and layout for better key information extraction from documents. In *Proceedings of the AAAI Conference on Artificial Intelligence*, volume 36, pages 10767–10775.

Yupan Huang, Tengchao Lv, Lei Cui, Yutong Lu, and Furu Wei. 2022. Layoutlmv3: Pre-training for document ai with unified text and image masking. In *Proceedings of the 30th ACM International Conference on Multimedia*, pages 4083–4091.

Yinhan Liu, Myle Ott, Naman Goyal, Jingfei Du, Mandar Joshi, Danqi Chen, Omer Levy, Mike Lewis, Luke Zettlemoyer, and Veselin Stoyanov. 2019. Roberta: A robustly optimized bert pretraining approach. *arXiv preprint arXiv:1907.11692*.

Kyle Lo, Zejiang Shen, Benjamin Newman, Joseph Z Chang, Russell Authur, Erin Bransom, Stefan Candra, Yoganand Chandrasekhar, Regan Huff, Bailey Kuehl, et al. 2023. Papermage: A unified toolkit for processing, representing, and manipulating visually-rich scientific documents. In *Proceedings of the 2023 Conference on Empirical Methods in Natural Language Processing: System Demonstrations*, pages 495–507.

Tengchao Lv, Yupan Huang, Jingye Chen, Lei Cui, Shuming Ma, Yaoyao Chang, Shaohan Huang, Wenhui Wang, Li Dong, Weiyao Luo, et al. 2023. Kosmos-2.5: A multimodal literate model. *arXiv preprint arXiv:2309.11419*.

Dheeraj Mekala, Chengyu Dong, and Jingbo Shang. 2022a. LOPS: Learning order inspired pseudo-label selection for weakly supervised text classification. In *Findings of the Association for Computational Linguistics: EMNLP 2022*, pages 4894–4908, Abu Dhabi, United Arab Emirates. Association for Computational Linguistics.

Dheeraj Mekala, Tu Vu, Timo Schick, and Jingbo Shang. 2022b. Leveraging QA datasets to improve generative data augmentation. In *Proceedings of the 2022 Conference on Empirical Methods in Natural Language Processing*, pages 9737–9750, Abu Dhabi, United Arab Emirates. Association for Computational Linguistics.

Dheeraj Mekala, Jason Wolfe, and Subhro Roy. 2023. ZEROTOP: Zero-shot task-oriented semantic parsing using large language models. In *Proceedings of the 2023 Conference on Empirical Methods in Natural Language Processing*, pages 5792–5799, Singapore. Association for Computational Linguistics.

Milad Nasr, Nicholas Carlini, Jonathan Hayase, Matthew Jagielski, A Feder Cooper, Daphne Ippolito, Christopher A Choquette-Choo, Eric Wallace, Florian Tramèr, and Katherine Lee. 2023. Scalable extraction of training data from (production) language models. *arXiv preprint arXiv:2311.17035*.

Vincent Perot, Kai Kang, Florian Luisier, Guolong Su, Xiaoyu Sun, Ramya Sree Boppana, Zilong Wang, Jiaqi Mu, Hao Zhang, and Nan Hua. 2023. Lmdx: Language model-based document information extraction and localization. *arXiv preprint arXiv:2309.10952*.

Colin Raffel, Noam Shazeer, Adam Roberts, Katherine Lee, Sharan Narang, Michael Matena, Yanqi Zhou, Wei Li, and Peter J Liu. 2020. Exploring the limits of transfer learning with a unified text-to-text transformer. *The Journal of Machine Learning Research*, 21(1):5485–5551.

QiuXing Michelle Tan, Qi Cao, Chee Kiat Seow, and Peter Chunyu Yau. 2023. Information extraction system for invoices and receipts. In *International Conference on Intelligent Computing*, pages 77–89. Springer.

Zineng Tang, Ziyi Yang, Guoxin Wang, Yuwei Fang, Yang Liu, Chenguang Zhu, Michael Zeng, Cha Zhang, and Mohit Bansal. 2023. Unifying vision, text, and layout for universal document processing.

In *Proceedings of the IEEE/CVF Conference on Computer Vision and Pattern Recognition*, pages 19254–19264.

Zilong Wang, Jiuxiang Gu, Chris Tensmeyer, Nikolaos Barmpalios, Ani Nenkova, Tong Sun, Jingbo Shang, and Vlad Morariu. 2022. Mgdoc: Pre-training with multi-granular hierarchy for document image understanding. In *Proceedings of the 2022 Conference on Empirical Methods in Natural Language Processing*, pages 3984–3993.

Thomas Wolf, Lysandre Debut, Victor Sanh, Julien Chaumond, Clement Delangue, Anthony Moi, Pierric Cistac, Tim Rault, Rémi Louf, Morgan Funtowicz, et al. 2019. Huggingface's transformers: State-of-the-art natural language processing. *arXiv preprint arXiv:1910.03771*.

Yang Xu, Yiheng Xu, Tengchao Lv, Lei Cui, Furu Wei, Guoxin Wang, Yijuan Lu, Dinei Florencio, Cha Zhang, Wanxiang Che, et al. 2021. Layoutlmv2: Multi-modal pre-training for visually-rich document understanding. In *Proceedings of the 59th Annual Meeting of the Association for Computational Linguistics and the 11th International Joint Conference on Natural Language Processing (Volume 1: Long Papers)*, pages 2579–2591.

Yiheng Xu, Minghao Li, Lei Cui, Shaohan Huang, Furu Wei, and Ming Zhou. 2020. Layoutlm: Pre-training of text and layout for document image understanding. In *Proceedings of the 26th ACM SIGKDD International Conference on Knowledge Discovery & Data Mining*, pages 1192–1200.

RedCoast: A Lightweight Tool to Automate Distributed Training of LLMs on Any GPU/TPUs

Bowen Tan[1], Yun Zhu[2], Lijuan Liu[2], Hongyi Wang[1], Yonghao Zhuang[1], Jindong Chen[2], Eric Xing[1,3,5], Zhiting Hu[4]

[1]Carnegie Mellon University, [2]Google Research, [3]Petuum Inc., [4]UC San Diego, [5]Mohamed bin Zayed University of Artificial Intelligence

Abstract

The recent progress of AI can be largely attributed to large language models (LLMs). However, their escalating memory requirements introduce challenges for machine learning (ML) researchers and engineers. Addressing this requires developers to partition a large model to distribute it across multiple GPUs or TPUs. This necessitates considerable coding and intricate configuration efforts with existing model parallel tools, such as Megatron-LM, DeepSpeed, and Alpa. These tools require users' expertise in machine learning systems (MLSys), creating a bottleneck in LLM development, particularly for developers without MLSys background. In this work, we present *RedCoast (Redco)*, a lightweight and user-friendly tool crafted to automate distributed training and inference for LLMs, as well as to simplify ML pipeline development. The design of Redco emphasizes two key aspects. Firstly, to automate model parallelism, our study identifies two straightforward rules to generate tensor parallel strategies for any given LLM. Integrating these rules into Redco facilitates effortless distributed LLM training and inference, eliminating the need of additional coding or complex configurations. We demonstrate the effectiveness by applying Redco on a set of LLM architectures, such as GPT-J, LLaMA, T5, and OPT, up to the size of 66B. Secondly, we propose a mechanism that allows for the customization of diverse ML pipelines through the definition of merely three functions, avoiding redundant and formulaic code like multi-host related processing. This mechanism proves adaptable across a spectrum of ML algorithms, from foundational language modeling to complex algorithms like meta-learning and reinforcement learning. Consequently, Redco implementations exhibit much fewer code lines compared to their official counterparts. [1]

1 Introduction

In recent years, the field of AI has witnessed profound advancements, predominantly attributed to the advent of LLMs with an impressive number of parameters, spanning from billions to hundreds of billions (Zhao et al., 2023a). Notable examples include GPT-4 (OpenAI, 2023) and LLaMA (Touvron et al., 2023). Yet, the size of these LLMs presents distinct challenges in terms of model deployment for ML researchers and engineers. The primary challenge arises from the substantial memory requirements of LLMs, often exceed the capability of a single GPU or TPU. This necessitates the use of model parallelism, a technique that partitions the LLMs into various shards, subsequently distributing them across multiple devices or even different hosts. However, achieving this partitioning requires intricate engineering, including the formulation of a tensor-specific splitting strategy. While several specialized tools like DeepSpeed (Rasley et al., 2020), Alpa (Zheng et al., 2022), and FSDP (Zhao et al., 2023b) provide diverse model parallelism solutions, but they demand significant additional coding and intricate configurations based on model architecture and hardware specifics, requiring in-depth understanding of MLSys. Such additional efforts make the deployment of LLMs particularly challenging, especially for users without MLSys expertise, such as algorithm developers or researchers. At times, the intricacy of coding for model parallelism proves to be even more daunting than the algorithm design itself.

In this work, we introduce *RedCoast (Redco)*[2], a lightweight and user-friendly tool designed to automate the distributed training and inference of LLMs, thereby users without MLSys expertise can also effortlessly use the tool without additional coding or intricate configurations. Furthermore, we

[1]`RedCoast (Redco)` has been released under Apache 2.0 license at `https://github.com/tanyuqian/redco`.

[2]For simplicity, we will use Redco more frequently in the rest of this paper.

Proceedings of the 2024 Conference of the North American Chapter of the Association for Computational Linguistics: Human Language Technologies (Volume 3: System Demonstrations), pages 137–147
June 16-21, 2024 ©2024 Association for Computational Linguistics

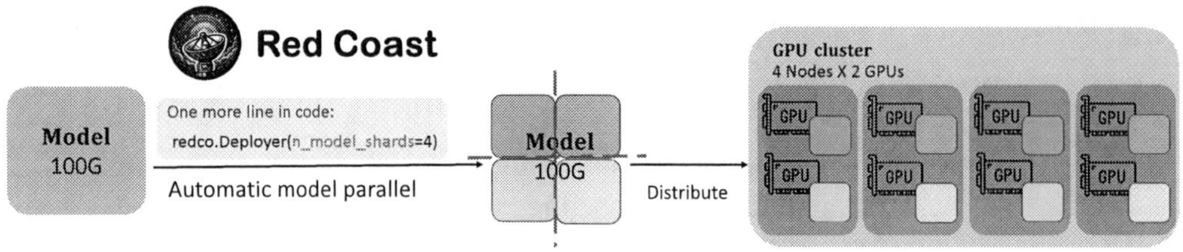

Figure 1: With a number of shards specified by user, Redco automatically conduct the model partitioning and distribution across hosts and devices.

propose a novel and neat mechanism to implement ML algorithms. This method necessitates users to define merely three functions as their pipeline design, with Redco managing all the remaining details in execution, such as data parallelism, multi-host related processing, checkpointing, etc.

Redco's design emphasizes two key aspects. The first is the automatic model parallelism. We identify two straightforward rules to generate the model parallel strategy for arbitrarily given transformer architecture, and integrate them into Redco. Unlike tools such as Megatron (Shoeybi et al., 2019) and DeepSpeed (Rasley et al., 2020) which require users to manipulate model forward function for different architecture and system specifics, Redco automates the process, where users only need to specify the desired number of shards to partition the model. We verified the effectiveness of Redco's model parallel strategy on multiple LLMs including LLaMA-7B (Touvron et al., 2023), T5-11B (Raffel et al., 2020), and OPT-66B (Zhang et al., 2022). Moreover, pipelines driven by Redco demonstrate efficiency superior to those implemented with FSDP (Zhao et al., 2023b), and closely matching the performance of Alpa (Zheng et al., 2022), the tool with state-of-the-art model parallel efficiency.

Another pivotal feature of Redco is the neat mechanism for ML pipeline development. With Redco, users only need to write three intuitive functions to define a ML pipeline: a collate function to convert raw data examples into model inputs (e.g., text tokenization); a loss function to execute the model and compute loss (e.g., cross-entropy); and a predict function to run the model and deliver outcomes (e.g., beam search). With the defined pipeline from a user, Redco automates all the remaining of pipeline execution such as data parallelism, multi-host related processing, checkpointing, log maintenance, and so forth. We demonstrate this neat mechanism is applicable to various ML paradigms, spanning from basic language modeling and sequence-to-sequence (seq2seq), to more complex algorithms like meta-learning and reinforcement learning. Redco-based implementations consistently exhibit substantially fewer lines of code compared to their official counterparts.

2 Related work

Distributed Machine Learning. Distributed machine learning refers to the utilization of multiple computing devices, typically GPUs or TPUs, for the efficient training and inference of ML models with large datasets or large models. It usually includes data parallelism and model parallelism. Data parallelism involves dividing a large dataset into multiple subsets, with each subset processed independently by a separate computing device, and every device maintains a full copy of the model parameters. However, data parallelism is limited in its ability to handle large models that exceed the memory constraints of individual devices. Model parallelism addresses this limitation by splitting and distributing the model across multiple devices, with each responsible for a portion of the model. Although it offers a solution for large models, model parallelism is more complex to implement than data parallelism due to the necessity of careful model partitioning. Tools such as Megatron-LM (Shoeybi et al., 2019; Narayanan et al., 2021), DeepSpeed (Rasley et al., 2020), FSDP (Zhao et al., 2023b), and Alpa (Zheng et al., 2022), have been developed to facilitate model parallelism. These tools support the model partitioning but still require significant coding and configuration efforts based on specific model architecture and hardware settings. In this work, Redco offers automatic data parallelism by default, and provides automatic model parallelism for LLMs, which is the majority of model parallelism use cases. Prioritizing user-friendliness, Redco enables users to execute distributed LLM training and inference by simply specifying the number of model shards for partitioning, without requiring users' MLSys expertise.

Pipeline development tools. In the development process using neural network libraries such as PyTorch (Paszke et al., 2019) and Flax (Heek et al., 2023), certain boilerplate code is consistently present. Common operations, such as backpropagation, gradient application, and batch iteration, recur in nearly every ML pipeline. A variety of tools aim to streamline pipeline development by eliminating repetitive code while maintaining as much development flexibility as possible. PyTorchLightning (Falcon et al., 2019) offers a default training loop within PyTorch, allowing users to customize their pipelines by inheriting a Trainer class and modifying hook functions such as loss function and checkpoint saving. However, this mechanism may not be intuitive for all users. For some people, it requires a learning curve to become comfortable. Furthermore, it may be unclear how to implement these hook functions for more complex algorithms, such as federated learning. HuggingFace-Transformers (Wolf et al., 2020) provides a Trainer for PyTorch models, but it heavily relies on models defined in its specific transformer classes and primarily focuses on natural language processing pipelines. Keras (Chollet et al., 2015) delivers higher-level APIs on top of TensorFlow (Abadi et al., 2015), enabling users to specify data, model, and loss functions. However, it is not well-suited for handling complex pipelines. Our proposed Redco is based on Flax, and uses a more intuitive and flexible approach for users to design their pipelines. This mechanism can be applied to a wide array of ML algorithms together with the automatic support for distributed training, including complex algorithms such as federated learning, meta-learning, and reinforcement learning.

3 Automatic Model Parallelism for LLMs

Model parallelism refers to distributing the computation of a large model across multiple GPUs or TPUs, in order to address the memory limitations of a single device. Two sub-paradigms within model parallelism are *pipeline parallelism* and *tensor parallelism*. Pipeline parallelism partitions the layers of the model across different devices, and tensor parallelism distributes every tensor in the model across multiple devices.

Model parallel tools like Megatron or Alpa require a bunch of intricate configurations and extensively modifying users' code based on the model architecture and the hardware setting. For example, Megatron requires users rewriting the model forward function to customize the tensor sharding for tensor parallelism and annotate breakpoints for pipeline parallelism. This demands substantial MLSys expertise, which is not possessed by most algorithm developers or researchers.

In this work, we develop an automatic model parallel strategy in Redco that applies across LLMs without requiring users' MLSys expertise or extra coding efforts.

3.1 Rules to Automate Tensor Parallelism

In Redco, we automate model parallelism via tensor parallelism. A tensor sharding strategy requires a dimension specified for each tensor. Along the dimension, the tensor is sharded and distributed across multiple devices. The objective of sharding strategy design is to minimize memory and time overhead associated with inter-device communication, which is usually brought by `reduce` or `gather` operations. For example, consider a tensor t is defined either as $t = t_1 + t_2$ or $t = (t_1, t_2)$ (concatenation), with t_1 and t_2 being stored on distinct devices. In this case, the computation of t requires message passing between the two devices (GPUs or TPUs).

Consider a dense layer in a neural network

$$y = \sigma(xA)$$

where x denotes the input tensor, σ is an element-wise activation function (e.g., ReLU, SiLU), and A is to the weight matrix, which is the model parameter of the dense layer. [3] When the weight matrix A is divided along its first dimension (dimension 0), a `reduce` operation becomes necessary to compute y. Formally,

$$A = \begin{pmatrix} A_1 \\ A_2 \end{pmatrix} \Longrightarrow y = \sigma(x_1 A_1 + x_2 A_2)$$

where x_1 and x_2 represent the first and second halves of the input tensor x's dimensions, respectively. The computation on two devices are indicated by the colors.

Conversely, when A is partitioned along its second dimension (dimension 1), a `gather` operation is required to obtain y:

$$A = (A_1, A_2) \Longrightarrow y = (\sigma(xA_1), \sigma(xA_2))$$

Therefore, when the weight parameter of each dense layer is partitioned across an arbitrary dimension, operations for reduction or gathering would

[3]The bias term is omitted here because its computation is non-significant.

Server	$2 \times$ 1080Ti	$4 \times$ A100	$2 \times$ TPU-v4	$16 \times$ TPU-v4
Device Memory	$2 \times$ 10G	$4 \times$ 40G	2 (hosts) $\times$ 4 (chips) $\times$ 32G	$16 \times 4 \times$ 32G
Models	BART-Large (1024) GPT2-Large (512)	LLaMA-7B (1024) GPT-J-6B (1024)	T5-XXL-11B (512) OPT-13B (1024)	OPT-66B (512)

Table 1: Runnable model finetuning on different servers. Numbers inside the brackets are the maxinum length in training. All the settings are with full precision (fp32) with AdamW optimizer.

occur within every dense layer. However, by examining a pair of consecutive dense layers

$$y = \sigma(\sigma(xA)B)$$

where A and B denote the respective weights, and partitioning A and B across dimensions 1 and 0, it becomes feasible to consolidate these operations with a single time of reduce operation:

$$A = (A_1, A_2), \quad B = \begin{pmatrix} B_1 \\ B_2 \end{pmatrix}$$

$$\begin{aligned} \Longrightarrow y &= \sigma(\sigma(xA)B) \\ &= \sigma\left((\sigma(xA_1), \sigma(xA_2))\begin{pmatrix} B_1 \\ B_2 \end{pmatrix}\right) \\ &= \sigma(\sigma(xA_1)B_1 + \sigma(xA_2)B_2) \end{aligned}$$

Consequently, the operations $\sigma(xA_1)B_1$ and $\sigma(xA_2)B_2$ can be performed independently on separate devices, which takes only a single reduce operation for two dense layers.

Based on the observation above, we get heuristic insights in terms of inter-device communication on the transformer architecture, specifically within feed-forward and attention layers. For feed-forward layers, given the nature of matrix multiplication, dividing two consecutive matrices along different dimensions is expected to require less inter-device communication than if they are divided along a same dimension. For the attention layers, the output matrix O is multiplied with each of the Q, K, V matrices, so the matrix O should be splitted along a dimension distinct from that chosen for Q, K, V. Based on these insights, we write two rules to determine the dimension along which to split each tensor in a model:

1. For fully-connected layers, alternate between splitting the parameter along dimension 1 and dimension 0.
2. For attention layers, split Q, K, V along dimension 0, and split the output projection matrix O along dimension 1.

Leveraging the rules above enables Redco to devise a model parallel strategy tailored for any given LLM architecture. This enables the distributed training of LLMs with almost zero user effort. Users only specify the number of shards to split the given model, without additional coding or configuration efforts.

Note that our proposed rules are similar to a part of suggested configurations of Megatron (Shoeybi et al., 2019), but they don't summarize their separate configurations into rules, so that only a few LLM architectures (BERT, GPT, and T5) are supported in their implmentation[4]. To customize any new architectures under Megatron, users still have to rewrite the model's forward function and manually implement their model parallel strategy.

3.2 Implementation inside Redco

We implement tensor parallelism with the proposed strategy on top of `jax.pjit` function. This function compiles the computational graph and it merges operations on the same device to reduce unnecessary communication overhead [5].

To integrate the proposed tensor parallel strategy, Redco has a function that takes in an arbitrary transformer architecture and produces a parameter sharding strategy based on the proposed rules. Moreover, in addition to automatically generating sharding strategies, Redco also enables their customization. This allows users with more advanced strategies to execute their approaches. Practical examples of the sharding strategies produced by Redco, applied to GPT-J and LLaMA, are showcased in the Appendix.

3.3 Evaluation

Applicability test We assess the applicability of our proposed automatic model parallel approach by applying Redco on an assorted collection of LLMs across various GPU and TPU servers. We conduct distributed training for LLMs without compromising the optimizer settings or precision. More precisely, we execute the distributed training under full precision (fp32) with the widely-used, yet memory-intensive, AdamW optimizer. We report all operable LLMs on GPU and TPU servers with varying memory capacities.

[4]https://github.com/NVIDIA/Megatron-LM/tree/main

[5]`https://jax.readthedocs.io/en/latest/notebooks/Distributed_arrays_and_automatic_parallelization.html`

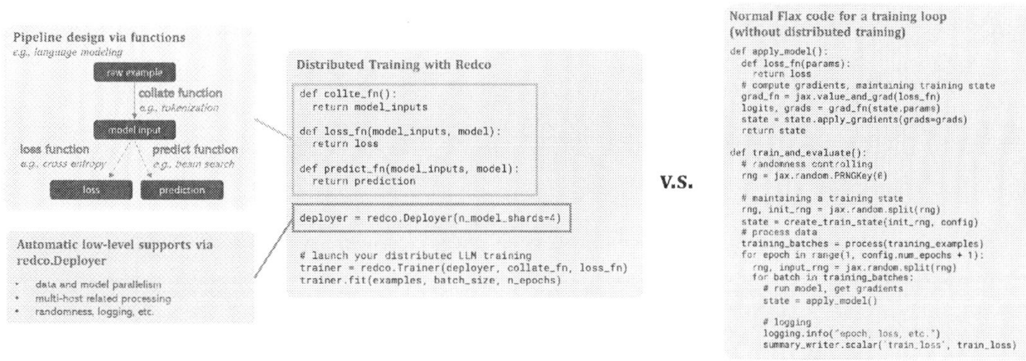

Figure 2: The template code of using redco to implement distributed training, where users only have to design a pipepine through three fucntions, without concerning data and model parallelism, multi-host related processing, randomness control, etc., which eliminates a lot of boilerplate coding.

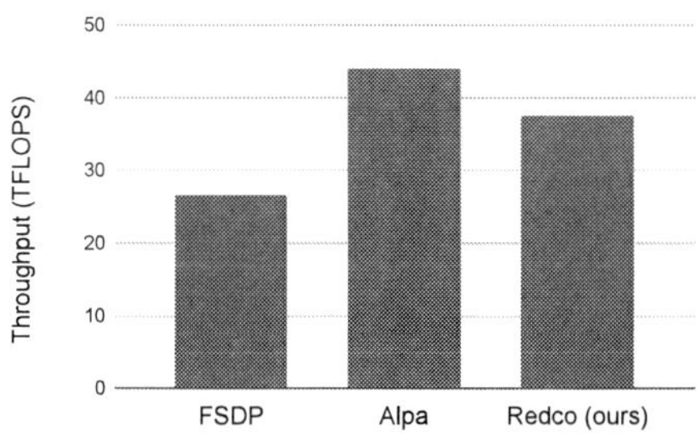

Figure 3: The comparison of throughput in the running of GPT-J-6B on a 4× A100 server. Redco's performance surpasses that of FSDP and is close to that of Alpa, the tool with state-of-the-art model parallel efficiency but intricate engineering.

The findings, as displayed in Table 1, indicate that our straightforward, yet effective, automatic model parallel strategy is highly applcable across LLMs. For example, on small servers, such as those equipped 2 × 1080Ti, our strategy successfully runs large versions of BART and GPT-2 with text lengths up to 512 and 1024, respectively. On the larger servers such as the one with 16 TPU-v4 hosts, Redco effectively handles the training of the giant OPT-66B.

Efficiency test We evaluate the efficiency of our proposed automatic model parallelism strategy in Redco on a server equipped 4 × A100 GPUs. We perform experiments by finetuning OPT-2.7B and GPT-J-6B, on the WikiText dataset, with full precision and AdamW optimizer. We compare Redco with two advanced model parallel tools: FSDP and Alpa. The experimental results are summarized in Figure 3. The observed throughput reveals that Redco surpasses FSDP and is close to Alpa, the state-of-the-art model parallel tool. Notably, Alpa's implementation requires advanced MLSys expertise and significant coding efforts.

4 RedCoast: Library Design

In addition to the complexities of implementing model parallelism, ML pipelines often contain repetitive boilerplate code that demands significant effort from developers. Examples of such code include back-propagation, gradient application, batch iteration, and so forth. Furthermore, the hardware upgrades usually require patches on existing codebase. For example, a code developed within a single-GPU setting needs data parallelism and multi-host related processing to be added when adapted to multi-GPU machines or clusters.

In Redco, we design a neat and user-friendly mechanism to simplify ML pipeline developments. Users only have to define their pipeline through three design functions, and Redco handles all the remaining of the pipeline execution. In this section, we will introduce the software design of Redco that enables this mechanism.

4.1 Pipeline Design Through Three Functions

As shown in the yellow brick in Figure 2, in our proposed mechanism, every ML pipeline can be decoupled into three simple functions: *collate function* to convert raw examples to model inputs, e.g., converting text sentences to be a batch of token indices via tokenization; *loss function* to convert the model inputs to a scalar loss; and *predict function* to convert the model inputs to the desired model outputs, such as running beam search for the language model. We demonstrate this framework with the implementation of image captioning and a meta-learning algorithm, MAML, as shown in Figure 4 and Figure 5. These examples showcase that both simple and complex algorithms can be naturally defined under the proposed mechanism.

```
def collate_fn(raw_examples):
  return {
      "pixel_values": # pixel values of the images
      "token_ids": # token indicies of captions
  }

def loss_fn(batch, params):
  logits = model(params, batch['pixel_values'], batch['token_ids']) # run model and get logits
  return cross_entropy(logits, batch['token_ids'])

def pred_fn(batch, params):
  return model.beam_search(params, batch['pixel_values'])
```

Figure 4: Pipeline design functions of image captioning under Redco.

```
def collate_fn(raw_examples):
  return {
      "train_data": # a batch of few-shot training tasks
      "eval_data": # a batch of few-shot evaluation tasks
  }

def loss_fn(batch, params):
  params_inner = params - alpha * jax.grad(inner_loss)(params, batch['train_data'])
  return inner_loss(params_inner, batch['eval_data'])

def pred_fn(batch, params, model):
  params_inner = params - alpha * jax.grad(inner_loss)(params, batch['train_data'])
  return model(params_inner, batch['eval_data'])
```

Figure 5: Pipeline design functions of meta-learning (MAML) for few-shot learning under Redco. MAML's loss $L = \mathcal{L}(\mathcal{T}_{eval}, \theta')$ and $\theta' = \theta - \alpha\nabla_\theta\mathcal{L}(\mathcal{T}_{train}, \theta)$, where $\mathcal{T}_{train}$, $\mathcal{T}_{eval}$ refer to the data of training and evaluation tasks, and $\mathcal{L}(\cdot, \cdot)$ refers to the original loss function (`inner_loss`), such as the cross-entropy loss for classification.

4.2 Pipeline Execution with Automatic Low-level Supports

For user-friendliness, there are merely three classes in Redco, i.e., `Deployer`, `Trainer`, and `Predictor`. As shown in the orange brick in Figure 2, Redco streamlines the management of low-level and boilerplate processing in pipeline development through the `Deployer` class. This includes automatic model parallelism, as discussed in the previous section, as well as automatic data parallelism, multi-host related processing, checkpointing, and other convenient features such as randomness control and logging management. The final execution of the pipeline is carried out by `Trainer` and `Predictor` of Redco. Supported by `Deployer`, they execute the training and inference of the pipeline defined by users via the functions as mentioned in Section 4.1. [6]

4.2.1 Multi-host Supports

Large-scale distributed training typically involves intricate processes to accommodate multiple hosts. These processes include allocating data samples to each node and aggregating gradients or parameters across hosts, etc. Redco offers automatic support for multi-host environments and demonstrates compatibility with various platforms, including SLURM (Yoo et al., 2003), XManager[7], as well as bare nodes interconnected via IP addresses. Notably, Redco allows users to maintain their existing pipeline design and execution code without additional efforts for multi-host environments.

4.2.2 Checkpointing

In distributed training frameworks, each typically employs a distinct formatting for checkpoint saving and loading, leading to a closed-loop system. For instance, Megatron utilizes a unique approach where model parameters and optimizer states are segmented based on the configuration of model parallelism. These checkpoints are inherently tied to Megatron, necessitating considerable effort for conversion into standard PyTorch checkpoint formats. Conversely, in Redco, we adopt a standardized and well-accepted checkpointing method. Here, both model parameters and optimizer states are encapsulated comprehensively within dictionaries of tensors. This approach is independent of the specific distributed training configurations, offering the advantage of simplicity in loading and utilization, even without Redco installation.

4.2.3 Lightweight and Flexible Dependency

Distributed training frameworks, such as Megatron and Alpa, often include modifications to foundational Python packages or CUDA kernels, resulting in stringent environment installation requirements. For instance, Alpa modifies the fundamental `jaxlib`[8] library, thereby limiting its compatibility to jaxlib version 0.3.22 and CUDA version 11.3. They have been outdated compared to advanced versions of jaxlib 0.4.32 and CUDA 12.2,

[6] We include a complete example in the Appendix implementing a distributed seq2seq pipeline with Redco.

[7] `https://github.com/google-deepmind/xmanager`

[8] `https://pypi.org/project/jaxlib/`

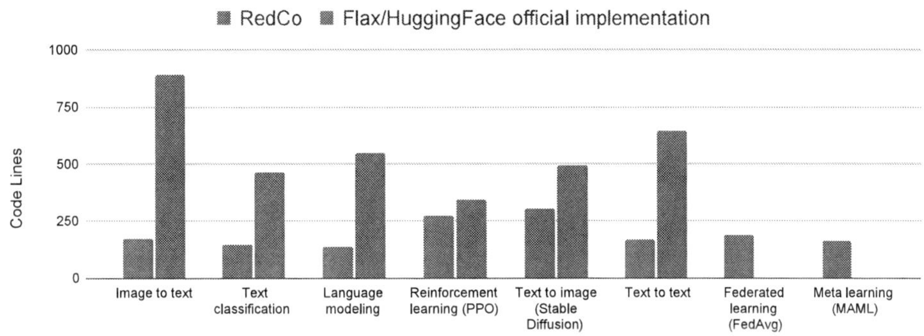

Figure 6: The comparison of code lines across a diverse set of ML algorithms. (There is no well-accepted official Flax implementations for FedAvg and MAML.)

which are prevalent in many cluster environments today. In contrast, Redco is developed on top of Jax and Flax, without any modification to existing packages. Consequently, Redco is able to support a wider range of versions of jax, flax, and CUDA, in addition to accommodating various device types, including GPUs and TPUs.

4.3 Evaluation

We implement a variety of machine learning paradigms using Redco, ranging from fundamental supervised learning techniques such as classification and regression, to more sophisticated algorithms including reinforcement learning and meta-learning. Figure 6 illustrates a comparison between the number of code lines in our implementation and those in officially published versions. The majority of these paradigms can be efficiently implemented using Redco with only 100 to 200 lines of code. This efficiency boost of development can be attributed to Redco's ability to significantly reduce the need for writing boilerplate code.

5 Conclusion

In this work, we present a lightweight and user-friendly toolkit, *RedCoast (Redco)*, designed to automate the distributed training of LLMs and simplify the ML pipeline development process. Redco incorporates an automatic model parallelism strategy, fundamentally based on two intuitive rules, without requiring additional coding efforts or ML-Sys expertise from the users. We evaluate its effectiveness on an array of LLMs, such as LLaMA-7B, T5-11B and OPT-66B. Furthermore, Redco has a novel and neat pipeline development mechanism. This mechanism requires users to specify only three intuitive pipeline design functions to implement a distributed ML pipeline. Remarkably, this mechanism is general enough to accommodate various ML algorithms and needs significantly fewer lines of code compared to their official implementations.

References

Martín Abadi, Ashish Agarwal, Paul Barham, Eugene Brevdo, Zhifeng Chen, Craig Citro, Greg S. Corrado, Andy Davis, Jeffrey Dean, Matthieu Devin, Sanjay Ghemawat, Ian Goodfellow, Andrew Harp, Geoffrey Irving, Michael Isard, Yangqing Jia, Rafal Jozefowicz, Lukasz Kaiser, Manjunath Kudlur, Josh Levenberg, Dandelion Mané, Rajat Monga, Sherry Moore, Derek Murray, Chris Olah, Mike Schuster, Jonathon Shlens, Benoit Steiner, Ilya Sutskever, Kunal Talwar, Paul Tucker, Vincent Vanhoucke, Vijay Vasudevan, Fernanda Viégas, Oriol Vinyals, Pete Warden, Martin Wattenberg, Martin Wicke, Yuan Yu, and Xiaoqiang Zheng. 2015. TensorFlow: Large-scale machine learning on heterogeneous systems. Software available from tensorflow.org.

François Chollet et al. 2015. Keras. `https://keras.io`.

William Falcon et al. 2019. PyTorch Lightning.

Jonathan Heek, Anselm Levskaya, Avital Oliver, Marvin Ritter, Bertrand Rondepierre, Andreas Steiner, and Marc van Zee. 2023. Flax: A neural network library and ecosystem for JAX.

Deepak Narayanan, Mohammad Shoeybi, Jared Casper, Patrick LeGresley, Mostofa Patwary, Vijay Korthikanti, Dmitri Vainbrand, Prethvi Kashinkunti, Julie Bernauer, Bryan Catanzaro, et al. 2021. Efficient large-scale language model training on gpu clusters using megatron-lm. In *Proceedings of the International Conference for High Performance Computing, Networking, Storage and Analysis*, pages 1–15.

OpenAI. 2023. Gpt-4 technical report. *ArXiv*, abs/2303.08774.

Adam Paszke, Sam Gross, Francisco Massa, Adam Lerer, James Bradbury, Gregory Chanan, Trevor Killeen, Zeming Lin, Natalia Gimelshein, Luca Antiga, et al. 2019. Pytorch: an imperative style, high-performance deep learning library. In *Advances in Neural Information Processing Systems*, pages 8024–8035.

Colin Raffel, Noam Shazeer, Adam Roberts, Katherine Lee, Sharan Narang, Michael Matena, Yanqi Zhou,

Wei Li, and Peter J Liu. 2020. Exploring the limits of transfer learning with a unified text-to-text transformer. *The Journal of Machine Learning Research*, 21(1):5485–5551.

Jeff Rasley, Samyam Rajbhandari, Olatunji Ruwase, and Yuxiong He. 2020. Deepspeed: System optimizations enable training deep learning models with over 100 billion parameters. In *Proceedings of the 26th ACM SIGKDD International Conference on Knowledge Discovery & Data Mining*, pages 3505–3506.

Mohammad Shoeybi, Mostofa Patwary, Raul Puri, Patrick LeGresley, Jared Casper, and Bryan Catanzaro. 2019. Megatron-lm: Training multi-billion parameter language models using model parallelism. *arXiv preprint arXiv:1909.08053*.

Hugo Touvron, Thibaut Lavril, Gautier Izacard, Xavier Martinet, Marie-Anne Lachaux, Timothée Lacroix, Baptiste Rozière, Naman Goyal, Eric Hambro, Faisal Azhar, Aur'elien Rodriguez, Armand Joulin, Edouard Grave, and Guillaume Lample. 2023. Llama: Open and efficient foundation language models. *ArXiv*, abs/2302.13971.

Thomas Wolf, Lysandre Debut, Victor Sanh, Julien Chaumond, Clement Delangue, Anthony Moi, Pierric Cistac, Tim Rault, Rémi Louf, Morgan Funtowicz, Joe Davison, Sam Shleifer, Patrick von Platen, Clara Ma, Yacine Jernite, Julien Plu, Canwen Xu, Teven Le Scao, Sylvain Gugger, Mariama Drame, Quentin Lhoest, and Alexander M. Rush. 2020. Transformers: State-of-the-art natural language processing. In *Proceedings of the 2020 Conference on Empirical Methods in Natural Language Processing: System Demonstrations*, pages 38–45, Online. Association for Computational Linguistics.

Andy B Yoo, Morris A Jette, and Mark Grondona. 2003. Slurm: Simple linux utility for resource management. In *Workshop on job scheduling strategies for parallel processing*, pages 44–60. Springer.

Susan Zhang, Stephen Roller, Naman Goyal, Mikel Artetxe, Moya Chen, Shuohui Chen, Christopher Dewan, Mona Diab, Xian Li, Xi Victoria Lin, et al. 2022. Opt: Open pre-trained transformer language models. *arXiv preprint arXiv:2205.01068*.

Wayne Xin Zhao, Kun Zhou, Junyi Li, Tianyi Tang, Xiaolei Wang, Yupeng Hou, Yingqian Min, Beichen Zhang, Junjie Zhang, Zican Dong, et al. 2023a. A survey of large language models. *arXiv preprint arXiv:2303.18223*.

Yanli Zhao, Andrew Gu, Rohan Varma, Liang Luo, Chien-Chin Huang, Min Xu, Less Wright, Hamid Shojanazeri, Myle Ott, Sam Shleifer, et al. 2023b. Pytorch fsdp: Experiences on scaling fully sharded data parallel. *arXiv preprint arXiv:2304.11277*.

Lianmin Zheng, Zhuohan Li, Hao Zhang, Yonghao Zhuang, Zhifeng Chen, Yanping Huang, Yida Wang, Yuanzhong Xu, Danyang Zhuo, Eric P Xing, et al. 2022. Alpa: Automating inter-and {Intra-Operator} parallelism for distributed deep learning. In *16th USENIX Symposium on Operating Systems Design and Implementation (OSDI 22)*, pages 559–578.

A Tensor Parallel Strategy Examples

We provide examples of the generated sharding strategies by Redco toward different architectures, where `PartitionSpec('mp', None)` indicates partioning a parameter by dimension 0 and `PartitionSpec(None, 'mp')` indicates partioning a parameter by dimension 1, and `None` means saving a copy of the parameter across every device.

```
params_sharding_rules_gptj = [
    (('fc_in', 'kernel'), PartitionSpec(None, 'mp')),  # Rule 1 in Section 3.1
    (('fc_out', 'kernel'), PartitionSpec('mp', None)),
    (('k_proj', 'kernel'), PartitionSpec(None, 'mp')), # Rule 2 in Section 3.1
    (('out_proj', 'kernel'), PartitionSpec('mp', None)),
    (('q_proj', 'kernel'), PartitionSpec(None, 'mp')),
    (('v_proj', 'kernel'), PartitionSpec(None, 'mp')),
    (('(bias|scale)',), None),                         # Parameters other than transformer blocks or bias or scale terms
    (('embedding',), PartitionSpec('mp', None)),
    (('lm_head', 'kernel'), PartitionSpec(None, 'mp'))
]
```

Figure 7: Sharding strategy for GPT-J generated by Redco.

```
params_sharding_rules_llama = [
    (('down_proj', 'kernel'), PartitionSpec('mp', None)), # Rule 1 in Section 3.1
    (('gate_proj', 'kernel'), PartitionSpec(None, 'mp')),
    (('up_proj', 'kernel'), PartitionSpec(None, 'mp')),
    (('k_proj', 'kernel'), PartitionSpec(None, 'mp')),    # Rule 2 in Section 3.1
    (('o_proj', 'kernel'), PartitionSpec('mp', None)),
    (('q_proj', 'kernel'), PartitionSpec(None, 'mp')),
    (('v_proj', 'kernel'), PartitionSpec(None, 'mp')),
    (('(bias|scale)',), None),                            # Parameters other than transformer blocks or bias or scale terms
    (('embedding',), PartitionSpec('mp', None)),
    (('lm_head', 'kernel'), PartitionSpec(None, 'mp')),
    (('norm', 'weight'), None),
    (('input_layernorm', 'weight'), None),
    (('post_attention_layernorm', 'weight'), None)
]
```

Figure 8: Sharding strategy for LLaMA generated by Redco.

B A Complete Distributed Training Example with Redco

We provide a complete example for the distributed training of a T5-XXL model, which is able to run on multi-host environments. It uses a modeling from HuggingFace, on a summarization dataset, evaluated by rouge scores, and it saves the checkpoints with best rouge-2 and rouge-L scores.

```
from functools import partial
import fire
import numpy as np
import jax
import jax.numpy as jnp
import optax
import datasets
from transformers import AutoTokenizer, FlaxAutoModelForSeq2SeqLM
import evaluate
from redco import Deployer, Trainer


def collate_fn(examples,
               tokenizer,
               decoder_start_token_id,
               max_src_len,
               max_tgt_len,
               src_key='src',
               tgt_key='tgt'):
    model_inputs = tokenizer(
        [example[src_key] for example in examples],
        max_length=max_src_len,
        padding='max_length',
        truncation=True,
        return_tensors='np')

    decoder_inputs = tokenizer(
        [example[tgt_key] for example in examples],
        max_length=max_tgt_len,
        padding='max_length',
        truncation=True,
        return_tensors='np')

    if tokenizer.bos_token_id is not None:
        labels = np.zeros_like(decoder_inputs['input_ids'])
        labels[:, :-1] = decoder_inputs['input_ids'][:, 1:]
        decoder_input_ids = decoder_inputs['input_ids']
        decoder_input_ids[:, 0] = decoder_start_token_id
    else:
        labels = decoder_inputs['input_ids']
        decoder_input_ids = np.zeros_like(decoder_inputs['input_ids'])
        decoder_input_ids[:, 1:] = decoder_inputs['input_ids'][:, :-1]
```

```
        decoder_input_ids[:, 0] = decoder_start_token_id

    model_inputs['labels'] = labels
    decoder_inputs['input_ids'] = decoder_input_ids

    for key in decoder_inputs:
        model_inputs[f'decoder_{key}'] = np.array(decoder_inputs[key])

    return model_inputs


def loss_fn(train_rng, state, params, batch, is_training):
    labels = batch.pop("labels")
    label_weights = batch['decoder_attention_mask']

    logits = state.apply_fn(
        **batch, params=params, dropout_rng=train_rng, train=is_training)[0]

    loss = optax.softmax_cross_entropy_with_integer_labels(
        logits=logits, labels=labels)

    return jnp.sum(loss * label_weights) / jnp.sum(label_weights)


def pred_fn(pred_rng, params, batch, model, gen_kwargs):
    output_ids = model.generate(
        input_ids=batch['input_ids'],
        attention_mask=batch['attention_mask'],
        params=params,
        prng_key=pred_rng,
        **gen_kwargs)
    return output_ids.sequences


def output_fn(batch_preds, tokenizer):
    return tokenizer.batch_decode(batch_preds, skip_special_tokens=True)


def eval_rouge(examples, preds, tgt_key):
    rouge_scorer = evaluate.load('rouge')

    return rouge_scorer.compute(
        predictions=preds,
        references=[example[tgt_key] for example in examples],
        rouge_types=['rouge1', 'rouge2', 'rougeL'],
        use_stemmer=True)


def main(n_processes=None,
         host0_address=None,
         host0_port=None,
         process_id=None,
         n_local_devices=None,
         dataset_name='xsum',
         src_key='document',
         tgt_key='summary',
         model_name_or_path='facebook/bart-base',
         n_model_shards=1,
         n_epochs=2,
         per_device_batch_size=8,
         eval_per_device_batch_size=16,
         accumulate_grad_batches=2,
         max_src_len=512,
         max_tgt_len=64,
         num_beams=4,
         learning_rate=4e-5,
         warmup_rate=0.1,
         weight_decay=0.,
         jax_seed=42,
         workdir='./workdir',
         run_tensorboard=False):
    deployer = Deployer(
        n_model_shards=n_model_shards,
        jax_seed=jax_seed,
        workdir=workdir,
        run_tensorboard=run_tensorboard,
        n_processes=n_processes,
        host0_address=host0_address,
        host0_port=host0_port,
        process_id=process_id,
        n_local_devices=n_local_devices)

    dataset = datasets.load_dataset(dataset_name)
    dataset = {key: list(dataset[key]) for key in dataset.keys()}

    with jax.default_device(jax.devices('cpu')[0]):
        model = FlaxAutoModelForSeq2SeqLM.from_pretrained(
            model_name_or_path, from_pt=True)
        model.params = model.to_fp32(model.params)

        tokenizer = AutoTokenizer.from_pretrained(model_name_or_path)
        gen_kwargs = {'max_length': max_tgt_len, 'num_beams': num_beams}

    lr_schedule_fn = deployer.get_lr_schedule_fn(
        train_size=len(dataset['train']),
        per_device_batch_size=per_device_batch_size,
        n_epochs=n_epochs,
        learning_rate=learning_rate,
        schedule_type='linear',
        warmup_rate=warmup_rate)
```

```
    optimizer = optax.adamw(
        learning_rate=lr_schedule_fn, weight_decay=weight_decay)
    if accumulate_grad_batches > 1:
        optimizer = optax.MultiSteps(
            optimizer, every_k_schedule=accumulate_grad_batches)

    trainer = Trainer(
        deployer=deployer,
        collate_fn=partial(
            collate_fn,
            tokenizer=tokenizer,
            decoder_start_token_id=model.config.decoder_start_token_id,
            max_src_len=max_src_len,
            max_tgt_len=max_tgt_len,
            src_key=src_key,
            tgt_key=tgt_key),
        apply_fn=model,
        loss_fn=loss_fn,
        params=model.params,
        optimizer=optimizer,
        lr_schedule_fn=lr_schedule_fn,
        accumulate_grad_batches=accumulate_grad_batches,
        params_sharding_rules=deployer.get_sharding_rules(params=model.params))

    predictor = trainer.get_default_predictor(
        pred_fn=partial(pred_fn, model=model, gen_kwargs=gen_kwargs),
        output_fn=partial(output_fn, tokenizer=tokenizer))

    trainer.fit(
        train_examples=dataset['train'],
        per_device_batch_size=per_device_batch_size,
        n_epochs=n_epochs,
        eval_examples=dataset['validation'],
        eval_per_device_batch_size=eval_per_device_batch_size,
        eval_loss=True,
        eval_predictor=predictor,
        eval_metric_fn=partial(eval_rouge, tgt_key=tgt_key),
        save_last_ckpt=True,
        save_argmax_ckpt_by_metrics=['rougeL'])


if __name__ == '__main__':
    fire.Fire(main)
```

Concept Over Time Analysis: Unveiling Temporal Patterns for Qualitative Data Analysis

Tim Fischer[†], **Florian Schneider**[†], **Robert Geislinger**[†], **Florian Helfer**[‡], **Gertraud Koch**[‡], **Chris Biemann**[†]
[†] Language Technology Group, Department of Informatics, Universität Hamburg, Germany
[‡] Institute of Anthropological Studies in Culture and History, Universität Hamburg, Germany
{firstname.lastname OR florian.schneider-1}@uni-hamburg.de

Abstract

In this system demonstration paper, we present the *Concept Over Time Analysis* extension for the Discourse Analysis Tool Suite. The proposed tool empowers users to define, refine, and visualize their concepts of interest within an interactive interface. Adhering to the Human-in-the-loop paradigm, users can give feedback through sentence annotations. Utilizing few-shot sentence classification, the system employs Sentence Transformers to compute representations of sentences and concepts. Through an iterative process involving semantic similarity searches, sentence annotation, and fine-tuning with contrastive data, the model continuously refines, providing users with enhanced analysis outcomes. The final output is a timeline visualization of sentences classified to concepts. Especially suited for the Digital Humanities, *Concept Over Time Analysis* serves as a valuable tool for qualitative data analysis within extensive datasets. The chronological overview of concepts enables researchers to uncover patterns, trends, and shifts in discourse over time.

1 Introduction

The Discourse Analysis Tool Suite (DATS) (Schneider et al., 2023) serves as an open-source operational platform designed for conducting digital qualitative discourse analysis within the realm of Digital Humanities (DH). Developed through collaborative efforts, the tool is tailored specifically for DH researchers. Its purpose is to democratize access to cutting-edge machine learning technologies derived from Computer Vision and Natural Language Processing. This initiative enables non-expert users to efficiently handle and analyze unstructured, large multi-modal data.

While the overarching design of the platform is catered to Grounded Theory-based research (Strauss and Corbin, 1990), particularly in alignment with approaches like the Sociology of Knowledge Approach to Discourse (Keller, 2011), numerous features extend its utility across various disciplines. Noteworthy functionalities include the automated pre-processing of multi-modal data (text, image, audio, and video), data exploration, and both manual and automatic annotation.

In this paper, we extend DATS with *Concept Over Time Analysis*, a machine-learning-based feature to identify concepts of interest in a large dataset and analyse their occurrences over time. The proposed system allows users to define concepts, assists them in identifying relevant sentences, refine the concept representation and finally visualize the results over time. The interactive User Interface (UI) follows the Human-in-the-loop paradigm (Holzinger, 2016), encouraging users to give feedback by annotating samples, which improves concept representations and analysis results.

The proposed system performs few-shot sentence classification, mapping each concept to a class. We use Sentence Transformers (Reimers and Gurevych, 2019) to compute representations of sentences and concept descriptions. Initially, a similarity search provides semantically relevant sentences for each concept that can be classified into concepts by the user. With few labeled examples, a contrastive dataset is generated to fine-tune a Sentence Transformer model. This is employed to update concept representations and similarity search results, providing the user with better suggestions. This iterative refinement step is repeated until the user is content. Finally, sentences classified to a concept with confidence above a specified threshold are visualized in a timeline.

The *Concepts Over Time Analysis* enables qualitative data analysis within large datasets. A chronological overview of custom concepts like events, topics, opinions or practices allows researchers to identify patterns, trends, and shifts in discourse over time. This temporal perspective can reveal how ideas, narratives, or cultural practices evolve, providing insights into the dynamics of discour-

Proceedings of the 2024 Conference of the North American Chapter of the Association for Computational Linguistics: Human Language Technologies (Volume 3: System Demonstrations), pages 148–157
June 16-21, 2024 ©2024 Association for Computational Linguistics

sive trends. By visualising such concepts along a timeline, researchers can identify clusters of related events, helping to create a nuanced understanding of how cultural phenomena unfold over time. Further, a timeline analysis can aid in contextualising and connecting different elements within a large dataset, making it easier to trace the lineage of ideas or the influence of past discourses on current ones. Though inspired by DH and discourse analysis, the proposed system is versatile, extending its utility to related analyses such as visualizing topics or sentiments over time.

While the *Concepts Over Time Analysis* is a powerful feature on its own, its integration within DATS can enable users to merge findings with existing analyses, utilize Memos or the Logbook for documentation and reflection, and identify concepts to be analyzed using search and filter functionalities.

The contributions of this paper are threefold: First, we develop the *Concept Over Time Analysis* extension, which facilitates the identification of concepts in large datasets and a chronological overview. Second, we describe a typical usage scenario, outlining the interaction with the system. Finally, we perform experiments on three datasets, demonstrating the feasibility of our system.

The DATS and *Concepts Over Time Analysis* are open-source and available on GitHub[1] where links to a demonstration and a video are provided.

2 Related Work

Qualitative Data Analysis tools that are frequently used in the DH include CATMA (Gius et al., 2022), MAXQDA and Atlas.ti. While offering various analysis tools, at the time of writing, none of them include means to semi-automatically identify concepts in large datasets or visualize concepts in a chronological overview. With the proposed extensions, DATS aims to close that gap.

However, there exist many tools and libraries that offer interesting timeline analysis functionalities. BERTopic (Grootendorst, 2022), a topic modeling tool, leverages Sentence Transformers to compute document or sentence embeddings, yielding easily interpretable topic representations through clustering. With Dynamic Topic Modeling, the tool offers a collection of techniques to analyse the development of topics over time. While BERTopic identifies prevalent topics automatically, our extension empowers users to define and analyze their own concepts or topics of interest across time.

SCoT (Haase et al., 2021) is an interactive web application to analyse the sense-clusters of a word and their evolution over time. SentiView (Wang et al., 2013) is an interactive visualization system for sentiment analysis. It visualizes changes over time of various attributes and relationships between demographics of interest as well as participants' sentiments on popular topics. Open Discourse is a web-platform for the analysis of the plenary minutes of the german federal parliament. It includes a topic analysis feature to investigate the political discourse over time, filterable by speaker, gender, party and other attributes.

LabelSleuth (Shnarch et al., 2022) serves as a no-code platform, making NLP accessible for a broad audience. It facilitates integrated model training and an intuitive, active learning-powered annotation interface. In contrast, our proposed extension supports the training of multi-class sentence classification models and enables a timeline analysis of the results.

3 Concept Over Time Analysis

The *Concept Over Time Analysis* extension is an interactive, machine-learning-based tool that semi-automatically identifies relevant sentences of user-defined concepts, adjusts accordingly to feedback, and visualizes concept occurrences in a timeline.

Its goal is to provide users with a chronological overview of their concepts of interest, with as few steps as possible. Integrating the feedback process into the workflow was a key requirement for the development of the UI.

3.1 Concepts

Concepts are defined by Strauss et al. (1996) as the basic building blocks of a theory. In grounded theory, open coding represents the analytical process through which concepts are identified and developed in terms of their properties and dimensions.

In this work, we employ the broad term *concept* to encompass various usage scenarios, such as categories, topics, sentiments, opinions, etc. In our terms, a concept refers to anything that serves to semantically group or classify sentences.

3.2 User Workflow

The *Concept Over Time Analysis* extension provides versatile functions for diverse applications. Illustratively, we present key features through a

[1] github.com/uhh-lt/dats

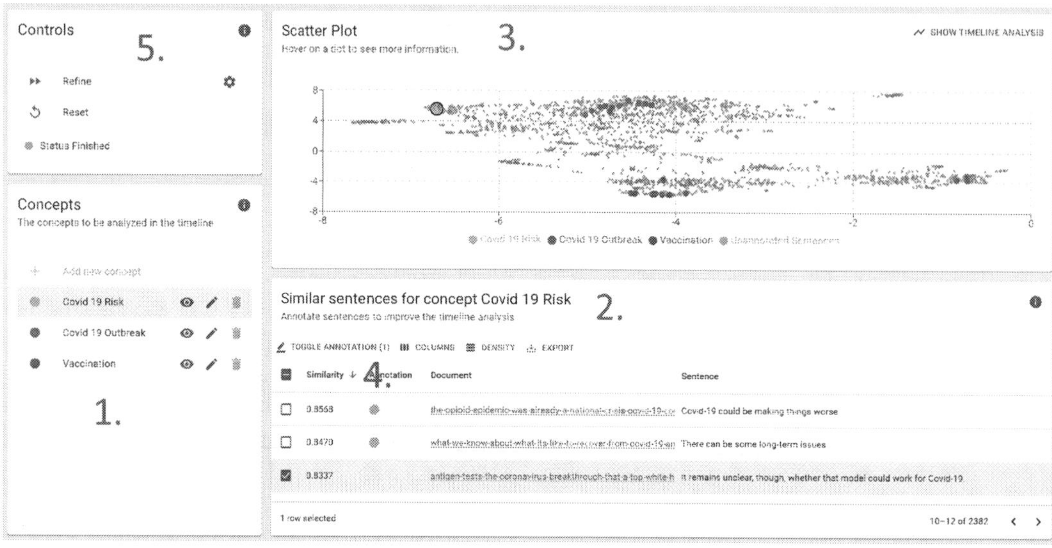

Figure 1: The annotation view of the *Concept Over Time Analysis* extension: (1) Define, edit, delete & toggle visibility of concepts. (2) + (4) Sentence Annotator: A ranked list sentences similar to the selected concept. (3) 2D visualization of the search space, annotated sentences are colored & highlighted. (5) Controls to manually start, reset & configure model training. Training status is updated live.

typical workflow. Consider Alice, a researcher exploring discourse on the COVID pandemic from 2020 to 2024. Using her web browser, she accesses DATS, registers, logs in, and creates a new project. Uploading material from various news websites, she ensures the presence of metadata indicating the publication date, which is required for *Concept Over Time Analysis*. To start her analysis, Alice locates the feature in the "Analysis" tab and creates an empty *Concept Over Time Analysis*.

Defining concepts Alice is presented with the annotation view of the *Concept over time analysis* view (see Figure 1). To initiate the analysis, she defines three concepts "Covid 19 as a risk", "Covid 19 Outbreaks", "Vaccinations", and provides a short description for each (1). To identify interesting concepts, DATS offers various dataset exploration features ranging from the distant, quantitative search, filter and statistics features to the close, qualitative reading and annotation of documents.

Concept annotation After inputting concepts and descriptions, Alice starts the first iteration of the analysis. The Sentence Annotator (2) displays ranked sentences based on similarity to the concept, accompanied by a scatter plot (3) visualizing all search space sentences. Clicking on a dot navigates to and highlights the corresponding sentence in the annotator. While exploring the search space, Alice realizes that the scatter plot lacks effective clustering for her concepts, primarily because, at this stage, a concept's representation relies solely on the initial description.

Alice enhances her defined concepts with more information by providing feedback through sentence annotations. While scrolling through lists of similar sentences, she annotates sentences with the respective concept (4), identifying fitting mentions, ideas, or paraphrases. This initial annotation is recognized as the most challenging part of the analysis, and we aim to assist by providing an initial similarity ranking.

Iterative concept refinement After annotating the minimum required sentences per concept (default is five), she proceeds to the next step by clicking the refine button (5). Through her feedback, the system improves its ability to distinguish between concepts and provides more relevant similar sentences for each. The scatter plot visualization is updated, showing clusters of sentences centered around the annotated ones. Annotated sentences are in Alice's defined color, while others are visualized in purple (3). With the improved scatter plot and sentence rankings, it becomes notably easier for Alice to identify additional relevant sentences for her concepts.

After annotating a few more relevant sentences, Alice is prompted to refine the Concept Over Time

Analysis again. Alice can continue this process until she's certain in the system's ability to distinguish between concepts. Typically, this is achieved if the scatter plot exhibits clear clustering, allowing for effective separation, and if most top similar sentences for a concept are deemed relevant.

Timeline analysis Satisfied with the clustering and the suggested similar sentences, Alice switches to the Timeline Analysis visualization (see Figure 2). This visualization (1) depicts the date on the x-axis and the aggregated count of similar sentences per concept on the y-axis, illustrating the development of her defined concepts over time. Alice customizes the aggregation (year, month, day) and adjusts the similarity threshold to filter out irrelevant sentences (2). Alice explores the results by clicking on several dots, which reveals all sentences of the selected concept on the chosen date in the Sentence Annotator (3).

4 System Implementation

The visualization is implemented using React and the Recharts[2] library. The asynchronous model training is implemented with Celery[3] and SetFit[4] (Tunstall et al., 2022).

The main challenges involve classifying concepts and adapting to limited user feedback while ensuring high performance and interactivity. Additionally, we noted that concepts are often nuanced and exist within the same domain, resulting in high inter-concept similarity. Therefore, key requirements considered during the implementation are fast training, the capacity to learn from a few labeled samples, and the ability to distinguish between topically similar instances.

The *Concept Over Time Analysis* workflow is internally structured as a three-step pipeline, encompassing: establishing the initial search space, fine-tuning the Sentence Transformer model, and computing the results. In the subsequent sections, we provide a detailed explanation of each step.

The initial search space To initiate the *Concept Over Time Analysis*, users provide concepts along with proper descriptions. The descriptions are embedded with a Sentence Transformer model to generate an initial representation of each concept. The model is configurable during the tool setup and defaults to a pretrained multilingual CLIP (Radford et al., 2021; Reimers and Gurevych, 2020) model.

Following this, the concept representations are employed to identify semantically similar sentences, leveraging the existing semantic similarity search feature within DATS. Each uploaded document runs through a multi-step pre-processing pipeline, including sentence splitting and sentence embedding, with the results stored in Weaviate[5], an open-source vector database. Consequently, the vector database is utilized to retrieve the top K similar sentences for each concept representation, along with their respective similarity scores. K is configurable in the UI and defaults to 1000.

The set of returned sentences is considered as the search space, which remains constant in the subsequent steps. However, the UI allows resetting the search space and restarting the analysis process.

The initial concept descriptions play a pivotal role in the entire analysis, determining the sentences considered during the analysis. This step is only executed once at the beginning, but crucial to the process as it limits the sentences to the concepts' domain and fastens the following steps.

Model fine-tuning Users provide feedback in terms of labeling sentences with concepts. This step is skipped, if there are insufficient annotations for any given concept. The minimum labeled examples per concept can be configured in the UI, however, our experiments suggest that 4, 8, and 16 are good thresholds to start the fine-tuning.

A contrastive training dataset is generated based on the users' annotations, which is then used to fine-tune a pre-trained Sentence Transformer model (more details in Section 5). The model trains asynchronously in the background for 1 epoch, the frontend is informed about status changes and displays them accordingly.

Results In the final step, we compute a 2D representation of the search space, update concept representations, re-rank sentences, and compute the timeline analysis.

To generate the 2D representation, displayed in the annotation view, the fine-tuned model computes sentence embeddings, which are then passed to UMAP (McInnes et al., 2020) or t-SNE (Van der Maaten and Hinton, 2008) for dimensionality reduction. Initially, the embeddings stored in the vector database represent the search space sentences. Throughout iterative refinement, models with im-

[2] https://recharts.org/
[3] https://docs.celeryq.dev/
[4] https://huggingface.co/docs/setfit
[5] https://weaviate.io/

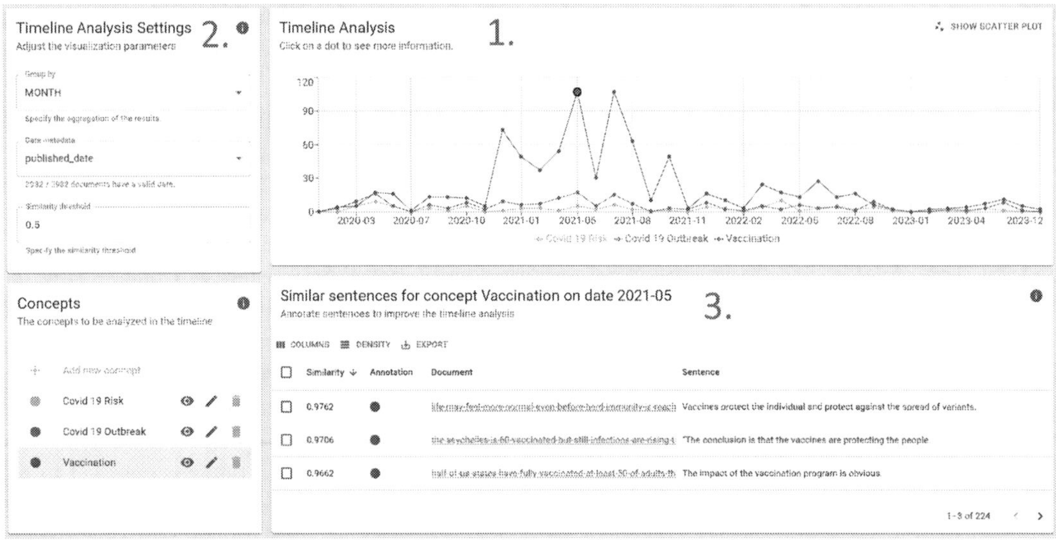

Figure 2: The timeline view of the *Concept Over Time Analysis* extension: (1) Aggregated occurrences of sentences similar to concepts over time. (2) Settings. (3) Sentence Annotator showing similar sentences of selected concept at selected date.

proved performance enhance the sentence representations, causing sentences to "move" toward their most similar concept and form clusters. Appendix B illustrates this process.

Initially, a concept is represented by its embedded description. An enhanced representation is derived by averaging the embeddings of labeled sentences for the concept. Next, we calculate the cosine similarity between concept representations and all embedded search space sentences. The sentences in the Sentence Annotator are then ranked based on the resulting similarity scores.

Finally, the timeline analysis is computed. For each concept, sentences below the similarity threshold are filtered out, and the remaining ones are aggregated and counted based on the specified time intervals (year, month, or day).

5 Experiments

Few-shot fine-tuning of Sentence Transformers has been shown to achieve high accuracy with few labeled data by Tunstall et al. (2022). Our following experiments assess the suitability of this approach for the *Concept Over Time Analysis* extension, while also gaining insights into its limitations.

We formulate the following requirements that our system should meet: Require few labeled samples, enabling users to quickly achieve satisfactory results. Ensure short training time to facilitate an interactive user experience with fast iterations. Improve performance with more training samples rather than more training time, allowing iterative refinement of the model.

5.1 Datasets

The 20 newsgroup dataset[6] (NG20), containing around 20,000 newsgroup posts across 20 topics, aligns with our users' domain. Given that concepts are commonly closely related and within the same domain, we align this experiment with the expected real-world setting by considering the classes "misc," "guns," and "mideast" in the politics subject. Similarly, we consider the related classes "Wellness", "Style & Beauty" and "Healthy Living" of the News Category dataset (Misra, 2022) (NCT). It contains around 210.000 news headlines from 2012 - 2022.

The Stanford Sentiment Treebank dataset (SST-5) (Socher et al., 2013), containing approximately 12,000 sentences from movie reviews, involves fine-grained sentiment classification with five labels ranging from "very negative" to "very positive." We explore this dataset to assess the applicability of our proposed system for Sentiment Analysis, a common need in DH research.

5.2 Setup

Following Tunstall et al. (2022), we fine-tune a Sentence Transformer model with few-shot training

[6] http://qwone.com/ jason/20Newsgroups/

data and train a Logistic Regression classifier on top. We use `paraphrase-mpnet-base-v2`[7] for all experiments.

The contrastive training data comprises sentence pairs, where a pair is deemed positive (1.0) if both sentences belong to the same class and negative (0.0) otherwise. Considering C classes with N sentences per class, all combinations $(N \times |C|)^2$ are evaluated, but duplicate $(A, B) = (B, A)$ and identical (A, A) sentence pairs are removed. To balance positive and negative pairs, positive examples are oversampled, resulting in a substantial training set even with limited labeled samples.

We mimic the iterative concept refinement step, by incrementally increasing the labeled training data. However, our experiments maintain a uniform label distribution in the labeled data, a condition not assured in real-world settings.

The model is fine-tuned for 1 epoch with cosine similarity loss, utilizing the AdamW optimizer with default parameters and a batch size of 16. Experiments are conducted on a single A100 GPU.

5.3 Evaluation

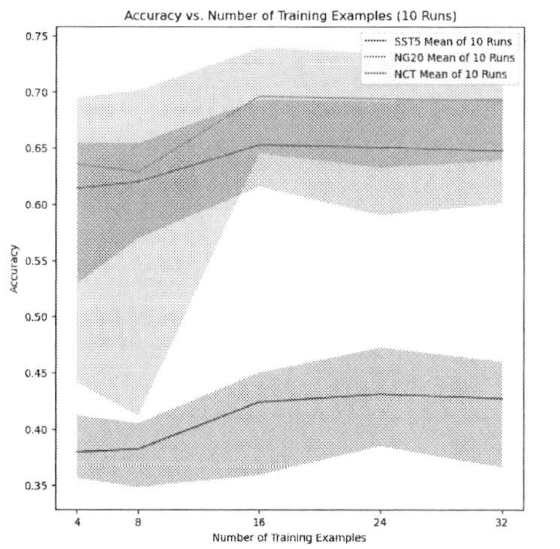

Figure 3: Accuracies over 10 runs of the experiments described in Section 5.

Figure 3 shows averaged accuracy from 10 runs of the SST-5, NG20 and NCT experiments. For all three experiments, we observe a steady improvement in accuracy up to 16 training examples per class. Labeling more examples does not improve the results. Additionally, we note that the quality of annotation significantly impacts our setup. In the 20 newsgroup experiment, there is a difference of over 30% accuracy between the best-performing and worst-performing run.

We acknowledge that the performance of our approach does not match state-of-the-art results on the datasets due to the few-shot nature of these experiments. To mitigate this, in the timeline analysis, users can define a similarity threshold to filter out irrelevant results. In addition, we provide an interface to assess the considered sentences for a given concept and time.

In summary, our implemented system achieves most of our requirements: It requires few labeled training data, the training times are fast (see Appendix A), and it scales with more training samples, but only up to 16 examples per class.

6 Conclusion

In this paper, we presented the *Concept Over Time Analysis* extension, a machine-learning-based tool facilitating the identification and analysis of user-defined concepts within large datasets over time. The proposed tool empowers users to define concepts, identify relevant sentences, and visualize results in a timeline through a unified and interactive interface that is fully integrated within the Discourse Analysis Tool Suite. Embracing the Human-in-the-loop paradigm, the system iteratively refines the underlying model and enhances the timeline analysis with the help of user feedback.

It employs few-shot sentence classification utilizing Sentence Transformer models for sentence and concept representations. With minimal human feedback, the model is fine-tuned on a contrastive dataset generated from the provided annotations.

This results in a powerful tool for qualitative data analysis in large datasets. The chronological overview of custom concepts allows researchers to identify patterns, trends, and shifts in discourse over time. Beyond discourse analysis, the extension supports various applications, including visualizing topics or sentiments over time.

This work centered on analyzing and visualizing concepts in texts over time. In the next iteration, we plan to support image data, i.e., using cross-modal Sentence Transformers powered by CLIP, and adapting the interface for image processing. We also aim to fine-tune Sentence Transformers with adapters to further reduce training time while maintaining comparable performance.

[7] https://huggingface.co/sentence-transformers/paraphrase-mpnet-base-v2

7 Acknowledgement

This work is supported by the D-WISE project, Universität Hamburg, funded by BMBF (grant no.01UG2124).

8 Ethics Statement

The proposed *Concept Over Time Analysis* extension of the DATS heavily relies on Machine Learning (ML) models and technology. We acknowledge that while ML models can provide valuable insights, they are not perfect and may produce errors. It is crucial to understand and accept the limitations of these models to avoid drawing false impressions or conclusions based on their outputs. We urge users to exercise caution and critical thinking when interpreting results generated by our tool. The accuracy and reliability of any findings depend heavily on the quality and appropriateness of the input data as well as the model's assumptions and parameters. Users should also consider potential biases that may exist within the training data used to develop the models. In addition, we emphasize the importance of validating all results through alternative methods such as manual coding or expert review. This step will help ensure the accuracy and robustness of the findings and prevent overreliance on automated tools.

References

Evelyn Gius, Jan Christoph Meister, Malte Meister, Marco Petris, Christian Bruck, Janina Jacke, Mareike Schumacher, Dominik Gerstorfer, Marie Flüh, and Jan Horstmann. 2022. CATMA: Computer Assisted Text Markup and Analysis.

Maarten Grootendorst. 2022. BERTopic: Neural topic modeling with a class-based TF-IDF procedure. *arXiv preprint arXiv:2203.05794*.

Christian Haase, Saba Anwar, Seid Muhie Yimam, Alexander Friedrich, and Chris Biemann. 2021. SCoT: Sense Clustering over Time: a tool for the analysis of lexical change. In *Proceedings of the 16th Conference of the European Chapter of the Association for Computational Linguistics: System Demonstrations*, pages 198–204, Online. Association for Computational Linguistics.

Andreas Holzinger. 2016. Interactive machine learning for health informatics: when do we need the human-in-the-loop? *Brain Informatics*, 3(2):119–131.

Reiner Keller. 2011. The sociology of knowledge approach to discourse (SKAD). *Human Studies*, 34:43–65.

Leland McInnes, John Healy, and James Melville. 2020. UMAP: Uniform Manifold Approximation and Projection for Dimension Reduction. *arXiv preprint arXiv:1802.03426*.

Rishabh Misra. 2022. News Category Dataset. *arXiv preprint arXiv:2209.11429*.

Alec Radford, Jong Wook Kim, Chris Hallacy, Aditya Ramesh, Gabriel Goh, Sandhini Agarwal, Girish Sastry, Amanda Askell, Pamela Mishkin, Jack Clark, et al. 2021. Learning Transferable Visual Models from Natural Language Supervision. In *International Conference on Machine Learning (ICML)*, pages 8748–8763, Online.

Nils Reimers and Iryna Gurevych. 2019. Sentence-BERT: Sentence Embeddings using Siamese BERT-Networks. In *Proceedings of the 2019 Conference on Empirical Methods in Natural Language Processing and the 9th International Joint Conference on Natural Language Processing (EMNLP-IJCNLP)*, pages 3973–3983, Hong Kong, China.

Nils Reimers and Iryna Gurevych. 2020. Making Monolingual Sentence Embeddings Multilingual using Knowledge Distillation. In *Proceedings of the 2020 Conference on Empirical Methods in Natural Language Processing (EMNLP)*, pages 4512–4525, Online.

Florian Schneider, Tim Fischer, Fynn Petersen-Frey, Isabel Eiser, Gertraud Koch, and Chris Biemann. 2023. The D-WISE Tool Suite: Multi-Modal Machine-Learning-Powered Tools Supporting and Enhancing Digital Discourse Analysis. In *Proceedings of the 61st Annual Meeting of the Association for Computational Linguistics (Volume 3: System Demonstrations)*, pages 328–335.

Eyal Shnarch, Alon Halfon, Ariel Gera, Marina Danilevsky, Yannis Katsis, Leshem Choshen, Martin Santillan Cooper, Dina Epelboim, Zheng Zhang, Dakuo Wang, Lucy Yip, Liat Ein-Dor, Lena Dankin, Ilya Shnayderman, Ranit Aharonov, Yunyao Li, Naftali Liberman, Philip Levin Slesarev, Gwilym Newton, Shila Ofek-Koifman, Noam Slonim, and Yoav Katz. 2022. Label Sleuth: From Unlabeled Text to a Classifier in a Few Hours. In *Proceedings of the 2022 Conference on Empirical Methods in Natural Language Processing: System Demonstrations*.

Richard Socher, Alex Perelygin, Jean Wu, Jason Chuang, Christopher D. Manning, Andrew Ng, and Christopher Potts. 2013. Recursive Deep Models for Semantic Compositionality Over a Sentiment Treebank. In *Proceedings of the 2013 Conference on Empirical Methods in Natural Language Processing*, pages 1631–1642, Seattle, Washington, USA. Association for Computational Linguistics.

Anselm Strauss and Juliet Corbin. 1990. *Basics of Qualitative Research: Grounded Theory Procedures and Techniques*. SAGE Publications, Inc.

Anselm Strauss, Juliet Corbin, Solveigh Niewiarra, and Heiner Legewie. 1996. *Grounded Theory: Grundlagen Qualitativer Sozialforschung*. Beltz, Psychologie-Verlag-Union Weinheim.

Lewis Tunstall, Nils Reimers, Unso Eun Seo Jo, Luke Bates, Daniel Korat, Moshe Wasserblat, and Oren Pereg. 2022. Efficient Few-Shot Learning Without Prompts. *arXiv preprint arXiv:2209.11055*.

Laurens Van der Maaten and Geoffrey Hinton. 2008. Visualizing data using t-SNE. *Journal of machine learning research*, 9(11).

Changbo Wang, Zhao Xiao, Yuhua Liu, Yanru Xu, Aoying Zhou, and Kang Zhang. 2013. SentiView: Sentiment Analysis and Visualization for Internet Popular Topics. *IEEE Transactions on Human-Machine Systems*, 43(6):620–630.

A Few-Shot Training Runtime

An important requirement for implementing usable tools is the time or latency. We measured the training times for the experiments described in Section 5 to get an estimate of the time users have to wait until they receive the results of the COTA Refinement in the UI. The results are shown in Figure 4. Here we can see that the runtime heavily depends on the lengths of the sentences (see Table 1) and the number of samples used for training. Since the sentences within our tool are created using spaCy[8], we can assume typical lengths. Hence, we expect the users of our tool to wait a maximum of two minutes when refining a COTA with 32 annotations per concept.

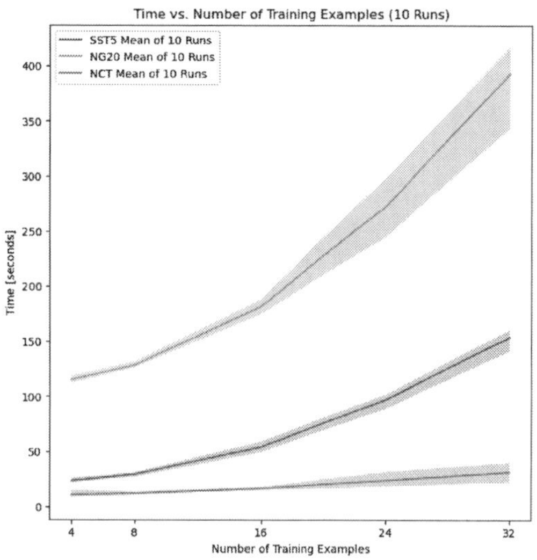

Figure 4: Average runtimes over 10 runs of the experiments described in Section 5.

Table 1: Number of white space separated words per dataset.

Dataset	mean	std	min	max
NG20	205.48	652.55	1.00	20082.00
SST-5	19.14	9.31	2.00	52.00
NCT	9.15	3.25	1.00	38.00

B Sentence Embedding Evolution

In this appendix section, we show the evolution of sentence embeddings produced during our experiment with the NG20 dataset. We use t-SNE (Van der Maaten and Hinton, 2008) to reduce the embeddings to 2D for better visualization.

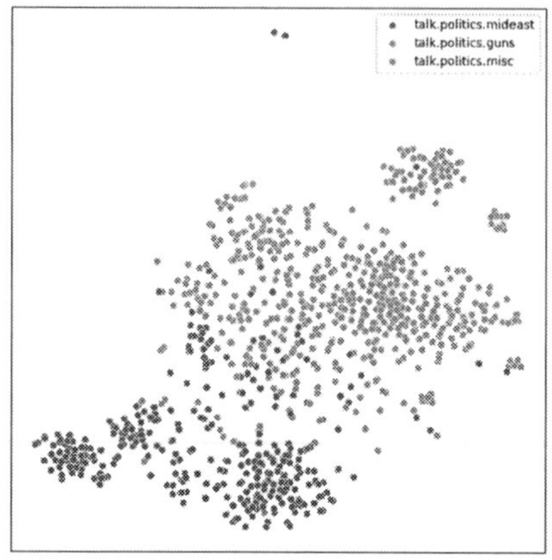

(a) Number of training samples per class: 4

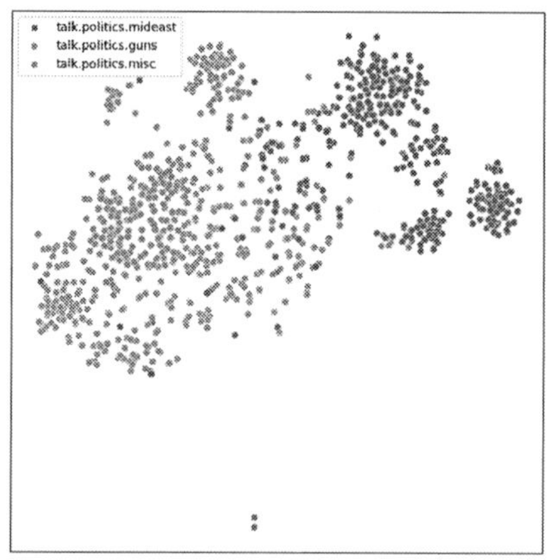

(b) Number of training samples per class: 8

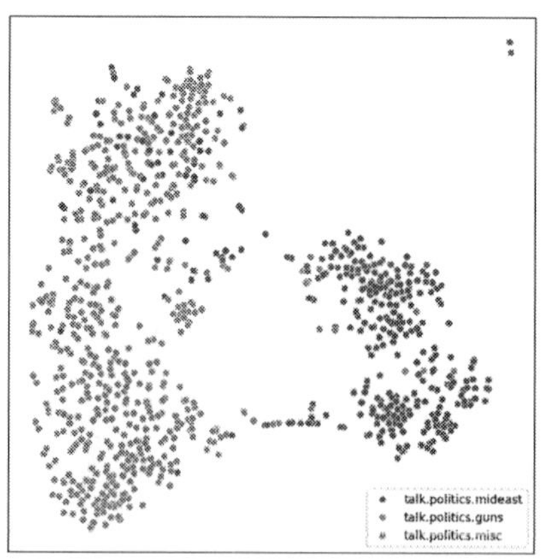

(c) Number of training samples per class: 16

[8] https://spacy.io/

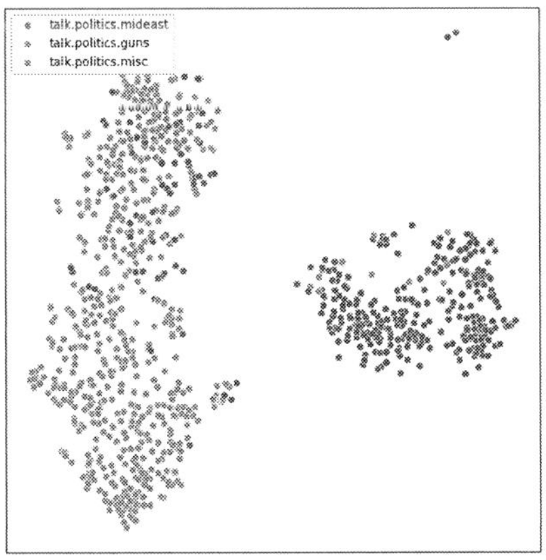

(d) Number of training samples per class: 24

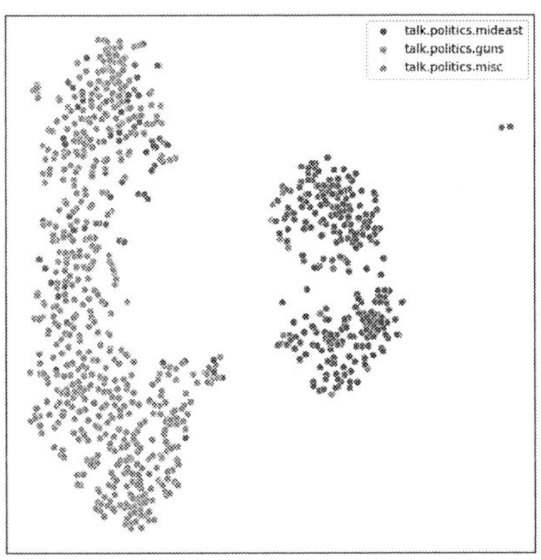

(e) Number of training samples per class: 32

Figure 5: The evolution of sentence embeddings produced during our experiment with the NG20 dataset.

pyvene: A Library for Understanding and Improving PyTorch Models via Interventions

Zhengxuan Wu[†], **Atticus Geiger**[‡], **Aryaman Arora**[†], **Jing Huang**[†], **Zheng Wang**[†], **Noah D. Goodman**[†], **Christopher D. Manning**[†], **Christopher Potts**[†]

[†]Stanford University [‡]Pr(Ai)^{2}R Group

{wuzhengx,atticusg,aryamana,hij,peterwz,ngd,manning,cgpotts}@stanford.edu

Abstract

Interventions on model-internal states are fundamental operations in many areas of AI, including model editing, steering, robustness, and interpretability. To facilitate such research, we introduce **pyvene**, an open-source Python library that supports customizable interventions on a range of different PyTorch modules. **pyvene** supports complex intervention schemes with an intuitive configuration format, and its interventions can be static or include trainable parameters. We show how **pyvene** provides a unified and extensible framework for performing interventions on neural models and sharing the intervened upon models with others. We illustrate the power of the library via interpretability analyses using causal abstraction and knowledge localization. We publish our library through Python Package Index (PyPI) and provide code, documentation, and tutorials at `https://github.com/stanfordnlp/pyvene`.

1 Introduction

When we *intervene* on a neural network, we make an in-place change to its activations, putting the model in a counterfactual state. This fundamental operation has emerged as a powerful tool for both understanding and improving models; interventions of various kinds are key to recent efforts in model robustness (He et al., 2019), model editing (Meng et al., 2022) and steering (Li et al., 2023a), causal abstraction (Geiger et al., 2020, 2021, 2023; Wu et al., 2023) or activation patching (Chan et al., 2022; Wang et al., 2023), circuit finding (Conmy et al., 2023; Goldowsky-Dill et al., 2023), and knowledge tracing (Geva et al., 2023).

As intervention-based techniques have matured, the need has arisen to run ever more complex interventions on ever larger models. Currently, there is no unified and generic intervention-oriented library to support such research. Existing libraries are often project-based (see implementations for Wang et al. 2023; Geiger et al. 2023 as examples) that lack extensibility and are hard to maintain and share, and current toolkits focus on single or non-nested interventions (e.g., ablation neurons in a single forward pass) and are often limited to interventions on Transformers (Vaswani et al., 2017) without natively supporting other neural architectures. Some of these existing libraries (Bau, 2022; Lloyd, 2023; Fiotto-Kaufman, 2023; Mossing et al., 2024) can

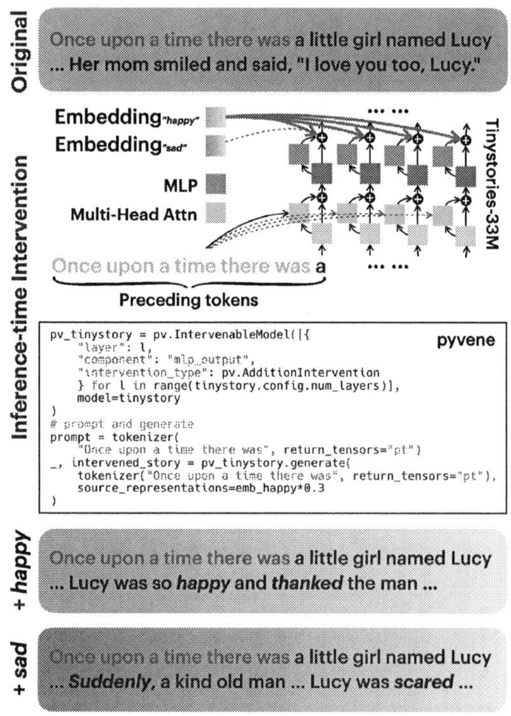

Figure 1: An inference-time intervention (Li et al., 2023a) on `TinyStories-33M`. The model is prompted with "Once upon a time there was a", and is asked to complete the story. We add a static word embedding (for "happy" or "sad") into the MLP output at each decoding step for all layers with a coefficient of 0.3. **pyvene**'s complete implementation is provided. The original and intervened generations use greedy decoding.

Proceedings of the 2024 Conference of the North American Chapter of the Association for Computational Linguistics: Human Language Technologies (Volume 3: System Demonstrations), pages 158–165
June 16-21, 2024 ©2024 Association for Computational Linguistics

support complex interventions such as exchanging activations across multiple forward passes yet they require sophisticated knowledge and heavy implementations.

To address these limitations, we introduce **pyvene**, an open-source Python library that supports customizable interventions on different neural architectures implemented in PyTorch. Different from previous libraries (Bau, 2022; Nanda and Bloom, 2022; Lloyd, 2023; Fiotto-Kaufman, 2023; Mossing et al., 2024), **pyvene** is intervention-oriented. It supports complex interventions by manipulating or exchanging activations across multiple model forward runs while allowing these interventions to be shared with a serialization configuration file. Specifically, **pyvene** has a number of advantages:

1. **Intervention as the primitive.** The intervention is the basic primitive of **pyvene**. Interventions are specified with a `dict`-based format, in contrast to previous approaches where interventions are expressed as code and executed during runtime (Bau, 2022; Lloyd, 2023; Fiotto-Kaufman, 2023; Mossing et al., 2024). All **pyvene** intervention schemes and models are serializable objects that can be shared through a public model hub such as HuggingFace.

2. **Complex intervention schemes. pyvene** supports interventions at multiple locations, involving arbitrary subsets of neurons, and interventions can be performed in parallel or in sequence. For generative use of LMs, **pyvene** supports interventions at decoding steps. Furthermore, activations can easily be collected for probe training.

3. **Support for recurrent and non-recurrent models.** Existing libraries offer only limited support for recurrent models. **pyvene** supports simple feed-forward networks, Transformers, and recurrent and convolutional neural models.

In this paper, we provide two detailed case studies using **pyvene** as well: (1) we fully reproduce Meng et al. (2022)'s locating factual associations in `GPT2-XL` (Figure 1 in the original paper) in about 20 lines of code, and (2) we show intervention and probe training with **pyvene** to localize gender in `Pythia-6.9B`. **pyvene** is published through the Python Package Index (PyPI),[1] and the project site[2] hosts more than 20 tutorials that cover interventions at different levels of complexity with various model architectures from simple feed-foward models to multi-modal models.

2 System Design and Architecture

Two primary components of **pyvene** are the **intervenable configuration**, which outlines which model components will be intervened upon, and the **intervenable model**, which decorates the original `torch` model with hooks that allow activations to be collected and overwritten.[3] Here is a setup for performing a zero-out intervention (often called a zero ablation; Li et al. 2023b) on the 10th, 11th, and 12th dimensions of the MLP output for 3rd token embedding of layer 0 in GPT-2:

```
import torch
import pyvene as pv
# built-in helper to get a HuggingFace model
_, tokenizer, gpt2 = pv.create_gpt2()
# create with dict-based config
pv_config = pv.IntervenableConfig({
  "layer": 0,
  "component": "mlp_output",
  "intervention_type": pv.VanillaIntervention})
# initialize model
pv_gpt2 = pv.IntervenableModel(
  pv_config, model=gpt2)
# run an intervened forward pass
intervened_outputs = pv_gpt2(
  # the base input
  base=tokenizer(
    "The capital of Spain is",
    return_tensors="pt"),
  # the location to intervene at (3rd token)
  unit_locations={"base": 3},
  # the individual dimensions targetted
  subspaces=[10,11,12],
  # the intervention values
  source_representations=torch.zeros(
    gpt2.config.n_embd)
)
# sharing
pv_gpt2.save("./tmp/", save_to_hf_hub=True)
```

The model takes a tensor input `base` and runs through the model's computation graph modifying activations in place to be other values `source`. In this code, we specified `source` in the forward call. When `source` is a constant, it can alternatively be specified in the `IntervenableConfig`. To target complete MLP output representations, one simply leaves out the `subspaces` argument. The final line of the code block shows how to serialize and share an intervened model remotely through a model hub such as HuggingFace.

[1] `pip install pyvene`

[2] `https://github.com/stanfordnlp/pyvene`

[3] Code snippets provided in the paper can be run on Google Colab at `https://colab.research.google.com/github/stanfordnlp/pyvene/blob/main/pyvene_101.ipynb`.

2.1 Interchange Interventions

Interchange interventions (Geiger et al., 2020; Vig et al., 2020; Wang et al., 2023, also known as activation patching) fix activations to take on the values they would be if a different input were provided. With minor changes to the forward call, we can perform an interchange intervention on GPT-2:

```
# run an interchange intervention
intervened_outputs = pv_gpt2(
  # the base input
  base=tokenizer(
    "The capital of Spain is",
    return_tensors = "pt"),
  # the source input
  sources=tokenizer(
    "The capital of Italy is",
    return_tensors = "pt"),
  # the location to intervene at (3rd token)
  unit_locations={"sources->base": 3},
  # the individual dimensions targeted
  subspaces=[10,11,12]
)
```

This forward call produces outputs for base but with the activation values for MLP output dimensions 10–12 of token 3 at layer 0 set to those that obtained when the model processes the source. Such interventions are used in interpretability research to test hypotheses about where and how information is stored in model-internal representations.

2.2 Addition Interventions

In the above examples, we replace values in the base with other values (`VanillaIntervention`). Another common kind of intervention involves updating the base values in a systematic way:

```
noising_config = pv.IntervenableConfig({
  "layer": 0,
  "component": "block_input",
  "intervention_type": pv.AdditionIntervention})
noising_gpt2 = pv.IntervenableModel(
  config, model=gpt2)
intervened_outputs = noising_gpt2(
  base=tokenizer(
    "The Space Needle is in downtown",
    return_tensors = "pt"),
  # target the first four tokens for intervention
  unit_locations={"base": [0, 1, 2, 3]},
  source_representations = torch.rand(
    gpt2.config.n_embd, requires_grad=False))
```

As in this example, we add noise to a representation as a basic robustness check. The code above does this, targetting the first four input token embeddings to a Transformer by using `AdditionIntervention`. This example serves as the building block of causal tracing experiments as in Meng et al. 2022, where we corrupt embedding inputs by adding noise to trace factual associations. Building on top of this, we reproduce Meng et al.'s result in Section 3. **pyvene** allows `Autograd` on the static representations, so this code could be the basis for training models to be robust to this noising process.

2.3 Activation Collection Interventions

This is a pass-through intervention to collect activations for operations like supervised probe training. Such interventions can be combined with other interventions as well, to support things like causal structural probes (Hewitt and Manning, 2019; Elazar et al., 2020; Lepori et al., 2023). In the following example, we perform an interchange intervention at layer 8 and then collect activations at layer 10 for the purposes of fitting a probe:

```
# set up a upstream intervention
probe_config = pv.IntervenableConfig({
  "layer": 8,
  "component": "block_output",
  "intervention_type":  pv.VanillaIntervention})
# add downstream collector
probe_config = probe_config.add_intervention({
  "layer": 10,
  "component": "block_output",
  "intervention_type": pv.CollectIntervention})
probe_gpt2 = pv.IntervenableModel(
  probe_config, model=gpt2)
# return the activations for 3rd token
collected_activations = probe_gpt2(
  base=tokenizer(
    "The capital of Spain is",
    return_tensors="pt"),
  unit_locations={"sources->base": 3})
```

2.4 Custom Interventions

pyvene provides a flexible way of adding new intervention types. The following is a simple illustration in which we multiply the original representation by a constant value:

```
# multiply base with a constant
class MultInt(pv.ConstantSourceIntervention):
  def __init__(self, **kwargs):
    super().__init__()
  def forward(self, base, source=None,
    subspaces=None):
    return base * 0.3

pv.IntervenableModel({
  "intervention_type": MultInt},
  model=gpt2)
```

The above intervention becomes useful when studying interpretability-driven models such as the Backpack LMs of Hewitt et al. (2023). The sense vectors acquired during pretraining in Backpack LMs have been shown to have a "multiplication effect", and so proportionally decreasing sense vectors could effectively steer the model's generation.

2.5 Trainable Interventions

pyvene interventions can include trainable parameters. `RotatedSpaceIntervention` implements Distributed Alignment Search (DAS; Geiger et al. 2023), `LowRankRotatedSpaceIntervention` is a more efficient version of that model, and BoundlessRotatedSpaceIntervention implements the Boundless DAS variant of Wu et al. (2023). With these primitives, one can easily train DAS explainers.

In the example below, we show a single gradient update for a DAS training objective that localizes the capital associated with the country in a one-dimensional linear subspace of activations from the Transformer block output (i.e., main residual stream) at the 8th layer by training our intervention module to match the gold counterfactual behavior:

```
das_config = pv.IntervenableConfig({
  "layer": 8,
  "component": "block_output",
  "low_rank_dimension": 1,
  "intervention_type":
    pv.LowRankRotatedSpaceIntervention})

das_gpt2 = pv.IntervenableModel(
    das_config, model=gpt2)

last_hidden_state = das_gpt2(
  base=tokenizer(
    "The capital of Spain is",
    return_tensors="pt"),
  sources=tokenizer(
    "The capital of Italy is",
    return_tensors="pt"),
  unit_locations={"sources->base": 3}
)[-1].last_hidden_state[:,-1]

# gold counterfacutual label as " Rome"
label = tokenizer.encode(
  " Rome", return_tensors="pt")
logits = torch.matmul(
  last_hidden_state, gpt2.wte.weight.t())

m = torch.nn.CrossEntropyLoss()
loss = m(logits, label.view(-1))
loss.backward()
```

2.6 Training with Interventions

Interventions can be co-trained with the intervening model for techniques like interchange intervention training (IIT), which induce specific causal structures in neural networks (Geiger et al., 2022):

```
pv_gpt2 = pv.IntervenableModel({
  "layer": 8},
  model=gpt2)
# enable gradients on the model
pv_gpt2.enable_model_gradients()
# run counterfactual forward as usual
```

In the example above, with the supervision signals from the training dataset, we induce causal structures in the residual stream at 8th layer.

2.7 Multi-Source Parallel Interventions

In the parallel mode, interventions are applied to the computation graph of the same base example at the same time. We can perform interchange interventions by taking activations from multiple source examples and swapping them into the base's computation graph:

```
parallel_config = pv.IntervenableConfig([
  {"layer": 3, "component": "block_output"},
  {"layer": 3, "component": "block_output"}],
  # intervene on base at the same time
  mode="parallel")

parallel_gpt2 = pv.IntervenableModel(
  parallel_config, model=gpt2)

base = tokenizer(
  "The capital of Spain is",
  return_tensors="pt")
sources = [
  tokenizer("The language of Spain is",
    return_tensors="pt"),
  tokenizer("The capital of Italy is",
    return_tensors="pt")]

intervened_outputs = parallel_gpt2(
  base, sources,
  {"sources->base": (
  # each list has a dimensionality of
  # [num_intervention, batch, num_unit]
  [[[1]],[[3]]],  [[[1]],[[3]]])}
)
```

In the example above, we interchange the activations from the residual streams on top of the second token from the first example ("language") as well as the fourth token from the second example ("Italy") into the corresponding locations of the base's computation graph. The motivating intuition is that now the next token might be mapped to a semantic space that is a mixture of two inputs in the source "The language of Italy". (And, in fact, "Italian" is among the top five returned logits.)

2.8 Multi-Source Serial Interventions

Interventions can also be sequentially applied, so that later interventions are applied to an intervened model created by the previous ones:

```
serial_config = pv.IntervenableConfig([
  {"layer": 3, "component": "block_output"},
  {"layer": 10, "component": "block_output"}],
  # intervene on base one after another
  mode="serial")

serial_gpt2 = pv.IntervenableModel(
  serial_config, model=gpt2)

intervened_outputs = serial_gpt2(
  base, sources,
  # src_0 intervenes on src_1 position 1
  # src_1 intervenes on base position 4
  {"source_0->source_1": 1,
   "source_1->base"    : 4}
)
```

In the example above, we first take activations at the residual stream of the first token ("language") at the 3rd layer from the first source example and swap them into the same location during the forward run of the second source example. We then take the activations of the 4th token ("is") at layer 10 at upstream of this intervened model and swap them into the same location during the forward run of the base example. The motivating intuition is that the first intervention will result in the model retrieving "The language of Italy" and the second intervention will swap the retrieved answer into the output stream of the base example. (Once again, "Italian" is among the top five returned logits.)

2.9 Intervenable Model

The `IntervenableModel` class is the backend for decorating `torch` models with intervenable configurations and running intervened forward calls. It implements two types of hooks: **Getter** and **Setter** hooks to save and set activations.

Figure 1 highlights **pyvene**'s support for LMs. Interventions can be applied to any position in the input prompt or any selected decoding step.

The following involves a model with recurrent (GRU) cells where we intervene on two unrolled recurrent computation graphs at a time step:

```
# built-in helper to get a GRU
_, _, gru = pv.create_gru_classifier(
  pv.GRUConfig(h_dim=32))
# wrap it with config
pv_gru = pv.IntervenableModel({
  "component": "cell_output",
  # intervening on time
  "unit": "t",
  "intervention_type": pv.ZeroIntervention},
  model=gru)
# run an intervened forward pass
rand_b = torch.rand(1,10, gru.config.h_dim)
rand_s = torch.rand(1,10, gru.config.h_dim)
intervened_outputs = pv_gru(
  base = {"inputs_embeds": rand_b},
  sources = [{"inputs_embeds": rand_s}],
  # intervening time step
  unit_locations={"sources->base": (6, 3)})
```

A hook is triggered every time the corresponding model component is called. As a result, a vanilla hook-based approach, as in all previous libraries (Bau, 2022; Lloyd, 2023; Fiotto-Kaufman, 2023; Mossing et al., 2024), fails to intervene on any recurrent or state-space model. To handle this limitation, **pyvene** records a state variable for each hook, and only executes a hook at the targeted time step.

3 Case Study I: Locating Factual Associations in GPT2-XL

We replicate the main result in Meng et al. (2022)'s Locating Factual Associations in GPT2-XL with **pyvene**. The task is to trace facts via interventions on fact-related datasets. Following Meng et al.'s setup, we first intervene on input embeddings by adding Gaussian noise. We then restore individual states to identify the information that restores the results. Specifically, we restore the Transformer block output, MLP activation, and attention output for each token at each layer. For MLP activation and attention output, we restore 10 sites centered around the intervening layer (clipping on the edges). Our Figure 2 fully reproduces the main Figure 1 (p. 2) in Meng et al.'s paper. To replicate their experiments, we first define a configuration for causal tracing:

```
def tracing_config(
    l, c="mlp_activation", w=10, tl=48):
  s = max(0, l - w // 2)
  e = min(tl, l - (-w // 2))
  config = IntervenableConfig(
    [{"component": "block_input"}] +
    [{"layer": l, "component": c}
      for l in range(s, e)],
    [pv.NoiseIntervention] +
    [pv.VanillaIntervention]*(e-s))
  return config
```

With this configuration, we corrupt the subject token and then restore selected internal activations to their clean value. Our main experiment is implemented with about 20 lines of code with **pyvene**:

```
trace_results = []
_, tokenizer, gpt = pv.create_gpt2("gpt2-xl")
base = tokenizer(
  "The Space Needle is in downtown",
  return_tensors="pt")
for s in ["block_output", "mlp_activation",
  "attention_output"]:
  for l in range(gpt.config.n_layer):
    for p in range(7):
      w = 1 if s == "block_output" else 10
      t_config, n_r = tracing_config(l, s, w)
      t_gpt = pv.IntervenableModel(t_config, gpt)
      _, outs = t_gpt(base, [None] + [base]*n_r,
        {"sources->base": ([None] + [[[p]]]*n_r,
          [[[0, 1, 2, 3]]] + [[[p]]]*n_r)})
      dist = pv.embed_to_distrib(gpt,
        outs.last_hidden_state, logits=False)
      trace_results.append(
        {"stream": s, "layer": l, "pos": p,
         "prob": dist[0][-1][7312]})
```

4 Case Study II: Intervention and Probe Training with Pythia-6.9B

We showcase intervention and probe training with **pyvene** using a simple gendered pronoun prediction task in which we try to localize gender in hidden representations. For trainable intervention, we use a one-dimensional Distributed Alignment Search (DAS; Geiger et al., 2023), that is, we seek to learn a 1D subspace representing gender. To localize gender, we feed prompts constructed from a template of the form "**[John/Sarah]** walked because **[he/she]**" (a fixed length of 4) where the name is sampled from a vocabulary of 47 typically male and 10 typically female names followed by the associated gendered pronoun as the output token. We use pythia-6.9B (Biderman et al., 2023)

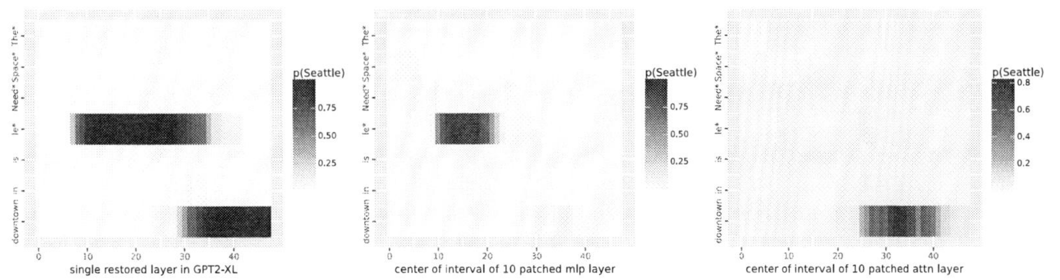

Figure 2: We reproduce the results in Meng et al. (2022)'s Figure 1 of locating early sites and late sites of factual associations in GPT2-XL *in about 20 lines of* **pyvene** *code*. The causal impact on output probability is mapped for the effect of each Transformer block output (left), MLP activations (middle), and attention layer output (right) .

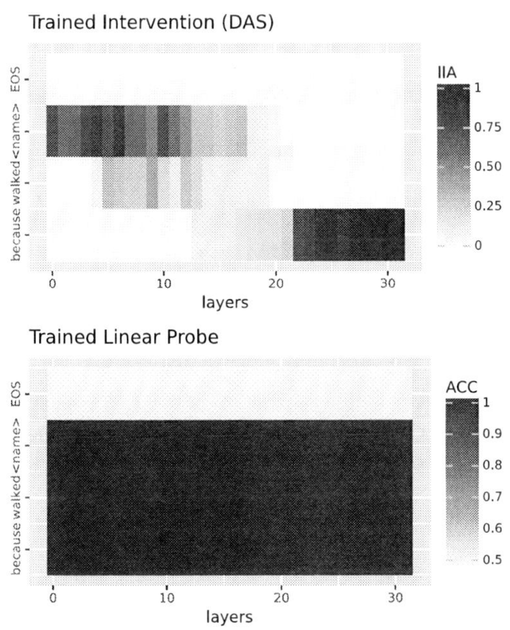

Figure 3: Results of interchange intervention accuracy (IIA) with the trainable intervention (DAS) and accuracy with the trainable linear probe on different model components when localizing gender information.

in this experiment, which achieves 100% accuracy on the task. We then train our interventions and probes at the Transformer block output at each layer and token position. For intervention training, we construct pairs of examples and train the intervention to match the desired counterfactual output (i.e., if we swap activations from an example with a male name into another example with a female name, the desired counterfactual output should be "he"). For linear probe training, we use activation collection intervention to retrieve activations to predict the pronoun gender with a linear layer.

As shown in Figure 3, a trainable intervention finds sparser gender representations across layers and positions, whereas a linear probe achieves 100% classification accuracy for almost all components. This shows that a probe may achieve high performance even on representations that are not causally relevant for the task.

5 Limitations and Future Work

We are currently focused on two main areas:

1. Expanding the default intervention types and model types. Although **pyvene** is extensible to other types, having more built-in types helps us to onboard new users easily.

2. **pyvene** is designed to support complex intervention schemes, but this comes at the cost of computational efficiency. As language models get larger, we would like to investigate how to scale intervention efficiency with multi-node and multi-GPU training.

6 Conclusion

We introduce **pyvene**, an open-source `Python` library that supports intervention-based research on neural models. **pyvene** supports customizable interventions with complex intervention schemes as well as different families of model architectures, and intervened models are shareable with others through online model hubs such as HuggingFace. Our hope is that **pyvene** can be a powerful tool for discovering new ways in which interventions can help us explain and improve models.

References

David Bau. 2022. BauKit. https://github.com/davidbau/baukit.

Stella Biderman, Hailey Schoelkopf, Quentin Gregory Anthony, Herbie Bradley, Kyle O'Brien, Eric Hallahan, Mohammad Aflah Khan, Shivanshu Purohit, USVSN Sai Prashanth, Edward Raff, Aviya Skowron, Lintang Sutawika, and Oskar Van Der Wal. 2023. Pythia: A suite for analyzing large language models across training and scaling. In *International Conference on Machine Learning (ICML)*.

Lawrence Chan, Adrià Garriga-Alonso, Nicholas Goldowsky-Dill, Ryan Greenblatt, Jenny Nitishinskaya, Ansh Radhakrishnan, Buck Shlegeris, and Nate Thomas. 2022. Causal scrubbing: a method for rigorously testing interpretability hypotheses. Alignment Forum Blog post.

Arthur Conmy, Augustine N Mavor-Parker, Aengus Lynch, Stefan Heimersheim, and Adrià Garriga-Alonso. 2023. Towards automated circuit discovery for mechanistic interpretability. In *Advances in Neural Information Processing Systems (NeurIPS)*.

Yanai Elazar, Shauli Ravfogel, Alon Jacovi, and Yoav Goldberg. 2020. Amnesic probing: Behavioral explanation with amnesic counterfactuals. In *Transactions of the Association of Computational Linguistics (TACL)*.

Jaden Fiotto-Kaufman. 2023. nnsight. `https://github.com/JadenFiotto-Kaufman/nnsight`.

Atticus Geiger, Hanson Lu, Thomas Icard, and Christopher Potts. 2021. Causal abstractions of neural networks. In *Advances in Neural Information Processing Systems (NeurIPS)*.

Atticus Geiger, Kyle Richardson, and Christopher Potts. 2020. Neural natural language inference models partially embed theories of lexical entailment and negation. In *Proceedings of the Third BlackboxNLP Workshop on Analyzing and Interpreting Neural Networks for NLP*, Online.

Atticus Geiger, Zhengxuan Wu, Hanson Lu, Josh Rozner, Elisa Kreiss, Thomas Icard, Noah Goodman, and Christopher Potts. 2022. Inducing causal structure for interpretable neural networks. In *International Conference on Machine Learning (ICML)*.

Atticus Geiger, Zhengxuan Wu, Christopher Potts, Thomas Icard, and Noah D. Goodman. 2023. Finding alignments between interpretable causal variables and distributed neural representations. In *Causal Learning and Reasoning (CLeaR)*.

Mor Geva, Jasmijn Bastings, Katja Filippova, and Amir Globerson. 2023. Dissecting recall of factual associations in auto-regressive language models. In *Empirical Methods in Natural Language Processing (EMNLP)*, Singapore.

Nicholas Goldowsky-Dill, Chris MacLeod, Lucas Sato, and Aryaman Arora. 2023. Localizing model behavior with path patching. *arXiv:2304.05969*.

Zhezhi He, Adnan Siraj Rakin, and Deliang Fan. 2019. Parametric noise injection: Trainable randomness to improve deep neural network robustness against adversarial attack. In *IEEE/CVF Conference on Computer Vision and Pattern Recognition (CVPR)*.

John Hewitt and Christopher D Manning. 2019. A structural probe for finding syntax in word representations. In *North American Chapter of the Association for Computational Linguistics (NAACL)*.

John Hewitt, John Thickstun, Christopher Manning, and Percy Liang. 2023. Backpack language models. In *Association for Computational Linguistics (ACL)*.

Michael A Lepori, Thomas Serre, and Ellie Pavlick. 2023. Uncovering intermediate variables in transformers using circuit probing. *arXiv:2311.04354*.

Kenneth Li, Oam Patel, Fernanda Viégas, Hanspeter Pfister, and Martin Wattenberg. 2023a. Inference-time intervention: Eliciting truthful answers from a language model. In *Advances in Neural Information Processing Systems (NeurIPS)*.

Maximilian Li, Xander Davies, and Max Nadeau. 2023b. Circuit breaking: Removing model behaviors with targeted ablation. *arXiv:2309.05973*.

Evan Lloyd. 2023. graphpatch. `https://github.com/evan-lloyd/graphpatch`.

Kevin Meng, David Bau, Alex Andonian, and Yonatan Belinkov. 2022. Locating and editing factual associations in GPT. In *Advances in Neural Information Processing Systems (NeurIPS)*.

Dan Mossing, Steven Bills, Henk Tillman, Tom Dupré la Tour, Nick Cammarata, Leo Gao, Joshua Achiam, Catherine Yeh, Jan Leike, Jeff Wu, and William Saunders. 2024. Transformer debugger. `https://github.com/openai/transformer-debugger`.

Neel Nanda and Joseph Bloom. 2022. Transformerlens. `https://github.com/neelnanda-io/TransformerLens`.

Ashish Vaswani, Noam Shazeer, Niki Parmar, Jakob Uszkoreit, Llion Jones, Aidan N Gomez, Łukasz Kaiser, and Illia Polosukhin. 2017. Attention is all you need. In *Advances in Neural Information Processing Systems (NeurIPS)*.

Jesse Vig, Sebastian Gehrmann, Yonatan Belinkov, Sharon Qian, Daniel Nevo, Yaron Singer, and Stuart Shieber. 2020. Investigating gender bias in language models using causal mediation analysis. In *Advances in Neural Information Processing Systems (NeurIPS)*.

Kevin Wang, Alexandre Variengien, Arthur Conmy, Buck Shlegeris, and Jacob Steinhardt. 2023. Interpretability in the wild: A circuit for indirect object identification in GPT-2 small. In *International Conference on Learning Representations (ICLR)*.

Zhengxuan Wu, Atticus Geiger, Thomas Icard, Christopher Potts, and Noah Goodman. 2023. Interpretability at scale: Identifying causal mechanisms in Alpaca. In *Advances in Neural Information Processing Systems (NeurIPS)*.

Newspaper Signaling for Crisis Prediction

Prajvi Saxena
German Research Center for Artificial Intelligence,
Saarbrücken, Germany
prajvi.saxena@dfki.de

Sabine Janzen
German Research Center for Artificial Intelligence,
Saarbrücken, Germany
sabine.janzen@dfki.de

Wolfgang Maaß
German Research Center for Artificial Intelligence;
Saarland University,
Saarbrücken, Germany
wolfgang.maass@dfki.de

Abstract

To establish sophisticated monitoring of newspaper articles for detecting crisis-related signals, natural language processing has to cope with unstructured data, media, and cultural bias as well as multiple languages. So far, research on detecting signals in newspaper articles is focusing on structured data, restricted language settings, and isolated application domains. When considering complex crisis-related signals, a high number of diverse newspaper articles in terms of language and culture reduces potential biases. We demonstrate MENDEL – a model for multi-lingual and open-domain newspaper signaling for detecting crisis-related indicators in newspaper articles. The model works with unstructured news data and combines multiple transformer-based models for pre-processing (STANZA) and content filtering (RoBERTa, GPT-3.5). Embedded in a Question-Answering (QA) setting, MENDEL supports multiple languages (>66) and can detect early newspaper signals for open crisis domains in real-time.

1 Introduction

Monitoring newspaper sources has a significant impact on companies, health organizations, and civil defense in preparing for and responding to emerging trends, conflicts, and crises situations effectively (Elliott and Timmermann, 2016; Dim et al., 2021). Nonetheless, up until now, newspaper signaling is not applied in crisis and risk management in practice as it is challenging due to the amount of unstructured data, media, cultural bias (Hanitzsch et al., 2020), and multiple languages (Asr and Taboada, 2019). So far, research on detecting potential signals for crisis-related events based on newspaper articles is focusing on structured data (Hassanzadeh et al., 2022; Huang et al., 2022, 2020; Sakaki et al., 2010; Rasouli et al., 2020; Asif et al., 2021), restricted language settings (Luca Barbaglia and Manzan, 2023), and isolated application domains, e.g., mobility, finances (Dim et al., 2021; Agrawal et al., 2022). The existing systems that monitors newspapers (GAIA-X, 2022; Eurostat, 2023) only aggregates and visualize current news, they don't posses advanced language processing capabilities. However, MENDEL distinguishes itself by processing unstructured newspaper data in real-time, and its use of large language models for multi-lingual content filtering and context-based crisis forecasting, offering a broader and more dynamic approach to early crisis signaling by encouraging organizational preparedness and supporting a rapid and effective response (Bundy et al., 2017).

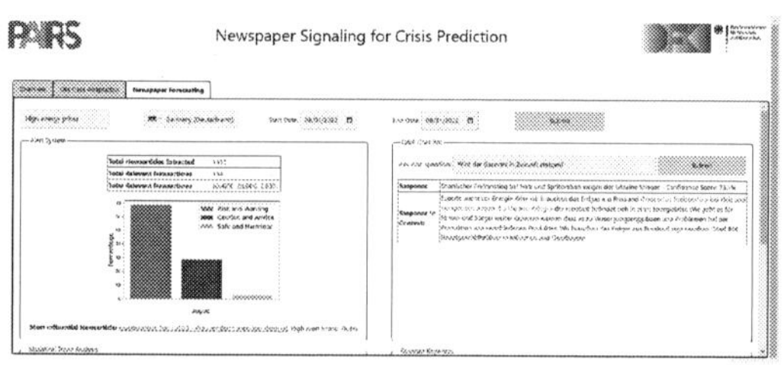

Figure 1: Demonstration of the user interface used for real-time newspaper signaling for detecting energy-related crisis signals.

The major challenge in using newspaper articles for crisis prediction is the management of unstructured data. Most approaches tackle this challenge by specifying a domain ontology for converting unstructured data into structured data, e.g., (Agrawal et al., 2022); facing all the well-known disadvantages in performance, flexibility, and openness with regard to domains. Thus, multi-lingual issues as well as media and cultural biases in newspaper articles written by diverse journalists for diverse newspapers in diverse countries on the same events cannot be captured (Hanitzsch et al., 2020). Furthermore, the media landscape in each country has an influence on how events are portrayed (Kalogeropoulos et al., 2019). Therefore,

Proceedings of the 2024 Conference of the North American Chapter of the Association for Computational Linguistics: Human Language Technologies (Volume 3: System Demonstrations), pages 166–173
June 16-21, 2024 ©2024 Association for Computational Linguistics

considering a high number of diverse newspaper resources in terms of language and culture reduces potential biases when seeking to identify complex crisis-related signals in newspaper articles. In this paper, we demonstrate MENDEL – a model for multi-lingual and open-domain newspaper signaling for detecting crisis-related indicators in newspaper articles (cf. Figure 1). Our model works with unstructured data of newspaper articles and combines multiple state-of-the-art transformer-based models (Vaswani et al., 2017) for pre-processing (STANZA (Qi et al., 2020)) and content filtering (XLM-RoBERTa (Conneau et al., 2020), GPT-3.5 (Brown et al., 2020)). MENDEL supports multiple of the most spoken languages in the world (>66) (e.g., Mandarin Chinese, Spanish, English, Hindi, Arabic). The model is able to detect newspaper signals for open domains, e.g., energy, finances, and supply chains, that can be directly adjusted by the user in terms of keywords. One appeal of the model is the usage of purely unstructured data on newspaper articles for processing signals in real-time in contrast to other approaches mixing those data with already existing structured data suffering from lower quality and timeliness, e.g., Wikidata (Hassanzadeh et al., 2022; Li et al., 2022; Shane E. Halse and Caragea, 2018; Mai and Quan, 2020). Furthermore, MENDEL covers a 2-step filtration pipeline based on RoBERTa (Conneau et al., 2020) and Cosine similarity for determining domain relevance and crisis reference enabling an extensive filtration of articles with high accuracy and less redundancy in distinction from other approaches, that use no filtration, restricted approaches and only sentiment analyses[1] (Agrawal et al., 2022). The model provides the risk and warnings, statistical trends of the crisis and is exemplified within a QA system as a natural language assistant in risk and crisis management (cf. Figure 1)[2]. We were able to evaluate the proposed approach by means of a set of newspaper articles (total: 18,673 news articles) in terms of performance in identifying potential signals for economic recession and energy-related crisis situations (i.e., availability and costs of energy like gas, oil, coal, solar, wind, supply chain disruption, mobility, etc) in Germany.

[1]https://eventregistry.org/products/intelligence/

[2]Link to demo video: `https://youtu.be/q2UTeQsBnDc`

2 Multi-lingual and Open-domain Newspaper Signaling for Crisis Prediction

We present MENDEL, a model for multi-lingual and open-domain newspaper signaling for crisis prediction powered with a real-time alert system, statistical trend visualization, and a QA chat-bot. In this paper, we explore crises defined as periods of substantial instability that disrupt the normal functioning of systems, leading to notable consequences; specifically, we concentrate on events that are predictable but challenging to influence, e.g. supply chain disruptions, mobility, rise in energy prices, economic crisis etc as outlined in various crisis taxonomies, including (Gundel, 2005). The framework consists of four main modules (cf. Figure 2): Data acquisitions, Data-processing pipeline, Two-stage data filtration, and Context-based reasoning and forecasting. MENDEL operates on domain-specific keywords given by a user with additional parameters such as language, country, and time frame. This serves as input to the data acquisition module which consists of several components, charged with generating domain-specific keywords, extracting newspaper articles, and a data parser. Outputs of these components are fed to the data-processing module which handles data cleaning by removing stopwords, punctuation followed by tokenizer and lemmatizer. This module processes the data that can be directly fed to our two-stage data filtration, which is responsible to filters the articles based on users specified crisis domain and by finding future and present tenses in articles. Outputs are further passed to the Context-based Reasoning and Forecasting module. It generates, risks and warnings for the filtered articles and also provide statistical trend visualization for six months period. It also provides relevant keywords and QA chat-bot. Overall, MENDEL pipeline uses completely unstructured data, i.e., newspaper articles, supports open crisis domain, multiple languages and provide early signaling and warnings.

To introduce the proposed approach in the demo, we give a short example course of detecting crisis-related indicators in newspaper articles, starting with the domain name provided by the user e.g. 'high energy prices' and ending with identified domain-specific newspaper signals. For the following, imagine a user, such as a company, looking for signals of energy-related crises due to reduced availability or rising costs of energy such as gas, oil, coal, supply chain disruption and mobility, etc. MENDEL would provide them with alert trends in the form of risk and warnings for rising energy prices. Additionally, it provides visualizations of the statistical crisis trend over 6 months period.

2.1 Data Acquisition

The data acquisition pipeline receives the specified domain name directly from the interface, i.e. 'high energy prices', which is given as a raw string input by the user. The keyword expansion model then generates a list of relevant keywords for the specified domain, e.g., energy shortage, energy cost surge, energy demand, and electricity blackouts. To do this, we are utilizing the openAI's[3] generative pre-trained transformer 3.5 (GPT-3.5) (Brown et al., 2020) model, which broaden the search scope and improve the precision of extracted articles over the manually collected list of keywords (Kyröläinen and Laippala, 2023). We then extract news articles for the curated list of relevant keywords using event registry news API[4]. It allows to obtain access to real-time as well as archive news articles. Additional filters such as time, date, country, and language can be provided from the user interface. Extracted articles are then passed through a data parser which extracts specific data from the entire news article such as title, URL, published date, and first four paragraphs; as typically an abstract of the article is given at the beginning. This helps to reduce the text size of the individual article and improves processing time.

2.2 Data Processing

Our data processing module mainly performs the pre-processing of the extracted news articles as shown in (cf. Figure 2). The data cleaning module handles the removal of special characters, converting them to lowercase, and removing duplicates and missing values. Followed by this, all the stop words and punctuation from the data is removed. STANZA (Qi et al., 2020) is used for tokenization and lemmatization of the data. It tokenizes and splits sentences, each of these sentences contains a list of tokens which is then converted to it's lemmatized form. In the example, the parsed news articles from section 2.1 are processed by removing punctuation, stop words, etc., and converting them into tokens and lemma form. The decomposed lemma represents the output as a set of single-word tokens, e.g., ['Household', 'will', 'face', 'energy-expensive', 'winter', ..., 'economic', 'stress'].

[3]https://openai.com/api/

[4]https://www.newsapi.ai

2.3 Two-Stage Data Filtration

News articles extracted from news API[5] generally contain irrelevant and noisy data. Hence, it is important to filter the articles based on the user's specified crisis domain. In this research, we propose a two-stage data filtering. First, to filter articles based on the use case, and second, to focus on articles that are related to future warnings. The domain-based articles matching module utilizes a state-of-the-art multilingual RoBERTa model (Conneau et al., 2020) to perform filtering based on the desired domain. For this, we derive embedding vectors of the articles by using its learned embedding representations from the RoBERTa model. Further we generate the embedding vectors of all the domain-relevant keywords and use cosine similarity to check if the embedding vectors of articles and domain keywords are close to each other. In this filtering stage, only articles with a cosine similarity greater than 70% arbitrary threshold are retained while the rest are discarded. Subsequently, we need to focus on articles related to future warnings, hence we propose a filtration method to only get articles that are in the future tense and present tense, and reject the articles which are in the past tense. To achieve this, we use the pre-trained zero-shot multilingual XLM-RoBERTa (Conneau et al., 2020) model to classify articles according to their tenses. We set up an arbitrary threshold of 70% combining both future and present tense confidence and discard the remaining articles.

For our example, we first input the sentence: [household will face energy expensive winter....economic stress] to the RoBERTa encoder along with the domain keywords (high energy prices, energy shortage, energy cost surge, energy demand, etc) and then we compute their likeness using cosine similarity. Here, we get a similarity of 93.7% which preceded the threshold of 70%, hence we pass this to the second filtration step where we give it to our tense-based classifier and got the confidence score of 94.1% for future and present tense. As the confidence is higher than the threshold of 70%, we include this article in our data set.

[5]https://www.newsapi.ai

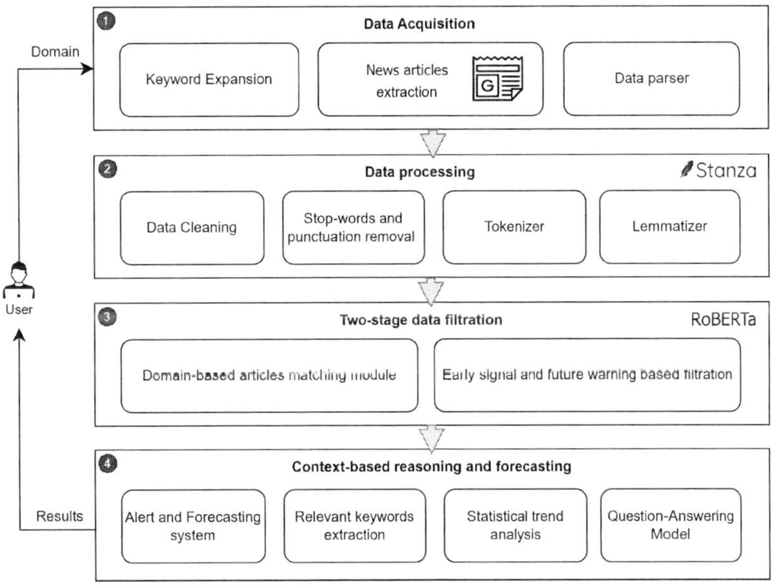

Figure 2: Architecture diagram of MENDEL: A model for multi-lingual and open-domain newspaper signaling for detecting early crisis-related indicators in the newspaper article.

2.4 Context-based Reasoning and Forecasting

Finally, the context-based reasoning and forecasting module receives the final set of embedding from two-stage data filtration2.3. Our alert system is based on the powerful GPT-3.5 (Brown et al., 2020) which classifies the article into three categories 'risk and warning', 'caution and advice', and, 'safe and harmless'. The classified articles are then statistically analyzed by computing the percentage and average confidence score of 'risk and warnings' articles to calculate the alerts. The predictions are delivered to users through the user interface along with visualization of the statistical crisis trend over 6 months period. For the 'high energy prices' example, users will be shown a percentage of 'risk and warnings' signals found with their mean confidence scores, and a graph showing the alert trends for 6 months. If the alerts percentage is high and the graph shows an exponential growth pattern, it is most likely to have an upcoming crisis related to 'high energy prices'. We further use KeyBERT [6] to extract the relevant keywords from the high-risk and warning articles. The resulting relevance for the selected example is ("gas price spikes: 92%", "energy-expensive: 72%", "supply chain disruptions: 78%", mobility: 43%]). Moreover, we also provide an extractive QA chatbot (Conneau et al., 2020; Rajpurkar et al., 2016) for users to interact and ask any questions related to filtered articles. It meets interactive needs of the users and provide more dynamic and responsive way to access crisis-related information.

[6]https://github.com/MaartenGr/KeyBERT

3 Implementation and Evaluation

Based on the proposed model MENDEL (cf. Figure 2), we implemented a newspaper signaling service for crisis and risk management [7]. The service architecture has been deployed using Python and Django while the client side interface has been designed as a web interface using HTML, CSS, and JavaScript. The system accepts keywords by the user in the form of plain text along with specific countries, languages, and time frames. In response, the system presents domain-specific crisis signals and highlights the most influential articles. Moreover, it delivers alerts with confidence and severity levels, along with the relevant keywords[8].

3.1 Settings

We evaluated the performance of the signaling service in identifying potential signals for economic recession and energy-related crisis situations (i.e., availability and costs of energy like gas, oil, coal, solar, and wind). Here, we selected a subset of

[7]Link to GitHub repo: `https://github.com/InformationServiceSystems/pairs-project/tree/main/Modules/NewspaperSignaling`

[8]Demo video: `https://youtu.be/q2UTeQsBnDc`

past and ongoing crises in Germany and represented with event (E) i.e., economic recession in mid-2023[9] (e_1), huge increase of energy prices in 2022[10] (e_2), and immense raise of gasoline prices in 2021[11] (e_3). The objective of the experiment was the identification of early signals regarding these crises in newspaper articles with high percentage and within notable time. We defined three-time horizons for test runs: four (t_{-1}), eight (t_{-2}), and twelve (t_{-3}) weeks before the crisis event occurred. Furthermore, the final set of articles went through the 'alert and forecasting' component and calculated the potential alerts by performing text classification. To assess the performance of our alert and forecasting model, we recruited three human annotators for creating an annotated text corpora due to the lack of crisis newspaper benchmarks. We focused on our crisis events (E) and generated ground truth from annotators. We provided clear instructions and examples for classification to ensure consistent labeling. They classified the articles into three categories: 'risk and warning', 'caution and advice', and 'safe and harmless'. These categories were motivated by existing crisis-related labels used in datasets like CrisisBench (Alam et al., 2021). The ground truth was then determined by selecting the majority label from the three annotator's inputs.

3.2 Data

To conduct the experiment, we collected the news articles for the three past events (E) using the event registry news API. The data acquisition module extracted a total of 18,673 articles in real-time from 01.07.2021 to 31.05.2023 (Table 1 displays article counts across different modules). For event (e_1) we input the keyword 'economic recession' and retrieved 12,265 articles. Following, for the event (e_2) we used the keyword 'high energy prices' and received 5,839 articles. Lastly, for the event (e_3) we got 569 articles for the keyword 'high gas prices'. The majority of articles consisted of German and English languages, but we also found multiple other languages such as Russian, Bulgarian, Spanish, Slovenian, Czech, Indonesian, and Chinese. The processed and parsed articles were fed to the two-stage data filtration, which narrowed down the relevant articles to a total of 4,002. On average, 67.37% of collected articles were irrelevant to the selected domains and future signals, highlighting the importance of the two-stage data filtration.

We also prepared a dataset for testing the performance of our 'alert and forecasting' system. We took a subset of the output of 2-stage filtered data for crisis events (E) and created datasets of total of 319 articles (e_1: 115, e_2: 100, e_3: 104) for annotations.

3.3 Results

Table 2 shows the performance of the signaling service in identifying newspaper signals for time intervals of 4 (t_{-1}), 8 (t_{-2}), and 12 (t_{-3}) weeks in advance of crisis events (E). For each point in time $t \in T$, we examined the monthly growth trend of risk and warning signals in newspaper articles, i.e., the Risk and Warning percentage ($RW\%$). It is defined as the percentage of articles classified as 'risk and warning' by our alert and forecasting module. Results show a generally growing trend in the frequency of risk and warning signals as indicators for recession and energy-related crises.

MENDEL was able to detect early signals at all points in time interval T, i.e., 4, 8, and 12 weeks before the crisis event. When points in time $t \in T$ are marked bold in Table 2, the signaling service detected newspaper signals for the respective crisis events $e \in E$. However, for the event e_3 at (t_{-3}) the $RW\%$ was weak maybe due to the fact that raising gasoline prices are quite popular and volatile compare to e_1, e_2. As people are familiar with volatile gasoline prices, the need for communicating about this issue is lower than with respect to immensely raising prices for electricity. e_1, e_2. Overall, the results of the run-time study indicate a positive evaluation of the newspaper signaling service implementing MENDEL.

To verify the quality of the results reported and to evaluate our alert and forecasting model performance we used the generated ground truth data. By experimenting with multiple state-of-the-art classification models to identify the most effective model for crisis signaling. Due to high-class imbalance in the results of events (e) with 'risk and warning' being the dominant class, we adopted the micro F1 score for the evaluation metric (Takahashi et al., 2022). Table 3 illustrates the model comparison, where the GPT-3.5 model outperformed other models, while Bart (Lewis et al., 2020) and De-

[9]https://www.dw.com/en/recession-in-germany-what-does-that-mean/a-63444401

[10]https://tradingeconomics.com/germany/electricity-price

[11]https://take-profit.org/en/statistics/gasoline-prices/germany/

Event (E)	#articles	#language	#German	#English	#data_processing	#2-stage_filtration
e_1	12265	02	9864	2399	12263	3371
e_2	5839	06	5486	298	5836	482
e_3	569	06	450	64	564	149

Table 1: Distribution of extracted and processed articles across different stages of MENDEL for all events (E).

Event (E)	Date of event (t_0)	Description	t_{-1}	$RW\%$	t_{-2}	$RW\%$	t_{-3}	$RW\%$
e_1	05/23	Economic Recession.	**04/23**	80.73	**03/23**	60	**02/23**	74.44
e_2	09/22	Peak in electricity price.	**08/22**	75.5	**07/22**	68.42	**06/22**	66.6
e_3	10/21	Peak in gasoline price.	**09/21**	73.7	**08/21**	59.09	07/21	30

Table 2: Results of run-time study for evaluating the performance of MENDEL in identifying newspaper signals for time intervals of 4 (t_{-1}), 8 (t_{-2}), and 12 (t_{-3}) weeks in advance of economic recession and past energy-related crisis events E between July 2021 and May 2023 in Germany. Domain-specific keyword: *['Economic recession', 'High energy prices', 'High gas Prices']*. (Legend: $RW\%$ = risk and warning percentage)

BERTaV3 (Laurer et al., 2024) also demonstrated promising results. Therefore, we used GPT-3.5 (Brown et al., 2020) for our alert and forecasting system.

Table 3: Performance of 'alert and forecasting' model for classifying the articles in 'risk and warning', 'caution and advice', and 'safe and harmless' categories. For the Events (E), numbers reported are micro-averaged f1 scores on different text classification models based on human-generated ground truth labels.

Model	e_1	e_2	e_3
XLM-RoBERTa$_{\text{Large}}$	0.46	0.37	0.27
DeBERTaV3	0.65	0.58	0.61
BART	0.6	0.68	0.63
GPT$_{3.5}$	**0.75**	**0.8**	**0.79**

4 Conclusion

We considered real-time newspaper signaling for detecting crisis-related indicators based on purely unstructured data. So far, research on detecting signals in newspaper articles is focusing on structured data, restricted language settings, and isolated application domains, giving little attention to the thereby induced potential biases. We introduced MENDEL – a model for multi-lingual and open-domain newspaper signaling for detecting crisis-related indicators in newspaper articles. The model works with unstructured data from newspaper articles and combines multiple transformer-based models for pre-processing (STANZA) and content filtering (XLM-RoBERTa, GPT-3.5). Embedded in a question-answering setting, MENDEL supports multiple spoken languages in the world (>66) and is able to detect newspaper signals for open domains in real time. We were able to evaluate the proposed approach by identifying potential signals for events (E), economic recession, and energy-related crisis situations. In terms of performance, we evaluated our alert and forecasting model by creating human-annotated data and achieved up to 80% average micro-F1 score. We also were able to identify the potential signals for recession and energy-related crisis, from four (t_{-1}), eight (t_{-2}), and twelve (t_{-3}) weeks before the crisis event occurred.

Ethics statement and limitations

MENDEL aims to make it easier to comprehend news articles about growing and rapidly updating crises, as it can be challenging for humans to keep up with emerging issues from extensive unstructured news data. It is not intended to make predictions, but rather to offer early warning signs of impending crises that would take humans too much time to detect. Verification of crisis warnings is a task that our system does not undertake and that we consider for future work. Our approach does not prove that all crises can be predicted with the same level of performance. It is highly influential on the quality and quantity of news articles due to its capability to deal only with unstructured data.

Acknowledgement

This work was partially funded by the German Federal Ministry of Economics and Climate Protection (BMWK) within the research project PAIRS (grant number: 01MK21008B) and by Saarland Ministry for Economics, Innovation, Digital and Energy (MWIDE) and European Regional Development Fund (ERDF) within the research project INTE:GRATE.

References

Garima Agrawal, Yuli Deng, Jongchan Park, Huan Liu, and Ying-Chih Chen. 2022. Building knowledge graphs from unstructured texts: Applications and impact analyses in cybersecurity education. *Information*, 13(11).

Firoj Alam, Hassan Sajjad, Muhammad Imran, and Ferda Ofli. 2021. Crisisbench: Benchmarking crisis-related social media datasets for humanitarian information processing. In *Proceedings of the Fifteenth International AAAI Conference on Web and Social Media, ICWSM 2021, held virtually, June 7-10, 2021*, pages 923–932. AAAI Press.

Amna Asif, Shaheen Khatoon, Md Maruf Hasan, Majed Alshamari, Sherif Abdou, Khaled Elsayed, and Mohsen Rashwan. 2021. Automatic analysis of social media images to identify disaster type and infer appropriate emergency response. *Journal of Big Data*, 8.

Fatemeh Torabi Asr and Maite Taboada. 2019. Big data and quality data for fake news and misinformation detection. *Big Data & Society*, 6(1):2053951719843310.

Tom Brown, Benjamin Mann, Nick Ryder, Melanie Subbiah, Jared D Kaplan, Prafulla Dhariwal, Arvind Neelakantan, Pranav Shyam, Girish Sastry, Amanda Askell, Sandhini Agarwal, Ariel Herbert-Voss, Gretchen Krueger, Tom Henighan, Rewon Child, Aditya Ramesh, Daniel Ziegler, Jeffrey Wu, Clemens Winter, Chris Hesse, Mark Chen, Eric Sigler, Mateusz Litwin, Scott Gray, Benjamin Chess, Jack Clark, Christopher Berner, Sam McCandlish, Alec Radford, Ilya Sutskever, and Dario Amodei. 2020. Language models are few-shot learners. In *Advances in Neural Information Processing Systems*, volume 33, pages 1877–1901. Curran Associates, Inc.

Jonathan Bundy, Michael D. Pfarrer, Cole E. Short, and W. Timothy Coombs. 2017. Crises and crisis management: Integration, interpretation, and research development. *Journal of Management*, 43(6):1661–1692.

Alexis Conneau, Kartikay Khandelwal, Naman Goyal, Vishrav Chaudhary, Guillaume Wenzek, Francisco Guzmán, Edouard Grave, Myle Ott, Luke Zettlemoyer, and Veselin Stoyanov. 2020. Unsupervised cross-lingual representation learning at scale. In *Proceedings of the 58th Annual Meeting of the Association for Computational Linguistics*, pages 8440–8451, Online. Association for Computational Linguistics.

Chukwuma Dim, Kevin Koerner, Marcin Wolski, and Sanne Zwart. 2021. Hot off the press: News-implied sovereign default risk. Available at SSRN: https://ssrn.com/abstract=3955052 or http://dx.doi.org/10.2139/ssrn.3955052.

Graham Elliott and Allan Timmermann. 2016. Forecasting in economics and finance. *Annual Review of Economics*, 8:81–110.

Eurostat. 2023. Businesses in the manufacturing sector. Available at `https://ec.europa.eu/eurostat/statistics-explained/index.php?title=Manufacturing_statistics_-_NACE_Rev._2&oldid=502915`.

GAIA-X. 2022. Gaia-x architecture document, release 22.04. Available at `https://gaia-x.eu/wp-content/uploads/2022/06/Gaia-x-Architecture-Document-22.04-Release.pdf`.

Stephan Gundel. 2005. Towards a new typology of crises. *Journal of contingencies and crisis management*, 13(3):106–115.

Thomas Hanitzsch, Josef Seethaler, Elizabeth A Skewes, Maria Anikina, Rosa Berganza, Incilay Cangöz, Mihai Coman, Basyouni Hamada, Folker Hanusch, Christopher D Karadjov, et al. 2020. Worlds of journalism: Journalistic cultures, professional autonomy, and perceived influences across 18 nations. In *The global journalist in the 21st century*, pages 473–494. Routledge.

Oktie Hassanzadeh, Parul Awasthy, Ken Barker, Onkar Bhardwaj, Debarun Bhattacharjya, Mark Feblowitz, Lee Martie, Jian Ni, Kavitha Srinivas, and Lucy Yip. 2022. Knowledge-based news event analysis and forecasting toolkit. In *Proceedings of the Thirty-First International Joint Conference on Artificial Intelligence, IJCAI-22*, pages 5904–5907. International Joint Conferences on Artificial Intelligence Organization. Demo Track.

Lida Huang, Gang Liu, Tao Chen, Hongyong Yuan, Panpan Shi, and Yujia Miao. 2020. Similarity-based emergency event detection in social media. *Journal of Safety Science and Resilience*, 2.

Lida Huang, Panpan Shi, Haichao Zhu, and Tao Chen. 2022. Early detection of emergency events from social media: a new text clustering approach. *Natural Hazards*, 111:1–25.

Antonis Kalogeropoulos, Jane Suiter, Linards Udris, and Mark Eisenegger. 2019. News media trust and news consumption: factors related to trust in news in 35 countries. *International Journal of Communication*, 13:22.

Aki-Juhani Kyröläinen and Veronika Laippala. 2023. Predictive keywords: Using machine learning to explain document characteristics. *Frontiers in Artificial Intelligence*, 5.

Moritz Laurer, Wouter van Atteveldt, Andreu Casas, and Kasper Welbers. 2024. Less annotating, more classifying: Addressing the data scarcity issue of supervised machine learning with deep transfer learning and bert-nli. *Political Analysis*, 32(1):84–100.

Mike Lewis, Yinhan Liu, Naman Goyal, Marjan Ghazvininejad, Abdelrahman Mohamed, Omer Levy, Veselin Stoyanov, and Luke Zettlemoyer. 2020. BART: Denoising sequence-to-sequence pre-training for natural language generation, translation, and comprehension. In *Proceedings of the 58th Annual Meeting of the Association for Computational Linguistics*, pages 7871–7880, Online. Association for Computational Linguistics.

Manling Li, Revanth Gangi Reddy, Ziqi Wang, Yishyuan Chiang, Tuan Lai, Pengfei Yu, Zixuan Zhang, and Heng Ji. 2022. COVID-19 claim radar: A structured claim extraction and tracking system. In *Proceedings of the 60th Annual Meeting of the Association for Computational Linguistics: System Demonstrations*, pages 135–144, Dublin, Ireland. Association for Computational Linguistics.

Sergio Consoli Luca Barbaglia and Sebastiano Manzan. 2023. Forecasting with economic news. *Journal of Business & Economic Statistics*, 41(3):708–719.

Trung Mai and Tho Quan. 2020. Ontology-based sentiment analysis for brand crisis detection on online social media. *Science Technology Development Journal - Engineering and Technology*, 3:First.

Peng Qi, Yuhao Zhang, Yuhui Zhang, Jason Bolton, and Christopher D. Manning. 2020. Stanza: A python natural language processing toolkit for many human languages. In *Proceedings of the 58th Annual Meeting of the Association for Computational Linguistics: System Demonstrations*, pages 101–108, Online. Association for Computational Linguistics.

Pranav Rajpurkar, Jian Zhang, Konstantin Lopyrev, and Percy Liang. 2016. SQuAD: 100,000+ questions for machine comprehension of text. In *Proceedings of the 2016 Conference on Empirical Methods in Natural Language Processing*, pages 2383–2392, Austin, Texas. Association for Computational Linguistics.

Elham Rasouli, Sajjad Zarifzadeh, and Amir Jahangard Rafsanjani. 2020. Webkey: a graph-based method for event detection in web news. *J. Intell. Inf. Syst.*, 54(3):585–604.

Takeshi Sakaki, Makoto Okazaki, and Yutaka Matsuo. 2010. Earthquake shakes twitter users: real-time event detection by social sensors. In *Proceedings of the 19th International Conference on World Wide Web*, WWW '10, page 851–860, New York, NY, USA. Association for Computing Machinery.

Anna Squicciarini Shane E. Halse, Andria Tapia and Cornelia Caragea. 2018. An emotional step toward automated trust detection in crisis social media. *Information, Communication & Society*, 21(2):288–305.

Kanae Takahashi, Kouji Yamamoto, Aya Kuchiba, and Tatsuki Koyama. 2022. Confidence interval for micro-averaged f1 and macro-averaged f1 scores. *Applied Intelligence*, 52.

Ashish Vaswani, Noam Shazeer, Niki Parmar, Jakob Uszkoreit, Llion Jones, Aidan N Gomez, Ł ukasz Kaiser, and Illia Polosukhin. 2017. Attention is all you need. In *Proceedings of the 31st International Conference on Neural Information Processing Systems*, volume 30. Curran Associates, Inc.

FastFit: Fast and Effective Few-Shot Text Classification with a Multitude of Classes

Asaf Yehudai ♢ ♣ **, Elron Bandel** ♢
IBM Israel Research Lab ♢, Hebrew University of Jerusalem ♣
{first.last}@ibm.com

Abstract

We present FastFit, a Python package designed to provide fast and accurate few-shot classification, especially for scenarios with many semantically similar classes. FastFit utilizes a novel approach integrating batch contrastive learning and token-level similarity score. Compared to existing few-shot learning packages, such as SetFit, Transformers, or few-shot prompting of large language models via API calls, FastFit significantly improves multi-class classification performance in speed and accuracy across various English and Multilingual datasets. FastFit demonstrates a 3-20x improvement in training speed, completing training in just a few seconds. The FastFit package is now available on GitHub, presenting a user-friendly solution for NLP practitioners.[1]

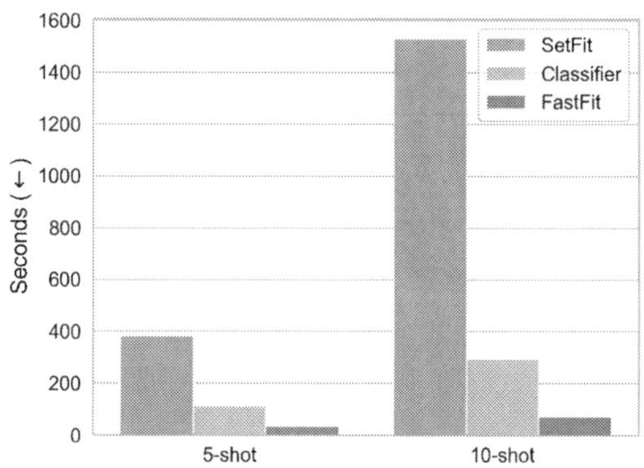

Figure 1: Training times (sec) for FastFit, SetFit, and standard classifier with MPNet model. FastFit training is 3-20x faster.

1 Introduction

Few-shot classification presents a unique challenge, especially when dealing with a multitude of classes that share similar semantic meanings. Expanding the training data can be both time-consuming and costly. To address this challenge, two primary categories of tools have been developed: few-shot prompting of large language models (LLMs) via API calls, or packages designed for fine-tuning smaller language models using the limited available data. However, we recognize the drawbacks of applying both of these approaches in practice.

Few-shot prompting of LLMs leverages their multitasking abilities to tackle data scarcity. However, in the presence of many classes, LLMs encounter three major challenges: (1) LLMs struggle to incorporate demonstrations of all classes within their context window. (2) Utilization of the long context for the classification task can be challenging (Liu et al., 2023). (3) Due to the model size, and prompt length the inference time is slow.

In contrast, the approach of fine-tuning smaller language models capitalizes on their adaptability to specific tasks, as demonstrated to be effective in recent works. However, these methods can be challenging to deploy as they require architectural adjustments (Yehudai et al., 2023) or, like SetFit, may prove less suitable for classification with many classes (Tunstall et al., 2022).

In this work, we present FastFit, a fast and accurate method, and a pip-installable Python package designed for fine-tuning small language models in few-shot classification tasks involving many classes. Through various experiments, we demonstrate that FastFit training is significantly faster, providing a 3-20x speedup. This enables training within seconds, as illustrated in Fig. 1. FastFit outperforms earlier packages, including SetFit, Transformer, and multi-task models like FLAN, or larger LLMs like LLama-70B, in both English and Multilingual settings.

The core contribution facilitating this speedup and improvement lies in FastFit's use of batch contrastive training, recognized for its efficiency and effectiveness (Khosla et al., 2021). This technique brings same-class texts closer while pushing apart

[1]FastFit GitHub

Proceedings of the 2024 Conference of the North American Chapter of the Association for Computational Linguistics: Human Language Technologies (Volume 3: System Demonstrations), pages 174–184
June 16-21, 2024 ©2024 Association for Computational Linguistics

all other texts. FastFit also incorporates token-level text similarity measures that leverage fine-grained information (Zhang et al., 2020; Khattab and Zaharia, 2020). Additionally, we integrate text augmentation techniques to enhance the robustness of the training process (Gao et al., 2021).

The FastFit package is easy to install and use, interfacing with standard training APIs (See §2). We hope that FastFit will help make text classification easier and faster for the benefit of the whole community.

2 The FastFit API

The FastFit Python package is available on PyPI and can be installed with: `$ pip install fast-fit`

To utilize FastFit, import the FastFit trainer, which inherits from the Hugging Face (HF) trainer. This enables FastFit to be customizable, inheriting all parameters from the HF trainer. FastFit supports loading datasets either by directly passing the dataset or providing file paths.

Here is a simple code example of loading and training FastFit. In App. §A, we provide a complete code example.

```
from fastfit import FastFitTrainer

trainer = FastFitTrainer(
  model_name_or_path=
    "roberta-large",
  label_column_name="label_text",
  text_column_name="text",
  dataset=dataset,
)

model = trainer.train()
results = trainer.evaluate()
```

As FastFit utilizes example texts and class names, it expects the data to have `text` and `label` fields or to map the existing fields to them using the `label_column_name` and `text_column_name` parameters of the `FastFitTrainer`. Our trainer also supports training with either CLS or token-level similarity metrics, set by the `sim_rep` parameter. The trainer allows to modify the number of augmentation repetitions with the `num_repeats` parameter. Then after training, we can easily save the model:

```
model.save_pretrained("fast-fit")
```

And later load it for inference, See App. §A.

3 Method

Given a few-shot text classification dataset containing texts and their corresponding classes denoted as $\{x_i, y_i\}_{i=1}^{N}$, let $C = \{c_j\}_{j=1}^{M}$ represent all possible classes. Our task is to classify each x_i into a class $y_i \in C$. To achieve this goal we aim to encode both texts and class names into a shared embedding space, where they are represented closely, according to a similarity metric S, when they belong to the same class and are represented further apart when they do not. To accomplish this, we optimize the following batch contrastive loss:

$$\mathcal{L} = \sum_{b \in [B]} \frac{-1}{|P(b)|} \sum_{p \in P(b)} \log \frac{e^{S(x^b, x^p)/\tau}}{\sum_{a \in [B] \setminus b} e^{S(x^b, x^a)/\tau}} \quad (1)$$

Here, $\{x_b\}_{b=1}^{B}$ represents a batch of B texts, and $P(b)$ refers to the set of texts in the same class as b in the batch, given by $P(b) = \{c \in [B], |, y_c = y_b\}$. The function S is the similarity metric, and τ is a scalar temperature parameter regulating the penalty for negative texts.

For each text in the batch, we augment the batch by including its class name as an additional example. Additionally, we repeat the texts in the batch r times as a data augmentation technique, following Gao et al. (2021) by treating the dropout as a minimal augmentation at the representation level. This method has demonstrated significant success in generating sentence embeddings, and we leverage it here to enhance representation for text classification.

In our data-scarce setting, we employ fine-grained token-level similarity metrics, leveraging textual details. This approach, successful in works like BERT-Score and ColBERT, defines the similarity metric between texts x_i and x_j as the sum of cosine similarities between x_i and the most similar tokens in x_j. Specifically, with tokens denoted as $x_i^1, \ldots, x_i^n$ and $x_j^1, \ldots, x_j^m$ respectively, the similarity score is computed as follows:

$$S(x_i, x_j) = \sum_{k=1}^{n} \max_{l=1}^{m} E_\theta(x_i^k) \cdot E_\theta(x_j^l) \quad (2)$$

where $E_\theta(x_i^k)$ is a dense representation of token x_i^k produced by a parametric encoder model with parameters θ.

During inference, when provided with a new text, x_u we classify it to the most similar class $y_i \in C$ with respect to a similarity metric S. This method draws inspiration from the way inference is conducted in retrieval systems, eliminating the need for a classification head and aligning the training and inference objectives.

4 Experiments

4.1 Datasets

We experiment with three English few-shot text classification datasets: Hwu64 (Liu et al., 2019a), Banking77 (Casanueva et al., 2020), and Clinc150 (Larson et al., 2019). The datasets have between 64 and 150 classes. Many classes are semantically similar, making the classification tasks much harder. We conduct our experiments in 5/10-shot scenarios where in the k-shot scenario the training set consisted of k examples per class. See App. §B for full data statistics.

4.2 Baselines

We compare FastFit with a few classification methods, including fine-tuning methods, like Standard and SetFit classifiers, and few-shot promoting of LLMs including Flan-XXL (Wei et al., 2022), Flan-ul2 (Tay et al., 2023), llama-2-70b-chat (Touvron et al., 2023), and Mistral-7b (Jiang et al., 2023). For all fine-tuning methods, we use small and large versions, where small is MPNet (110M parameters) (Song et al., 2020), and large is Roberta-large (355M parameters)(Liu et al., 2019b) or equivalent.

Standard classifier. A simple yet strong baseline is a standard fine-tuning of an encoder-only model. Since we assume no validation sets, we use best practices as described in previous works, and train for 40 epochs, with a learning rate of $1e-5$, and batch size of 16 (Lin et al., 2023). We recovered runs that didn't converge.

SetFit. Sentence Transformer Fine-tuning (SetFit) (Tunstall et al., 2022) is a two-stage method for training a Sentence Transformer model (Reimers and Gurevych, 2019), specifically designed for few-shot classification tasks. In the first stage, the encoder undergoes fine-tuning using triplet loss, and in the second stage, the classification head is trained. For the small model we use `paraphrase-mpnet-base-v2`[2], and for the large model, we used `all-Roberta-Large-v1`[3], both trained with sentence transformer objective before. We trained the model with a learning rate of $1e-5$, a batch size of 16, for one epoch, based on the parameters defined in SetFit's paper.

Flan. Flan language models are fine-tuned on a diverse range of NLP tasks and datasets, making them adaptable for various NLP tasks in a few-shot manner. Here, we experimented with Flan-XXL (11B) and Flan-ul2 (20B) models. These models have a 4K tokens context window.

Llama. Llama-2-chat is a set of large language models developed for conversational applications and has strong multi-task few-shot capabilities. Here, we experimented with a Llama model that supports a 4K tokens context window.

Mistral. Mistral is a strong 7B open-source large language model. Here, we used the instruct-tuned version. Mistral supports an 8K tokens context window.

4.3 Experimental Setup

Training Setup. We fine-tune the FastFit model with a learning rate of $1e-5$, a batch size of 32, and a maximum sequence length of 128 tokens, for 40 epochs. We used AdamW optimizer, 16-bit floating-point (FP16) precision, and applied 4 batch repetitions that acts as augmentations.

All LLMs, except Mistral, have a context window of 4K. We were able to fit 1 example into their context for Clinc150 and Banking77, and 3 examples for Hwu64. Mistral, with an 8K context window allows for 2, 3, and 5 examples from Clinc150, Banking77, and Hwu64, respectively.

Evaluation Setup. Few-shot evaluations can be noisy due to variations in the small datasets (Dodge et al., 2020; Zhang et al., 2021). To address this challenge, we perform all our experiments using 5 random training split variations and report the mean results.

4.4 Results

In Table 1, we present the results of FastFit, SetFit, and the standard classifier for three datasets under 5/10-shot settings. FastFit large outperforms SetFit by 2.1% and the standard classifier by 3.4%. FastFit small outperforms SetFit by 3.4% and the standard classifier by 5.1%, achieving comparable results to SetFit large. Notably, FastFit shows

[2]ST-MPNet

[3]ST-Roberta-Large

Method	Size	CLINC150		BANKING77		HWU64		Average
		5	10	5	10	5	10	
FastFit	S	90.2	93.3	80.1	85.4	79.8	84.7	85.6
	L	**92.2***	**94.8***	**83.0***	**87.9***	**82.9***	**86.3***	**87.9***
SetFit	S	86.9	90.5	74.3	81.9	77.8	81.8	82.2
	L	90.7	93.1	79.1	86.4	81.0	84.6	85.8
Classfier	S	86.0	91.4	68.1	80.4	74.4	82.9	80.5
	L	89.2	94.0	75.9	86.1	76.3	85.5	84.5

Table 1: Accuracy results of FastFit and baselines on 5/10-shot text classification. Results show that FastFit outperforms SetFit and standard classfier. Moreover, FastFit small is comparable to SetFit large. Results with * are statistically significant by t-test ($p < 0.05$) compared to the large standard classifier.

Model	C150	B77	H64	Avg.
Flan-ul2	80.3	71.5	**76.2**	76.0
Flan-XXL	**82.1**	**72.1**	74.9	**76.3**
Llama-2-13B-chat	53.0	42.6	53.2	49.6
Llama-2-70B-chat	60.8	45.7	62.8	56.4
Mistral-7B	63.5	46.8	71.7	60.7

Table 2: Accuracy results of a few LLMs models. The Flan models outperform the other LLMs. Llama-70B scores higher than Llama-13B but less than Mistral, which has a larger context window.

greater improvement in the 5-shot case compared to the 10-shot case and for the small model compared to the large one.

Table 2 displays the results of few-shot prompting for several LLMs. The Flan models exhibit higher performance than other LLMs, likely due to the presence of many classification datasets in the Flan dataset, which do not include our test sets. This observation aligns with findings in zero-shot classification (Gretz et al., 2023). Although Llama-70B outperforms Llama-13B, it falls short of Mistral-7B's performance, possibly due to Mistral's larger context length, allowing it to incorporate more examples per class.

The results suggest that in our setting, where numerous classes are present, even the best-performing LLMs we tested (Flan's) underperform compared to large standard classifiers and face challenges compared to FastFit. It's important to note that, due to the model's size and the length of the few-shot prompt, inference time can be slow, with throughput exceeding 1 second per input, in contrast to about 1 millisecond with FastFit.

5 Multilingual Experiments

5.1 Datasets

To evaluate FastFit's multilingual classification abilities we adopt Amazon Multilingual MASSIVE dataset (FitzGerald et al., 2022). From the 51 available languages, we selected six typologically diverse languages: English, Japanese, German, French, Spanish, and Chinese. MASSIVE is a parallel dataset, with 60 classes (See App. §B).

5.2 Baselines

For multilingual training, we utilized paraphrase-multilingual-mpnet-base-v2 as a small model and XLM-Roberta-Large as a large model. Both models underwent pretraining in a large number of languages. Notably, to the best of our knowledge, there is no multilingual sentence transformer model equivalent to Roberta-Large for SetFit training. Monolingual and XLM-Roberta-Large models were tested, but they yielded lower performance than the small model; hence, their results are detailed in Appendix §C. In English experiments, we maintained the use of monolingual models (see §4.2), conducting training and evaluation with the same setup outlined in §4.3.

5.3 Results

In Table 3, we present the results on MASSIVE in 5/10-shot scenarios using FastFit, SetFit, and the standard classifier. FastFit consistently outperforms both SetFit and the standard classifier in both 5-shot and 10-shot settings, across small and large models. In the 5-shot scenario, FastFit large achieve an 8% improvement over SetFit small and a 12.4% improvement over the standard classifier. Meanwhile, FastFit small shows a 2.7% improvement over SetFit small and a 7.1% improvement over the standard classifier. In the 10-shot case,

Method	Size	En	De	Ja	Es	Fr	Zh	Average
				5-shot				
FastFit	S	72.3	65.0	68.7	65.9	68.0	68.4	68.1
	L	**77.6***	**70.5***	**73.7***	**71.7***	**73.1***	**73.7***	**73.4***
SetFit	S	67.9	62.2	66.8	64.0	65.0	66.7	65.4
Classfier	S	61.2	56.8	59.7	58.4	59.8	61.4	59.5
	L	66.4	56.0	65.3	56.6	60.0	61.9	61.0
				10-shot				
FastFit	S	77.6	70.5	73.7	71.7	73.1	73.7	73.4
	L	**79.2***	**74.8***	**77.4**	**74.1***	**75.7***	**74.9***	**76.0***
SetFit	S	74.7	69.8	73.5	71.4	72.0	72.9	72.4
Classfier	S	72.2	67.7	71.0	68.6	69.7	70.0	69.9
	L	77.5	71.2	74.3	71.3	72.5	72.7	73.3

Table 3: Accuracy results for FastFit and baselines across six languages, under 5/10-shot settings. Results show that FastFit consistently outperforms SetFit and the standard classifier. Notably, FastFit small consistently surpasses SetFit's small and standard large classifiers. Results marked with an asterisk (*) are statistically significant according to t-test ($p < 0.05$) when compared to the large standard classifier.

FastFit large outperforms SetFit small by 3.6% and the standard large classifier by 2.7%. Similarly, FastFit small exhibits improvements of 1.9% and 3.5% over SetFit small and the standard classifier, respectively.

It is noteworthy that FastFit demonstrates improvement when scaling from a small to a large model, with gains of 5.3% and 2.6% in the 5-shot and 10-shot settings, respectively. This enhancement highlights the fact that FastFit is not model-specific and thus is highly flexible for different sizes and types of models, unlike SetFit. Such flexibility is particularly crucial in few-shot settings where limited examples are available, highlighting the potential to train enhanced classifiers using domain- or language-specific models. Moreover, if unlabeled or pairwise data is available, using it for pretraining can lead to even further improvement.

Training Times for FastFit, SetFit, and the standard classifier are illustrated in Figure 1. FastFit exhibits faster training times compared to both SetFit and the standard classifier, with a 3-20x decrease, and training ranging between 35-70 seconds (See more results at App. §D). This can be attributed to a combination of technical and methodological factors. The improved implementation includes pretraining tokenization and FP16 training. Furthermore, the methodological advantage stems from using batch contrastive training, which leverages in-batch examples as negatives, in contrast to the triplet loss utilized by SetFit.

6 FastFit Ablation & Full Training

To further examine the contribution of some of our method modifications, we compare training with CLS and token-level similarity metrics, as well as training with a different number of batch repetitions. We conduct these experiments on three datasets: Hwu64, Banking77, and Clinc150, with 5 random splits, and average their results. We assess the effect of these modifications for both small and large models, with 5 and 10 shots.

In Table 4, we present the differences in performance caused by our changes; full results are available in App. §E. The Token-level similarity metric proves beneficial across all settings, with a more pronounced effect for smaller models and when less data is available (5-shot compared to 10-shot). Concerning the number of repetitions, we observe that, in most cases, adding repetitions helps. Additionally, it appears that overall, four repetitions are more effective than two. Regarding the relationship between the number of shots and the effectiveness of repetition, no clear connection is apparent. While an increase in the number of shots enhances effectiveness in small models, the opposite is observed for large models, where the effect decreases. Nevertheless, it seems that, in general, larger models benefit more from batch repetition.

Although our primary focus is few-shot classification, we also wanted to examine the effectiveness of FastFit when training on the full dataset. We conducted two sets of experiments. In the first,

Model	Shot	Similarity Level	Repetitions	
		Token	2	4
FastFit-S	5	1.33	-0.28	0.09
FastFit-S	10	0.85	0.09	0.24
FastFit-L	5	0.65	0.72	1.04
FastFit-L	10	0.36	0.55	0.78

Table 4: FastFit ablation experiments; Accuracy differences in training with token-level versus CLS similarity metrics and increasing augmentations repetitions. Token-level enhancements are more prominent in smaller models, especially in the 5-shot setting.

Model	C150	B77	H64	Avg.
Classfier-L	96.8	93.7	92.1	94.2
FastFit-S	97.1	93.8	92.7	94.5
FastFit-L	**97.5**	**94.2**	**93.0**	**94.9**

Table 5: FastFit accuracy results when training on the full data.

Model	EN	DE	JP	ES	FR	CN	Avg.
Classfier-B	88.3	85.7	83.9	86.9	86.3	84.9	86.0
mT5-B T2T	87.9	86.2	83.5	86.7	86.9	85.2	86.1
mT5-B Enc	89.0	86.8	85.8	86.8	87.2	85.8	86.9
FastFit-S	88.8	87.4	87.0	**87.9**	87.6	**86.7**	87.6
FastFit-L	**89.5**	**88.5**	**88.5**	87.4	**88.5**	**86.7**	**88.2**

Table 6: FastFit and baselines accuracy results on MASSIVE with full data training.

we compared FastFit-small, FastFit-large, and a large standard classifier on Hwu64, Banking77, and Clinc150. In the second, we compared FastFit-small and FastFit-large with a few base-sized multilingual baseline models on Msstive, using the set of six languages mentioned in §5.1. These baselines are based on the Msstive paper, where Classifier-B and mT5-B Encoder are standard classifiers based on XLM-R-BASE and mT5-Base with 270M and 258M parameters, respectively. mT5-B T2T is a text-2-text classifier with 580M parameters.

Results in Table 5 demonstrate that when training on all the data, FastFit-Small outperforms the large Classifier, and FastFit-Large performs even better. From Table 6, we can see that FastFit-Small outperforms all other baselines even with fewer than half the number of parameters. Moreover, FastFit-Large further improves performances by 0.6% on average. These results indicate that FastFit is not only a fast few-shot classifier but can also outperform even larger classifiers when training on the full dataset.

7 Related Work

For fine-tuning baselines, we focus on readily available methods. , including SetFit with its package, a standard classifier accessible through HF Transformers (Wolf et al., 2019), or LLMs through API calls. However, there are various few-shot classifiers, and we will briefly discuss a couple of them. QAID (Yehudai et al., 2023) proposed pre- and fine-tuning training stages with unsupervised and supervised loss, using ColBERT architecture, achieving SOTA results. T-Few (Liu et al., 2022), a parameter-efficient fine-tuning method based on T0 (Sanh et al., 2021), claims to be better and cheaper than In-Context Learning.

Regarding few-shot prompting of LLMs approaches, a question arises about whether our results will withstand stronger LLMs or improved prompting techniques. According to Loukas et al. (2023) we can deduce that FastFit outperforms GPT4 (OpenAI et al., 2023) with a fraction of the cost. Additionally, Milios et al. (2023) demonstrate that retrieval-based few-shot prompts can lead to improved results. However, it's worth noting that currently, these models remain slow and costly.

8 Conclusions

In this paper, we introduce FastFit, a novel few-shot text classification method accompanied by a Python package. Our results demonstrate that FastFit outperforms large language models (LLMs) such as Flan-XXL and Llama-2-chat-70B, as well as fine-tuning methods, including both standard and SetFit classifiers, readily available in existing packages. Notably, FastFit exhibits fast training and inference. We provide evidence that these results hold for both Multilingual and full-data training setups. We hope that FastFit's speed and simplicity will enhance its usability.

References

Iñigo Casanueva, Tadas Temčinas, Daniela Gerz, Matthew Henderson, and Ivan Vulić. 2020. Efficient intent detection with dual sentence encoders. *arXiv preprint arXiv:2003.04807*.

Jesse Dodge, Gabriel Ilharco, Roy Schwartz, Ali Farhadi, Hannaneh Hajishirzi, and Noah Smith. 2020. Fine-tuning pretrained language models: Weight initializations, data orders, and early stopping.

Jack FitzGerald, Christopher Hench, Charith Peris, Scott Mackie, Kay Rottmann, Ana Sanchez, Aaron

Nash, Liam Urbach, Vishesh Kakarala, Richa Singh, Swetha Ranganath, Laurie Crist, Misha Britan, Wouter Leeuwis, Gokhan Tur, and Prem Natarajan. 2022. Massive: A 1m-example multilingual natural language understanding dataset with 51 typologically-diverse languages.

Tianyu Gao, Xingcheng Yao, and Danqi Chen. 2021. SimCSE: Simple contrastive learning of sentence embeddings. In *Proceedings of the 2021 Conference on Empirical Methods in Natural Language Processing*, pages 6894–6910, Online and Punta Cana, Dominican Republic. Association for Computational Linguistics.

Shai Gretz, Alon Halfon, Ilya Shnayderman, Orith Toledo-Ronen, Artem Spector, Lena Dankin, Yannis Katsis, Ofir Arviv, Yoav Katz, Noam Slonim, and Liat Ein-Dor. 2023. Zero-shot topical text classification with LLMs - an experimental study. In *Findings of the Association for Computational Linguistics: EMNLP 2023*, pages 9647–9676, Singapore. Association for Computational Linguistics.

Albert Q. Jiang, Alexandre Sablayrolles, Arthur Mensch, Chris Bamford, Devendra Singh Chaplot, Diego de las Casas, Florian Bressand, Gianna Lengyel, Guillaume Lample, Lucile Saulnier, Lélio Renard Lavaud, Marie-Anne Lachaux, Pierre Stock, Teven Le Scao, Thibaut Lavril, Thomas Wang, Timothée Lacroix, and William El Sayed. 2023. Mistral 7b.

Omar Khattab and Matei Zaharia. 2020. Colbert: Efficient and effective passage search via contextualized late interaction over bert.

Prannay Khosla, Piotr Teterwak, Chen Wang, Aaron Sarna, Yonglong Tian, Phillip Isola, Aaron Maschinot, Ce Liu, and Dilip Krishnan. 2021. Supervised contrastive learning.

Stefan Larson, Anish Mahendran, Joseph J Peper, Christopher Clarke, Andrew Lee, Parker Hill, Jonathan K Kummerfeld, Kevin Leach, Michael A Laurenzano, Lingjia Tang, et al. 2019. An evaluation dataset for intent classification and out-of-scope prediction. *arXiv preprint arXiv:1909.02027*.

Yen-Ting Lin, Alexandros Papangelis, Seokhwan Kim, Sungjin Lee, Devamanyu Hazarika, Mahdi Namazifar, Di Jin, Yang Liu, and Dilek Z. Hakkani-Tür. 2023. Selective in-context data augmentation for intent detection using pointwise v-information. In *Conference of the European Chapter of the Association for Computational Linguistics*.

Haokun Liu, Derek Tam, Mohammed Muqeeth, Jay Mohta, Tenghao Huang, Mohit Bansal, and Colin Raffel. 2022. Few-shot parameter-efficient fine-tuning is better and cheaper than in-context learning. *ArXiv*, abs/2205.05638.

Nelson F. Liu, Kevin Lin, John Hewitt, Ashwin Paranjape, Michele Bevilacqua, Fabio Petroni, and Percy Liang. 2023. Lost in the middle: How language models use long contexts.

Xingkun Liu, Arash Eshghi, Pawel Swietojanski, and Verena Rieser. 2019a. Benchmarking natural language understanding services for building conversational agents. *arXiv preprint arXiv:1903.05566*.

Yinhan Liu, Myle Ott, Naman Goyal, Jingfei Du, Mandar Joshi, Danqi Chen, Omer Levy, Mike Lewis, Luke Zettlemoyer, and Veselin Stoyanov. 2019b. Roberta: A robustly optimized bert pretraining approach.

Lefteris Loukas, Ilias Stogiannidis, Odysseas Diamantopoulos, Prodromos Malakasiotis, and Stavros Vassos. 2023. Making llms worth every penny: Resource-limited text classification in banking. *Proceedings of the Fourth ACM International Conference on AI in Finance*.

Aristides Milios, Siva Reddy, and Dzmitry Bahdanau. 2023. In-context learning for text classification with many labels. *ArXiv*, abs/2309.10954.

OpenAI, :, Josh Achiam, Steven Adler, Sandhini Agarwal, Lama Ahmad, Ilge Akkaya, Florencia Leoni Aleman, Diogo Almeida, Janko Altenschmidt, Sam Altman, Shyamal Anadkat, Red Avila, Igor Babuschkin, Suchir Balaji, Valerie Balcom, Paul Baltescu, Haiming Bao, Mo Bavarian, Jeff Belgum, Irwan Bello, Jake Berdine, Gabriel Bernadett-Shapiro, Christopher Berner, Lenny Bogdonoff, Oleg Boiko, Madelaine Boyd, Anna-Luisa Brakman, Greg Brockman, Tim Brooks, Miles Brundage, Kevin Button, Trevor Cai, Rosie Campbell, Andrew Cann, Brittany Carey, Chelsea Carlson, Rory Carmichael, Brooke Chan, Che Chang, Fotis Chantzis, Derek Chen, Sully Chen, Ruby Chen, Jason Chen, Mark Chen, Ben Chess, Chester Cho, Casey Chu, Hyung Won Chung, Dave Cummings, Jeremiah Currier, Yunxing Dai, Cory Decareaux, Thomas Degry, Noah Deutsch, Damien Deville, Arka Dhar, David Dohan, Steve Dowling, Sheila Dunning, Adrien Ecoffet, Atty Eleti, Tyna Eloundou, David Farhi, Liam Fedus, Niko Felix, Simón Posada Fishman, Juston Forte, Isabella Fulford, Leo Gao, Elie Georges, Christian Gibson, Vik Goel, Tarun Gogineni, Gabriel Goh, Rapha Gontijo-Lopes, Jonathan Gordon, Morgan Grafstein, Scott Gray, Ryan Greene, Joshua Gross, Shixiang Shane Gu, Yufei Guo, Chris Hallacy, Jesse Han, Jeff Harris, Yuchen He, Mike Heaton, Johannes Heidecke, Chris Hesse, Alan Hickey, Wade Hickey, Peter Hoeschele, Brandon Houghton, Kenny Hsu, Shengli Hu, Xin Hu, Joost Huizinga, Shantanu Jain, Shawn Jain, Joanne Jang, Angela Jiang, Roger Jiang, Haozhun Jin, Denny Jin, Shino Jomoto, Billie Jonn, Heewoo Jun, Tomer Kaftan, Łukasz Kaiser, Ali Kamali, Ingmar Kanitscheider, Nitish Shirish Keskar, Tabarak Khan, Logan Kilpatrick, Jong Wook Kim, Christina Kim, Yongjik Kim, Hendrik Kirchner, Jamie Kiros, Matt Knight, Daniel Kokotajlo, Łukasz Kondraciuk, Andrew Kondrich, Aris Konstantinidis, Kyle Kosic, Gretchen Krueger, Vishal Kuo, Michael Lampe, Ikai Lan, Teddy Lee, Jan Leike, Jade Leung, Daniel Levy, Chak Ming Li, Rachel Lim, Molly Lin, Stephanie Lin, Mateusz Litwin, Theresa Lopez, Ryan Lowe, Patricia Lue,

Anna Makanju, Kim Malfacini, Sam Manning, Todor Markov, Yaniv Markovski, Bianca Martin, Katie Mayer, Andrew Mayne, Bob McGrew, Scott Mayer McKinney, Christine McLeavey, Paul McMillan, Jake McNeil, David Medina, Aalok Mehta, Jacob Menick, Luke Metz, Andrey Mishchenko, Pamela Mishkin, Vinnie Monaco, Evan Morikawa, Daniel Mossing, Tong Mu, Mira Murati, Oleg Murk, David Mély, Ashvin Nair, Reiichiro Nakano, Rajeev Nayak, Arvind Neelakantan, Richard Ngo, Hyeonwoo Noh, Long Ouyang, Cullen O'Keefe, Jakub Pachocki, Alex Paino, Joe Palermo, Ashley Pantuliano, Giambattista Parascandolo, Joel Parish, Emy Parparita, Alex Passos, Mikhail Pavlov, Andrew Peng, Adam Perelman, Filipe de Avila Belbute Peres, Michael Petrov, Henrique Ponde de Oliveira Pinto, Michael, Pokorny, Michelle Pokrass, Vitchyr Pong, Tolly Powell, Alethea Power, Boris Power, Elizabeth Proehl, Raul Puri, Alec Radford, Jack Rae, Aditya Ramesh, Cameron Raymond, Francis Real, Kendra Rimbach, Carl Ross, Bob Rotsted, Henri Roussez, Nick Ryder, Mario Saltarelli, Ted Sanders, Shibani Santurkar, Girish Sastry, Heather Schmidt, David Schnurr, John Schulman, Daniel Selsam, Kyla Sheppard, Toki Sherbakov, Jessica Shieh, Sarah Shoker, Pranav Shyam, Szymon Sidor, Eric Sigler, Maddie Simens, Jordan Sitkin, Katarina Slama, Ian Sohl, Benjamin Sokolowsky, Yang Song, Natalie Staudacher, Felipe Petroski Such, Natalie Summers, Ilya Sutskever, Jie Tang, Nikolas Tezak, Madeleine Thompson, Phil Tillet, Amin Tootoonchian, Elizabeth Tseng, Preston Tuggle, Nick Turley, Jerry Tworek, Juan Felipe Cerón Uribe, Andrea Vallone, Arun Vijayvergiya, Chelsea Voss, Carroll Wainwright, Justin Jay Wang, Alvin Wang, Ben Wang, Jonathan Ward, Jason Wei, CJ Weinmann, Akila Welihinda, Peter Welinder, Jiayi Weng, Lilian Weng, Matt Wiethoff, Dave Willner, Clemens Winter, Samuel Wolrich, Hannah Wong, Lauren Workman, Sherwin Wu, Jeff Wu, Michael Wu, Kai Xiao, Tao Xu, Sarah Yoo, Kevin Yu, Qiming Yuan, Wojciech Zaremba, Rowan Zellers, Chong Zhang, Marvin Zhang, Shengjia Zhao, Tianhao Zheng, Juntang Zhuang, William Zhuk, and Barret Zoph. 2023. Gpt-4 technical report.

Nils Reimers and Iryna Gurevych. 2019. Sentence-bert: Sentence embeddings using siamese bert-networks.

Victor Sanh, Albert Webson, Colin Raffel, Stephen H. Bach, Lintang Sutawika, Zaid Alyafeai, Antoine Chaffin, Arnaud Stiegler, Teven Le Scao, Arun Raja, Manan Dey, M Saiful Bari, Canwen Xu, Urmish Thakker, Shanya Sharma Sharma, Eliza Szczechla, Taewoon Kim, Gunjan Chhablani, Nihal V. Nayak, Debajyoti Datta, Jonathan D. Chang, Mike Tian-Jian Jiang, Han Wang, Matteo Manica, Sheng Shen, Zheng-Xin Yong, Harshit Pandey, Rachel Bawden, Thomas Wang, Trishala Neeraj, Jos Rozen, Abheesht Sharma, Andrea Santilli, Thibault Févry, Jason Alan Fries, Ryan Teehan, Stella Biderman, Leo Gao, Tali Bers, Thomas Wolf, and Alexander M. Rush. 2021. Multitask prompted training enables zero-shot task generalization. *ArXiv*, abs/2110.08207.

Kaitao Song, Xu Tan, Tao Qin, Jianfeng Lu, and Tie-Yan Liu. 2020. Mpnet: Masked and permuted pre-training for language understanding.

Yi Tay, Mostafa Dehghani, Vinh Q. Tran, Xavier Garcia, Jason Wei, Xuezhi Wang, Hyung Won Chung, Siamak Shakeri, Dara Bahri, Tal Schuster, Huaixiu Steven Zheng, Denny Zhou, Neil Houlsby, and Donald Metzler. 2023. Ul2: Unifying language learning paradigms.

Hugo Touvron, Louis Martin, Kevin Stone, Peter Albert, Amjad Almahairi, Yasmine Babaei, Nikolay Bashlykov, Soumya Batra, Prajjwal Bhargava, Shruti Bhosale, Dan Bikel, Lukas Blecher, Cristian Canton Ferrer, Moya Chen, Guillem Cucurull, David Esiobu, Jude Fernandes, Jeremy Fu, Wenyin Fu, Brian Fuller, Cynthia Gao, Vedanuj Goswami, Naman Goyal, Anthony Hartshorn, Saghar Hosseini, Rui Hou, Hakan Inan, Marcin Kardas, Viktor Kerkez, Madian Khabsa, Isabel Kloumann, Artem Korenev, Punit Singh Koura, Marie-Anne Lachaux, Thibaut Lavril, Jenya Lee, Diana Liskovich, Yinghai Lu, Yuning Mao, Xavier Martinet, Todor Mihaylov, Pushkar Mishra, Igor Molybog, Yixin Nie, Andrew Poulton, Jeremy Reizenstein, Rashi Rungta, Kalyan Saladi, Alan Schelten, Ruan Silva, Eric Michael Smith, Ranjan Subramanian, Xiaoqing Ellen Tan, Binh Tang, Ross Taylor, Adina Williams, Jian Xiang Kuan, Puxin Xu, Zheng Yan, Iliyan Zarov, Yuchen Zhang, Angela Fan, Melanie Kambadur, Sharan Narang, Aurelien Rodriguez, Robert Stojnic, Sergey Edunov, and Thomas Scialom. 2023. Llama 2: Open foundation and fine-tuned chat models.

Lewis Tunstall, Nils Reimers, Unso Eun Seo Jo, Luke Bates, Daniel Korat, Moshe Wasserblat, and Oren Pereg. 2022. Efficient few-shot learning without prompts.

Jason Wei, Maarten Bosma, Vincent Y. Zhao, Kelvin Guu, Adams Wei Yu, Brian Lester, Nan Du, Andrew M. Dai, and Quoc V. Le. 2022. Finetuned language models are zero-shot learners.

Thomas Wolf, Lysandre Debut, Victor Sanh, Julien Chaumond, Clement Delangue, Anthony Moi, Pierric Cistac, Tim Rault, Rémi Louf, Morgan Funtowicz, and Jamie Brew. 2019. Huggingface's transformers: State-of-the-art natural language processing. *ArXiv*, abs/1910.03771.

Asaf Yehudai, Matan Vetzler, Yosi Mass, Koren Lazar, Doron Cohen, and Boaz Carmeli. 2023. Qaid: Question answering inspired few-shot intent detection.

Tianyi Zhang, Varsha Kishore, Felix Wu, Kilian Q. Weinberger, and Yoav Artzi. 2020. Bertscore: Evaluating text generation with bert.

Tianyi Zhang, Felix Wu, Arzoo Katiyar, Kilian Q Weinberger, and Yoav Artzi. 2021. Revisiting few-sample {bert} fine-tuning. In *International Conference on Learning Representations*.

A Full Code Example

Any dataset can be loaded directly from Huggingface Hub, For example:

```
from datasets import load_dataset
dataset =
load_dataset("mteb/banking77")
```

Then fast fit library can sample it down to the 5 or 10 shot format:

```
from fastfit import sample_dataset

dataset["train"] =sample_dataset(
  dataset["train"],
  label_column="label",
  num_samples=5
)
```

Then once the data is ready it can be serve as input to the Fast-Fit trainer together with other important inputs:

```
from fastfit import FastFitTrainer

trainer = FastFitTrainer(
  model_name_or_path=
    "roberta-large",
  label_column_name="label_text",
  text_column_name="text",
  dataset=dataset,
)

model = trainer.train()
results = trainer.evaluate()
```

Then we can save the model:

```
model.save_pretrained("fast-fit")
```

And could be loaded for inference with:

```
from fastfit import FastFit from
transformers import (
  AutoTokenizer,
  pipeline
)

model = FastFit.from_pretrained(
  "fast-fit"
)
tokenizer =
AutoTokenizer.from_pretrained(
  "roberta-large"
)

classifier = pipeline(
  "text-classification",
  model=model,
  tokenizer=tokenizer
)

print(classifier("Hello World!"))
```

B Data Statistics

In Table 7, we provide the data statistics for the classification datasets used in our work.

Dataset	#Train	#Vaild	#Test	#Intents	#Domains
Clinc150	15,000	3,000	4,500	150	10
BankingG77	8,622	1,540	3,080	77	1
Hwu64	8,954	1,076	1,076	64	21
MASSIVE	11,514	2,033	2,974	60	18

Table 7: Data statistics of the few-shot classification datasets.

C Multilingual Results

In Table 10, we present the experimental results using various backbone models for SetFit. We evaluated three models: (1) Monolingual sentence-transformer (ST) large, referred to as ST-L. (2) Regular Multilingual RoBERTa-large, denoted as XLM-R-L or simply L. (3) RoBERTa-Base Multilingual sentence-transformer model, labeled as ST-XB.

The results indicate that ST-L encounters difficulties with all non-English datasets, resulting in overall inferior performance. XLM-R-L exhibits lower proficiency in English but demonstrates improved results across all other languages. Lastly, ST-XB, with a comparable size to the small models

(125M vs. 110M), achieved similar, albeit slightly lower, results. These findings underscore SetFit's dependence on ST pre-trained models and highlight its limitations when such a model is unavailable, as in this experiment.

D Training Run Times Results

Here we present more training run time results for FastFit, SetFit, and a standard classifier. In 2 we present the run time for the small and large settings. In Table 9 we show the average training run time results.

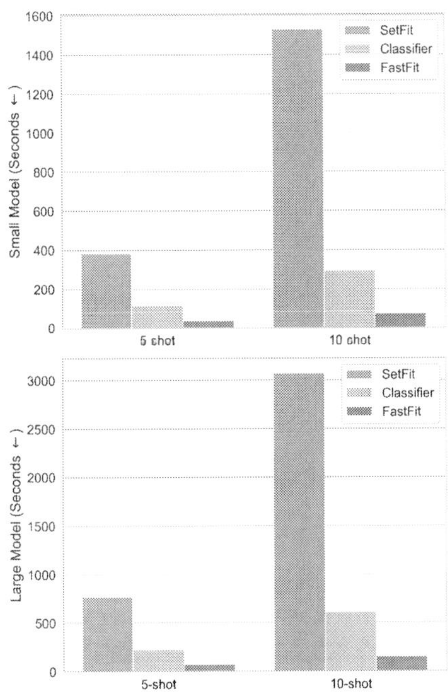

Figure 2: Training times (sec) for FastFit, SetFit, and standard classifier. FastFit training is faster both for the small model (top) and for the large model (bottom).

Table 8: Results

Model	Small		Large	
	5-shot	10-shot	5-shot	10-shot
FastFit	35.5	73.2	72.7	151.0
SetFit	384.1	1530.5	767.1	3073.7
classifier	112.0	294.8	230.6	606.7

Table 9: Training times (sec) for FastFit, SetFit, and standard classifier.

E Ablation Results

Here, we present the results for the ablations associated with Table 4. The first ablation is designed to measure the effect of the similarity metrics. Table 11 shows the results of the experiments with both CLS and token-level similarity metrics. In Table 12, we present the results without augmentation repetitions (1), and with 2 and 4 repetitions. Both ablations support our claim that the token-level similarity metric and an increased number of augmentation repetitions help.

F Short Video

Click here for our short presentation.

Method	Model	En	De	Ja	Es	Fr	Zh	Average
				5-shot				
FastFit	S	72.3	65.0	68.7	65.9	68.0	68.4	68.1
	L	**77.6***	**70.5***	**73.7***	**71.7***	**73.1***	**73.7***	**73.4***
SetFit	S	67.9	62.2	66.8	64.0	65.0	66.7	65.4
	ST-L	74.0	50.3	41.3	53.6	52.1	39.6	51.8
	L	66.1	60.8	64.8	50.1	61.3	43.6	57.8
	ST-XB	74.0	62.3	64.8	62.0	62.3	65.1	65.1
				10-shot				
FastFit	S	77.6	70.5	73.7	71.7	73.1	73.7	73.4
	L	**79.2***	**74.8***	**77.4**	**74.1***	**75.7***	**74.9***	**76.0***
SetFit	S	74.7	69.8	73.5	71.4	72.0	72.9	72.4
	ST-L	78.3	61.4	53.4	64.0	63.2	48.3	61.4
	L	74.5	69.1	72.5	69.7	70.7	59.2	69.3
	ST-XB	78.3	68.7	72.9	70.1	70.5	72.3	72.1

Table 10: Accuracy results for FastFit and baselines across six languages, under 5/10-shot settings. Results with few SetFit versions but no one surpasses SetFit small. We experimenting here with sentence-transformer (ST) large monolingual, multilingual base, and non-ST multilingual large.

Method	Shots	Sim. metric	C150	B77	H64	Average
FastFit-small	5	CLS	88.9	78.6	78.5	82.0
	5	TOK.	90.2	80.0	79.7	**83.3**
	10	CLS	92.4	84.7	83.8	86.9
	10	TOK.	93.3	85.4	84.7	**87.8**
FastFit-large	5	CLS	91.6	81.7	82.4	85.2
	5	TOK.	92.3	82.9	82.4	**85.9**
	10	CLS	94.1	87.6	86.3	89.4
	10	TOK.	94.8	88.0	86.4	**89.7**

Table 11: Ablation results with CLS and token-level similarity metrics. The average results that scored the highest for each model size and shot number are highlighted in bold.

Method	Shots	Repet.	C150	B77	H64	Average
	5	1	90.3	80.3	79.1	83.2
FastFit-small	5	2	89.8	79.8	79.2	82.9
	5	4	90.2	80.0	79.7	**83.3**
	10	1	93.3	85.3	84.1	87.6
FastFit-small	10	2	93.2	85.3	84.5	87.6
	10	4	93.3	85.4	84.7	**87.8**
	5	1	91.6	82.0	81.0	84.8
FastFit-Large	5	2	92.0	82.4	82.3	85.6
	5	4	92.3	82.9	82.4	**85.9**
	10	1	94.2	87.3	85.2	88.9
FastFit-Large	10	2	94.6	87.7	86.1	89.5
	10	4	94.8	88.0	86.4	**89.7**

Table 12: Ablation results with varying repetition numbers. The bolded values represent the highest-scoring average results for each model size and shot number.

AgentQuest: A Modular Benchmark Framework to Measure Progress and Improve LLM Agents

Luca Gioacchini[1,2], Giuseppe Siracusano[1], Davide Sanvito[1], Kiril Gashteovski[1,3], David Friede[1], Roberto Bifulco[1], Carolin Lawrence[1]
[1] NEC Laboratories Europe, Heidelberg, Germany
[2] Politecnico di Torino, Turin, Italy
[3] CAIR, Ss. Cyril and Methodius University, Skopje, North Macedonia

Abstract

The advances made by Large Language Models (LLMs) have led to the pursuit of LLM agents that can solve intricate, multi-step reasoning tasks. As with any research pursuit, benchmarking and evaluation are key corner stones to efficient and reliable progress. However, existing benchmarks are often narrow and simply compute overall task success. To face these issues, we propose AgentQuest[1] – a framework where (i) both benchmarks and metrics are modular and easily extensible through well documented and easy-to-use APIs; (ii) we offer two new evaluation metrics that can reliably track LLM agent progress while solving a task. We exemplify the utility of the metrics on two use cases wherein we identify common failure points and refine the agent architecture to obtain a significant performance increase. Together with the research community, we hope to extend AgentQuest further and therefore we make it available under `https://github.com/nec-research/agentquest`.

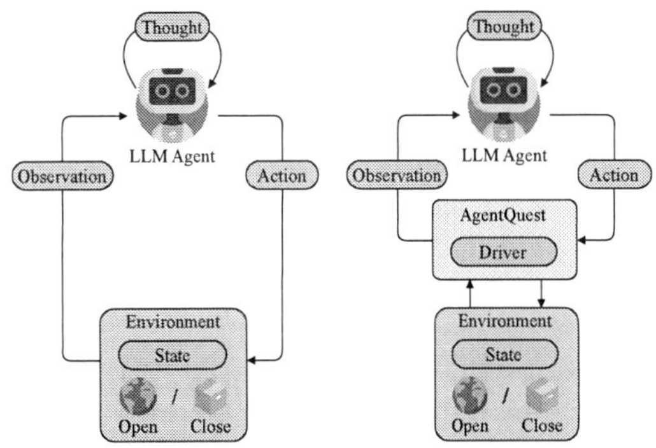

(a) Existing (b) AgentQuest

Figure 1: Overview of agent-benchmark interactions in existing frameworks and in AgentQuest. AgentQuest defines a common interface to interact with the benchmarks and to compute progress metrics, easing the addition of new benchmarks and allowing researchers to evaluate and debug their agent architectures.

1 Introduction

Generative Agents (Kiela et al., 2023) are software systems that leverage foundation models like Large Language Models (LLMs) to perform complex tasks, take decisions, devise multi-steps plans and use tools (API calls, coding, etc.) to build solutions in heterogeneous contexts (Wang et al., 2023; Weng, 2023). The potential ability to solve heterogeneous tasks with high degrees of autonomy has catalysed the interest of both research and industrial communities. Nonetheless, it is still unclear to which extent current systems are successfully able to fulfil their promises. In fact, methodologies to benchmark, evaluate and advance these systems are still in their early days.

We identify a couple of gaps. Firstly, benchmarking agents requires combining different benchmark types (Liu et al., 2023; Chalamalasetti et al., 2023). For example, some benchmarks focus on specific capabilities and provide gaming environments, which we refer to as "closed-box" – i.e. with a finite set of actions (Liu et al., 2023; Patil et al., 2023; Chalamalasetti et al., 2023) – whereas other benchmarks provide open-ended tasks and access to general tools, like web browsing (Zhuang et al., 2023; Zheng et al., 2023; Mialon et al., 2023). As benchmarks are developed independently, significant effort goes into custom integration of new agent architectures with each benchmark.

Secondly, and more critically, existing benchmarks mostly focus on providing a *success rate* measure, i.e. a binary success/fail evaluation for each of the proposed tasks. While success rate is helpful to measure overall advances of an agent technology, it has limited use in guiding improvements for new generative agent architectures. Here, it is important to consider that generative agents often combine foundation models with multiple other components, such as memory and tools. Develop-

[1]Demo provided at `https://youtu.be/0JNkIfwnoak`.

Proceedings of the 2024 Conference of the North American Chapter of the Association for Computational Linguistics: Human Language Technologies (Volume 3: System Demonstrations), pages 185–193
June 16-21, 2024 ©2024 Association for Computational Linguistics

ers can reason about these individual components in terms of architecture and their inter-dependence, and could actively change and evolve them using deeper insights about how an agent performs in a benchmark. That is, developers need benchmarks to both evaluate and *debug* agents.

For example, current benchmarks make it hard to answer questions like *does the agent fail completely the tasks or does it partially solve them? Does the agent fail consistently at a certain step? Would extra run time lead to finding a solution?* Answering these questions would require tracing and inspecting the execution of the agent. We argue that providing a more efficient approach that is consistent over multiple benchmarks is a stepping stone towards evolving generative agents.

We address these gaps introducing AgentQuest, a modular framework to support multiple diverse benchmarks and agent architectures (See Figure 1), alongside with two new metrics – i.e. progress rate and repetition rate – to debug an agent architecture behaviour. AgentQuest defines a standard interface to connect an arbitrary agent architecture with diverse benchmarks, and to compute progress and repetition rates from them.

We showcase the framework, implementing 4 benchmarks in AgentQuest: ALFWorld (Shridhar et al., 2020), Lateral Thinking Puzzles (Sloane, 1992), Mastermind and Sudoku. The latter two are newly introduced with AgentQuest. Additional benchmarks can be easily added, while requiring no changes to the tested agents.

Our final contribution is to present our experience leveraging the proposed metrics to debug and improve existing agent architectures as implemented in LangChain (Chase, 2022). In particular, we show that in the Mastermind benchmark the combination of progress rate and repetition rate identifies a limitation in the ability of the agent to explore the full space of potential solutions. Guided by this insight we could improve the success rate in this benchmark by up to $\approx$20%. In Lateral Thinking Puzzles we show that partially repeating actions is part of the agent strategy, whereas in ALFWorld, we show that monitoring the progress rate makes it possible to identify that the final success rate is limited by the allowed runtime of the agent, and that more steps lead to a better performance. Finally, in the Sudoku benchmark, we show that the low success rate is actually paired with low progress rate, making clear that the tested agent is unable to solve this type of tasks.

2 Generative AI Agents in a Nutshell

Generative AI agents are automated systems relying on software components integrated with LLMs pre-trained on large amount of data for language understanding and processing. When assigned a task, an agent engages in a systematic process: it iteratively formulates self-generated instructions, executes them, and observes the outcomes until the ultimate objective is achieved. Next, we showcase the basic interaction between agents and the environment in which they operate and describe the standard benchmarking techniques.

2.1 Agent-Environment interaction

Closely following the terminology in Reinforcement Learning (RL)[2] (Sutton and Barto, 2018), the core elements defining the agent-environment interaction are *environment*, *state*, *observation* and *action* (see Figure 1a).

Environment and states. The environment refers to the external system the agent interacts with. In this context, we treat the benchmark and the environment as synonyms. It is typically described through a finite set of hidden *states*, which are not directly observable by the agent and represent the benchmark configuration.

Observations and actions. The agent interacts with the environment for multiple execution steps. At each step, the environment produces an *observation* providing information about its current hidden state. The agent uses the internal LLM to process the received observation. Being pre-trained on general knowledge data, the LLM engages a reasoning process generating a *thought* on the observation (e.g. the planned strategy to follow in the current step or the usage of a tool). According to this thought, the agent provides the environment an *action* to modify the current hidden state. [3]

The following is an example of an agent interacting with a closed-box environment to solve a code-breaking challenge, i.e. the Mastermind game (Stuckman and Zhang, 2005). The agent is tasked to guess a four-digit code. At each step, the agent devises a strategy and acts accordingly to guess the code. The environment provides a feedback on the number of guessed digits in correct

[2]Unlike RL scenarios, the agent does not need a further training process. It relies on the pre-trained LLM and does not perform an action under the influence of any reward.

[3]Unlike RL, the LLM outputs are unconstrained, and any provided action is considered valid.

and wrong positions. The process continues until a stopping condition is met.

```
ENVIRONMENT: Initializing a new environment...
OBSERVATION: Start guessing the 4 digits code.
THOUGHT: I'll start by guessing 1234 to get an idea of which
of these numbers are in the secret number and if any are in
the correct position.
ACTION: 1234

ENVIRONMENT: Comparing the guessed code with the truth...
OBSERVATION: Your guess has 1 correct numbers in the wrong
position and 0 correct numbers in the correct position.
Keep guessing...
THOUGHT: One of the digits 1, 2, 3, or 4 is correct but in
the wrong position. I'll try to move each digit to a
different position to see if I can get a correct position.
ACTION: 2143
...
```

2.2 Benchmarking an agent

When evaluating agents performance on a benchmark, the following two metrics are commonly used (Liu et al., 2023): (i) Success Rate (SR), i.e. the ratio of successful tasks to the total instances; (ii) Time to Success, i.e. the average time required to obtain a solution. While important and trending metrics (Chalamalasetti et al., 2023; Hessel et al., 2022; Zhang et al., 2020a), they exclusively address the final success. They cannot measure intermediate success or failure and therefore make it difficult to understand why agents might systematically fail and how they can be improved. In contrast, we want to define intermediate metrics that allow us to easily assess and compare the performance of agents across a wide range of tasks.

3 AgentQuest Overview

We designed AgentQuest as a separation layer between agent and environment (see Figure 1b). Essentially, it offers (i) a unified interface (i.e. the *driver*) ensuring compatibility between different agent architectures and benchmarks with minimal programming efforts (Section 3.1); (ii) the implementation of two metrics beyond task success (i.e. *progress rate* and *repetition rate*) aimed at monitoring the agent advancement toward the final goal and allowing us to understand the reasons behind failures (Section 3.2); (iii) a unique vantage point and interface for implementing new metrics to monitoring and measuring the execution (Section 3.3).

3.1 Benchmarks common interface

Different benchmarks require invoking distinct functions, using specific formats, and performing parsing and post-processing of observations and agent actions. To integrate different agent architectures, the common trend is hardcoding such benchmark-specific requirements directly in the framework (Liu et al. 2023; Chalamalasetti et al. 2023, *inter alia*). This results in many custom interfaces tailored on each environment, making it difficult to easily move to other benchmarks and agent architectures.

Instead, AgentQuest exposes a single unified Python interface, i.e. the `Driver` and two classes reflecting the agent-environment interaction components (i.e. `Observation`, `Action`).

Observations and actions. We provide two simple classes: `Observation` and `Action`. The first has two required attributes: (i) `output`, a string reporting information about the environment state; (ii) `done`, a Boolean variable indicating if the final task is currently accomplished or not. The `Action` class has one required attribute, `action_value`. It is a string directly output by the agent. Once processed and provided to the environment, it triggers the environment change. To customise the interactions, developers can define optional attributes.

Driver. We provide the `Driver` class with two mandatory methods: (i) the `reset` method initialises a new instance of the environment and returns the first observation; (ii) the `step` method performs one single execution step. It accepts one instance of the `Action` class from the agent, processes the action (e.g. parses the `action_value` string) and uses it to modify the environment state. It always returns an observation. The driver supports also the benchmark-specific `state` attribute, acting as a simple API. It exposes the environment state at step t, useful to compute the progress rate.

We here provide an example of the implemented interaction for Mastermind:

```python
from agentquest.drivers import MasterMindDriver
from agentquest.utils import Action
from agentquest.metrics import get_progress, get_repetition

agent = ... # Initialize your agent
actions, progress, repetitions = [], [], []
# Initialize the environment and reset round
driver = MasterMindDriver(truth='5618')
obs = driver.reset()
# Agent loop
while not obs.done:
    guess = agent(obs.output) # Get the agent output
    action = Action(action_value=guess) # Create action
    actions.append(action.action_value) # Store action
    obs = driver.step(action) # Execute step
    # Compute current progress and repetition
    progress.append(get_progress(driver.state, '5618'))
    repetitions.append(get_repetitions(actions))
    # Extend with your custom metrics here ...
# Compute final metrics
PR = [x/len('5618') for x in progress]
RR = [x/(len(actions)-1) for x in repetitions]
```

3.2 Understanding agent advancements

Getting insights on how they tackle a specific task is key to comprehend agent behaviours, capabilities and limitations. Furthermore, identifying systematic agent failures allows to pinpoint necessary adjustments within the architecture to effectively address the underlying issues.

AgentQuest contributes towards this direction introducing two cross-benchmark metrics, the *progress rate* and the *repetition rate*. While the first expresses *how much* the agent is advancing towards the final goal, the latter indicates *how* it is reaching it, with a specific focus on the amount of repeated (i.e. similar) actions the agent performs.

Milestones and progress rate. To quantify the agent advancement towards the final goal, AgentQuest uses a set of *milestones* $\mathcal{M}$. In a nutshell, we break down the final solution into a series of environment hidden states the agent needs to reach to get the final solution of the task, hence, $\mathcal{M} \subseteq \mathcal{S}$, where $\mathcal{S}$ is the set of hidden states. The magnitude of $\mathcal{M}$ determines the level of *granularity* in the evaluation process. Specifically, when $\mathcal{M}$ aligns closely with $\mathcal{S}$, it offers a more comprehensive insight into the agent progress, resulting in finer granularity, whereas for $|\mathcal{M}| = 1$ the evaluation coincides with the success rate.

We assign a score to all the states included in $\mathcal{M}$ through a scoring function f and, at execution step t, we define the *progress rate* $\text{PR}_t : \mathcal{S} \rightarrow [0, 1]$ dependant of such scoring function, as an indication of how far the agent is from the goal, allowing to track agent progress over time. Depending on the benchmark, the progress rate might also decrease during the execution. Milestones can either be manually annotated, or internally computed.

Repetition rate. The repetition rate RR_t is a measure of the agent tendency of repeating actions. Depending on the benchmark, we do not consider repetitions as a limitation, – e.g. solving a maze requires repetitions, such as going left repeatedly. See also Section 4 for a positive and negative example of repetitions.

At execution step t, we consider the set of unique actions taken by the agent up to $t-1$, $\mathcal{A}_{t-1}$. Then, we compute the similarity function g between the current action a_t and all the previous ones in $\mathcal{A}_{t-1}$. As any action generated by the LLM is considered valid, we consider the action a_t as *repeated* if it exists at least one previous action $a \in \mathcal{A}_{t-1}$ such that $g(a_t, a) \geq \theta_a$, where $\theta_a \in [0, 1]$ is the *resolution*.[4] If the action is not repeated, we update the set of unique actions as $A_t = A_{t-1} \cup a_t$.

Based on this, we define the repetition rate at step t as the cumulative number of repeated actions normalised by the number of execution steps, T, except for the first. Formally, $\text{RR}_t = \frac{t-|A_t|}{T-1}$.

Table 1: Attributes exposing components of the agent-environment interaction useful to define new metrics.

Class	Attribute	Access to
`Driver`	`state`	Hidden states
`Observation`	`output`	Observations
`Action`	`action_value`	Agent actions

3.3 Adding new metrics

We rely on the progress and repetition rates to show how AgentQuest can be extended with new metrics through a simple function template. We then show the implementations of the functions adapted to the considered benchmark.

Metric function template. We use a Python function template to easily define the elements of the agent-environment interactions required for computing a given metric. Table 1 provides a recap of the main attributes and reference classes that can be used as input for the custom metrics. Additionally, users can provide external data, like milestones or action history.

Implement progress rate. Depending on the benchmark, developers need to implement the custom scoring function f through the `get_progress` function and define the set of milestones $\mathcal{M}$. Milestones can either be user-defined or internally computed within `get_progress`. Here, we show the definition of `get_progress` to quantify the achieved milestones for Mastermind. The milestones are the digits of the final solution and the progress indicates the count of correctly guessed digits in their positions:

```
def get_progress(state, milestones):
    reached_milestones = 0 # Digits in correct position
    for i, j in zip(state, milestones):
        if i == j: reached_milestones += 1
    return reached_milestones

# Usage example. The code to guess is '5618'
progress = get_progress('2318', '5618') # Reached milestones
>>> 2
progress/len('5618') # Compute Progress Rate
>>> 0.5
```

[4] A higher resolution demands closer matches for classification as repeated actions, while lower values broaden the spectrum of qualifying action similarities.

Table 2: Overview of the benchmarks provided in AgentQuest.

Benchmark	Description	Milestones
Mastermind	Guessing a numeric code with feedback on guessed digits and positions.	Digits of the code to guess.
LTP	Solving riddles by asking Yes/No questions.	Guessed riddle key aspects.
ALFWorld	Finding an object in a textual world and using it.	Sequence of actions.
Sudoku	9x9 grid puzzle. Digits 1-9 fill each column, row, and 3x3 sub-grid without repetition.	Total number of correct inserted digits.

Implement repetition rate. To determine if an action is repeated, the end user must define the similarity function g according to the considered benchmark. We provide the `get_repetitions` template function to compute the number of repeated actions. Here, we illustrate its implementation in Python and provide a usage example for Mastermind, where g is the Levenshtein similarity (Levenshtein, 1966).

```
from Levenshtein import ratio as g

def get_repetitions(actions, THETA_A):
    unique_act = set() # Initialise unique actions
    for i,a in enumerate(actions):
        # Check for repetitions
        if all([g(a,actions[x])<THETA_A for x in range(i)]):
            unique_act.add(a)
    return len(actions)-len(unique_act)

# Usage example. The code to guess is '5618'
actions = ['1234', '2143', '1234', '5618'] # Actions history
repetitions = get_repetitions(actions, 1.0)
>>> 1 repeated action
# Compute Repetition Rate
repetitions/(len(actions)-1)
>>> 0.33
```

In other cases, where a can be any text string, we can use standard metrics, such as BLEU (Papineni et al., 2002), ROGUE (Lin, 2004) or BERTScore (Zhang et al., 2020b).

4 Insights via AgentQuest

We investigate agent behaviours in different reasoning scenarios by proposing a starting set of four benchmarks. We implemented from scratch Sudoku (Felgenhauer and Jarvis, 2006) and Mastermind (Stuckman and Zhang, 2005) environments, while ALFWorld (Shridhar et al., 2020) and Lateral Thinking Puzzles (LTP)(Sloane, 1992) are existing implementations (Liu et al., 2023). Table 2 provides an overview of the benchmarks and their respective milestones used to measure progress.

We emphasise that this evaluation is not aimed at providing a thorough evaluation and comparison of agent architectures, but rather to show how to use AgentQuest and how monitoring progress and action repetition can provide relevant insights to developers, even after a few executions.

Table 3: Average existing and proposed metrics for the tested benchmarks. We report the metrics, Success Rate (SR), Steps, Progress Rate at step 60 (PR_{60}) and Repetition Rate at final step 60 (RR_{60}). We denote with * the improved results after modifying the agent architecture.

	Existing Metrics		AgentQuest	
	SR	Steps	PR_{60}	RR_{60}
Mastermind	0.47	41.87	0.62	0.32
LTP	0.20	52.00	0.46	0.81
ALFWorld	0.86	21.00	0.74	0.06
Sudoku	0.00	59.67	0.08	0.22
Mastermind*	0.60	39.73	0.73	0.00
ALFWorld*	0.93	25.86	$0.80^{\dagger}$	$0.07^{\dagger}$

† Metrics referred to the extended runtime up to 120 steps, hence PR_{120} and RR_{120}.

Experimental setup. We use as reference architecture the off-the-shelf chat agent provided by LangChain (Chase, 2022) powered by GPT-4 (OpenAI, 2023b) as LLM because it is intuitive, easy to extend and open source. We run 15 instances of the four benchmarks within AgentQuest, setting the maximum number of execution steps as 60[5]. In Appendix B we provide examples on how to use AgentQuest with two additional agent architectures and GAIA (Mialon et al., 2023) as open-ended environment.

Experimental results. For Mastermind, Figure 2a shows the progress rate PR_t and repetition rate RR_t. In the first 22 steps, the agent explores different solutions ($RR_{[0,22]} < 5\%$). This leads to growing progress towards the final goal, reaching half of the milestones ($PR_{22} \approx 55\%$). Then, the agent starts performing the same actions, exhibiting a repetitive pattern (see also Figure 3a rightmost part) and failing to reach the final goal within the

[5] We limit the number of instances in our experiments for two main reasons: (i) the work primarily serves as a demonstration of the developed framework itself, rather than an extensive evaluation of the agent performance; (ii) extensive tests could have significantly impacted the ability to reproduce the experiments due to the expensive nature of API calls.

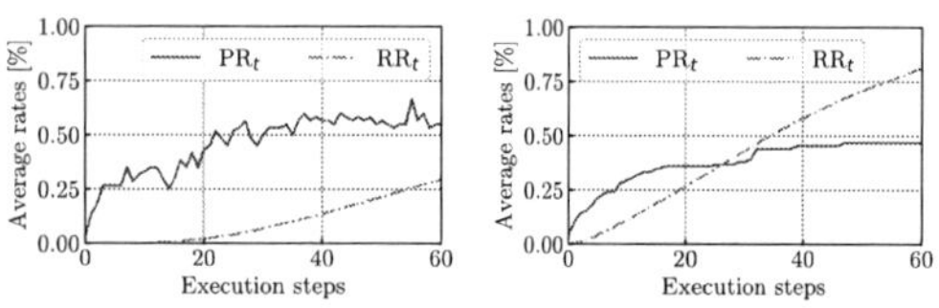

(a) Mastermind (b) LTP

Figure 2: Average Progress rate PR_t and the repetition rate RR_t on Mastermind and LTP. Mastermind: It starts out with a low RR_t but this increases after step 22 while the progress rate also stall at 55%. LTP: at first a higher RR_t allows the agent to progress by making small variations that lead to success, but later this plateaus.

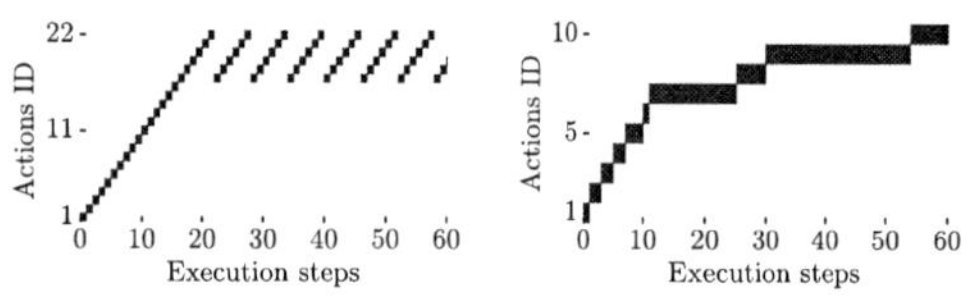

(a) Mastermind (b) LTP

Figure 3: Examples of repeated actions in Mastermind and LTP. Mastermind: there is a set of unique actions at first, but then gets stuck repeating the same actions over and over. LTP: repeated actions are small variations of the same question that lead to progress.

next 38 steps. This results in a rise of the repetitions to $RR_{60} = 30\%$ and a saturation of the progress rate at $PR_{60} = 55\%$. Hence, AgentQuest offered us a crucial insights on why the current agent cannot solve the Mastermind game.

To overcome this agent limitation we incorporate a memory component (Park et al., 2023) into the agent architecture. The agent stores the past guesses in a local buffer. Then, at each step, if the agent outputs an action already in the buffer, it is prompted to provide a new one. Table 3 (Mastermind*) shows that this simple change in agent architecture has a big impact: the agent can now solve more instances, increasing the final SR from 47% to 60% and preventing repetitions ($RR_{60} = 0\%$). This highlights how studying the interplay between progress and repetition rates can allow us to improve agent architecture, sometimes even with simple remedies. We support our intuition extending the evaluation to more instances of Mastermind from 15 to 60 achieving comparable results – i.e. 43% of SR with the standard architecture and 62% with the simple memory (19% of improvement).

For LTP, the AgentQuest metrics reveal a different agent behaviour, where repetitions are part of the agent reasoning strategy, enhancing the progress rate (Figure 2b). From the initial steps, the agent changes aspects of the same questions until a local solution emerges. This leads to horizontal indicators in Figure 3b and $RR_{20} \approx 30\%$. Despite solving only a few riddles (SR=0.2), these repetitions contribute to progress, achieving 46% of the milestones by the end of the execution, with a final repetition rate of $RR_{60} = 81\%$. This shows us how the interplay of progress and repetition rates provides an insight on how agents behave across the different time steps.

Consider the benchmark ALFWorld in Table 3 (we report the metrics trend in Appendix A). It requires the exploration of a textual world to locate an object. While the agent explores the solution space and limits action repetitions ($RR_{60} = 6\%$), it fails to solve all the games ($PR_{60} = 74\%$). This discrepancy may arise from the more exploration steps required to discover the object. We support this intuition extending the benchmark runtime to 120 steps resulting in a success and progress rates increase by 6% (ALFWorld* in Table 3). This confirms the usefulness of AgentQuest in understanding the agent failures.We support our intuition also extending the evaluation to more instances of ALFWorld from 15 to 60 achieving comparable results – i.e. 83% of SR with 60 steps as limit and 87% with 120 steps as limit (4% of improvement).

Finally, we look at Sudoku, known for its high level of difficulty (Felgenhauer and Jarvis, 2006). The low progress and repetition rates achieved after 60 steps ($PR_{60} = 8\%$ and $RR_{60} = 22\%$) indicate that the current agent architecture struggles in finding correct solutions solving this task. We report the metrics trend in Appendix A.

5 Conclusions

AgentQuest allows the research community to keep track of agent progress in a holistic manner. Starting out with a first set of four benchmarks and two new metrics, AgentQuest is easily extendable. Furthermore, the two proposed metrics, progress and repetition rates, have the great advantage of allowing to track how agents advance toward the final goal over time. Especially studying their interplay can lead to important insights that will allow the research community to improve agent performance. Finally, we believe that promptly sharing AgentQuest with the research community will facilitate benchmarking and debugging agents, and will foster the creation and use of new benchmarks and metrics.

Ethical Considerations

The complexity of LLM agents poses challenges in comprehending their decision-making processes. Ethical guidelines must demand transparency in such systems, ensuring that developers and end-users comprehend how decisions are reached.

We are not aware of any direct ethical impact generated by our work. However, we hope that insights into Generative AI agents' decision-making processes will be applied to improve and promote transparency and fairness.

Acknowledgements

This project has received funding from the European Union's Horizon Europe research and innovation programme (SNS-JU) under the Grant Agreement No 101139285 ("NATWORK").

References

Kranti Chalamalasetti, Jana Götze, Sherzod Hakimov, Brielen Madureira, Philipp Sadler, and David Schlangen. 2023. Clembench: Using Game Play to Evaluate Chat-Optimized Language Models as Conversational Agents.

Harrison Chase. 2022. LangChain - Building applications with LLMs through composability.

Bertram Felgenhauer and Frazer Jarvis. 2006. Mathematics of Sudoku I. *Mathematical Spectrum*.

Jack Hessel, Ari Holtzman, Maxwell Forbes, Ronan Le Bras, and Yejin Choi. 2022. CLIPScore: A Reference-free Evaluation Metric for Image Captioning.

Douwe Kiela, Tristan Thrush, Kawin Ethayarajh, and Amanpreet Singh. 2023. Plotting Progress in AI. *Contextual AI Blog*.

Vladimir I. Levenshtein. 1966. Binary codes capable of correcting deletions, insertions, and reversals. In *Soviet Physics Doklady*.

Chin-Yew Lin. 2004. ROUGE: A Package for Automatic Evaluation of Summaries.

Xiao Liu, Hao Yu, Hanchen Zhang, Yifan Xu, Xuanyu Lei, Hanyu Lai, Yu Gu, Hangliang Ding, Kaiwen Men, Kejuan Yang, et al. 2023. AgentBench: Evaluating LLMs as Agents.

Grégoire Mialon, Clémentine Fourrier, Craig Swift, Thomas Wolf, Yann LeCun, and Thomas Scialom. 2023. GAIA: a benchmark for General AI Assistants.

OpenAI. 2023a. Assistants API.

OpenAI. 2023b. GPT-4 Technical Report.

Kishore Papineni, Salim Roukos, Todd Ward, and Wei-Jing Zhu. 2002. Bleu: a Method for Automatic Evaluation of Machine Translation.

Joon Sung Park, Joseph O'Brien, Carrie Jun Cai, Meredith Ringel Morris, Percy Liang, and Michael S Bernstein. 2023. Generative Agents: Interactive Simulacra of Human Behavior.

Shishir G. Patil, Tianjun Zhang, Xin Wang, and Joseph E. Gonzalez. 2023. Gorilla: Large Language Model Connected with Massive APIs.

Mohit Shridhar, Xingdi Yuan, Marc-Alexandre Côté, Yonatan Bisk, Adam Trischler, and Matthew Hausknecht. 2020. ALFWorld: Aligning Text and Embodied Environments for Interactive Learning.

Paul Sloane. 1992. *Lateral Thinking Puzzlers*. Sterling Publishing Company, Inc.

Jeff Stuckman and Guo-Qiang Zhang. 2005. Mastermind is NP-complete.

Richard S Sutton and Andrew G Barto. 2018. *Reinforcement Learning: An Introduction*. MIT press.

Lei Wang, Chen Ma, Xueyang Feng, Zeyu Zhang, Hao Yang, Jingsen Zhang, Zhiyuan Chen, Jiakai Tang, Xu Chen, Yankai Lin, et al. 2023. A Survey on Large Language Model based Autonomous Agents.

Lilian Weng. 2023. LLM-powered Autonomous Agents.

Shunyu Yao, Jeffrey Zhao, Dian Yu, Nan Du, Izhak Shafran, Karthik Narasimhan, and Yuan Cao. 2022. ReAct: Synergizing Reasoning and Acting in Language Models.

Tianyi Zhang, Varsha Kishore, Felix Wu, Kilian Q. Weinberger, and Yoav Artzi. 2020a. BERTScore: Evaluating Text Generation with BERT.

Tianyi Zhang, Varsha Kishore, Felix Wu, Kilian Q. Weinberger, and Yoav Artzi. 2020b. BERTScore: Evaluating Text Generation with BERT.

Lianmin Zheng, Wei-Lin Chiang, Ying Sheng, Siyuan Zhuang, Zhanghao Wu, Yonghao Zhuang, Zi Lin, Zhuohan Li, Dacheng Li, Eric Xing, et al. 2023. Judging LLM-as-a-judge with MT-Bench and Chatbot Arena.

Yuchen Zhuang, Yue Yu, Kuan Wang, Haotian Sun, and Chao Zhang. 2023. ToolQA: A Dataset for LLM Question Answering with External Tools.

A Appendix: ALFWorld and Sudoku benchmarks

In this section we report the detailed metrics for each step for the ALFWorld and Sudoku benchmarks, omitted for the sake of brevity from the main paper.

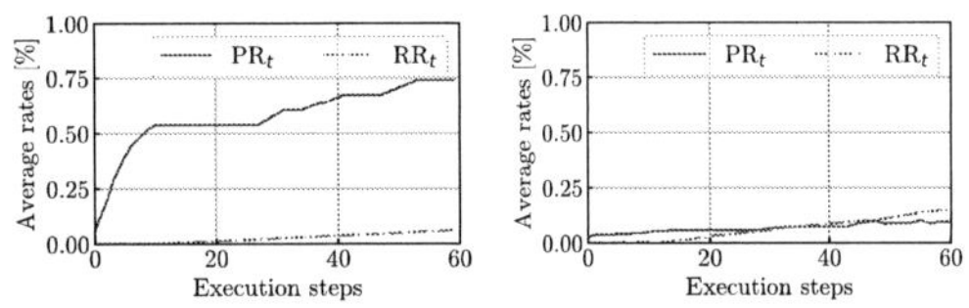

(a) ALFWorld (b) Sudoku

Figure 4: Progress rate PR_t and the repetition rate RR_t on ALFWorld and Sudoku averaged over 15 runs. ALFWorld: It starts out with a low repetition rate and quick increase of the progress rate. Then a slow increase of the repetition rate enables to further increase the progress rate although less quickly. Sudoku: The progress rate quickly reaches 8%. The repetition rate then slowly increases without any positive change in the progress rate.

Figure 4a reports the progress rate and repetition rate for ALFWorld. The repetition rate is close to 0% for the first 20 steps, then it slowly increases up to 6% after 60 steps. The progress rate quickly reaches over 50% in 10 steps, then keeps increasing, although slowly, up to 74%. The consistent improvement of the progress rate even for steps close to 60 together with the low repetition rate suggests that higher values may be reached by increasing the maximum number of steps. We validate this hypothesis by extending the benchmark runtime to 120 steps. As previously reported in Table 3, this results in an improvement of 6 percentage points for both the success rate the progress rate, i.e. SR$=93\%$ and $\text{PR}_{120} = 80\%$.

Figure 4b includes the two metrics for the Sudoku benchmark. We can observe that the progress rate quickly reaches a plateau at 8% in very few steps. The repetition rate is close to 0% for the first 10 steps, then it slowly increases up to 22% after 60 steps without any improvement of the progress rate.

B Appendix: Additional agents architectures and benchmarks

In this section we highlight the plug-and-play aspect of AgentQuest showing the implementation of Mastermind with two additional agents architectures, i.e. ReAct (Yao et al., 2022) as the most used architecture in literature and OpenAI Assistant (OpenAI, 2023a), as the most recent proprietary architecture. Additionally, we show how to implement the open-ended benchmark GAIA (Mialon et al., 2023) requiring the usage of external tools. For brevity, in the following snippets we omit details, like error handling or full agent definition. The complete code is available in the GitHub repository.

B.1 ReAct for Closed-box Environments

We show an example of how to execute a closed-box benchmark (i.e. ALFWorld) with an agent based on the ReAct architecture (Yao et al., 2022). Such architecture forces the agent decision making process to generate both textual reasoning traces and actions pertaining to a task in an interleaved manner. Common implementations (Chase, 2022; Yao et al., 2022) rely on external tools to perform actions. Here, we ensure compatibility with existing implementations providing a single tool (i.e. `ProxyTool`) that forwards the actions to the driver. In a nutshell, the agent reflects on the action to take and invokes the tool. Then, we feed the tool input to the driver to perform the interaction with the environment. At each step, we provide the agent the updated history of the actions and observations through the `intermediate_steps` variable.

```
from agentquest.drivers import MasterMindDriver
from agentquest.metrics import ...
from agentquest.utils import Action
...

# Define a dummy tool for closed-box environments
class ProxyTool(BaseTool):
    name = "proxytool"
    description = "Provide the action you want to perform"
    def _run(self):
        pass

# Instantiate custom prompt
prompt = CustomPromptTemplate(
    template=..., # LLM prompt
    tools=[ProxyTool()],
    input_variables=["intermediate_steps", ...]
)
# Initialise the agent
agent = create_react_agent(llm, [ProxyTool()], prompt)
intermediate_steps = []
# Initialise the driver
driver = MasterMindDriver(game)
# Get the first observation
obs = driver.reset()
# Agent Loop
while not obs.done:
    # Retrieve the agent output
    agent_choice = agent.invoke(
        {'input':obs.output,
         'intermediate_steps':intermediate_steps}
    )
    action = Action(action_value=agent_choice.tool_input)
    # Perform the step
    obs = driver.step(action)
    # Update intermediate steps
    intermediate_steps.append((agent_choice, obs.output))
    # Get current metrics ...
```

B.2 OpenAI Assistant for Closed-box Environments

The OpenAI Assistant (OpenAI, 2023a) is a proprietary architecture. It allows users to define custom agents by specifying the tasks to accomplish and the set of tools the agent can use. While the decision-making process is not directly accessible by the end-users (the agent and the LLM are hosted on the proprietary cloud environment), the tools can be invoked both remotely or locally. In the latter, users have control on the tool invocation managing the agent loop.

Similarly to ReAct, we here rely on the `ProxyTool`, acting as a proxy between the agent and the environment. We invoke the remote agent with the initial task (e.g. first ALFWorld observation) and process the output of its decision making process, i.e. the action to perform provided as tool input. Then, we bypass the tool invocation, directly forwarding the action to the driver to perform the execution step and retrieve the next observation. Finally, we invoke the agent with the new observation concluding the execution step.

```
from agentquest.drivers import MasterMindDriver
from agentquest.metrics import ...
from agentquest.utils import Action
...

# Define a dummy tool for closed-box environments
class ProxyTool(BaseTool):
    name = "proxytool"
    description = "Provide the action you want to perform"
    def _run(self):
        pass

# Initialise the agent
agent = OpenAIAssistantRunnable.create_assistant(
    instructions=... # LLM prompt
    tools=[ProxyTool()],
    model=... # Chosen LLM
    as_agent=True
)
# Initialise the driver
driver = MasterMindDriver(game)
# Get the first observation
obs = driver.reset()
# Get the first action
response = agent.invoke({"content": obs.output})
# Agent Loop
while not obs.done:
    # Retrieve the agent output
    agent_guess = response[0].tool_input
    action = Action(action_value=agent_guess)
    # Perform the step
    obs = driver.step(action)
    # Get current metrics ...
    # Manage Proxy Tool output
    tool_outputs = [
        {"output": obs.output,
         "tool_call_id": response[0].tool_call_id}
    ]
    # Invoke the agent to get the next action
    response = agent.invoke(
        {"tool_outputs": tool_outputs,
         "run_id": response[0].run_id,
         "thread_id": response[0].thread_id}
    )
```

B.3 OpenAI Assistant for Open-ended Environments

When interacting with an open-ended environment, the agent is not restricted to the pre-defined actions of the closed-box environment and it is allowed to select any user-defined tool (e.g. retrieving information online or executing code). Hence, we provide the agent the list of tools via the `tool` variable. The agent relies on its reasoning process to choose which tool to invoke. Omitted here for the sake of brevity, we rely of the manual annotations of the GAIA questions (Mialon et al., 2023) as milestones to compute the progress rate.

```
from agentquest.drivers import GaiaDriver
from agentquest.metrics import ...
from agentquest.utils import Action
...

# Define the tools
tools=[
    OnlineSearch(), # Retrieve a web page link
    WebContentParser(), # Read the web page
    FinalAnswerRetriever(), # Provide the final answer
    ...
]
# Initialise the agent
agent = OpenAIAssistantRunnable.create_assistant(
    instructions=... # LLM prompt
    tools=tools,
    model=... # Chosen LLM
    as_agent=True
)
# Initialise the driver
driver = GaiaDriver(question, tools)
# Get the first observation
obs = driver.reset()
# Get the first action
response = agent.invoke({"content": obs.output})
# Agent Loop
while not obs.done:
    # Retrieve the agent output
    act = f'{response[0].tool}:{response[0].tool_input}'
    action = Action(action_value=act)
    # Perform the step invoking the local tool
    obs = driver.step(action)
    # Get current metrics ...
    # Manage tool output as observation
    tool_outputs = [
        {"output": obs.output,
         "tool_call_id": response[0].tool_call_id}
    ]
    # Invoke the agent to get the next action
    response = agent.invoke(
        {"tool_outputs": tool_outputs,
         "run_id": response[0].run_id,
         "thread_id": response[0].thread_id}
    )
```

Here, the driver acts as a wrapper, executing the tool with the parameters provided by the agent (`tool_input`) and forwards the output to the agent in the correct format:

```
class GaiaDriver():
    def __init__(self, question, tools, ...):
        # Initialise the tool lookup
        self.tool_lookup = {x.name:x for x in tools}
    ...
    def step(self, action):
        # Parse the action
        tool, tool_input = action.action_value.split(':')
        # Invoke the tool
        tool_out = self.tool_lookup[tool]._run(tool_input)
        # Parse the tool output here ...
        return Observation(output=tool_out)
```

ZhuJiu-Knowledge: A Fairer Platform for Evaluating Multiple Knowledge Types in Large Language Models

Pengfan Du[1,2*], **Sirui Liang**[1*], **Baoli Zhang**[1*], **Pengfei Cao**[1], **Yubo Chen**[1,2†], **Kang Liu**[1,2,3†] and **Jun Zhao**[1,2]

[1]Institute of Automation, Chinese Academy of Sciences

[2]School of Artificial Intelligence, University of Chinese Academy of Sciences

[3]Shanghai Artificial Intelligence Laboratory

{baoli.zhang,pengfei.cao,yubo.chen,kliu,jzhao}@nlpr.ia.ac.cn

{dupengfan22}@mails.ucas.ac.cn, liangsirui2024@ia.ac.cn

Abstract

The swift advancement in large language models (LLMs) has heightened the importance of model evaluations. LLMs have acquired a substantial amount of knowledge, and evaluating the knowledge of these LLMs is crucial. To address this, we introduce the ZhuJiu-Knowledge benchmark which carefully considers the following factors: (1) **For knowledge scope**, we concentrate on three domains: commonsense knowledge, world knowledge, language knowledge, which comes from ATOMIC, Conceptnet, Wikidata, and Wordnet. (2) **For data construction**, to prevent data contamination, we utilize knowledge derived from corpora and knowledge graphs to formulate novel questions that are ensured not to appear in the training corpus. A multitude of prompts is purposefully devised to mitigate the impact of prompt design on evaluation and to further analyze the LLMs' sensitivity to various prompts. (3) **For evaluation criteria**, we propose a novel voting methodology for assessing generative text, aligning the model's evaluation with human preferences to reduce biases inherent in individual model assessments. We evaluate 14 current mainstream LLMs and conduct a comprehensive discussion and analysis of their results. The ZhuJiu-Knowledge benchmark and open-participation leaderboard are publicly released at http://zhujiu-knowledge.top/ and we also provide a demo video at https://youtu.be/QJp4qlEHVH8.

1 Introduction

The unprecedented performance of LLMs, such as GPT4 (Achiam et al., 2023) and Llama2 (Touvron et al., 2023), has garnered significant attention and made their evaluation a focal point as the field progresses(Guo et al., 2023; Chang et al., 2023). LLMs have acquired a substantial amount of knowledge, and evaluating the knowledge of these LLMs is crucial. Existing efforts have focused on evaluating the knowledge stored within the model (e.g., Petroni et al., 2019; Yu et al., 2023). However, these works still face several challenges.

Constructing a reasonable benchmark for evaluating knowledge involves careful consideration of several key factors: (1) **Knowledge Scope**. Most evaluations are limited to world knowledge related to entities and relations, lacking assessments of commonsense knowledge and language knowledge (Liang et al., 2022; Zhang et al., 2023). This limitation arises because these two types of knowledge are often expressed in the form of events or sentences. Currently, making unbiased evaluations of the generated sentences is still a difficult problem for LLMs. (2) **Data Constructinon**. Most evaluation platforms have limitations on assessing data. Firstly, the evaluated data usually are leaked and embedded in the target LLMs in the process of pre-training or SFT, after such data are released publicly. As a result, making an evaluation on such data would be biased (Brown et al., 2020; Zhou et al., 2023a). Secondly, existing knowledge probing strategies usually relied on the given prompts heavily. Existing methods only used just one prompt for each piece of knowledge. If the target LLM does not understand the given prompt well, it will not obtain better results (Webson and Pavlick, 2021; Abdou et al., 2022). (3) **Evaluation Criteria**. Evaluating knowledge using multiple-choice questions and true or false questions may introduce certain biases obviously. Assessing generated text with QA questions requires a reasonable evaluation metric for the generated content. Traditional evaluation criteria such as GLUE (Wang et al., 2018), ROUGE (Lin, 2004), and RECALL have inherent limitations, often leading to a gap between evaluation results and users' subjective experiences. While manual evaluation is highly

[1]*Co-first authors, they contributed equally to this work.

[2]†Corresponding author

Proceedings of the 2024 Conference of the North American Chapter of the Association for Computational Linguistics: Human Language Technologies (Volume 3: System Demonstrations), pages 194–206
June 16-21, 2024 ©2024 Association for Computational Linguistics

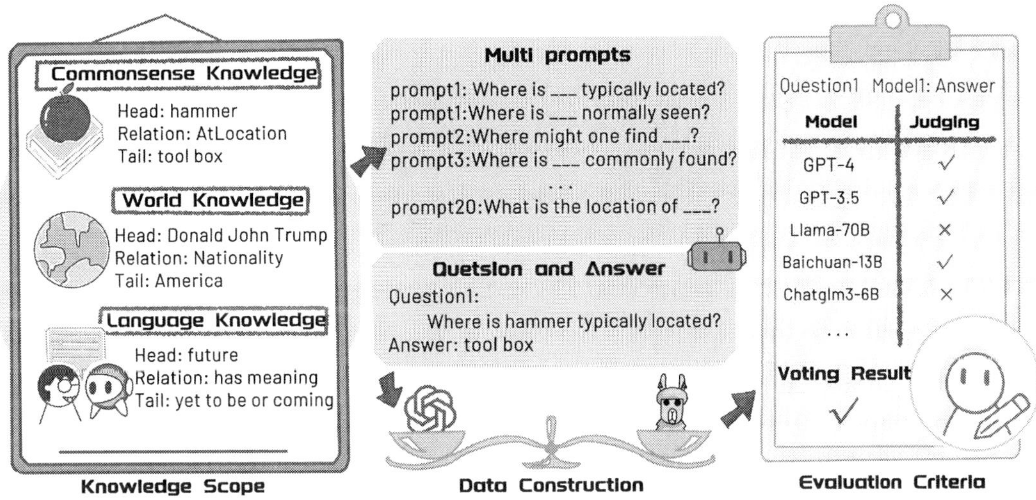

Figure 1: The evaluation process of LLM using ZhuJiu-Knowledge.

reliable, it is time-consuming and labor-intensive (Karpinska et al., 2021). Therefore, designing a rational evaluation metric is also a critically important issue.

This paper constructs ZhuJiu-Knowledge, a fairer platform for evaluating multiple Knowledge types in LLMs, which is designed to assess LLMs' capabilities in commonsense knowledge, world knowledge, and language knowledge. During the construction process, we fully consider the aforementioned three factors.

For Knowledge Scope, we choose to evaluate commonsense knowledge, world knowledge, and language knowledge for the following reasons: (i) Commonsense knowledge is often implicitly embedded in the texts, which presents a challenge for LLMs to acquire substantially from textual corpora. A proficient understanding of commonsense is fundamental for LLMs to generate reasonable responses (Davis, 2023). (ii) World knowledge plays a critical role in LLMs' performance. Based on memory and manipulation for world knowledge, LLMs can provide more accurate and relevant responses to user questions (Hendrycks et al., 2020; Zhong et al., 2023). (iii) A deep understanding of grammar, semantics, and pragmatics enables LLMs to grasp language nuances and process text effectively (Chuang et al., 2020; Dentella et al., 2023).

For data construction, we simultaneously address data contamination(Zhou et al., 2023b; Sainz et al., 2023) and prompt sensitivity issues. (i) To address data contamination, some studies adopt machine-unreadable (Huang et al., 2023) data or constantly evolving data. Considering the pressing demand for high-quality data in the training process of LLMs, it can be foreseen that these data will also be trained by LLMs in the near future. To overcome this limitation, the paper proposes to leverage knowledge from existing knowledge graphs and corpora to construct evaluation questions. The advantage of this method is to allow for the automatic generation of questions tailored to the targeted knowledge domains. (ii) To better assess LLMs' prompt sensitivity, we propose designing multiple prompts for each piece of knowledge. For each knowledge, we design multiple prompts to investigate whether an LLM can consistently generate correct answers when given varying prompts

For evaluation criteria, conventional methods typically relied on traditional evaluation metrics or more advanced models. However, these methods often fail to fully capture LLMs' comprehensive abilities and users' subjective experiences (Li et al., 2023; Chiang and Lee, 2023), while purely manual evaluations are labor-intensive. To bridge the gap between objective metrics and subjective preferences, we propose an innovative approach integrating human-computer collaboration, which employs a vote-like evaluation strategy. Multiple LLMs are employed to evaluate the given answers, where some pivot LLMs are selected as the evaluation models because they have higher correlations with human evaluations. The final result is obtained through voting.

We also release an online evaluation platform that supports multiple functions including visualizations of evaluation results and submission of evaluation models, etc. Moreover, we evaluate 14 publicly available LLMs. Based on the experimental results, we obtain some intriguing observations and summarize them in Section 4.

In summary, the contributions of this paper are as follows:

- We construct ZhuJiu-Knowledge, a fairer platform for evaluating commonsense knowledge, language knowledge, and world knowledge in LLMs.
- We present a novel benchmark construction technique to evaluate LLMs in commonsense knowledge, world knowledge, and language knowledge. This benchmark is designed to reduce data contamination and prompt sensitivity, accompanied by a human-aligned evaluation strategy to yield more reliable results.
- Using the ZhuJiu-Knowledge benchmark, we evaluate 14 current LLMs across three types of knowledge, providing insights for the improvement and enhancement of LLM.

2 ZhuJiu-Knowledge Benchmark

As stated above, the ZhuJiu-Knowledge benchmark conducts precise evaluations of models across three knowledge types. This section provides a detailed introduction to the ZhuJiu-Knowledge benchmark covering the knowledge selection, task design, data construction, and evaluation method. We also detailed the process of problem construction in Appendix A. The Evaluation framework is shown in Figure 1.

2.1 Knowledge Scope

The remarkable proficiency exhibited by the LLM has propelled evaluations towards more challenging and diverse tasks. The excessive pursuit of broadening task coverage has resulted in the neglect of knowledge itself within the evaluation process (Suzgun et al., 2022). To address these challenges, we advocate for classifying knowledge, designing tasks tailored to different knowledge types, and evaluating the model's ability in this knowledge with finer granularity. We have chosen the following three kinds of knowledge as our focus of assessment.

2.1.1 Commonsense Knowledge

We start with two commonsense knowledge graphs, Atomic (Hwang et al., 2021) and ConceptNet (Speer et al., 2017). (i) Atomic captures diverse relations on every day and inferences about others' mental states in symbolic form, it is represented by triples, e.g., *(PersonX adopts a dog, xNeed, to go to the pet store.)* (ii) ConceptNet encompasses the general attributes of common entities, also represented as triplets, e.g., *(single rose, HasProperty, beautiful)*. By contextualizing knowledge from these knowledge graphs, we transform abstract knowledge into specific questions, thereby assessing the model's ability to comprehend and apply this abstract knowledge in a contextualized manner.

2.1.2 World Knowledge

This paper employs Wikidata[1] as the knowledge source for generating evaluation queries. This knowledge base is renowned for its high quality and comprises billions of data triples. Additionally, we have introduced two refined evaluation metrics to gauge the model's knowledge proficiency. (i) To evaluate the model's understanding of knowledge at different frequencies, we have classified knowledge into three categories: (1) High-frequency Knowledge, characterized by interlinking occurrences exceeding 1000; (2) Common-frequency Knowledge, with interlinking occurrences between 100 and 1000; and (3) Low-frequency Knowledge, where interlinking occurrences are fewer than 100. (ii) To access LLMs' sensitivity to timeliness, temporally relevant knowledge triples are selected.

2.1.3 Language Knowledge

Our evaluation of language knowledge is divided into three aspects: semantics evaluation, syntax evaluation, and pragmatics evaluation, with WordNet (Miller, 1995) serving as the knowledge corpus for language knowledge. WordNet, a comprehensive English lexical database, organizes vocabulary based on sense and establishes a semantic network through word relationships (Miller et al., 1990). Given the extensive scope of syntax, semantics, and pragmatics, we have designed four knowledge corpus-based tasks (tasks 1-4) and four combined natural language understanding (NLU) and natural language generation (NLG) tasks (tasks 5-8) for the knowledge capability evaluation of large

[1] https://www.wikidata.org

language models (LLMs). (i) For semantics evaluation, we establish *(1) Semantic Selection Task* to choose or provide sentences that contain a specific meaning of a polysemous word. *(2) Similar Words Task* to provide near-synonyms for a particular sense of a word. *(3) Idiom Explanation Task* to explain the meanings of idioms. (ii) For syntax evaluation, we establish *(4) Part-of-speech Analysis Task* to analyze the parts of speech and meanings of words within sentences. *(5) Grammatical Correction Task* to correct grammatical errors in sentences. (iii) For pragmatics evaluation, we establish *(6) Specialized Formats Task*, which entail completing writing tasks in specific formats. *(7) Sentiment Analysis Task* to analyze the emotions of characters in sentences. *(8) Writing Style Task* to complete text generation following specific stylistic writing guidelines.

2.2 Data Construction

Ensuring fairness and objectivity is paramount in constructing reliable evaluation methods for LLMs. Our approach to data construction addresses two critical issues: data leakage and prompt sensitivity.

2.2.1 Knowledge-based Question Generation

Previous research has highlighted the severity of data contamination, where models answer questions through memorization rather than genuine knowledge mastery (Marie, 2023; Li, 2023; Sainz et al., 2023). Many existing benchmarks, e.g., CLEVA (Li et al., 2023), keep the evaluation data confidential from users during the assessment process. However, with the abundance of training data for LLMs, such practices cannot guarantee that the data has not been exposed during training. Kola (Yu et al., 2023) addresses this issue by employing continuously evolving data. However, it is foreseeable that such data will soon be utilized in training large models, potentially diminishing this approach's effectiveness.

We propose a knowledge-based question construction method using knowledge from the aforementioned knowledge bases, wherein the knowledge is typically formulated as triplets, denoted as <head, relation, tail>. We design question templates for relation, into which we insert heads from the triplets, thereby creating questions with answers. Additionally, recognizing the unsuitability of this approach for evaluating certain specialized tasks, such as some pragmatic tasks in language knowledge, we use GPT-4 to customize evaluation questions specifically for these types of tasks.

2.2.2 Prompt-based Question Expansion

An ideal large language model should be able to comprehend various prompts for the same knowledge. Nevertheless, current research indicates that the sensitivity of LLMs to prompts significantly influences their performance (Wei et al., 2022). It is reasonable to assert that evaluating LLMs using a single prompt may introduce bias in the evaluation results due to the sensitivity of different LLMs to the prompt. However, most current evaluation methods have not taken this issue into consideration.

To address the aforementioned issues, we propose a prompt-based question expansion method. This method involves the augmentation of a set of question prompts through the utilization of four advanced models, namely Llama-2-70B, Claude-instant, GPT3.5-turbo[2], and GPT-4. For each prompt set, we manually selected 20 prompts that are both universal and diverse. By utilizing the generated prompts, we construct a variety of questions targeting the same knowledge. A detailed description of the question construction process is shown in Appendix A. Furthermore, we explore which models exhibit heightened robustness in responding to prompts based on their performance on these questions.

To assess the sensitivity of different models to various prompts, we computed the entropy for each LLM's responses to different prompts for the same knowledge. Specifically, upon completing multiple-choice questions, we obtained $\Omega = \{\ldots, \omega_j, \ldots, \omega_k\}$ clusters for the n responses and the number of each cluster ω_k is $c(\omega_k)$. We calculate the entropy of the answer distribution as:

$$\text{entropy}(R(q)) = \sum_j \frac{c(\omega_j)}{n} \log\left(\frac{c(\omega_j)}{n}\right) \quad (1)$$

The entropy measures the degree of divergence between the responses for different prompts of the same knowledge. A higher entropy value indicates greater randomness in the answering process, which is associated with the model's uncertainty regarding that particular knowledge.

2.3 Evaluation Criteria

To alleviate biases from individual model evaluations and align assessment results more closely

[2]https://platform.openai.com/overview

with human perception, our evaluation system integrates two key components: multi-model voting evaluation and manual alignment.

2.3.1 Multi-model Voting Evaluation

Owing to the variations in knowledge scope among different models, evaluating results outside a model's knowledge range can introduce biases (Zhao et al., 2023).

We advocate the adoption of collaborative evaluation involving multiple LLMs to mitigate such potential biases. Specifically, the responses from different models to the same question form a set of answers $A = \{a_i\}_{i=1}^{|A|}$ for a question and an evaluation model ensemble $M = \{m_j\}_{j=1}^{|M|}$, we can obtain a set of evaluation results $R = \{(m_1^i), (m_2^i), \ldots, (m_j^i)\}_{i=1}^{|A|}$ for each answer. Then the final evaluation result of each answer is $F = argmax(R)$.

Considering the ultimate goal of LLMs is to cater to human needs, ensuring the generation of evaluation that aligns with human preferences becomes a paramount expectation. We incorporate a manual alignment step into the model evaluation process to achieve this. Specifically, for each type of knowledge, we selected some questions for manual evaluation. Subsequently, we adopt Pearson correlation coefficients between the manual evaluation results set and model evaluation results set R to measure the evaluation performance of different models. Considering that different LLMs excel in different types of knowledge, we selected the top five models of each knowledge type that are most closely aligned with manual evaluation results. The outcome will be determined by a voting process involving these five models. This approach aims to enhance the model's ability to produce evaluations that resonate more closely with human preferences and expectations.

2.4 Scoring Method

Each knowledge has different target views to evaluate LLMs' performance. For example, we have common-frequency, high-frequency, low-frequency, and timeliness to evaluate world knowledge. Since the metrics of different tasks are incomparable and differently sensitive, different results cannot be directly merged. Therefore, we propose to introduce Min-Max normalization to get a unified ranking of LLMs. Specifically, given a model set $M = \{m_j\}_{j=1}^{|M|}$ and the task set $D = \{d_j\}_{j=1}^{|D|}$, we get accuracy matrix a_{ij}. We first compute the Min-Max normalization of a_{ij} as z_{ij}.

$$z_{ij} = 100\frac{a_{ij} - min(a_j)}{max(a_j) - max(a_j)} \tag{2}$$

Then the standardized score S can be calculated as:

$$S_i = avg(z_i) \tag{3}$$

We use S_{QA} to represent the QA question score, and S_{CQ} to represent the Choices Question score.

3 Platform

We have developed an online platform that offers a diverse array of services to the community, as outlined below:

Evaluation process and questions We provide a detailed introduction for our evaluation process in Figure 5 and present a subset of evaluation questions in Figure 7.

Visualizations of evaluation results We show the overall scores (detailed in Figure 6) and metric scores of LLMs across three knowledge assessments (detailed in Figure 2.4), comprehensively analyzing the LLMs' strengths and weaknesses of each type of knowledge.

Submission of Evaluation Model We also invite all participants to engage actively in our evaluations and contribute to the leaderboard.

4 Experiment

4.1 Evaluated Models

In order to promote the development of LLMs, our primary focus for evaluation lies in open-source models with a parameter scale of approximately 10 billion, including ChatGLM3-6b, Baichuan2-13B-Chat (Yang et al., 2023), Baichuan-13B-Chat, Baichuan2-7B-Chat, Qwen-7B-Chat (Bai et al., 2023), Qwen-14B-Chat, Yi-6B-Chat (AI et al., 2024), WizardLM-13B-V1.2 (Xu et al., 2023), Vicuna-7b-v1.5 (Zheng et al., 2024), Vicuna-13B-v1.5 (Zheng et al., 2024), LLaMa2-7b-Chat, LLaMa2-13b-Chat, Mistral-7B-Instruct-v0.2 (Jiang et al., 2023), Mistral-7B-Instruct-v0.1.

4.2 Overall Performance

We report the overall performance in Table 1. S_{CQ} and S_{QA} represent the Choices question score and the QA question score respectively, which are defined in Section 2.4. H represents prompt sensitivity, which is defined in Equation 1. A more detailed

Metrics \ Knowledge / LLMs	Commonsense Knowledge			World Knowledge			Language Knowledge		
	S_{CQ}	S_{QA}	H	S_{CQ}	S_{QA}	H	S_{CQ}	S_{QA}	H
Yi-6B-Chat	85.54	19.62	0.49	87.53	50.62	0.34	70.65	92.45	0.21
ChatGLM3-6b	38.88	77.4	0.55	46.63	19.21	0.55	58.56	71.07	0.22
WizardLM-13B-V1.2	24.11	90.59	0.45	27.06	67.13	0.70	71.64	**94.5**	0.30
Baichuan-13B-Chat	16.38	88.84	0.47	12.96	64.7	0.85	59.78	80.61	0.27
Baichuan2-13B-Chat	43.28	57.32	0.53	54.79	47.84	0.58	72.02	69.11	0.25
Baichuan2-7B-Chat	41.95	**93.21**	0.53	68.95	50.53	0.87	71.21	15.17	0.27
Vicuna-13b-v1.5	72.08	24.72	0.44	87.66	**78.06**	0.42	73.02	93.98	0.25
Vicuna-7b-v1.5	64.78	47.41	0.46	52.01	59.25	0.61	51.8	89.67	0.27
LLaMa2-13b-chat	22.3	67.76	0.43	79.6	37.75	0.43	64.2	89.02	0.24
LLaMa2-7b-chat	25.85	65.77	0.47	6.32	0	0.87	52.28	54.16	0.30
Mistral-7B-Instruct-v0.1	68.63	21.01	0.42	27.4	36.71	0.67	62.82	61.67	0.24
Mistral-7B-Instruct-v0.2	78.85	68.99	0.47	**96.64**	74.38	0.31	86.81	89.57	0.22
Qwen-14B-Chat	**96.78**	42.06	0.48	91.44	51.54	0.37	**93.62**	91.61	0.18
Qwen-7B-Chat	54.1	15.49	0.48	68.68	46.67	0.46	80.36	89.05	0.22

Table 1: The overall performance based on three knowledge abilities of the LLMs participating in the ZhuJiu-Knowledge evaluation. S_{CQ}: multiple choice question score, S_{QA}: QA question score, H: entropy.

assessment result can be found on our platform. The results reveal several noteworthy findings:

(1) **Evaluating with QA questions is fairer:** We compare the results of model responses to multiple-choice questions and QA questions across three knowledge abilities, revealing a significant difference. This suggests that LLMs may make correct choices through random selection or co-occurrence frequency calculation, which does not indicate that the LLM has mastered the knowledge. Employing multiple-choice questions as the evaluation method for models can lead to bias.

(2) **LLMs exhibit a preference for their own generated text:** We compare the evaluation results that the model assigned to itself with the evaluations from other LLMs. The specific calculation method and results can be found in Appendix B. The experimental results indicate that the model's self-assigned evaluations are significantly better than the evaluations it receives from other models. This suggests that models exhibit a clear preference for the text they generate, emphasizing the importance of using a voting mechanism for a fair evaluation.

(3) **LLMs is more prompt sensitive to hard question:** Entropy score represents prompt sensitivity, with higher entropy indicating greater model sensitivity. Table 1 shows that LLMs are most sensitive to world knowledge, followed by commonsense knowledge and then language knowledge. This sensitivity ranking aligns with the difficulty of the tasks, as depicted in Figures 2, 3, and 4. LLMs perform the poorest in the world knowledge task, followed by commonsense knowledge and language knowledge. This suggests that prompt sensitivity is higher in challenging tasks, emphasizing the need for carefully designed prompts to improve performance.

5 Conclusion and Future Work

In this work, we presented ZhuJiu-Knowledge, a fairer benchmark for evaluating multiple knowledge types of LLMs. Zhujiu-Knowledge extends the current knowledge evaluation scope to commonsense knowledge, language knowledge, and world knowledge. We introduce a novel data construction methodology that mitigates the risks of data contamination and prompt sensitivity and proposes a novel voting methodology to evaluate generative text. Our comprehensive evaluation of 14 mainstream LLMs provides significant insights into their performance, revealing the strengths and weaknesses of each model of various knowledge abilities. Finally, we provide a comprehensive knowledge evaluation platform for LLMs in the ZhuJiu-Knowledge.

In the future, our objectives include: (1) broadening the scope of the ZhuJiu-Knowledge benchmark to cover a wider array of knowledge assessment dimensions; and (2) enhancing our evaluation platform by integrating more features and improving the user interface, which will facilitate more efficient and user-friendly assessments.

6 Acknowledgements

This work is supported by the National Key Research and Development Program of China (No. 2022ZD0160503), the National Natural Science Foundation of China (No. 62176257). This work is also supported by the Youth Innovation Promotion Association CAS.

References

Mostafa Abdou, Vinit Ravishankar, Artur Kulmizev, and Anders Søgaard. 2022. Word order does matter and shuffled language models know it. In *Proceedings of the 60th Annual Meeting of the Association for Computational Linguistics (Volume 1: Long Papers)*, pages 6907–6919.

Josh Achiam, Steven Adler, Sandhini Agarwal, Lama Ahmad, Ilge Akkaya, Florencia Leoni Aleman, Diogo Almeida, Janko Altenschmidt, Sam Altman, Shyamal Anadkat, et al. 2023. Gpt-4 technical report. *arXiv preprint arXiv:2303.08774*.

01. AI, :, Alex Young, Bei Chen, Chao Li, Chengen Huang, Ge Zhang, Guanwei Zhang, Heng Li, Jiangcheng Zhu, Jianqun Chen, Jing Chang, Kaidong Yu, Peng Liu, Qiang Liu, Shawn Yue, Senbin Yang, Shiming Yang, Tao Yu, Wen Xie, Wenhao Huang, Xiaohui Hu, Xiaoyi Ren, Xinyao Niu, Pengcheng Nie, Yuchi Xu, Yudong Liu, Yue Wang, Yuxuan Cai, Zhenyu Gu, Zhiyuan Liu, and Zonghong Dai. 2024. Yi: Open foundation models by 01.ai.

Jinze Bai, Shuai Bai, Yunfei Chu, Zeyu Cui, Kai Dang, Xiaodong Deng, Yang Fan, Wenbin Ge, Yu Han, Fei Huang, et al. 2023. Qwen technical report. *arXiv preprint arXiv:2309.16609*.

Tom Brown, Benjamin Mann, Nick Ryder, Melanie Subbiah, Jared D Kaplan, Prafulla Dhariwal, Arvind Neelakantan, Pranav Shyam, Girish Sastry, Amanda Askell, et al. 2020. Language models are few-shot learners. *Advances in neural information processing systems*, 33:1877–1901.

Yupeng Chang, Xu Wang, Jindong Wang, Yuan Wu, Linyi Yang, Kaijie Zhu, Hao Chen, Xiaoyuan Yi, Cunxiang Wang, Yidong Wang, Wei Ye, Yue Zhang, Yi Chang, Philip S. Yu, Qiang Yang, and Xing Xie. 2023. A survey on evaluation of large language models.

Cheng-Han Chiang and Hung-yi Lee. 2023. Can large language models be an alternative to human evaluations? *arXiv preprint arXiv:2305.01937*.

Yung-Sung Chuang, Shang-Yu Su, and Yun-Nung Chen. 2020. Lifelong language knowledge distillation.

Ernest Davis. 2023. Benchmarks for automated commonsense reasoning: A survey. *arXiv preprint arXiv:2302.04752*.

Vittoria Dentella, Elliot Murphy, Gary Marcus, and Evelina Leivada. 2023. Testing ai performance on less frequent aspects of language reveals insensitivity to underlying meaning.

Zishan Guo, Renren Jin, Chuang Liu, Yufei Huang, Dan Shi, Supryadi, Linhao Yu, Yan Liu, Jiaxuan Li, Bojian Xiong, and Deyi Xiong. 2023. Evaluating large language models: A comprehensive survey.

Dan Hendrycks, Collin Burns, Steven Basart, Andy Zou, Mantas Mazeika, Dawn Song, and Jacob Steinhardt. 2020. Measuring massive multitask language understanding. *arXiv preprint arXiv:2009.03300*.

Yuzhen Huang, Yuzhuo Bai, Zhihao Zhu, Junlei Zhang, Jinghan Zhang, Tangjun Su, Junteng Liu, Chuancheng Lv, Yikai Zhang, Jiayi Lei, et al. 2023. C-eval: A multi-level multi-discipline chinese evaluation suite for foundation models. *arXiv preprint arXiv:2305.08322*.

Jena D Hwang, Chandra Bhagavatula, Ronan Le Bras, Jeff Da, Keisuke Sakaguchi, Antoine Bosselut, and Yejin Choi. 2021. (comet-) atomic 2020: on symbolic and neural commonsense knowledge graphs. In *Proceedings of the AAAI Conference on Artificial Intelligence*, volume 35, pages 6384–6392.

Albert Q Jiang, Alexandre Sablayrolles, Arthur Mensch, Chris Bamford, Devendra Singh Chaplot, Diego de las Casas, Florian Bressand, Gianna Lengyel, Guillaume Lample, Lucile Saulnier, et al. 2023. Mistral 7b. *arXiv preprint arXiv:2310.06825*.

Marzena Karpinska, Nader Akoury, and Mohit Iyyer. 2021. The perils of using mechanical turk to evaluate open-ended text generation. *arXiv preprint arXiv:2109.06835*.

Yanyang Li, Jianqiao Zhao, Duo Zheng, Zi-Yuan Hu, Zhi Chen, Xiaohui Su, Yongfeng Huang, Shijia Huang, Dahua Lin, Michael R Lyu, et al. 2023. Cleva: Chinese language models evaluation platform. *arXiv preprint arXiv:2308.04813*.

Yucheng Li. 2023. An open source data contamination report for llama series models. *arXiv preprint arXiv:2310.17589*.

Percy Liang, Rishi Bommasani, Tony Lee, Dimitris Tsipras, Dilara Soylu, Michihiro Yasunaga, Yian Zhang, Deepak Narayanan, Yuhuai Wu, Ananya Kumar, et al. 2022. Holistic evaluation of language models. *arXiv preprint arXiv:2211.09110*.

Chin-Yew Lin. 2004. Rouge: A package for automatic evaluation of summaries. In *Text summarization branches out*, pages 74–81.

Benjamin Marie. 2023. The decontaminated evaluation of gpt-4.

George A Miller. 1995. Wordnet: a lexical database for english. *Communications of the ACM*, 38(11):39–41.

George A Miller, Richard Beckwith, Christiane Fellbaum, Derek Gross, and Katherine J Miller. 1990. Introduction to wordnet: An on-line lexical database. *International journal of lexicography*, 3(4):235–244.

Fabio Petroni, Tim Rocktäschel, Patrick Lewis, Anton Bakhtin, Yuxiang Wu, Alexander H. Miller, and Sebastian Riedel. 2019. Language models as knowledge bases?

Oscar Sainz, Jon Ander Campos, Iker García-Ferrero, Julen Etxaniz, Oier Lopez de Lacalle, and Eneko Agirre. 2023. Nlp evaluation in trouble: On the need to measure llm data contamination for each benchmark. *arXiv preprint arXiv:2310.18018*.

Robyn Speer, Joshua Chin, and Catherine Havasi. 2017. Conceptnet 5.5: An open multilingual graph of general knowledge. In *Proceedings of the AAAI conference on artificial intelligence*, volume 31.

Mirac Suzgun, Nathan Scales, Nathanael Schärli, Sebastian Gehrmann, Yi Tay, Hyung Won Chung, Aakanksha Chowdhery, Quoc V Le, Ed H Chi, Denny Zhou, et al. 2022. Challenging big-bench tasks and whether chain-of-thought can solve them. *arXiv preprint arXiv:2210.09261*.

Hugo Touvron, Louis Martin, Kevin Stone, Peter Albert, Amjad Almahairi, Yasmine Babaei, Nikolay Bashlykov, Soumya Batra, Prajjwal Bhargava, Shruti Bhosale, et al. 2023. Llama 2: Open foundation and fine-tuned chat models. *arXiv preprint arXiv:2307.09288*.

Alex Wang, Amanpreet Singh, Julian Michael, Felix Hill, Omer Levy, and Samuel R Bowman. 2018. Glue: A multi-task benchmark and analysis platform for natural language understanding. *arXiv preprint arXiv:1804.07461*.

Albert Webson and Ellie Pavlick. 2021. Do prompt-based models really understand the meaning of their prompts? *arXiv preprint arXiv:2109.01247*.

Jason Wei, Xuezhi Wang, Dale Schuurmans, Maarten Bosma, Fei Xia, Ed Chi, Quoc V Le, Denny Zhou, et al. 2022. Chain-of-thought prompting elicits reasoning in large language models. *Advances in Neural Information Processing Systems*, 35:24824–24837.

Can Xu, Qingfeng Sun, Kai Zheng, Xiubo Geng, Pu Zhao, Jiazhan Feng, Chongyang Tao, and Daxin Jiang. 2023. Wizardlm: Empowering large language models to follow complex instructions.

Aiyuan Yang, Bin Xiao, Bingning Wang, Borong Zhang, Ce Bian, Chao Yin, Chenxu Lv, Da Pan, Dian Wang, Dong Yan, et al. 2023. Baichuan 2: Open large-scale language models. *arXiv preprint arXiv:2309.10305*.

Jifan Yu, Xiaozhi Wang, Shangqing Tu, Shulin Cao, Daniel Zhang-Li, Xin Lv, Hao Peng, Zijun Yao, Xiaohan Zhang, Hanming Li, et al. 2023. Kola: Carefully benchmarking world knowledge of large language models. *arXiv preprint arXiv:2306.09296*.

Baoli Zhang, Haining Xie, Pengfan Du, Junhao Chen, Pengfei Cao, Yubo Chen, Shengping Liu, Kang Liu, and Jun Zhao. 2023. Zhujiu: A multi-dimensional, multi-faceted chinese benchmark for large language models.

Wayne Xin Zhao, Kun Zhou, Junyi Li, Tianyi Tang, Xiaolei Wang, Yupeng Hou, Yingqian Min, Beichen Zhang, Junjie Zhang, Zican Dong, et al. 2023. A survey of large language models. *arXiv preprint arXiv:2303.18223*.

Lianmin Zheng, Wei-Lin Chiang, Ying Sheng, Tianle Li, Siyuan Zhuang, Zhanghao Wu, Yonghao Zhuang, Zhuohan Li, Zi Lin, Eric P. Xing, Joseph E. Gonzalez, Ion Stoica, and Hao Zhang. 2024. Lmsys-chat-1m: A large-scale real-world llm conversation dataset.

Wanjun Zhong, Ruixiang Cui, Yiduo Guo, Yaobo Liang, Shuai Lu, Yanlin Wang, Amin Saied, Weizhu Chen, and Nan Duan. 2023. Agieval: A human-centric benchmark for evaluating foundation models. *arXiv preprint arXiv:2304.06364*.

Kun Zhou, Yutao Zhu, Zhipeng Chen, Wentong Chen, Wayne Xin Zhao, Xu Chen, Yankai Lin, Ji-Rong Wen, and Jiawei Han. 2023a. Don't make your llm an evaluation benchmark cheater. *arXiv preprint arXiv:2311.01964*.

Kun Zhou, Yutao Zhu, Zhipeng Chen, Wentong Chen, Wayne Xin Zhao, Xu Chen, Yankai Lin, Ji-Rong Wen, and Jiawei Han. 2023b. Don't make your llm an evaluation benchmark cheater.

A Data construction

A.1 Prompt construction

We use GPT-4, GPT3.5, LLaMa70B, and Claude instance to build prompts. The specific instructions are as follows:

Now I would like you to provide me with some templates, and I will give you some examples to illustrate my requirements: OWant represents, as a result, Y or others want For relationships<Event, oWant, Result>, construct the following question: What do PersonalY or others want to do next? <Event, oWant, Result>can be: PersonX admissions PersonY's work, oWant, to be acknowledged PersonX admissions PersonY was wrong, oWant, to apologize PersonX options a child, oWant, to decorate room Please provide me with more questions

Table 2: An example of building multiple prompts

A.2 ConceptNet Question Construction

Table 3 displays a prompt for formulating an LLM query derived from a ConceptNet triple.

Triplet	<hammer , AtLocation , tool box>
Prompt	Where is ______ typically located?
Question	Where is hammer typically located?
Answer	Tool box

Table 3: ConceptNet data construction process

Metrics \ Knowledge / LLMs	Conceptnet		
	A_{CQ}	A_{QA}	H
Yi-6B-Chat	43.47	71.29	0.40
TChatGLM3-6b	38.17	73.59	0.63
WizardLM-13B-V1.2	39.62	74.18	0.48
Baichuan-13B-Chat	35.43	74.23	0.54
Baichuan2-13B-Chat	38.21	73.7	0.65
Baichuan2-7B-Chat	39.26	74.85	0.61
Vicuna-13b-v1.5	43.18	73.05	0.50
Vicuna-7b-v1.5	42.13	72.59	0.53
LLaMa2-13b-chat	37.94	73.75	0.49
LLaMa2-7b-chat	39.8	74.69	0.55
Mistral-7B-Instruct-v0.1	42.58	72.41	0.47
Mistral-7B-Instruct-v0.2	44.12	73.28	0.57
Qwen-14B-Chat	43.56	72.33	0.57
Qwen-7B-Chat	38.62	72.05	0.56

Table 4: The specific performance of the LLMs in ConceptNet. A_{CQ}: multiple choice question accuracy, A_{QA}: QA question accuracy, H: entropy.

A.3 ATOMIC Question Construction

During the process of constructing questions, we attempted to replace person variables (e.g., PersonX, PersonY) from ATOMIC with common human names. However, this led the model to treat them as real individuals and refuse to answer. Therefore, we directly use person variables in the questions to refer to human beings, thereby obtaining more objective answers.

Triplet	<PersonX accepts thanks , xReact , happy>
Prompt	______. How does PersonX feel?
Question	PersonX accepts thanks. How does PersonX feel?
Answer	happy

Table 5: ConceptNet data construction process

B Model self-preference value

To measure whether the model exhibits a preference for its own generated results, we use $rank(i, j)$ to represent the ranking assigned by evaluation model i to evaluation model j. We calculated the P as the self-preference value and $G(P)$ as the global self-preference value of models for their generated results in each knowledge domain and present the top five results in Table 7.

Metrics \ Knowledge / LLMs	Conceptnet		
	A_{CQ}	A_{QA}	H
Yi-6B-Chat	51.68	48.96	0.40
Chatglm3-6b	45.52	51.66	0.44
WizardLM-13B-V1.2	36.69	52.18	0.33
Baichuan-13B-Chat	42.95	51.92	0.37
Baichuan2-13B-Chat	47.11	49.71	0.45
Baichuan2-7B-Chat	44.30	41.46	0.43
Vicuna-13b-v1.5	47.19	46.88	0.35
Vicuna-7b-v1.5	46.71	49.97	0.37
LLaMa2-13b-chat	39.69	50.4	0.34
LLaMa2-7b-chat	36.96	48.79	0.38
Mistral-7B-Instruct-v0.1	47.19	47.44	0.33
Mistral-7B-Instruct-v0.2	47.71	51.23	0.40
Qwen-14B-Chat	55.77	49.79	0.39
Qwen-7B-Chat	50.33	47.39	0.39

Table 6: The specific performance of the LLMs in ATOMIC. A_{CQ}: multiple choice question accuracy, A_{QA}: QA question accuracy, H: entropy.

$$P(i) = \frac{1}{k-1}\sum_{\substack{j=1 \\ j\neq i}}^{k}(rank(j,i) - rank(i,i)) \tag{4}$$

$$G(P) = \frac{1}{k}\sum_{i=1}^{k}(P(i)) \tag{5}$$

C The Performance of LLMs in World Knowledge and Language Knowledge

We conducted a detailed analysis of the performance of LLMs on world knowledge. As illustrated in Figure 2, the models exhibit significantly better performance on high-frequency knowledge compared to low-frequency knowledge, indicating a certain challenge in mastering low-frequency world knowledge. Additionally, the models exhibit low sensitivity to time-sensitive knowledge, implying a potential confusion of temporal occurrence times.

We also conducted a detailed analysis of the performance of LLMs in the scope of language. As illustrated in Figure 4, compared to other tasks, these models exhibit significantly better performance in pos-analysis tasks, indicating that the models are well-versed in more traditional natural language processing tasks like POS analysis. However, they exhibit lower proficiency in reverse tasks and tasks requiring deeper understanding and application of the knowledge corpus.

Model Name	Total Score	common-frequency	high-frequency	low-frequency	timeliness
01ai/Yi-34B-Chat	**79.85**	47.75	45.5	27.45	37.5
lmsys/vicuna-13b-v1.5	**78.06**	45.5	42.4	37.3	24.45
qwen/Qwen-72B-Chat	**75.3**	42.95	36.6	27.25	49.3
mistralai/Mistral-7B-Instruct-v0.2	**74.38**	44.05	39.6	39.55	20.25
WizardLM/WizardLM-13B-V1.2	**67.13**	44.85	43.7	31.2	16.3
baichuan-inc/Baichuan-13B-Chat	**64.7**	37.8	34.05	33.85	30.65
lmsys/vicuna-7b-v1.5	**59.25**	40.3	34.5	33.4	18.4
meta/llama2-70b-chat	**58.75**	43	37.2	16.75	39.7
qwen/Qwen-14B-Chat	**51.54**	37.65	31.85	31.1	17.05
01ai/Yi-6B-Chat	**50.62**	33.2	32	18.15	44.4
baichuan-inc/Baichuan2-7B-Chat	**50.53**	33.35	32.35	31.3	20.2
baichuan-inc/Baichuan2-13B-Chat	**47.84**	37.15	34.35	23.3	22
qwen/Qwen-7B-Chat	**46.67**	33.9	29.85	31	17.1
meta/llama2-13b-chat	**37.75**	31.85	31.95	24.4	13.95
mistralai/Mistral-7B-Instruct-v0.1	**36.71**	30.15	28.9	25.7	16.5
THUDM/chatglm3-6b	**19.21**	22.7	23.5	20.4	14.7
meta/llama2-7b-chat	**0**	17.5	15.85	16.3	8

Figure 2: The performance of LLMs on common-frequency, high-frequency, low-frequency, and timeliness in world knowledge.

Model Name	Total Score	commonsense_ConceptNet
baichuan-inc/Baichuan2-7B-Chat	100	74.85
meta/llama2-7b-chat	**95.51**	74.69
baichuan-inc/Baichuan-13B-Chat	**82.58**	74.23
WizardLM/WizardLM-13B-V1.2	**81.18**	74.18
meta/llama2-13b-chat	**69.1**	73.75
THUDM/chatglm3-6b	**64.61**	73.59
baichuan-inc/Baichuan2-13B-Chat	**61.24**	73.47
mistralai/Mistral-7B-Instruct-v0.2	**55.9**	73.28
lmsys/vicuna-13b-v1.5	**49.44**	73.05
lmsys/vicuna-7b-v1.5	**36.52**	72.59
mistralai/Mistral-7B-Instruct-v0.1	**31.46**	72.41
qwen/Qwen-14B-Chat	**29.21**	72.33
qwen/Qwen-7B-Chat	**21.35**	72.05
01ai/Yi-6B-Chat	**0**	71.29

Figure 3: The performance of LLMs on ConceptNet in commonsense knowledge.

Model Name	Total Score	idiom_explanation	pos_analysis	semantic_selection	similar_words
01ai/Yi-34B-Chat	**96.92**	95.6	98.88	93.98	94.29
openai/chatgpt	**95.48**	85.71	100	97.14	93.75
WizardLM/WizardLM-13B-V1.2	**94.5**	85.19	98.86	97.48	93.94
qwen/Qwen-72B-Chat	**94.05**	86.41	98.8	94.07	94.63
lmsys/vicuna-13b-v1.5	**93.98**	79.2	99.4	97.48	95.36
01ai/Yi-6B-Chat	**92.45**	92.38	98.21	94.08	90.2
qwen/Qwen-14B-Chat	**91.61**	85.96	99.38	89.44	93.02
lmsys/vicuna-7b-v1.5	**89.67**	74.78	100	92.02	93.38
mistralai/Mistral-7B-Instruct-v0.2	**89.57**	72.45	98.87	95.42	94.05
qwen/Qwen-7B-Chat	**89.05**	85.05	98.8	92.31	88.95
meta/llama2-13b-chat	**89.02**	81.9	97.31	90.59	93.41
meta/Llama-2-70b-chat	**81.21**	67.27	96.17	83.67	94.44
baichuan-inc/Baichuan-13B-Chat	**80.61**	79.57	96.92	83.78	86.5
THUDM/chatglm3-6b	**71.07**	77.52	88.58	73.61	90.48
baichuan-inc/Baichuan2-13B-Chat	**69.11**	71.55	92.9	63.76	90
mistralai/Mistral-7B-Instruct-v0.1	**61.67**	20.51	96.79	73.78	93.18
tiiuae/falcon-40b-instruct	**60.64**	53.33	92.53	63.95	86.89
meta/llama2-7b-chat	**54.16**	65.57	92.12	68.18	69.74
baichuan-inc/Baichuan2-7B-Chat	**15.17**	66.06	73.21	30.49	58.87

Figure 4: The four knowledge corpus-based tasks performance of LLMs in language knowledge.

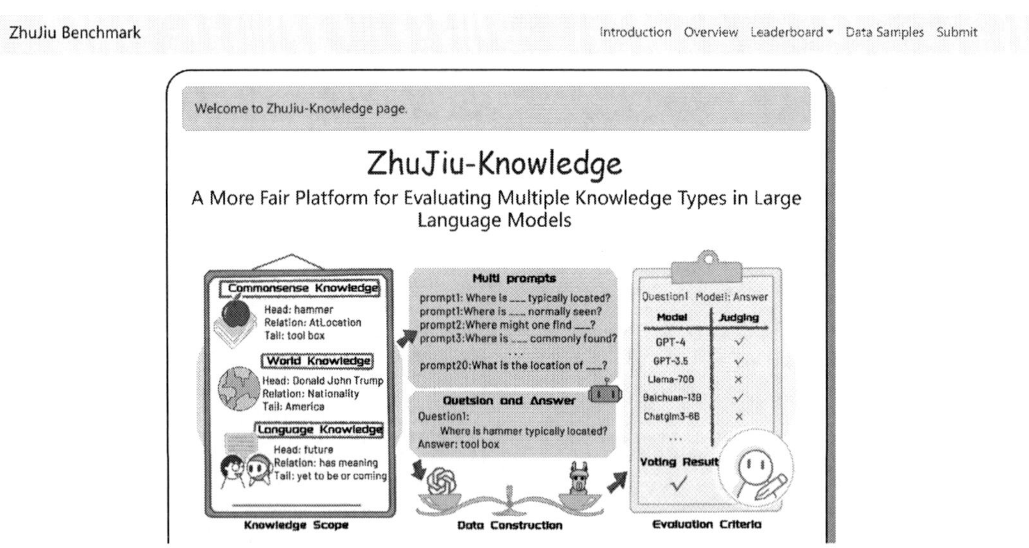

Figure 5: The introduction page of Zhujiu-knowledge platform.

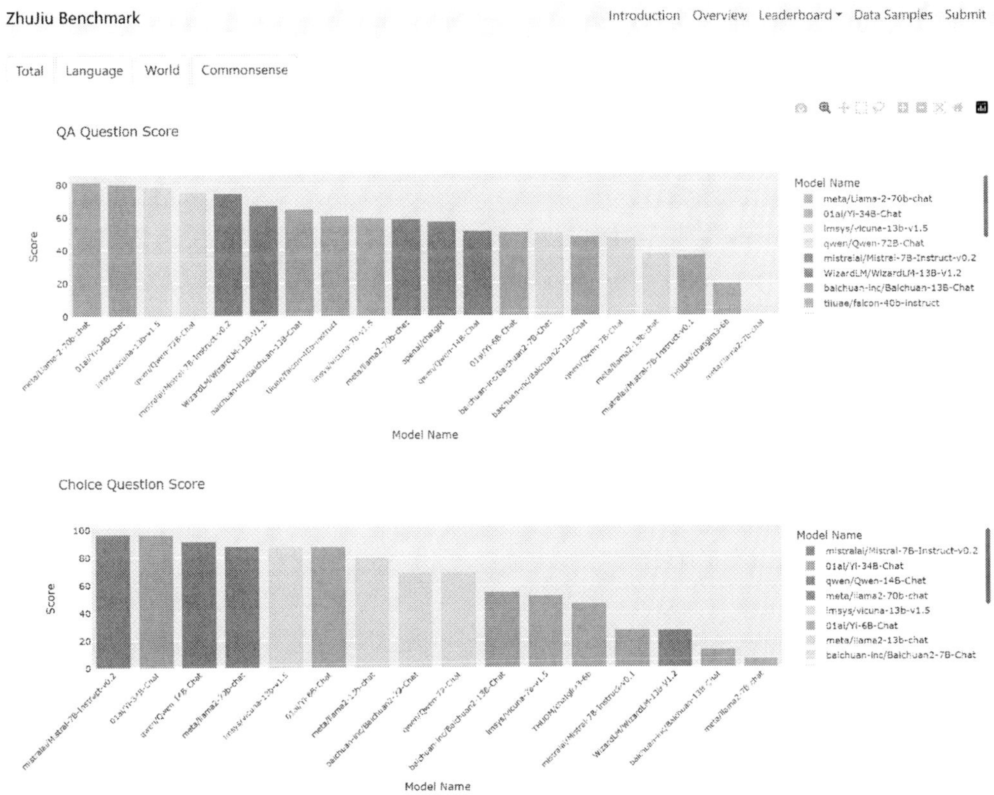

Figure 6: Overview Performance: The total score of LLMs in QA question and Choice question.

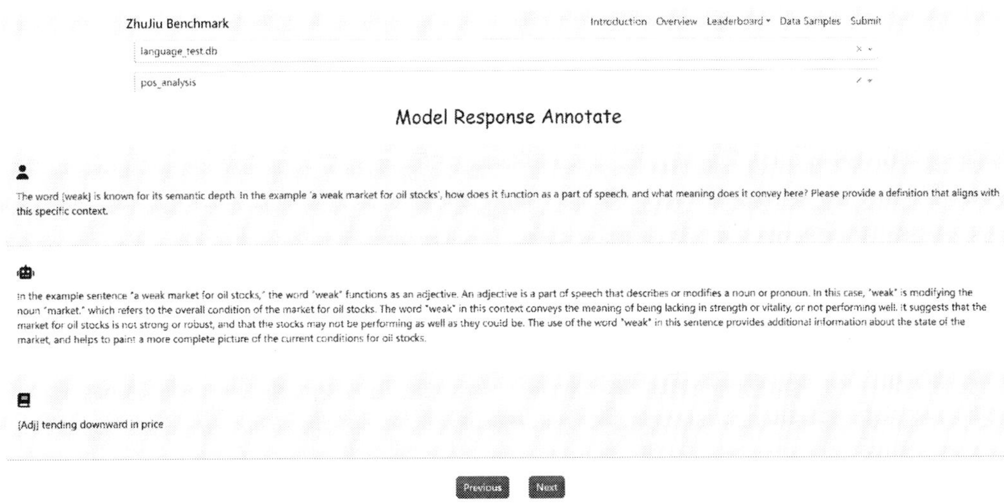

Figure 7: The dataset demonstration page.

evalmodel	commonsense	world	lanauage
top-model1	-3.2	-8.6	6.6
top-model2	0.2	4.4	4.4
top-model3	4.6	0.6	-6.2
top-model4	0.4	-0.75	0.4
top-model5	-1.4	6.8	-1.8
global-self-preference	0.1	0.5	0.6

Table 7: The self-preference value of the top five LLMs in three knowledge evaluations

Unitxt: Flexible, Shareable and Reusable Data Preparation and Evaluation for Generative AI

Elron Bandel **Yotam Perlitz** **Elad Venezian** **Roni Friedman-Melamed**
Ofir Arviv **Matan Orbach** **Shachar Don-Yehiya** **Dafna Sheinwald**
Ariel Gera **Leshem Choshen** **Michal Shmueli-Scheuer** **Yoav Katz**
IBM Research
elron.bandel@ibm.com

Abstract

In the dynamic landscape of generative NLP, traditional text processing pipelines limit research flexibility and reproducibility, as they are tailored to specific dataset, task, and model combinations. The escalating complexity, involving system prompts, model-specific formats, instructions, and more, calls for a shift to a structured, modular, and customizable solution. Addressing this need, we present Unitxt, an innovative library for customizable textual data preparation and evaluation tailored to generative language models. Unitxt natively integrates with common libraries like HuggingFace and LM-eval-harness and deconstructs processing flows into modular components, enabling easy customization and sharing between practitioners. These components encompass model-specific formats, task prompts, and many other comprehensive dataset processing definitions. The Unitxt Catalog centralizes these components, fostering collaboration and exploration in modern textual data workflows. Beyond being a tool, Unitxt is a community-driven platform, empowering users to build, share, and advance their pipelines collaboratively. Join the Unitxt community;
Project: https://github.com/IBM/unitxt.
UI: https://bit.ly/unitxt-explore
Video: https://bit.ly/unitxt-video

1 Introduction

Textual data processing has always been at the heart of NLP, but in the current landscape it has taken on new roles. A prominent one comes from LLMs' role as general interfaces, that receive an example, but also the task they should perform, general system instruction and other specifications, all in natural language. Thus, the inputs – or *prompts* – that a model receives now consist of many components, that can be combined in different ways: task instructions (Wei et al., 2022), in-context demonstrations (Brown et al., 2020), system prompts and more. At the same time, for text generation models, model outputs are themselves rich textual data, and thus can be processed and evaluated with a range of different approaches and paradigms. Therefore, textual data processing for LLMs is growing increasingly complex. It incorporates a large number of non-trivial design choices and parameters, which pose new challenges for maintaining flexibility and reproducibility in LLM research.

Broadly, research in computer science, and in particular within NLP, thrives on that combination of flexibility and reproducibility. On the one hand, it should be simple to try new ideas: to compare different approaches, choose parameters, and easily switch out one workflow or architecture with another. On the other hand, the results of these explorations must be shared in such a way that others are able to – and crucially, are likely to – reproduce and try them. To enable the above, code reuse, a well-defined API and ease of use are pivotal, ensuring reproducibility and applicability in practice. How such traits allow for widespread adoption is epitomized by the Hugging Face transformers library (Wolf et al., 2020). Today, a modest set of hyperparameters is sufficient to reproduce a training or inference workflow. This has had an undeniable and dramatic impact on the ability to make progress in the field.

Such is not the case, however, for textual data pipelines. Unfortunately, data-preparation for LLMs has no standards, Processing model inputs or outputs of the same data often comes with rewriting the code, leading to mismatches in reported values (Post, 2018), unanswerable examples and hidden bugs (Fourrier et al., 2023) and general time waste. Crucially, the additional components beyond traditional processing, such as in-context demonstrations, have no canonical API. This prevents fair comparisons between different studies, discourages exploring combinations, hinders integrating a particular approach (say, a new type of system prompt) into an existing NLP system, and prevents major

Proceedings of the 2024 Conference of the North American Chapter of the Association for Computational Linguistics: Human Language Technologies (Volume 3: System Demonstrations), pages 207–215
June 16-21, 2024 ©2024 Association for Computational Linguistics

scale-ups in terms of datasets, tasks and metrics.

To address these gaps, we introduce a new collaborative framework for unified textual data processing named `Unitxt`. This new Python library supports multilingual textual data processing through flexible pipelines called *recipes*. A recipe (see §4.1 and examples in §3) is a sequence of textual data processing operators, including, among others, operators that load data, pre-process it, handle the preparation of different parts of a prompt, or evaluate model predictions (see Figure 1).

Aiming for reuse, `Unitxt` ships with a catalog containing a wide variety of pre-defined recipes for various tasks. These are all based on a diverse set of built-in operators that are also shared in the catalog. Having a centralized location for these components, where anyone can add new ingredients (such as recipes or operators), or share existing ones, fosters collaboration, transparency and reproducibility.

As fitting a Recipe, the modularity of `Unitxt` enables mixing and matching of ingredients to create new recipes. This ability to mix and match ingredients enables `Unitxt` to support 100K+ recipe configurations, allowing users to experiment with a large set of such recipes by to obtain multiple configurations of tasks, datasets and new formatting (see §3 for example).

Changing libraries is always a nuisance; therefore, `Unitxt` is designed to seamlessly integrate with preexisting code, offering a hassle-free experience without even needing a pip install. For instance, `Unitxt` can load HuggingFace datasets and produce outputs that adhere to the same format, allowing it to integrate seamlessly with other parts of your codebase (§4.4.1). Demonstrating this, incorporating `Unitxt`, with all its tasks, datasets, templates and metrics into LM-eval-harness (Gao et al., 2023) required only 30 lines of code, while preserving the current API and ensuring a smooth transition and compatibility with existing workflows (App. A).

`Unitxt`, an open-source library, is under active development by IBM and the community. The code and documentation are available on GitHub at: `https://github.com/IBM/unitxt`, the UI, at `https://bit.ly/unitxt-explore` while the demo video is at `https://bit.ly/unitxt-video`.

2 Use cases

`Unitxt` for evaluation: The increasing capabilities of LLMs require evaluation frameworks that test models over an unprecedented number of datasets, tasks and configurations (Liang et al., 2022; Gao et al., 2023; Contributors, 2023). `Unitxt` can serve as the backbone of such evaluation efforts, by supporting easy changes across multiple important axes, including tasks, languages, prompt structure (e.g. instructions, verbalizations, etc.), augmentation robustness and more. Moreover, with the `Unitxt Catalog`, different distinct projects can share their full evaluation pipelines, making their data-preparation and evaluation metrics reproducible.

`Unitxt` for training: Modern LLM training frameworks have extensive data requirements to attain state-of-the-art performance. Multiple datasets across diverse domains and languages need to be leveraged to impart broad capabilities; Various prompt formulations and *verbalizations* are necessary to enable instruction-following, where verbalizations are the final text form. However, combining heterogeneous data sources and textual representations poses significant engineering challenges. Without a common underlying framework, data augmentation, multitask learning and few-shot tuning become prohibitively complex. This is where `Unitxt` steps in, as an indispensable data backend.

`Unitxt` enables seamless fusion of diverse datasets. Moreover, the standardized format also facilitates changes to the datasets, dynamic prompt generation, data augmentations and model-specific format, to name just a few. By handling the data wrangling complexity, `Unitxt` empowers researchers to focus on creating performant, robust and safe LLMs.

For both evaluation and training, `Unitxt` *has already been adopted* as a core utility for LLMs in IBM by multiple teams working on various NLP tasks, including classification, extraction, summarization, generation, question answering, code, biases and more. In total, the open source catalog contains more than 100K possible pipeline configurations.

3 Unitxt: Library Tour

To introduce unitxt, we begin with a tour of the library, and specifically, with the creation of a recipe. A recipe contains all the data-processing and metric configurations needed, including the data, task,

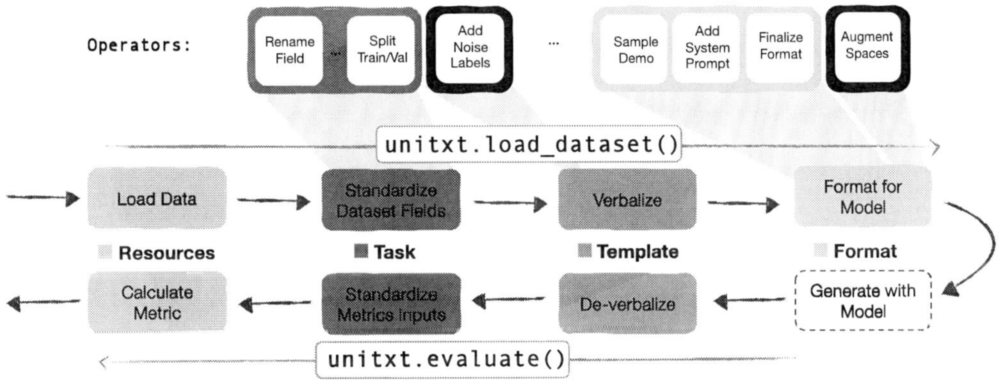

Figure 1: `Unitxt` flow: The upper section illustrates the data-preparation pipeline §4.4.1, encompassing raw dataset loading, standardization according to the task interface, verbalization using templates, and application of formatting. The lower section showcases the evaluation pipeline §4.4.2, involving de-verbalization operations and output standardization before performance evaluation with task-defined metrics. All components are described in §4.2.

template and formatting (see details in §4). Here we define a recipe that loads the STS-B dataset for a sentence similarity task:

```
recipe = """
    card=cards.stsb, # dataset info card
    template=templates.text_similarity,
    sys_prompt=prompts.helpful,
    format=formats.user_agent,
    num_demos=1
"""
```

With a recipe, a concrete dataset can be loaded:

```
dataset = unitxt.load_dataset(recipe)
```

Importantly, every data instance in a dataset loaded with a unitxt recipe contains a fully prepared source text, which can be directly passed as input to the model. For example, here is such source text for one sentence-similarity data instance, integrated with three formatting decisions, a "helpful model" system-prompt, a user-agent response schema and one demonstration:

```
[System] you are helpful model [/System]
[User]: for the following texts rank the
        similarity between 1 to 5.
        Text 1: "i love ice cream"
        Text 2: "i like ice cream"
[Agent]: 4.8
[User]: Text 1: "i hate pizza"
        Text 2: "i like pizza"
[Agent]:
```

Loading a dataset with a unitxt recipe also adds a metric-ready target text (created from the original target) to each data instance. To Evaluate the model's textual predictions, we call:

```
results = unitxt.evaluate(
    dataset,
    predictions=predictions,
)
```

The evaluation results are a dictionary of task defined metric names and the values computed for them.

4 Design

In this section we outline the design of `Unitxt`. `Unitxt` processes data by applying a modular sequence of operators, which are segmented into 5 key ingredients (§4.2) color-coded as in Fig. 1: ■ Resources, ■ Task, ■ Template, ■ Format and ■ Extensions. These ingredients are then used to build the **data preparation** (§4.4.1) and **evaluation** (§4.4.2) pipelines.

4.1 `Unitxt` Building Blocks

When loading a dataset (as demonstrated in §3), the `Unitxt` ingredients are retrieved based on a *Data-Task Card* and a *Recipe*.

■■ Data-Task Card Defines how raw data (inputs and targets) are standardized for a certain task. Typically, this includes data wrangling actions, e.g. renaming fields, filtering data instances, modifying values, train/test/val splitting etc. It also describes the resource from which the data is loaded.

■■■■■ Recipe A *Recipe* holds a complete specification of a `Unitxt` pipeline: including the Resources, Task, Template, Format and Extensions.

4.2 Unitxt Ingredients

Resources Raw data and metrics are external resources utilized by Unitxt. Unitxt implements several APIs for raw-data and metric loading (e.g., from Huggingface Hub, local files, and cloud storage).

Task A Unitxt *Task* follows the formal definition of an NLP task, such as multi-label classification, named entity extraction, abstractive summarization or translation. A task is defined by its standard interface – namely, input and output fields – and by its evaluation metrics. Given a dataset, its contents are standardized into the fields defined by an appropriate task by a Data-Task Card (§4.1).

As an example of a defined task, consider sentence similarity: it has two input fields (named "sentence1" and, "sentence2"), one output field (named "label") and the conventional metric is Spearman correlation (Spearman, 1904).

Template A Unitxt *Template* defines the verbalizations to be applied to the inputs and targets, as well as the de-verbalization operations over the model predictions. For example, in Fig 2, applying the template to `I like toast` verbalizes it into `classify the sentence: "I like toast"`.

In the other direction, template de-verbalization involves two steps. First, a general standardization of the output texts: taking only the first non-empty line of a model's predictions, lowercasing, stripping whitespaces, etc. The second step standardizes the output to the specific task at-hand. For example, in Sentence Similarity, a prediction may be a quantized float number outputted as a string (e.g "2.43"), or a verbally expressed numeric expression (e.g "two and a half"). This depends on the verbalization defined by the template and the in-context demonstrations it constructs. Both types of outputs should be standardized before evaluation begins – e.g. to a float for sentence similarity. Having the de-verbalization steps defined within the template enables templates reuse across different models and datasets.

Crucially, in contrast to existing solutions (e.g., Bach et al., 2022) the templates, datasets and tasks in Unitxt are not exclusively tied. Each task can harness multiple templates and a template can be used for different datasets. Thus, the modularity of Unitxt allows mixing and matching, significantly enhancing re-usability and flexibility.

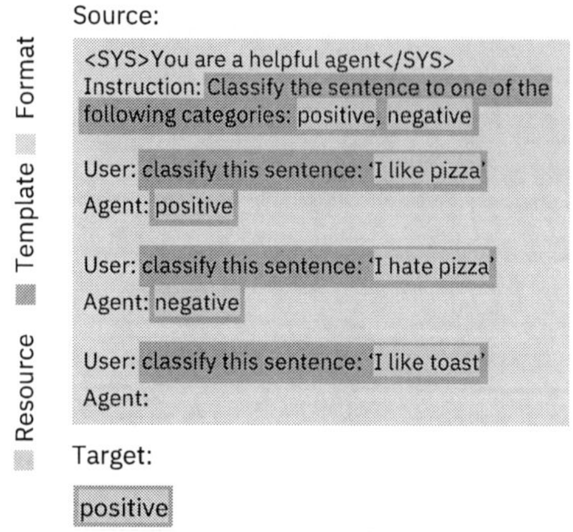

Figure 2: Illustration of the data preparation pipeline (§4.4.1), depicting the transformation from raw data and formatting specifications to the final text output. Components include Resources (raw data), Format (model-specific formatting requirements), and Template (verbalization).

Format A Unitxt *Format* defines a set of extra formatting requirements, unrelated to the underlying data or task, including those pertaining to system prompts, special tokens or user/agent prefixes, and in-context demonstrations. Continuing the example from Figure 2, the Unitxt format receives the text produced by the template `classify the sentence: "I like toast"`, and adds the system prompt `<SYS>You are a helpful agent</SYS>`, the Instruction-User-Agent schema cues, and the two presented demonstrations.

Extensions Unitxt supports *Extensions* such as *input-augmentation* (for example, adding random whitespace, introducing spelling mistakes, or replacing words with their synonyms) or *label-noising* (replaces the labels in the demonstrations randomly from a list of options). Such extensions can be added anywhere in the data-preparation pipeline between any two operators, depending on the desired logic (see Fig. 1). Unitxt supports the addition of custom extensions to the Catalog. Each extension is an independent unit, reusable across different datasets and tasks, templates and formats.

4.3 Unitxt Catalog

All Unitxt artifacts – recipes, data-task cards, templates, pre-processing operators, formats and metrics – are stored in the Unitxt Catalog. In addition to the open-source catalog, that can be found in the documentation, users can choose to define a private catalog. This enables teams and organizations to harness the open `Unitxt Catalog` while upholding organizational requirements for additional proprietary artifacts.

4.4 `Unitxt` Pipelines

4.4.1 Data Preparation Pipeline

The data preparation pipeline (top part ot Fig. 1) begins with standardizing the raw data into the task interface, as defined in the data-task card (§4.1). The examples are then verbalized by the template, and the format operator applies system prompts, special tokens and in-context learning examples (§4.2), as illustrated in Figure 2. To maintain compatibility, the output of this pipeline is an HF dataset, that can be saved or pushed to the hub.

4.4.2 Evaluation Pipeline

The evaluation pipeline (bottom part of Fig. 1) is responsible for producing a list of evaluation scores that reflect model performance. It includes a deverbalization of the model outputs (as defined in the template, see §4.2), and a computation of performance by the metrics defined in the task. The standardization of the task interface, namely, having fixed names and types for its input and output fields, allows the use of any metric that accept such fields as input. In addition to the computed evaluation scores, `Unitxt` metrics supports a built in mechanism for confidence interval reporting, using statistical bootstrap (Perlitz et al., 2023).

5 `Unitxt` UI: Explore & Preview

The objective of the user interface is to guide users through the essential steps of recipe creation, illustrated with pertinent examples. Additionally, it allows for catalog exploration. The UI complements the experience with the option to execute the examples on some pre-set model (e.g., flan-t5-base), get the predictions and associated scores.

The interaction entry point is the tasks. Upon clicking, the tasks taxonomy is presented, and the users have the option to choose the applicable task type. Selecting a task results in showing only the relevant datasets and templates. Once the user selects a dataset, and a template, and presses "Generate Prompts" a random example enhanced with the template is loaded. If the user wants to augment the input with system prompt, or response-schema those will be instantly added when opted for. As in-context learning evaluations are supported, the user can select the preferred number of shots. Once satisfied with the example, the user has the option to proceed with executing it on a model, wherein the predictions and corresponding scores will be displayed for this specific example. Further, going to the code tab, the user can copy the associated code into a notebook and run. Users have the option to explore various examples, enhancing their comprehension and confidence in the chosen configuration.

6 Related work

Standardized data processing for evaluation and training has been a longstanding need in the NLP community and has been repeatedly addressed in the past. Datasets (Lhoest et al., 2021) and Evaluate[1] are community-driven libraries, providing a standardized interface to diverse corpora and metrics, as well as supporting many data processing operations. These packages, however, fall short of providing a standardized, shareable and reproducible framework to cast the raw data into textual prompts and cast them back from text to a metric digestible format. The lack of such a framework hinders reproducibility, as often slight variations in ad-hoc text processing code may yield significantly different evaluation scores. Moreover, it also prevents users from easily scaling up their experiment, as each task and dataset often requires specific code for processing and evaluation. `Unitxt` builds on top of these frameworks, harnessing them as resources (§4.1) to produce a full data-preparation and evaluation framework.

While several existing frameworks have contributed to data pipeline management workflows, a common drawback, for those we are aware of, is the absence of a well-defined and flexible modularity in their design, such as the ability to define specific components for system prompts, task instructions and model-specific formats. This absence of clearly defined components makes it challenging to share and customize such pipelines effectively, across different datasets and tasks.

Like `Unitxt`, Tasksource (Sileo, 2023) supplies tools for consistent preprocessing over different datasets, simplifying their usage. However, it is primarily designed for discriminative tasks, uses fixed formats and lacks a modular design that enables sharing, mixing and matching, and overall

[1] `https://github.com/huggingface/evaluate/`

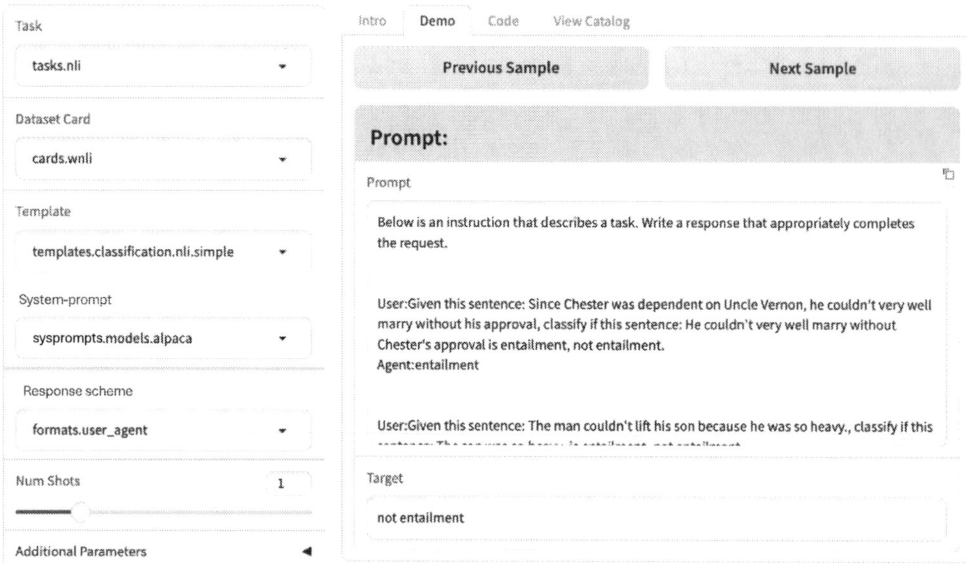

Figure 3: Exploration UI showcasing configuration options for model input creation on the left, including parameters such as task, dataset card, template, system-prompt, response-schema, number of examples, and optional augmentations. The resulting model input is displayed in the prompt window.

flexibility in processing steps. Promptsource (Bach et al., 2022) focuses on making and sharing natural language prompts but doesn't handle other types of data processing. Each prompt is tied to just one dataset, making it hard to reuse and share. Furthermore, prompts aren't split into system, instruction, and format parts, limiting options for flexibility and reuse. SeqIO (Roberts et al., 2022), offers task-based pipelines encompassing pre-processing, post-processing, and handling metrics. However, a structured breakdown of these processing steps is absent, limiting the creation of shareable catalogs within the community. In this framework, each process is a generic function and specialized steps are missing, like those designed for system prompts.

A different branch of solutions are language model evaluation frameworks such as OpenCompass (Contributors, 2023), HELM (Liang et al., 2022) and LM-eval-harness (Gao et al., 2023) also implement their own standardized data processing pipelines in order to obtain verbalized prompts for LMs. These, however, are highly coupled with the inference engine and cannot be used as standalone data-processing pipelines or integrated into other code bases.

7 Conclusion

In this paper, we have introduced `Unitxt`, an open-source Python library aimed at unifying textual data processing pipelines for large language models. `Unitxt` provides a modular, flexible framework that enables mixing and matching of various pipeline components like loaders, templates, formats and metrics. `Unitxt` key capabilities are, standardization, flexibility, collaboration and scale.

`Unitxt` has already been successfully deployed for large language model evaluation and training within IBM. As the library matures through open-source community involvement, we hope its adoption will grow to push the frontiers of textual data processing for LLMs. We believe `Unitxt` has the potential to significantly impact research and development of large language models by unifying textual data processing. Through its emphasis on flexibility, reproducibility and collaboration, unitxt can help drive progress towards more capable, safer and trustworthy LLMs.

8 Limitations

While unitxt makes significant progress towards unified textual data processing for LLMs, some limitations still remain:

- The `Unitxt Catalog`, while already substantial in coverage, needs expansion to encompass more datasets, languages, and niche tasks. Community contributions will be key to enhancing catalog diversity.

- Coverage of evaluation metrics, especially for generative tasks, needs improvement. We plan to incorporate more reference-free and LLM-based metrics going forward.
- Training data augmentation abilities, while flexible currently, can be expanded further with techniques like back-translation for multilinguality.
- While using `Unitxt` recipes is as simple as specifying the recipe ingrediants, adding new datasets or operators requires learning the `Unitxt` operator language. Additional documentation, examples and IDE support could help alleviate this.

Addressing these limitations through open-source community involvement is the major focus going forward. By tapping into collective expertise, we envision unitxt becoming an indispensable textual data processing backbone for the responsible development, evaluation and deployment of large language models.

References

Stephen H. Bach, Victor Sanh, Zheng-Xin Yong, Albert Webson, Colin Raffel, Nihal V. Nayak, Abheesht Sharma, Taewoon Kim, M Saiful Bari, Thibault Fevry, Zaid Alyafeai, Manan Dey, Andrea Santilli, Zhiqing Sun, Srulik Ben-David, Canwen Xu, Gunjan Chhablani, Han Wang, Jason Alan Fries, Maged S. Al-shaibani, Shanya Sharma, Urmish Thakker, Khalid Almubarak, Xiangru Tang, Xiangru Tang, Mike Tian Jian Jiang, and Alexander M. Rush. 2022. Promptsource: An integrated development environment and repository for natural language prompts.

Tom Brown, Benjamin Mann, Nick Ryder, Melanie Subbiah, Jared D Kaplan, Prafulla Dhariwal, Arvind Neelakantan, Pranav Shyam, Girish Sastry, Amanda Askell, Sandhini Agarwal, Ariel Herbert-Voss, Gretchen Krueger, Tom Henighan, Rewon Child, Aditya Ramesh, Daniel Ziegler, Jeffrey Wu, Clemens Winter, Chris Hesse, Mark Chen, Eric Sigler, Mateusz Litwin, Scott Gray, Benjamin Chess, Jack Clark, Christopher Berner, Sam McCandlish, Alec Radford, Ilya Sutskever, and Dario Amodei. 2020. Language models are few-shot learners. In *Advances in Neural Information Processing Systems*, volume 33, pages 1877–1901. Curran Associates, Inc.

OpenCompass Contributors. 2023. Opencompass: A universal evaluation platform for foundation models. `https://github.com/open-compass/opencompass`.

Clémentine Fourrier, Alex Cabrera, Stella Biderman, Nathan Habib, and Thomas Wolf. 2023. Open llm leaderboard: Drop deep dive.

Leo Gao, Jonathan Tow, Baber Abbasi, Stella Biderman, Sid Black, Anthony DiPofi, Charles Foster, Laurence Golding, Jeffrey Hsu, Alain Le Noac'h, Haonan Li, Kyle McDonell, Niklas Muennighoff, Chris Ociepa, Jason Phang, Laria Reynolds, Hailey Schoelkopf, Aviya Skowron, Lintang Sutawika, Eric Tang, Anish Thite, Ben Wang, Kevin Wang, and Andy Zou. 2023. A framework for few-shot language model evaluation.

Quentin Lhoest, Albert Villanova del Moral, Yacine Jernite, Abhishek Thakur, Patrick von Platen, Suraj Patil, Julien Chaumond, Mariama Drame, Julien Plu, Lewis Tunstall, Joe Davison, Mario Šaško, Gunjan Chhablani, Bhavitvya Malik, Simon Brandeis, Teven Le Scao, Victor Sanh, Canwen Xu, Nicolas Patry, Angelina McMillan-Major, Philipp Schmid, Sylvain Gugger, Clément Delangue, Théo Matussière, Lysandre Debut, Stas Bekman, Pierric Cistac, Thibault Goehringer, Victor Mustar, François Lagunas, Alexander Rush, and Thomas Wolf. 2021. Datasets: A community library for natural language processing. In *Proceedings of the 2021 Conference on Empirical Methods in Natural Language Processing: System Demonstrations*, pages 175–184, Online and Punta Cana, Dominican Republic. Association for Computational Linguistics.

Percy Liang, Rishi Bommasani, Tony Lee, Dimitris Tsipras, Dilara Soylu, Michihiro Yasunaga, Yian Zhang, Deepak Narayanan, Yuhuai Wu, Ananya Kumar, et al. 2022. Holistic evaluation of language models. *arXiv preprint arXiv:2211.09110*.

Yotam Perlitz, Elron Bandel, Ariel Gera, Ofir Arviv, Liat Ein-Dor, Eyal Shnarch, Noam Slonim, Michal Shmueli-Scheuer, and Leshem Choshen. 2023. Efficient benchmarking (of language models). *arXiv preprint arXiv:2308.11696*.

Matt Post. 2018. A call for clarity in reporting BLEU scores. In *Proceedings of the Third Conference on Machine Translation: Research Papers*, pages 186–191, Brussels, Belgium. Association for Computational Linguistics.

Adam Roberts, Hyung Won Chung, Anselm Levskaya, Gaurav Mishra, James Bradbury, Daniel Andor, Sharan Narang, Brian Lester, Colin Gaffney, Afroz Mohiuddin, Curtis Hawthorne, Aitor Lewkowycz, Alex Salcianu, Marc van Zee, Jacob Austin, Sebastian Goodman, Livio Baldini Soares, Haitang Hu, Sasha Tsvyashchenko, Aakanksha Chowdhery, Jasmijn Bastings, Jannis Bulian, Xavier Garcia, Jianmo Ni, Andrew Chen, Kathleen Kenealy, Jonathan H. Clark, Stephan Lee, Dan Garrette, James

Lee-Thorp, Colin Raffel, Noam Shazeer, Marvin Ritter, Maarten Bosma, Alexandre Passos, Jeremy Maitin-Shepard, Noah Fiedel, Mark Omernick, Brennan Saeta, Ryan Sepassi, Alexander Spiridonov, Joshua Newlan, and Andrea Gesmundo. 2022. Scaling up models and data with `t5x` and `seqio`. *arXiv preprint arXiv:2203.17189*.

Damien Sileo. 2023. tasksource: Structured dataset preprocessing annotations for frictionless extreme multi-task learning and evaluation. *arXiv preprint arXiv:2301.05948*.

C. Spearman. 1904. The proof and measurement of association between two things. *The American Journal of Psychology*, 15(1):72–101.

Jason Wei, Maarten Bosma, Vincent Zhao, Kelvin Guu, Adams Wei Yu, Brian Lester, Nan Du, Andrew M. Dai, and Quoc V Le. 2022. Finetuned language models are zero-shot learners. In *International Conference on Learning Representations*.

Thomas Wolf, Lysandre Debut, Victor Sanh, Julien Chaumond, Clement Delangue, Anthony Moi, Pierric Cistac, Tim Rault, Remi Louf, Morgan Funtowicz, Joe Davison, Sam Shleifer, Patrick von Platen, Clara Ma, Yacine Jernite, Julien Plu, Canwen Xu, Teven Le Scao, Sylvain Gugger, Mariama Drame, Quentin Lhoest, and Alexander Rush. 2020. Transformers: State-of-the-art natural language processing. In *Proceedings of the 2020 Conference on Empirical Methods in Natural Language Processing: System Demonstrations*, pages 38–45, Online. Association for Computational Linguistics.

A LM Eval Harness Integration

LM-eval-harness (Gao et al., 2023) is one of the most commonly used open source evaluation frameworks. It leverages a yaml-based declarative language which defines loading of the dataset, the dataset splits, the prompt used and the metrics in a single file for each task. Many tasks are supported, including multi-class classification, multiple choice question answering, and generation tasks. Unitxt was integrated into LM-eval-harness to extend LM-eval-harness to support new tasks and metrics that currently are not supported, including multi-label classification, named entity extraction, and target sentiment analysis.

Since `Unitxt` recipes can be loaded as standard HF datasets, no code changes were required to add the `Unitxt` data preparation pipeline to LM-eval-harness. Adding a `Unitxt` recipe requires only one line change in a LM-eval-harness yaml (see Figure 4 in Appendix). Adding the `Unitxt` metrics required about 30 lines of code, to register the `Unitxt` metrics to the LM-eval-harness metrics registry.

```
1  group: glue
2  task: unitxt_unfair_tos
3  dataset_path: unitxt/data
4  dataset_name: card=cards.unfair_tos,template_card_index=templates.classification.
       multi_label.default,format=formats.user_agent
5  output_type:  generate_until
6  training_split: train
7  validation_split: validation
8  doc_to_text: "{{source}}"
9  doc_to_target: target
10 generation_kwargs:
11   until:
12     - "</s>"
13 metric_list:
14   - metric: unitxt_f1_micro_multi_label
15 metadata:
16   version: 1.0
```

Figure 4: **Unitxt and LM-eval-harness integration**. A Unitxt recipe can be integrated as an LM-eval-harness task, by setting the *dataset_path* (line 3) to *unitxt/data* and the setting the recipe in the *dataset_name* (line 4). Unitxt metrics can be used like any other metric (line 14).

Author Index

Association for Computational Linguistics
209 N. Eighth Street
Stroudsburg, Pennsylvania 18360

ISBN 978-1-7138-9896-2

CURRAN ASSOCIATES INC.
proceedings.com